MYTHIC FRONTIERS

Cultural Heritage Studies

UNIVERSITY PRESS OF FLORIDA

Florida A&M University, Tallahassee
Florida Atlantic University, Boca Raton
Florida Gulf Coast University, Ft. Myers
Florida International University, Miami
Florida State University, Tallahassee
New College of Florida, Sarasota
University of Central Florida, Orlando
University of Florida, Gainesville
University of North Florida, Jacksonville
University of South Florida, Tampa
University of West Florida, Pensacola

MYTHIC FRONTIERS

Remembering, Forgetting, and Profiting
with Cultural Heritage Tourism

DANIEL R. MAHER

Foreword by Paul A. Shackel

University Press of Florida

Gainesville · Tallahassee · Tampa · Boca Raton

Pensacola · Orlando · Miami · Jacksonville · Ft. Myers · Sarasota

First cloth printing, 2016
First paperback printing, 2019

24 23 22 21 20 19   6 5 4 3 2 1

Library of Congress Cataloging-in-Publication Data
Names: Maher, Daniel R., author. | Shackel, Paul A., Author of introduction, etc.
Title: Mythic frontiers : remembering, forgetting, and profiting with cultural heritage
tourism / Daniel R. Maher ; foreword by Paul A. Shackel.
Other titles: Cultural heritage studies.
Description: Gainesville : University Press of Florida, [2016] | Series: Cultural heritage
studies | Includes bibliographical references and index.
Identifiers: LCCN 2015041910 | ISBN 9780813062532 (cloth : alk. paper)
ISBN 9780813064185 (pbk.)
Subjects: LCSH: Heritage tourism—Arkansas—Fort Smith. | Culture and tourism—
Arkansas—Fort Smith. | Fort Smith (Ark.)—Historiography. | Tourism—Arkansas—Fort
Smith. | Frontier and pioneer life—Arkansas—Fort Smith.
Classification: LCC F419.F7 M28 2016 | DDC 976.7/36—dc23
LC record available at http://lccn.loc.gov/2015041910

The University Press of Florida is the scholarly publishing agency for the State University
System of Florida, comprising Florida A&M University, Florida Atlantic University, Florida
Gulf Coast University, Florida International University, Florida State University, New
College of Florida, University of Central Florida, University of Florida, University of North
Florida, University of South Florida, and University of West Florida.

University Press of Florida
2046 NE Waldo Road
Suite 2100
Gainesville, FL 32609
http://upress.ufl.edu

For Richard and Mary Maher

Contents

Figures

Foreword

Daniel Maher's *Mythic Frontiers: Remembering, Forgetting, and Profiting with Cultural Heritage Tourism* provides a compelling story about how a federal agency, the National Park Service, along with private entities and the city of Fort Smith, Arkansas, combine to create a memory that is used to promote cultural tourism. Since the mid-1950s, Fort Smith has been marketed as a frontier, western town, and today the town showcases outlaws and deputies as well as brothels and judges. It also has a full-size gallows to reinforce the "justice" that Judge Isaac Parker allegedly meted out. These stories associated with Fort Smith and the frontier perpetuate popular narratives of courage, fortitude, and nation building, often at the expense of other perspectives, notably from nondominant groups.

Borrowing from Lowenthal, Maher writes, "Heritage is not an inquiry into the past but a celebration of it, not an effort to know what actually happened but a profession of faith in a past tailored to present-day purposes." Using that definition of heritage, Maher examines the myth building associated with the western frontier and deconstructs these myths by performing detailed, rigorous, intense historical research. His work explores and deconstructs issues related to race, racism, and gender inequities that are associated with Fort Smith as well as other heritage sites. He provides powerful examples that allow us to think about ways heritage is used in nation building.

The United States was built on a consensus history that was prevalent in museums and in landscapes throughout the country. It was not until the 1960s and 1970s that scholars began to think about history from the bottom up, hidden histories, and representation of the subaltern. Maher's scholarship comes at a time when critical histories that challenge traditional American narratives are being contested. Let us not forget that Lynne Cheney, chair of the National Endowment for the Humanities in the 1980s, argued in her report to Congress that scholars were occupying themselves with issues related to gender, race, and class.[1] She discouraged funding projects that encouraged a pluralistic view of the past. Her appointed advisory council rejected proposals if they questioned consensus history. In the 1980s the NEH sharply curtailed support for projects dealing with women, labor, or racial groups or any others that might conflict with the national collective memory.[2] At about the same time, columnist George Wills wrote that these scholars were "forces . . . fighting against the conservation of the common culture that is the nation's social cement."[3]

During the George W. Bush administration, Cheney also had a powerful role in the NEH and helped to develop the "We the People" initiative. In a CNN interview in 2003 she suggested that the NEH could be used to help foster an "American history that's taught in as positive and upbeat a way as our national story deserves."[4] Eric Foner, a history professor at Columbia University, explains that Cheney "always saw history in terms of generating a kind of patriotism for the country."[5]

Recently, Mitch Daniels, the former governor of Indiana (2005–2013) and later president of Purdue University, attempted to purge Howard Zinn's *A People's History of the United States* from the Indiana curriculum. A Freedom of Information Act request for e-mails indicates that when Daniels was governor he wrote to the state's top education officials describing the book as anti-American: "Can someone assure me that it is not in use anywhere in Indiana? If it is, how do we get rid of it before more young people are force-fed a totally false version of our history?"[6]

Undaunted by the disparagement of these critical histories, scholars continue to step forward to examine the stories of the making of our country, revealing explicit and implicit forms of racism, sexism, and imperialism that continue to contribute to nation building. For instance, Mark Spence writes about how the making of several national parks was also a product of policies of Indian removal.[7] Teresa Bergman critically evaluates the way patriotism is exhibited at nationally significant places like Mount Rushmore and the USS *Arizona* Memorial.[8] Seth C. Bruggeman examines the contested public memory that surrounds the George Washington Birthplace National Monument in Virginia and explains that national parks have not always welcomed all Americans.[9]

With this ongoing struggle to control the national public memory, *Mythic Frontiers* is part of a larger dialogue about the meaning of our past in the present. The detailed primary research, the solid deconstruction and critique of the frontier complex in general and at Fort Smith specifically, is quite refreshing and exciting to read. It follows the growing tradition of scholarship that critically evaluates the way national parks and national monuments are used to foster the national narrative. Much of the narrative related to nation building ignores the effects of imperialism, racism, and sexism, thereby reinforcing and perpetuating social inequalities. Maher challenges these created pasts head on and implores us to think of space and place and the American narrative in different ways.

Paul A. Shackel
Series editor

Foreword Notes

1. Lynne V. Cheney, *The Humanities in America: A Report to the President, the Congress, and the American People* (Washington, D.C.: National Endowment for the Humanities, 1988).

2. Gary B. Nash, Charlotte Crabtree, and Ross E. Dunn, *History on Trial: Culture Wars and the Teaching of the Past* (New York: Knopf, 1998), 103.

3. George F. Wills, "The Politicization of Higher Education," *Newsweek*, April 22, 1991, 72.

4. Interview with Lynne Cheney, *CNN Late Edition with Wolf Blitzer*, September 28, 2003, http://www.cnn.com/transcripts/0309/28/le.00.html.

5. Mary Jacoby, "Madame Cheney's Cultural Revolution: How the Vice President's Powerful Wife Makes Sure that Historians and Other Scholars Follow the Right Path," *Salon*, August 26, 2004, http://dir.salon.com/story/news/feature/2004/08/26/lynne_cheney/index.html.

6. Joseph A. Palmero, "Mitch Daniels, Howard Zinn, and the Politics of History," *Huffington Post*, August 30, 2013, http://www.huffingtonpost.com/joseph-a-palermo/mitch-daniels-howard-zinn_b_3677477.html.

7. Mark David Spence, *Dispossessing the Wilderness: Indian Removal and the Making of the National Parks* (New York: Oxford University Press, 2000).

8. Teresa Bergman, *Exhibiting Patriotism: Creating and Contesting Interpretations of American Historic Sites* (Walnut Creek, Calif.: Left Coast Press, 2013).

9. Seth C. Bruggeman, *Here, George Washington Was Born: Memory, Material Culture, and the Public History of a National Monument* (Athens: University of Georgia Press, 2008).

Acknowledgments

It took five years of intensive research and writing for the frontier complex to come into focus for me. It did so only with the assistance of a great many people who offered comments, contributions, and insights, without which this book would never have come to be. I would like to thank Paul Shackle and Meredith Morris-Babb for their vision of what this project could become and the support and encouragement they provided in making this a reality.

Kirstin Erickson was invaluable in working through earlier versions of this project, and JoAnn D'Alisera, Ted Swedenburg, and Patrick Williams were likewise key in shaping my theoretical understanding and handling of the material.

Invaluable archival assistance was provided me by Joshua Youngblood at the University of Arkansas, Connie Manning at the Fort Smith Museum of History, Loren McLane at the Fort Smith National Historic Site, and Matt Myers and Shelly Blanton at the Pebley Historical and Cultural Center at the University of Arkansas–Fort Smith. Special thanks goes to Sharon Freeman, who processed hundreds of interlibrary loans for me, and to all of the library staff who helped me keep those due dates in order. Colleagues who gave unwavering encouragement and support throughout this process include Mike Crane, Matt McCoy, Bob Willoughby, Henry Rinne, and Rita Barrett.

Those employed in the Fort Smith frontier complex provided me with courteous and easy access to the sites, and I am thankful for their assistance. They include Lisa Conard-Frost, Michael Groomer, Pat Schmidt, Cody Faber, Jeremy Lynch, Leisa Gramlich, Caroline Speir, Jessica Hougen, Julie Moncrief, Catherine Foreman Gray, Roy Hamilton, and Candessa Tehee. Numerous reenactment groups and reenactors welcomed me to their events and monthly meetings. Though I suspect many in this number will disagree entirely with my interpretation of the frontier complex and their role in it, I am extremely indebted to them for their hospitality and their patience with me. Had it not been for Baridi Nkokheli's portrayal of Bass Reeves, this project would never have begun. To Mr. Nkokheli and to the memory of his father, Sgt. Henry Wesley Kellough, I owe a debt of respect and gratitude beyond measure.

Many mentors patiently showed me a path to writing, among them Larry Nelson, Margaret Miller, Jerilyn Strohecker, Michael Kuelker, Dave Van Mierlo, and Dick Stivers. For this particular project, Jacqulyn Harper West provided unique analytical discussions and important editorial suggestions. I am very appreciative of Lisa Knoche Kite, whose close reading and thoughtful comments brought the final draft of the manuscript into sharper relief. I am indebted to Colette St. Mary, Billy Higgins, Shandine Maines, Bradley Kidder Sr., Steve Kite, Jay Casey, and Kevin Jones, who provided important feedback and reader critiques at various stages of research and writing. Linda Mills Boyd's fine-toothed-comb editing of the manuscript was extraordinarily timely and beneficial.

For the underlying form and structure that I was able to bring to this project, I must thank my dear friends Darvin Curtis and Billy Higgins. For the wisdom each has shared with me—about gardening, motorcycles, guitars, chainsaws, and axes as well as about ideas, insights, and perspective on life—and ultimately for their friendship, I am forever grateful. My only regret is that Ed Levy was not here to mercilessly joke with us throughout the project.

In the final months of the project, Michele Gibson helped to remind me what this was all about, and I thank her for that. My children, Allyson, Thor, Atticus, and Jonah, have been patient and supportive while I've sorted things out, and I am thankful for their forgiveness and love. To my parents, Richard and Mary Maher—who in their own way taught me and their other children, Christine, Patrick, and Michael, the Maher DDS: discipline, desire, and structure—this book is a manifestation of what I have inherited from you both, and I dedicate it to you.

1

///////////////////////////////////

The Significance of the Frontier Complex
in American History

Oh give me a home where the buffalo roam,
Where the deer and the antelope play,
Where seldom is heard a discouraging word,
And the sky is not cloudy all day.

Brewster Higley, 1873

The winter wind howled as the Indians crept slowly toward the edge of the stockade military fort. From the blockhouse came the muffled scream of the night watch as his Indian assailant took his life with the quiet of a knife. Red Cloud cupped his hands and blew the faint call of a morning dove—the sign to take the fort. War Eagle led a waiting pack of Indians through the gate only to be met with the ferocious blast of a cannon followed by a volley of bullets. Sergeant Thomas had anticipated this late-night attack and preemptively loaded the cannon before dusk. The Indians responded with ear-piercing war cries as they raised their hatchets to the air and sprang upon the mounted cavalry. Drawn swords and rifles met the bows and arrows and clubs as the warriors breached the stockade. The battle might have gone on for hours, but just before Fort Apache was taken, a great string of pops were heard—pop-pop, pop, pop-pop, pop, pop—interrupting the fierce battle.

The smell of popcorn hung heavy in the air as we succumbed to the temptation of the buttery afternoon snack. And so my friends and I would while away many winter hours inhabiting the imagined space of the Wild West frontier, immersing ourselves in what I now refer to as the frontier complex. Today, when I inspect the action figures that came with the popular play sets that entranced generations for decades, such as Fort Apache and Fort Cheyenne, several features stand out.[1] Most obvious, there are no

Figure 1.1. Figures from Fort Apache, the once-popular Marx Toys play set. The violent confrontation they depict precludes civil discourse. Photo by the author.

women. This action is clearly only for the men to decide. Second, the postures presented by the characters make it hard to imagine how any of them could be used to construct a diorama depicting peaceful diplomacy. Instead, savage Indians paw the ground with raised hatchets, bows are drawn taut by arrows ready to fly, and clubs twirl in time to a frenetic war dance. Their opponents hold the tools of advancing civilization—rifles—and ride on saddled horses, not bareback, and hats, not feathers, adorn the men's heads. In contrast to the Indians, with their stylized tipi and totem pole, the soldiers stand uniformed and poised in their fortified structure, with their refined instruments of military prowess; these are not mere natural objects of rocks and sticks fashioned into crude weapons, shelter, and objects of worship.

The social history of the Wild West American frontier was of course much more complex and nuanced than the binary possibilities contained in such egregiously essentializing toys and in their counterpart narratives told in pulp fiction, on television shows, and on the movie screen. Regardless of medium, these popular, iconic representations of the Wild West frontier continue to constitute a "frontier complex" in our national imagination. In addition to being created in fiction, the frontier complex takes material forms that are visited by millions of domestic and foreign tourists each year. They view the frontier complex in places ranging from the fantastical at Disneyland's Frontierland on the Pacific coast to the campy Frontier Town Campground near Ocean City, Maryland; from the OK Corral in Tombstone, Arizona, to the reconstructed Front Street of the quintessential 1870s cowboy town of Dodge City, Kansas; and from Deadwood, South Dakota, to the infamous Hanging Judge Isaac Parker's reconstructed gallows in Fort Smith, Arkansas. Many visitors come to these sites expecting to see the real-life highlight reel from the Fort Apache play set, and many sites cater to that expectation. This frontier complex is one of many "tourism imaginaries" that are the direct and intended result of decades of the consciously planned "tourismification" of the Wild West frontier.[2]

The frontier complex is a companion concept to Tony Horwitz' *Confederates in the Attic*. Horwitz shows that by perpetually reenacting the Civil War on a life-size theatrical stage, many Americans are able to act out pent-up frustration and anger while working through felt grievances from the past up through today. Likewise, "frontiers in the attic" represents a mental and physical space in which to work out fears and anxieties that are not necessarily grounded in reality. As "attic" might connote a pathology, "fantasy" may be a better descriptor. The key difference between the Confederate and frontier attics is that in the case of the frontier there was and is a clear victor: white Anglo men definitively won claims to property and power as each frontier space was bent to the will of manifest destiny.

Reenacting the frontier inherently re-creates a unifying win for America and specifically for white Americans. Reenacting the Civil War, despite the facts in the matter, does not provide as clear a resolution for all the involved white social actors. Despite the racialized legacy of white Anglos, British, Spanish, and French supplanting legions of Indian groups on the leading edge of the frontier for centuries, somehow the frontier complex is not performed within as racially charged a context as the Civil War. Consequently, it is purveyed as a more socially acceptable landscape in which one can find city leaders publicly boasting about their heritage in unison—a very white heritage.

Heritage, Cultural Memory, and Myth

The ever-rolling wave of the frontier border that spread from east to west in the nation's history enables virtually every state in the Union, and any city within it, to lay claim to some point in time in which it sat squarely on the border of the frontier. This imagined moment in history creates a marker between an advancing western civilization on one side of it and a wild savagery that lay beyond it. Annual Frontier Days, also called Pioneer Days or Founders Days, thus function as an origin myth for communities as they tell the tale of how white Anglo-Saxon settlers came to dominate the landscape.

Such events can be found across the country from Steubenville, Ohio, to Arlington Heights, Illinois; Wetumpka, Alabama; Charlotte, Michigan; Cheyenne, Wyoming; and Willits, California. Practically every state is host to such an event. As such, this frontier complex resides in the nation's collective psyche, in its attic. It provides a simplified, overarching narrative history of the nation that selectively remembers and portrays some details as it conveniently forgets others. This practice of "silencing the past" and "imagineering otherness" is embodied in many popular conceptions of cultural heritage.[3]

The narratives for cultural heritage tourism in the frontier complex are frequently attached to historical places or artifacts from the middle to late nineteenth century. While they are presented to the public as historically impeccable, in fact they are often reproducing fictionalized, sensationalized, impeachable accounts of the frontier past.[4] In *The Heritage Crusade and the Spoils of History*, David Lowenthal observes, "In fact, heritage is not history at all; while it borrows from and enlivens historical study, heritage is not an inquiry into the past but a celebration of it, not an effort to know what actually happened but a profession of faith in a past tailored to present-day purposes."[5] Though quite different, heritage and history are consistently interwoven in tourist discourses.

In practice, the frontier complex emerges from this process of mixing contemporary imaginings of what the frontier was like with historical and material artifacts from a specific period to create ostensibly authentic reproductions for tourists to consume. In other words, it is created in the process that is commonly thought to be describing it. The frontier complex is performed into existence and maintained both materially and mentally through this perpetual interaction.[6] It manifests materially in buildings, monuments, and artifacts that can be visited and seen in reconstructed log stockade forts, blacksmith shops, historic homes, gallows, and covered wagons. The frontier complex takes mental shape in the ideas and memories with which the material forms are imbued through spoken, visual, and textual interpretations that represent contemporary ideologies of power, class, gender, and race. The primary narrative of the frontier complex minimizes the devastating consequences that imperialism, racism, and sexism have had on social minorities in the past and still today as it elevates and legitimizes the privilege bestowed to white men past and present.

Heritage thus creates a selective and exaggerated cultural memory in which flesh-and-blood mortals are turned into legends, just beyond normal human abilities, and facts take wing and fly to mythic heights, often beyond common sense, yet frequently are believed nonetheless. In *Remembering the Alamo*, Richard Flores suggests that it is difficult to tease out the difference between the historical facts and the mythic narrative that shapes cultural memory because "cultural memory refers to those aspects of memory that exist outside of official historical discourse, yet are 'entangled' with them."[7] Grounded in grains of truth, life is breathed into myths by their perpetual performance, and as Roland Barthes argues, these myths become "deeply grounded narratives through which communities express their heartfelt convictions."[8] Myths therefore are not precisely fallacies; they convey the felt truths of the lived social experience for those who believe them. It is this variety of mythic narratives that converts history into the cultural memory and heritage found in the frontier attic.

The Wild West frontier complex is particularly adept at creating mythic narratives and wrapping them in the protective cloak of heritage. In order to untangle facts from heritage, cultural memory, and myths, they must be grounded in historical context. A general sketch of the American western frontier will allow us to measure the disconnection between the historical record and popular tourist narratives.

Frontier Complex

The frontier complex under discussion here is of a particular variety, and observations of it may not be true of other frontier regions. Frontier environments are found all over the world and can come from any direction on the compass.[9] The specific frontier complex in question stems from circumstances set in motion after the 1803 Louisiana Purchase and continuing until Oklahoma statehood in 1907, in lands spanning from the Mississippi River to the Rocky Mountains. It is from this time and region that many of the iconic American images in the popular imagination of cowboys, Indians, wagon trains, and military forts are derived. The frontier of the Old Northwest Territory, for example, may share some of these attributes, but that specific frontier is not the focus of this study.[10] Nor do I claim this work to be an exhaustive inquiry into the hundreds of forts, battles, and campaigns west of the Mississippi.[11]

What follows is a template of five frontier eras that I will use to examine how the frontier complex has been exploited for different purposes throughout American history. This model is a modified version of that found in Robert Frazer's *Forts of the West*.[12] The precise time frames are slightly different from Frazer's, and I have added two more periods to bring the stages of the frontier complex up to the present time. None of these five time frames has a hard and fast beginning or ending. They are general time frames that in some cases overlap.

The first three time frames relate to Indian removal (1804–1848), restraint (1848–1887), and reservation (1887–1934). Over the course of these three periods the U.S. Army was employed to clear the path for white immigrants inspired by a succession of economic bonanzas, prominently fur, grazing land, gold and silver, timber, railroads, coal, and homesteads. The history that unfolded in the first three periods was converted into new riches, as popular entertainment for tourists in the recreation period (1920–1980); those efforts were redoubled (1980–present) in drastically altered national and global economies.

The recreation period that began in the 1920s saw a burst of tourism within the frontier complex. This era of converting nineteenth-century military forts and westward trails into twentieth-century tourist attractions began in earnest with the advent of affordable automobiles and grew in tandem with the explosion of western films and television shows after World War II. The fifth period, of redoubling, began in response to a shift in economic policies typically discussed as neoliberalism, globalization, and deindustrialization that resulted in the loss of manufacturing jobs and a decline in middle-class families' disposable incomes for summer vacations.

Given the economic shift, producers of frontier-complex tourism faced two new dilemmas: well-established tourist sites had to attract new tourists who had less money to spend than generations before them, and cities desperate to fill the economic void caused by losses in the manufacturing sector became more reliant on cultural heritage tourism to improve otherwise eroding tax bases. Compounding this economic crisis was a heightened competition within the tourism sector of the economy as an effect of the Reagan era of deregulation. As a result of the 1988 Indian Gaming Regulatory Act, Indian gaming from bingo halls to casinos burst onto the scene in the 1990s, giving the long-established frontier tourism industry a run for its money.[13]

Frontier Era of Removal, 1804–1848

The namesake of the military fort and then city of Fort Smith, General Thomas Adams Smith, was a principal architect in the creation of the national frontier complex here in question. After the War of 1812 the U.S. military could focus on the nation's newly acquired land west of the Mississippi. Within three years of the war's end, while stationed in St. Louis veteran Smith directed Army explorer Stephen H. Long to locate the best sites for military forts along this new frontier.[14] The ultimate result was an array of strategically located forts on a north-south axis from Fort Snelling, Minnesota, to Fort Jessup, Louisiana.

Many of the forts were positioned along key waterways: Fort Crawford was built in 1816 at the confluence of the Mississippi and Wisconsin Rivers; Fort Smith was established in 1817 where the Arkansas and Poteau Rivers meet; in 1819 Forts Snelling and Atkinson were built respectively at the confluence of the Mississippi and Minnesota Rivers and of the Missouri and Boyer Rivers; Fort Jessup was built in 1822 between the Red and Sabine Rivers. Sitting in the three-forks region of the Arkansas, Verdigris, and Neosho Rivers, Fort Gibson was garrisoned by troops from Fort Smith after it closed in 1824. Fort Leavenworth, the only active fort remaining from this time and region, was built on the banks of the Missouri in 1827 near where it meets the Kansas River. These forts had commanding views of the new frontier not only for military maneuvers but also for future commerce and travel.[15]

They were among the first forts in the West, and they clearly had more than one mission. Ostensibly they were constructed to oversee the so-called permanent Indian frontier to which Indian groups from the Southeast and the Old Northwest could be moved, opening more land for white settlement along the frontier line.[16] The precise western boundaries of the United States with Britain, France, Spain, Mexico, and Texas had yet to be resolved. The early western forts served as a bulwark against foreign invasion as well as springboards for military and trading forays into foreign territories.[17]

During this era the American public became accustomed to popular narratives depicting the frontier. James Fenimore Cooper's *Leatherstocking*

Tales (1823–1841) helped shape perceptions of the Old Northwest Territory frontier. In 1833 Davy Crockett himself, one of America's first frontier legends, sat in the audience in Washington D.C. watching a visage of his frontiersman self in James Paulding's play *The Lion of the West*.[18] In the western frontier created by the Louisiana Purchase the policies of Indian removal had a popular narrative that served as tacit if not manifest support for this government action. Washington Irving's 1834 *Tour of the Prairies* is his account of the 1832 journey into Indian Territory in a region that was part of Missouri Territory (1812–1819), Arkansas Territory (1819–1824), then formally Indian Territory (1824–1907). He began near Fort Smith, at Fort Gibson. Irving's travelogue reinforced misconceptions proffered as early as 1820 by both Zebulon Pike and Stephen Long that the region was a sparsely inhabited, wild part of the "great American desert" and unfit for Anglo habitation.[19]

Published just in time to buttress an Indian removal policy, Irving's popular story caught the attention of eager eastern Americans whose appetite for new lands had been whetted in 1827 by the discovery of gold in Georgia. They could be rid of the "Indian problem" by relegating tribes in that eastern region to this faraway and reportedly inhospitable, unusable land to the west. It is interesting to note here that the popular imagination had a literary narrative paralleling the political process of Indian removal. This pattern of popular narratives accompanying political and economic machinations is a recurring theme in all the frontier eras.

Toward the end of the removal period several forts were added to assist with the permanent Indian frontier. In present-day Oklahoma, Fort Coffee opened in 1834 and Fort Wayne in 1838. Construction began on a second Fort Smith in 1838; Forts Scott (in present-day Kansas) and Washita (in present-day Oklahoma) were added in 1842 and Fort Des Moines (in present-day Iowa) in 1843. Though ideally suited for the dual purposes of Indian removal and defense against threatening political states, land acquisitions by battle and treaty quickly made the two missions of the newly established line of forts obsolete, and most closed within a few years of opening.

Frontier Era of Restraint, 1848–1887

The 1845 annexation of Texas, the acquisition of the Oregon Territory from Britain in 1846, and the 1848 Mexican Cession made the manifest destiny of a nation stretching from the Atlantic Ocean to the Pacific Ocean attainable. By the start of the Civil War in 1861, all of what today constitutes the lower forty-eight states had been incorporated as states or territories. Subsequently, the mission of the western frontier military forts shifted from overseeing Indian removal and defending against foreign political states to restraining Indians as white immigrants passed through or settled on their lands, causing open conflict. The era of restraint is marked in both history and the popular imagination by a series of wagon trails, cattle trails, and rail lines crisscrossing the plains to accommodate an ever-expanding white American population.

The Santa Fe, California, Oregon, and Mormon Trails led migrants to boom-and-bust towns settled to profit from gold, silver, copper, and cattle. All of these economic ventures necessitated protection by the U.S. Army along the way as settlers cut through and took possession of more Indian land and resources. In this period of westward migration, some old military forts were revived and new ones were established to create a corridor of protection for white travelers on the road west. The second Fort Smith, Arkansas, was built in part to service the war with Mexico and then California-bound gold seekers. Troops at Fort Snelling (in present-day Minnesota) restrained Dakota Indians to establish safe passage for immigrants on the northern plains.[20] Fort Kearny (in present-day Nebraska) sprang up in 1848 on the Oregon Trail, and Fort Larned (in present-day Kansas) was established in 1859 on the Santa Fe Trail.[21] To the south, Fort Davis, Texas, protected migrants beginning in 1854 traveling between San Antonio and El Paso.

The Civil War occurred during the frontier era of restraint, and I leave the bulk of Civil War history to other scholars. My main objective here is to examine how the Wild West frontier, not the Civil War, is used in tourism discourses today.[22] The Civil War did play a crucial role in shaping the frontier complex, especially in its aftermath when there was a new focus on westward movement; the war altered U.S. relations with Indian nations that had sided with the Confederacy, particularly the five nations residing adjacent to Fort Smith in Indian Territory (present-day Oklahoma): Cherokee, Choctaw, Creek, Seminole, and Chickasaw.[23] The leaders of these tribes, some of them slave owners, sided with the rebels, but all of the tribes experienced divided loyalties.

It was also during the frontier era of restraint that Texas longhorn cattle were herded through Indian Territory on trails such as the Shawnee, Chisolm, and Western to Kansas railheads where they would be shipped by train to feed a growing nation, giving birth to the legendary Dodge City, Kansas. These cattle trails and subsequent railroads caused an enormous amount of turmoil in Indian Territory. It is from these cattle trails that the mythic cowboy was born, Dodge City and other places came to fame, and western fiction like Larry McMurtry's *Lonesome Dove* captured America's imagination. In Fort Smith, whose very identity stems from its relation to neighboring Indian Territory, these cattle trails are not mentioned in tourism narratives although they contributed to the supposed lawlessness against which Fort Smith needed defending.[24] Such is the picking and choosing of facts that are then disconnected from their historical contexts and represented to the public in oversimplified tourism discourses.

A more pointed way to look at this would be to consider people's reactions to reading the first stanza of "Home on the Range." Some might at least imagine or maybe even sing the chorus, "Home, home on the range." If so, then they have tapped into their frontier complex. This song comes from Brewster Higley's 1873 poem. Higley was proudly describing in these quaint lyrics his new home in Kansas that he acquired through the Homestead Act of 1862.[25] The irony of the lyrical lines reveals the prestidigious feat accomplished by the song. White Anglos could only make their home on the range after the buffalo no longer roamed and the previous residents had been evicted. The irony within "Home on the Range" hides in the dark recesses of the frontier attic. Cowboys, cattle trails, and catchy tunes mute the voices of those most adversely affected by westward expansion.

The head of steam for pushing white immigrants into the western frontier had been building for several decades. The end of the Civil War was followed by the completion of the transcontinental railroad in 1869 and subsequent rail lines, making western migration easier. It was made inevitable by tapping into the popular imagination and creating the lure of the western frontier. As soon as the physical engineering of the railroad was complete, a parallel mental imagineering followed suit, showing Americans how to access the West by rail. Travel journals and advertisements of the West played a key role in creating conceptions for how Americans might make use of western lands.

Within a year of completion, the transcontinental railroad possessed a popular travel narrative. George Crofutt was among the first to promote the West as a tourist destination. His *Great Continental Tourist's Guide*, first published in 1870, gave Americans a vision of how to take advantage of the West.[26] In the same year, after making a living killing buffalo to feed railroad workers, William Cody parlayed his skills and reputation into showmanship. His Wild West shows were only possible because the western frontier was no longer quite so wild and rather quite industrialized; but the popular imagination did not need to know that. Likewise, the professional rodeos that began in the 1880s gave unemployed cowboys work as entertainers. Rodeos and Wild West shows were the Branson, Missouri, of the age.

The parallel of popular narratives following the trajectory of the political economy held true for the three great iconic Wild West towns of Dodge City, Deadwood, and Tombstone. These boom-and-bust towns were quickly constituted in popular mythic form as early as 1877, in Edward Wheeler's *Deadwood Dick, the Prince of the Road*; 1883 in Joseph Badger Jr.'s *The Old Boy of Tombstone*; and 1888 in *The Dandy of Dodge, or, Rustling for Millions*, by A. K. Simms. Kevin Britz brilliantly illustrates how these three iconic towns in particular were first constituted in fiction as Wild West towns full of shootouts, gamblers, and prostitutes—all exaggerations of historical facts—well before their respective town leaders embraced their legendary reputations as a strategy for luring tourists to their fair cities.[27]

Early visitors were disappointed when they could not find the legendary frontier imagery that had been planted in their minds by pulp fiction. Within a few decades these three iconic Wild West towns embraced not their history but rather their frontier-complex mythologies and began packaging their exaggerated reputations for tourists accordingly. Britz shows, "The key to a successful tourism industry as promoters soon discovered, was meeting expectations of visitors as tourists arrived in search of the authentic Old West."[28] It was the imaginative literary and theatrical voices of the frontier era of restraint that gave rise to the recreation era of touring the frontier complex. The busted towns of Deadwood and Tombstone were saved from fading into the sunset, and Dodge City's thriving meatpacking industry was supplemented by the rise of frontier tourism.

Frontier Era of Reservation, 1887–1934

The precise ending of the era of restraint could easily vary ten years on either side of 1887. I chose this year because it officially marks the beginning of a shift in control of land. The Dawes Severalty Act of 1887, also known as the General Allotment Act, codified what many white Americans had been wanting for decades—a legal pathway to acquiring land owned by Indians. The other existing method used by many white men leading up to the Dawes Act was marrying an Indian woman to become an adopted member of her nation, thus gaining access to her clan's property. Notably, this marital approach necessarily excluded non-Indian women from becoming property owners, for a white woman marrying an Indian man was anathema.

From the 1887 Dawes Act to the Indian Reorganization Act of 1934, settlement of the land of the western frontier fell under the auspices and enforcement of federal property laws. Thoughts of a permanent Indian frontier were long forgotten. The period of mass migration and military restraint was shifting into permanent settlements for whites and Indians alike. The frontier complex was being reserved, more tightly bound to fixed property designations, an important step for solidifying ownership of natural resources, including grazing lands, timber, coal, natural gas, and oil.

The early reservation era in the history of the frontier complex fosters some of its most potent popular images, and it is these images, exaggerated and incorrect as they may have been, that are frequently mistaken for historical facts of the time when looking back on them decades later. Though something of a Johnny-come-lately by 1893, Frederick Jackson Turner articulated how the frontier had made America exceptional; his was a white audience hungry for an explanation that would legitimate a century of expansion across the continent.[29] Turner's "frontier thesis" was delivered in tandem with the 1893 World's Columbian Exposition, or simply the Chicago World's Fair. Attended by an audience nearly half the size of the entire American population, the masses of people at the fair were able to see on full display the stages of human development that were so mistakenly conceived by nineteenth-century anthropologists and sociologists such as Herbert Spencer, Edward Burnett Tylor, and Louis Henry Morgan, not to mention Franz Boas.

In essence and physical layout of the Chicago World's Fair allowed visitors to walk through the theoretical stages of unilinear social development from savagery to barbarism and finally to civilization. True to its name, the Columbian Exposition constituted in dramatic form the steps of social advancement traversed since Christopher Columbus charted a route to North America. From the human exhibits of "the primitives" on the Midway Plaisance, to Buffalo Bill Cody's Wild West show performing adjacent to the fairgrounds, to the great industrial exhibition halls, Chicago had become one great big theatrical stage on which the pinnacle reached by western civilization could be demonstrated. This choreography of crowning imperialism was no accident, and anthropology was complicit in this imagineering of otherness.[30]

The fact that 27 million people were physically able to attend the fair in Chicago underscores the realization that by 1893, much of the United States, including the so-called Wild West frontier, had been industrialized by sheer miles of railroad tracks alone. To think of America in the late nineteenth century as wild and untamed is to confuse the theater of William Cody with the reality of firmly established industrialization. Despite events such as the 1890 massacre at Wounded Knee and Apache raids occurring into the 1920s, the West was quite urban.[31] Tourist behavior from this time reveals how safe, tame, and commoditized the West had already become.

Americans of elite economic circles had been using their position to tour the great vistas of the West before Turner declared it closed. While touring Yosemite Park in 1889, for example, Rudyard Kipling encountered what could be described as a full-scale parade of ugly-American tourists. He called them a "ghastly vulgarity [of] rampant ignorance" plaguing the countryside.[32] Trains, stagecoaches, and fancy hotels at Yosemite, Sequoia, Yellowstone, and the Grand Canyon were marketed to and accommodating wealthy visitors as quickly as railroad tracks were laid.[33] Thus, the reservation era of the frontier not only allowed for white settlement but also expanded white tourism. Mythic frontier imagery from the likes of Frederic Remington's art and Owen Wister's best-selling novel, *The Virginian*, coupled with widespread diagnoses of neurasthenia, enticed many citified East Coast residents to venture westward and reawaken their dormant, bureaucratized beings.[34]

Read in tandem, Christine Bold's *Frontier Club: Popular Westerns and Cultural Power, 1880–1924*, and Marguerite Shaffer's *See America First: Tourism and National Identity, 1880–1940*, reveal the full extent to which the western frontier was used as a template for rationalizing and legitimating white male hegemony. Bold exquisitely shows how Frederic Remington, Owen Wister, George Bird Grinnell, Theodore Roosevelt, and the rest of the "frontier club" used the western genre to "shore up their cultural power by influencing public opinion and federal policy in the key areas of land control, race politics, and emerging mass culture."[35] Pulp fiction, paintings, and sculpted imagery of the frontier complex constituted ideological propaganda from its inception.

Likewise, Shaffer shows in great detail that what came first in this process of tourists visiting the West were the advertising promotions selling the new commodity of sightseeing travel. The tourists came second. Train companies beginning with the Great Northern Railway and the Union Pacific Railroad created a demand for the ever-expanding supply of traveling that their routes could fill. It would take a few more decades before railroad fares shrank, automobile production expanded, and roads were improved so that middle-class Americans would have a chance to tour the West.

Frontier Era of Recreation, 1920–1980

Between 1893 and 1915 mythic groundwork was being laid for the soon-to-be-motoring middle class. Zane Grey was filling America's imagination with western vistas and mythic characters, and the 1904 Louisiana Purchase Exposition in St. Louis and the 1915 Panama-Pacific International Exposition in San Francisco reiterated the message delivered in Chicago in 1893 that America was exceptional. With the concern for traveling abroad in the midst of World War I, the San Francisco World's Fair showed Americans that touring America was not only feasible but downright patriotic.[36] Thanks to Henry Ford, automobiles became more affordable. With the completion of roads such as the Lincoln Highway in 1913 and the first Federal Highway Act in 1916, tourism was on the verge of becoming commonplace. Local infrastructures of America connected cultural heritage tourism and commerce. Groups like the Daughters of the American Revolution actively lobbied for improved roads so that key heritage sites could be visited.[37] By the early 1920s, "tourist parks" and other facilities sprang up in communities across the country to accommodate the temporary visitors.[38]

The Great Depression aside, the interwar period saw the United States poised for a tourism explosion. The frontier era of recreation had its infrastructure well under way before World War II; Route 66 was built in 1927, and the Works Progress Administration (WPA) projects created jobs and destinations for Americans. After the war, several factors combined to create a veritable cornucopia of frontier tourists: a burgeoning middle class with disposable incomes, a growing Interstate Highway System, and an explosion of Wild West frontier films and television shows.

All of this converged amid the start of the Cold War. The binary images in frontier westerns of good guys and bad guys assisted the political objective of building a Cold War consensus as threats of routing communists influenced Hollywood studios, directors, and actors.[39] Thus primed, America was ready to embark on family vacations that would retrace the steps of conquering the western frontier a century after it began in earnest.

Figure 1.2. Roadside exhibit at the Harrison County Historical Village and Iowa Welcome Center. Here the Lincoln Highway, a means to access tourist experiences, becomes a tourist stop in and of itself. Photo by the author.

The mythic frontier imaginary was about to be constructed on a one-to-one scale.

It is not that tourists came first looking for frontier forts and then the films and other fiction followed. Rather, the fiction came first, and then the tourists arrived to inhabit the imagined spaces of the frontier complex. With the advent of film, the fantastical Wild West narratives of the Buffalo Bill shows and dime-store novels found new audiences in movie theaters. The imagined frontier began to be solidified in early films including *The Great Train Robbery* (1903), *The Passing of the Oklahoma Outlaws* (1915), *The Covered Wagon* (1923), *The Iron Horse* (1924), and *Tumbleweeds* (1925). One of the most influential architects of the frontier complex, John Ford, began making westerns in 1917.[40]

A few classics such as *Stagecoach*, *Frontier Marshal*, *Union Pacific*, and *Dodge City* were all released in 1939, not long before the United States entered World War II. After the war, westerns came rapid-fire, one after the next, and were readily viewed on increasingly affordable home television sets and at movie and drive-in theaters.

Many films and television shows from this era, destined to capture America's mythic-frontier imagination for generations to come, were made within a dozen years, from 1948 to 1960. A few of the most popular were the film *Fort Apache* (1948), followed in 1951 by the Marx Toys play set of the same name; TV series *The Lone Ranger* (1949–1957), *The Life and Legend of Wyatt Earp* (1955–1961), *Cheyenne* (1955–1963), *Gunsmoke* (1955–1975), *Wagon Train* (1957–1965), *The Rifleman* (1958–1963), *Rawhide* (1959–1965), and *Bonanza* (1959–1973); and Hollywood films *High Noon* (1952), *Shane* (1953), *The Searchers* (1956), *Gunfight at the O.K. Corral* (1957), *The Magnificent Seven* (1960), and *The Alamo* (1960). Two notable films relevant to Fort Smith came later: *Hang 'Em High* (1968) with Clint Eastwood and *True Grit* (1969) starring John Wayne.

These and other westerns created fanciful and memorable, yet factually mistaken, conceptions of the historical American West, but their purpose was not to educate—it was to entertain. Americans consumed westerns en masse and had their minds filled with expectations of what to see upon visiting the Wild West frontier. Towns seeking those tourist dollars made changes to accommodate tourists' expectations. Dodge City still reaps the financial rewards from *Gunsmoke*, and Fort Smith often leverages *True Grit* in the name of profit.

Capitalizing on the frontier fever that was sweeping the nation, commercial enterprises opened from coast to coast. On the Pacific coast, Walt Disney's Frontierland opened in 1955; in the mid-continent, Frontier City opened in Oklahoma City in 1958; and on the Atlantic coast near Ocean City, Maryland, Frontier Town opened in 1959. These frontier amusement parks, still open today, featured stereotypical images from the frontier complex that resembled stages upon which visitors could replay scenes from their favorite western TV shows and movies. These included the quintessential log military fort with stockades and elevated blockhouses, pretend frontier towns complete with false-front saloons and dance-hall girls, stagecoaches, covered wagons, steam locomotives, rifles, cowboys, a "boot hill," Indians, tipis, and totem poles. The parks provided tourists with a theater of props that visitors could use to locate themselves within the frontier complex.

After a solid decade of frontier-complex imagery pervading American culture and proving its commercial promise, state and national parks began catering to these intentionally cultivated desires. The first military forts west of the Mississippi that were designated as National Historic Sites in

1960 were Bent's Old Fort National Historic Site in La Junta, Colorado, and Fort Laramie National Historic Site in Wyoming. Fort Smith, Fort Davis in Texas, and Fort Vancouver in Washington followed in 1961; Fort Bowie in Arizona and Fort Larned in 1964; Fort Point in California in 1970; and Fort Scott in Kansas in 1978. One of the most iconic parks dedicated to westward expansion is the Jefferson National Expansion Memorial in St. Louis, which memorializes the starting point of the Lewis and Clark Expedition. First authorized by the National Park Service in 1954, the Gateway Arch opened in 1967 and the Museum of Westward Expansion in 1976. Old military forts also were designated as state parks in close order: Fort Kearny in Nebraska in 1960, then Fort Snelling in Minnesota and Fort Jessup in Louisiana in 1961.

This vast array of pulp fiction, western films and television shows, theme parks, entire towns catering to tourists in search of the Wild West (Dodge City, Deadwood, and Tombstone, in particular), with national parks, and state parks reconstructing nineteenth-century forts—taken as a whole—constituted the frontier complex for tourists to physically and mentally inhabit. This is the "tourismification of peoples and places" of which Noel Salazar has written.[41]

Not all the people involved in this tourismification of the frontier complex necessarily recognized the role they were playing in its construction, but some, like the creators and promoters of the Frontier Club, were acutely aware, as Christine Bold describes. Until 1933, most parks in the National Park System were centered around the natural wonders of North America, among them Yellowstone, Sequoia, and Yosemite. After this point, new parks were focused on interpreting the wonders of the nation instead of nature and were consciously crafted as a pedagogy for a national curriculum.[42] However, this national classroom was not accessible to all, and it traded in highly essentialized notions of gender and race that reinforced the status quo of the American power structure. In the early years of this process, for example, some park managers took specific measures to not attract African Americans when at the very same time they would employ local Native Americans to perform their "Indian-ness," their otherness, for the tourists.[43] The national narrative that was being taught to and performed by tourists in the frontier complex was one of whiteness, and by going through the motions, tourists were unwittingly reenacting the westward claiming of North America by white men.

The idea of the American West is a stage upon which the project of national identity, power struggles, race, and gender are negotiated. As the political state expanded, a trove of symbolic elements was created with which to weave myths of savagery being overtaken by civilization. The trope of the wagon train is used in countless popular novels and films. Much like the Pony Express, wagon-train imagery has been used for far more years than the convoys existed in reality. Regardless, the recurring narrative of "savage Indian Others" warring against white migrants—who were literally and figuratively packing the advancement of western civilization in their wagons—is neither simply historical description nor coincidental.

Narratives surrounding the so-called Five Civilized Tribes are rear-ranged to reinforce this same righteousness of whiteness crossing the landscape. Although they were "civilized" before they were removed from their homes in the southeastern United States, after removal they had to be re-othered as savages to legitimate the intrusion and interference by the troops at Fort Smith and decisions by the federal court of "Hanging Judge" Isaac Parker. Richard Flores argues, "One of the strategies of state violence is to reproduce its competition as 'primitive' and 'other' so as to feign a kind of frontier imagery of savagery that rationalizes violence."[44] Consequently, manifest destiny is naturalized; it becomes inevitable and immutable by the collective impact of decades of stereotypical frontier imagery. It is this same process that creates and validates the "frontiers in the attic" as a safe public space to openly revel in the domination of whiteness.

The continued growth of frontier tourism in the 1950s and '60s was not only legitimating the imperialism of the past but also reinforcing binary images against the new enemy, the Soviet Union and its "primitive" eco-nomic form of communism. John Wayne made a career out of embodying this twofold dynamic that reinforced the righteousness of America in all its military actions, past and present.[45] The frontier complex is the result of an ongoing, interactive process between its producers and consumers. Capital-ists supplied popular culture conceptions of the frontier complex, which in turn constructed the demand for it. National and state parks picked up the surplus supply of tourists spilling out of commercial frontier theme parks. With this burgeoning demand, local nonprofit entities such as local histori-cal societies, museums, and historic home preservationists set their sights on attracting these new "tourists of history."[46]

The tourist is the key element in this economic equation, without which the entire frontier complex would close. Middle-class families found access to suburbia and annual vacations in a Cold War economy. Once they filled up on imagery from television and found the on-ramp to the new Inter-state Highway System, their journeys into the mythically imagined frontier Wild West were virtually on autopilot. Between 1955 and 1975 tourist businesses in the frontier complex flourished to accommodate the throngs of seekers who found simplistic, comfortable narratives explaining America's violent and complex past.

Literature on tourism in the United States reveals nearly all contemporary tourist hot spots to be intentionally contrived spaces for tourists to enter and live out fantasies and expectations associated with that site.[47] The illusion created by a visit to Beale Street in Memphis, a stroll through the French Quarter in New Orleans, or a stop in New Glarus, Wisconsin, for a locally brewed beer amid faux Swiss chalets can be blown off as easily as the head of foam from a poorly poured draught.

These socially constructed tourist sites have been around so long that many have forgotten they were in fact fabricated with the purpose of attracting tourists back to otherwise blighted cities. The same social forces that took families on vacation into the West also moved them to the suburbs. Many tourist sites were constructed as part of urban renewal plans to attract them, albeit for a visit rather than to live. The tourist site became something to be made and something to be performed. Likewise, those who traveled to these sites quickly learned that their role was to perform the expected behaviors of "tourist."

It is unclear exactly when "tourist site" and "tourist" became something expected to be performed, perhaps as long as there has been long-distance travel, but Earl Pomeroy clearly describes their presence in the frontier complex in 1956. In a manner reminiscent of Erving Goffman's dramaturgical analysis outlined in *Presentation of Self in Everyday Life*, Pomeroy says of the tourist, "He never simply tours through the West: he changes the West when he looks at it, not only because he wears out the highway pavements, but because Westerners change the West into what they think he wants it to be or, with less commercial intent, even change themselves into what they think he is."[48] What is clear is that the assortment of frontier military forts, history museums, restored historical homes, and monuments to nineteenth-century figures is staging preconceived notions and theatrical expectations believed to be held by tourists.

This chameleon process of towns catering to what the tourist wants is articulated in the title and story that unfolds in the documentary film on Branson, Missouri, *We Always Lie to Strangers*.[49] Why is there a hillbilly in overalls in so many Branson shows? Because if you come to Branson, Missouri, that's what you expect to see. Why do you see a hula dance every time a trip to Hawaii is referenced? Exactly. In the frontier complex, why does every site have to have a blacksmith shop or a saloon or an outlaw or a brothel or deputies strolling the street? For the same reason: tourists demand to see it, so the tourist attractions supply it regardless of whether the imagery squares with the historical reality or, more pointedly, fails to give a more accurate, complex, and nuanced depiction of the place and time. The extent to which sites will cater to commercially prefabricated notions for tourists depends upon how they are funded and their mission. Disneyland's commitment to historical accuracy, in other words, will be far different from that of a National Historic Site, but regardless of funding source, the fact is that consumer/tourist taste drives even the most historically conscientious sites. No tourist stop will stay open if nobody shows up for it, whether it be Colonial Williamsburg, the St. Louis Arch, or the Old Cowtown Museum in Wichita, Kansas.

In *Devil's Bargains: Tourism in the Twentieth-Century American West*, Hal Rothman points out that there is a wager implicit in tourism ventures.[50] The wager made is that if a particular commodity is packaged to sell for visiting tourists, whether it be history, blues, or beer, then tourists will arrive to consume it. Towns that are successful in this venture often develop an ambivalent, ironic relationship to the tourists.[51] Pomeroy says of towns peddling the western frontier complex to the tourist that "they sometimes resent being dependent on him. They may sometimes mistreat him, offering him what he wants to see instead of what he should see, or what he should see instead of what he wants to see . . . but in the main they welcome the first of the species each year as they welcome spring lambs and winter wheat." The economic comparison here is deliberate, as the tourist "himself is a crop, . . . is capital; he is income; he is market for gasoline and ice-cream cones and real estate, for the West itself; he is the East sitting in judgment on the West when he comes, and conferring the approval that Westerners crave when he comes again."[52] Still, other towns suffering a poor economy may be all too happy to sell their historical souls to the proverbial devil in exchange for a little coin in the coffers. While many towns and cities are still willing to do so, the economic odds of cashing in on this wager today, in the redoubling era of the frontier complex, are not nearly as good as they were in the recreation era that preceded it.

Frontier Era of Redoubling, 1980–Present

The frontier complex entered a new era with a shift in economic policies generally framed as neoliberalism. This is a well-documented shift in the global political economy led by Ronald Reagan, Margaret Thatcher, Deng Xiaoping, and Augusto Pinochet, most generally characterized by less regulation.[53] The net result in the United States was an exodus of manufacturing jobs, a deindustrialization that left behind a gutted manufacturing sector of the economy. Local economies that saw a decline in revenue streams and jobs, such as that found in Fort Smith, increasingly turned toward producing the commodity of cultural heritage tourism to sell to out-of-towners. "You can't ship our history to Mexico," is a quip heard in Fort Smith since the Whirlpool Corporation closed its doors and did just that to thousands of local jobs. Though local history could not be shipped abroad, new markets within the tourism industry grew in this same era. Tourists began mirroring the breaking down of national borders in the global economy by engaging in "eco" and "cultural" tourism abroad as alternatives to domestic travel.[54]

Three observations apply to the era of efforts to sell the frontier complex as cultural heritage tourism. First, although tourism industry publications and promotional materials extol growth in this sector, there are many examples of failed attempts at fostering it and even more examples of struggling local museums and historic homes. Just because "you build it" does not guarantee that they will come. Cultural heritage tourism is simply not the magical boon it is hyped to be. Almost every town is likely to have a struggling cultural heritage attraction.

Second, what precisely qualifies as "heritage" is up for discussion. The National Trust for Historic Preservation defines cultural heritage tourism as "traveling to experience the places, artifacts, and activities that authentically represent the stories and people of the past."[55] Who decides what is and what is not heritage or authentic? Whose heritage are we talking about, and does it need to be accurate or only give the feel of authenticity? Is there any assurance that what is being presented is historically accurate? Perhaps these are only academic questions if all that matters is improving the bottom line for local revenues. If tourists come and spend money, what difference does it make if the tourist narrative is a bit inaccurate? What if it is biased against women and people of color as it reinforces a matrix of white male domination? To what extent should problematic narratives such as these be tolerated if they improve the tax base?

Another economic dynamic at play here is that virtually no cultural heritage tourist site can operate on admission fees alone. At one of the biggest tourist draws in Arkansas, Crystal Bridges Museum of American Art, underwritten by the Walton family, there is no admission fee. National Historic Sites are in essence fully subsidized by the federal government. Some cultural heritage tourist sites are supported by state taxes, others by county or city resources. Most require significant donations and preferably have an endowment or two. Many small institutions are so strapped for resources they find it extremely difficult if not impossible to hire and retain qualified, credentialed staff. Towns are often left with organizations with poorly designed, outdated exhibits with questionable interpretations that are propped up by and large with taxpayer money and run by well-intentioned yet unqualified individuals. Where that is the case, it must then be asked, Do we truly value cultural heritage tourism? If so, where is the value in that sort of commodity except for increased revenues? These questions will resurface as the Fort Smith frontier complex is dismantled for analysis.

The third observation on the current frontier era of redoubling is that there is something of a lag in the faith being placed in cultural heritage tourism. The same formula that worked so marvelously between 1920 and 1980 is often expected to create and sustain the same results in a much changed economy. The heyday of baby boom family vacation tourism that worked so well in a post–World War II economy simply does not work the same today. Moreover, frontier tourist sites of the 1950s, '60s, and '70s were not trumped by Indian casinos, as many are today. There is some of what Lauren Berlant calls "cruel optimism" in a city that trusts cultural heritage tourism to bring a return of the good life when in fact it is a precarious venture. Further, while operating on the faith that cultural heritage tourism will bring an economic boom, other projects are put on hold.[56]

Whether the fecundity of the frontier complex knows any end remains to be seen, but from the American Wild West to *Star Trek*, the frontier has decidedly captured our imaginations. Though technically the frontier is simply a border, it becomes much more than that in our minds when we imagine and fantasize about what is happening on either side of the arbitrarily drawn line. Connecting our imagined fantasies of life on the other side of that border, whether it be to another era, another culture, or another ecosystem or to traveling away from the domain of our everyday, normal domestic sphere is a potent formula for identity formation by an individual or a nation. This process has long been exploited by the tourism industry for the American West. Indeed, purveyors of the tourism industry have learned from anthropology, as illustrated in textbooks such as *Travel, Tourism, and Hospitality Research: A Handbook for Managers and Researchers*.[57] This large tome of fifty-two chapters covers topics from "Crafting a Destination Vision" to "Evaluating the Effectiveness of Trade Shows and Other Tourism Sales-Promotion Techniques."

Chapter 20 of the textbook, "Anthropological Research on Tourism," translates anthropological concepts and theories into industry lingo. Arnold Van Gennep and Victor Turner are cited for explaining the "push factors" associated with why individuals seek out tourist experiences. The text is illustrated with a diagram indicating that an individual living in the "mundane, profane, everyday work" sphere seeks out tourist experiences in a "special, sacred" space resembling the liminality stage of a ritual. In this betwixt and between time and space the tourist is allowed and encouraged to do things he or she does not normally do. Upon completion of the trip, the tourist returns to his or her mundane, profane, everyday work. Thus, individuals seek out tourist experiences as something akin to a religious ritual or pilgrimage.

The textbook recommends that promoters of potential tourist sites actively use this knowledge and make adjustments to provide what the tourist is seeking. The tourist industry creates "pull factors" that provide "otherness, authenticity, and nostalgia" for travelers seeking an escape or respite from their normal lives. Cultural heritage tourism is thus orchestrated for the desired effect. The textbook even offers this succinct assessment: "Tourism is the commoditization of experience."[58]

As such, tourism is susceptible to market forces, and without first capturing the imagination of potential tourists with the right combination of push-pull factors, its economic benefits will not be realized. In Fort Smith much downtown riverfront development has been on hold for years as the city awaits construction of the U.S. Marshals Museum, which is assumed to automatically have the pull factor to draw an abundance of visitors once it is opened.[59] Fort Smith has wagered on frontier-complex tourism since 1955. It has added key frontier attractions every decade or so, banking on presumed dividends from the Wild West frontier complex.

In 2003 the city went all-in on the belief that the Marshals Museum would be a royal flush for the local economy. What was not openly discussed in Fort Smith was that when the Marshals Museum was housed in the Wyoming Territorial Park in Laramie, Wyoming, from 1991 to 2001, it proceeded and ended very badly, with lawsuits filed by the park and the Marshals Service against one another. Also never spoken of is the failed attempt in 1989 to have a Marshals Memorial and Museum in Oklahoma City or the tepid response to Fort Smith's efforts at upping the ante to a $53 million museum facility. When the $91 million spent on the still-unfinished American Indian Cultural Center and Museum in Oklahoma City is mentioned, there is little comment, muting what should be a clear alarm that the wager on cultural heritage tourism is no sure bet.

Cary Carson in "The End of History Museums: What's Plan B?" points out what should be an obvious trend: there has been a consistent decline in visitors to cultural heritage sites for decades. Carson has a list of otherwise flagship tourist institutions that have had to make adjustments because of a decline in visitorship. Among them are Colonial Williamsburg, the Museum of the Confederacy, Great Camp Sagamore, Monticello, Mount Vernon, Old Sturbridge Village, the Mariners' Museum, the City Museum of Washington, D.C., and Conner Prairie. Carson puts a brave face on this decline and explores alternative ways to attract visitors, but he stops short of locating the decline of tourism in the larger economic context.

Following Frederick Jackson Turner's lead in his 1893 essay "The Significance of the Frontier in American History," I am declaring the era of frontier-complex tourism closed. The first four eras of the frontier complex—removal, restraint, reservation, and recreation—all represented economic bonanzas in the forms of fur, cattle, gold, silver, copper, land, entertainment, and tourism. The result each time was that a small number of Americans became exceptionally wealthy from these shifts in the national economy and popular imaginary. From the Chouteaus' fur trade to Carnegie's steel and railroad tycoons, a handful of individuals situated themselves to profit handsomely from the systematically imagineered dreams of the masses.

The economic policies and practices of the redoubling era have dealt a significant blow to both the middle class and the frontier complex. Vestiges of the frontier complex remain by sheer inertia, but the mental driving force behind the frontier complex is found chiefly in the minds of those born before 1980. Short of capturing the imaginations of younger generations wired to the Internet and their smart phones, as Carson advocates, it is just a matter of time before the door to frontier-complex tourism is closed.

2

///////////////////////////

The Frontier Complex
in Fort Smith, Arkansas

But the magazines of today do not know a good story when they see
one. They would rather print trash. They say my article is too long and
"discursive." Nothing is too long or too short either if you have a true and
interesting tale and what I call a "graphic" writing style combined with
educational aims.

Mattie Ross, *True Grit*

For the grand finale of the tour, we were led to the end of a hallway where
a miniature gallows stood on a table. The model was about two feet high
and two feet wide and complete with a little stairwell that ascended to a
platform covered with a vaulted roof. Four little wooden gingerbread men,
each with a hangman's noose around its neck, stood on the trap door awaiting execution. Above these pretend gallows hung the portrait of the man
said to be the architect of this entire scene—Judge Isaac C. Parker—widely
referred to as the Hanging Judge. With his head cocked to the left, his
trademark white goatee and moustache finely combed, and his eyes sternly
focused in the distance, Parker's austere visage presided over the tourist
proceedings at these miniature gallows in Miss Laura's Visitor Center.

The tour guide asked if we knew who Judge Parker was and if we had
visited the National Historic Site to see his courtroom. She suddenly grew
a sideways grin on her face and looked squarely into the eyes of a young
teenage girl whom she had conspicuously ignored up to this point in the
tour of this historic bordello. "Would you like to pull the lever?" she said to
her. "Sure," the girl sardonically replied. With the switch of the lever a trap
door swung open and the four gingerbread men fell to their fates. With
their little ropes cinched around their necks, the hangman's knot did its
designated duty causing each of them to forcefully lurch to one side, which
is said to be what breaks the neck in an actual hanging. In this case the

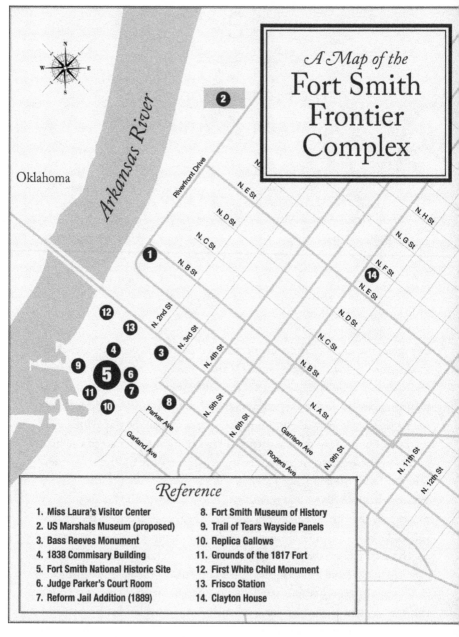

Figure 2.1. Key sites in the Fort Smith frontier complex. Map by Katie Harper.

knot only set the gingerbread men to comically Weeble-Wobbling back and forth on their ropes for several seconds.

A similar scene has been replayed for tourists in the frontier complex of Fort Smith many times. What does it mean to reduce an instrument of capital punishment into a child's plaything? What does it mean for a young teenage girl to tour a brothel and be ignored the entire way? Why did it suddenly become acceptable to engage the girl when the subject turned to hangings and gleefully request that she pull the lever? Moreover, what does it mean for a city to intentionally build its entire tourist marketing scheme around gallows and a brothel? These are the sorts of questions that need to be asked and answered.

The Fort Smith frontier complex consists of one star attraction, the Fort Smith National Historic Site, with a few satellites revolving around it: the Fort Smith Museum of History, Miss Laura's Visitor Center, the Clayton House, and the Bass Reeves Legacy Monument. Numerous nine-teenth-century frontier-complex narratives are projected into and out of the mythic imaginary of the Wild West frontier from these sites. The U.S. Marshals Museum is working to join this frontier complex constellation with a new building shaped like a badge on the edge of the Arkansas River.

Presently, the actions and ethos of each of the principal characters in the Fort Smith frontier complex are represented by their associations with the period when military forts were established (1817–1871) and that of the U.S. District Court for the Western District of Arkansas (1871–1896). Material remains from each period are contained on the present-day grounds of the Fort Smith National Historic Site. Today, the city features fantastic stories of "Hanging Judge" Parker, *True Grit* Deputy Rooster Cogburn, "Invincible Marshal" Bass Reeves, "Hello Bordello Madam" Laura Zeigler, and "Amazon Bandit Queen" Belle Starr.

Each of these tourist narratives is tied uniquely to Fort Smith and told in such a way as to circumvent any other vantage point of the historical events being conveyed, as if the wider world revolved around Fort Smith. This must be done to entice tourists to come to the city and hear the stories that cannot be heard anywhere else. In fact, the stories told in the Fort Smith frontier complex are very similar to the stories told at all the other sites within the frontier complex of the United States: lawbreakers and peacemakers, pioneers and prostitutes, immigrants and Indians, and frontier justice at the end of a rope.

An overarching frontier complex can be accessed by almost any city in the nation that can draw images and characters from the same deep well of this mythic heritage. David Lowenthal observes, "Each people supposes their newly inflated heritage concerns to be unique, reflecting some trait or character or circumstance, some spirit of veneration or revenge that is peculiarly their own." He continues, "Vaunting our own legacy, we are unaware how strikingly concurrent it often is with those of our neighbors."[1] To rephrase "Tip" O'Neill's political aphorism, "All tourism is local." Tourist narratives must foster the illusion that what is being sold cannot be purchased or experienced anywhere else. Superlatives follow, such as "most dangerous," "most lawless," "most arrests," "most hangings," and "most saloons," manufactured to produce the desired effect of more visitors.

Fort Smith Frontier Eras

Framing the Fort Smith frontier complex within the five frontier eras assists in dismantling the subjective uniqueness of its narratives by seeing them within the wider national context. At its inception in 1817, Fort Smith was a key strategic point in the removal era of the frontier complex. The fort was situated in the Missouri Territory in the Arkansas River Valley in what was then the middle of land inhabited by displaced Cherokee. This geographical location had long been inhabited and still contains many prehistoric Indian sites, including one at present-day Spiro, Oklahoma, less than ten miles from downtown Fort Smith, where a settlement flourished during the Mississippian Period (800–1450 CE). Groups of Quapaws, Caddos, and Osages lived and hunted in the area in the seventeenth and eighteenth centuries, interacting with Spanish and French explorers, clergy, and diplomats for two full centuries before the United States formed and became interested in the region.[2]

By the time the Arkansas River Valley fell into the national frontier complex with the Louisiana Purchase in 1803, the local Indians were well versed in European customs and institutions. The Louisiana Purchase doubled the size of the country and precipitated an initially gradual, then rapid, and finally systematic advance of the nation westward. It took fourteen more years before Fort Smith was established.[3] The military fort was the catalyst for the growth of the Belle Point community that became the city of Fort Smith in 1842. Though fundamentally symbiotic, the relationship between the civilians and the soldiers, between the captains of the local economy and the captains of the fort, was never clear or certain, seldom congenial, and most often contentious.[4]

From 1817 to the present, the Fort Smith economy has been inextricably bound to political and military decisions made in Washington, D.C. The political economy of a nation at war necessitates a particular balance between the military and civilian uses of its resources. Fort Smith was founded as a direct result of the War of 1812 to protect the nation's ill-defined southwest border, then given a second life by the U.S.–Mexican War (1846–1848). In the frontier era of restraint Fort Smith troops escorted California gold seekers to Santa Fe, New Mexico, and the U.S. District Court for the Western District of Arkansas imposed federal restraints in Indian Territory from 1851 to 1896. From 1851 to 1871 the court was located in the nearby city of Van Buren before being relocated to Fort Smith.

It is from the era of restraint that Fort Smith acquired its "Hell on the Border" identity while federal Judge Isaac C. Parker presided over parts of Indian Territory from 1875 to 1896. Before that, in 1865, Fort Smith had hosted a post–Civil War Indian Council that led to an 1866 treaty, which laid the groundwork for railroad access and privatization of land in Indian Territory, clearing the brush for the wholesale land runs that would come after the Dawes Severalty Act of 1887. It was these actions that facilitated white intrusion into Indian Territory and the spike in lawlessness that Judge Parker was then tasked with curbing. As such, Fort Smith played a key role in the national transition from the frontier eras of removal and restraint to the era of reservation.

Likewise, the economy of Fort Smith fluctuated with the shifting imperialist impulses of the United States as it breached the continental borders by 1900. Forests near Fort Smith in the Ozark and Ouachita Mountains, which span into Oklahoma, and lumberyards in the Arkansas River Valley supplied the wood for wagons and rifle butts during World War I and gliders in and after World War II. From 1941 to 1961, Camp Chaffee, renamed Fort Chaffee in 1956, adjacent to the city of Fort Smith, readied soldiers for World War II, held German POWs, and then became a base of operations in the Cold War military buildup. In 1953 Fort Smith was designated the base of the 184th Tactical Reconnaissance Squadron, which became the 188th Fighter Wing, commonly referred to as the Flying Razorbacks. During the frontier era of recreation Fort Smith continued to benefit from federal monies spent for military operations abroad while it began repackaging its old military history. It was in 1955 that city leaders began to intentionally brand it with its nineteenth-century frontier history of the military fort and the federal court reign of Judge Parker, with big dreams of cashing in on the nascent boom in frontier tourism.

The Fort Smith–area economy has thus ridden tightly on the vicissitudes of U.S. military involvements and its subsequent frontier complex, from the fort's founding in 1817 to the present. Besides the profound social and economic shifts of the times, the 1975 Indian Self-Determination and Education Assistance Act and the 1988 Indian Gaming Regulatory Act created many new opportunities for Indian nations, especially in attracting tourists with the lure of casino gambling.

In Fort Smith this radically altered the tourism landscape within the frontier complex. Cherokee Casino opened in Roland, Oklahoma, in 1990, just six miles from downtown Fort Smith. In 2014 an $80 million expansion from 50,000 to 170,000 square feet was announced.[5] The Choctaw Casino in Pocola, Oklahoma, completed a $60 million expansion in 2012 that includes a seven-story hotel that employs more than eight hundred people.[6] Technically, the Choctaw Casino does sit in Oklahoma, but it is so close to the state line that its parking lot is literally in Arkansas, just across the Fort Smith city limits. The problem for Fort Smith is that those hundreds of thousands of dollars are being spent very close to it but not in the city or even in the state. Though gaming has been on the ballot at least eight times in Fort Smith, it was voted down each time with vocal opposition coming first from Governor Mike Huckabee, then Governor Mike Beebe as well as the mayor of Fort Smith.[7]

In Fort Smith the message has been very clear, to redouble efforts to attract tourists to its frontier complex. In January 2013 this point was driven home in Fort Smith when it became clear that national defense cuts would remove the 188th Flying Razorbacks from the city, placing more than a thousand jobs in jeopardy and setting the local economy reeling with uncertainty. Months later it was announced that the former home of the 188th was targeted to become a training base for MQ-9 Reaper drones designed for intelligence, reconnaissance, and surveillance missions.[8]

Though the city was somewhat relieved by this news, it remains to be seen how this transition will translate into local jobs. The dependence on federal monies in the Fort Smith economy has been manifest at every turn, yet this fact is virtually absent in both the popular history and cultural memory of the town. Rather than looking eastward toward Washington,

D.C., for its history and its economic well-being, all eyes in Fort Smith are redirected westward in the diversionary narratives of the frontier complex.

Fort Smith Cultural Heritage Tourism

City officials embrace the popular frontier brand and market the city as such frequently. In December 2013 the city introduced Western Heritage Month as May 2014 with the slogan "Relive the Heritage, Restore the Pride."[9] To announce the event, Mayor Sandy Sanders stood atop the restored gallows wearing a Rooster Cogburn eye patch and flanked by historical reenactors representing Judge Parker and Deputy U.S. Marshal Bass Reeves.[10] In tourist discourse and performance, Fort Smith symbolically turns its back on the federal government and its law, order, and money in favor of reenacting deputies and outlaws from Indian Territory to revel in a lawless Wild West. This westward focus affords a mental escape from the reality of the political economy as it veils both the eastern and northern origins of key Fort Smith historical elements, including its dependence on federal money, the carpetbagger background of Judge Parker, the industrialist Jay Gould's northern railroad interests, and the complexity and legacy of slavery, the Civil War, and segregation of the South.

The reality of the political economy of Fort Smith and the nation become entangled with the mythology of the frontier complex. Despite its heavy reliance on federal monies, the region votes heavily Republican, features an active tea party presence, and has strong antitax and antiregulation attitudes. Instead of directly acknowledging Fort Smith's reliance on subsidies from the federal government, many residents toss their socially and politically conservative views on Washington up into the frontier attic, embracing the cocksure independent attitude of the most righteous John Wayne western persona.

To be clear, Fort Smith has its fair share of what Tony Horwitz describes as "Confederates in the attic,"[11] but what I am suggesting here is that the frontier complex, in all its various manifestations across the country, creates another social and mental space for conflicted individuals to exorcise their frustrations with contemporary social structures. Many frontier-complex reenactors in Fort Smith retreat into this frontier attic, where they can express their antigovernment attitudes under the guise of keeping their history alive. The head of the local tea party chapter, for example, is also the leader of a frontier reenactment group, the Sons and Daughters of the Old West.

Public remnants of the Confederate attic can still be found in Fort Smith, such as the Jefferson Davis Highway memorial at the intersection of Garrison Avenue and Highway 22 (Rogers Avenue), the First White Child monument near the old footings of the Albert Pike Free Bridge, and the Southside High School Johnny Rebel mascot and the school song "Dixie," which were used until 2015. More inflammatory markers exist, such as the rebel battle flag that was once the background for the Southside High School scoreboard before it was painted over. Nearly every year surrounding small towns have a day or two when high school boys sport rebel battle flags from their pickup trucks as they parade to and from school. In the rural areas as well as in Fort Smith proper the battle flag can still be spotted. On the grounds of the Fort Smith National Historic Site there are both Union and Confederate reenactment groups to be found on a regular basis. But by and large the dominant imagery used publicly today in Fort Smith to fantasize about pride in heritage and the good old days derives from the more socially acceptable frontier attic.

In similar fashion, tourist discourses in the Fort Smith frontier complex direct attention away from the ills of imperialism, racism, and sexism and are made more palatable for attracting tourist dollars by emphasizing the role the region played in building the nation. The iconographies and narratives of tourism cultivated for popular consumption do this by inscribing binary messages of civilization/savagery, whiteness/other, and masculinity/femininity onto the Fort Smith border and all of its iconic representations—the Parker court and gallows, Miss Laura and her prostitutes, the Bass Reeves story and the monument to him—in the process of imagineering otherness.[12]

Highly stylized and dualistic frontier narratives are offered up as historically authentic products to be consumed by cultural heritage tourists. Thus they fundamentally legitimate, rationalize, and disguise discourses that locate the role of Fort Smith as a champion of westward expansion. This is accomplished in part by mythologizing the life stories of Judge Isaac C. Parker of the U.S. District Court for the Western District of Arkansas, 1875–1896; Deputy U.S. Marshal Bass Reeves, African American lawman of Indian Territory, 1875–1907; Laura Zeigler, madam of a Fort Smith brothel, 1903–1911; and Myra Maybelle Shirley, better known as Belle Starr, a convicted horse thief murdered in 1889. The stories told in the frontier complex about these individuals function to generate an overall narrative in the frontier complex that distracts from and serves as an alibi for the trauma caused by westward expansion and the altered lives left in its wake.[13]

Instead of invoking thoughts of state-induced trauma, the mythic discourse of the frontier border town conjures a carnivalesque atmosphere that sends the imagination reeling far from the facts of misfortune found in the fulfillment of manifest destiny. It is a place of refuge and exoneration from these past and contemporary traumas of the political state for which some may otherwise feel culpable. The frontier complex resonates deeply for many individuals today, serving as a talisman for protecting narrow notions of race, gender, and justice, as it elides their complexity, ignores their ambiguity, and reinforces the social inequalities they create. What is comforted in this frontier attic is the privilege of whiteness, particularly as it relates to white male identity. From what other vantage point could the late nineteenth century be considered the good old days? For social minorities, the frontier attic was a horror.

This is in no way meant to suggest that the individuals or institutions in the frontier complex are the conscious architects of some complex cover-up. On the contrary, individually there is no conspiracy here. Within the national cultural memory of the western frontier, however, there is a collective narrative that bears little resemblance to the historical facts of the nineteenth century. Dime novelists, the frontier club of publishers, and Hollywood, not historians, have generated an overriding frontier narrative that is very hard to escape regardless of how inaccurate it may be.

Fort Smith has its share of books that have misinformed the so-called historical narrative; principal among them is *Hell on the Border*, the 1898 book that in essence is the genesis account for the Fort Smith frontier complex.[14] There is very little scholarly writing on the city, and residents have not discriminated when it comes to poorly conceived or executed amateur writing. Tourists arrive expecting to find the frontier, and the staff, interpreters, volunteers, and reenactors at the various sites of memory unwittingly describe and corroborate many of those expectations while representing the western frontier. In other words, the frontier complex does not simply exist in toto for tourists to be delivered by an interpreter. The meaning of the frontier is created in the interrelationship of the consumers and producers of the frontier complex.[15] Just as I say all the human agents construct the frontier complex by interacting within it, so too have I circumscribed it in my research and in this writing.

Winnowing History from Mythic Heritage

Parsing fact from fiction in frontier tourism discourses can be quite difficult because the manner in which historical facts are appropriated, manipulated, and represented for maximum public impact and tourism dollars in the Fort Smith frontier complex oftentimes exceeds the limits of their signification. Historical facts get lost in the grist, as myths and legends are milled into memories for the tourist who visits these sites. Sociologist Émile Durkheim and anthropologist Paul Rabinow would remind us that even though these "facts" may be socially created and lack scientific, empirical evidence to support their origin, once they are repeated and represented in social reality enough times they become social facts, cultural facts, that are as real to people as gravity.[16] The persona of the Lone Ranger, for example, was suggested by Art Burton to be based on the life of Bass Reeves.[17] The legend has been repeated in the Fort Smith frontier complex so many times that it has become a social fact.

The local newspaper has become complicit in this construction. It has run stories like this one in 2012 quoting a resident as saying, "Experts think that Bass Reeves was the person producers based the Lone Ranger character from. Bass Reeves had an Indian sidekick, he knew Indian languages, and he used disguises when he went after people to arrest them."[18] This social fact swirled in the wake of the dismal box-office showing for Gore Verbinski's 2013 film *The Lone Ranger* and drew national attention to the point that African American scholar Henry Louis Gates Jr. perpetuated it.[19] What was once conjecture by one person is now canon. The historical veracity of this claim merits interrogation, as do the more intriguing questions of why this social fact has been incorporated into the myth of Bass Reeves and why it is repeated so frequently.

Marita Sturken's work on how the attack of September 11, 2001, and the Oklahoma City bombing are memorialized provides a larger context through which to understand the popularity of tropes of the mythic frontiers—they conceal traumas.[20] Connecting Bass Reeves to the Lone Ranger is much more pleasant than talking about him being born into slavery and enduring racism his entire life. Frontier myths function as vehicles for postponing the collective mourning and honest reckoning of the traumatic events and consequences of colonization, slavery, and manifest destiny.

Entering the Frontier Complex

Between August 2009 and October 2014 I talked with reenactment group members, historical interpreters, and consumers of frontier tourism at various sites of memory.[21] I researched archives of primary documents of the Fort Smith frontier complex. I traveled to other frontier complexes, interpretive centers, and towns as well, in Indian nations in Oklahoma; restored military forts in Arkansas, Oklahoma, Kansas, Nebraska, Iowa, Minnesota, and Wisconsin; and Dodge City, Old Cowtown at Wichita, Kansas, and Fort Dodge, Iowa. Following scholars such as Ivan Karp and Steven Lavine and Barbara Kirshenblatt-Gimblett, I have devoted a great deal of attention to the material exhibits at these various frontier complex sites.[22]

When I first moved to Fort Smith in 1997 I was slow to interact in the frontier complex. The Fort Smith National Historic Site was closed for remodeling. It had been struck by a devastating tornado that ripped through the downtown area in April 1996, destroying many buildings and homes. With matching federal monies, the site's directors took the opportunity to remodel and develop the grounds and exhibits. I recall visiting it with my young family shortly after it reopened in 2000; I was nonplused if not flat-out repulsed by this ghoulish site featuring gallows, jails, and the Hanging Judge. I did not return to the frontier complex for many years, and even then I did so only quite reluctantly. It was only after I heard the personal story of Baridi Nkokheli that I propelled myself headlong into the frontier complex.

I began following Nkokheli for research in August 2009 when he was caught in a public paradox of racial ideologies. In one instance, he would be widely respected in his reenactment portrayals of Deputy Marshal Bass Reeves; in the next, he was being told publicly by a member of Fort Smith's elected board of directors—the equivalent of a city council—that in his capacity as head of the Fort Smith Department of Sanitation, Nkokheli could "only serve one master." For four months a series of newspaper articles unfolded in which Nkokheli had to defend himself as not being "an angry black man," all the while being fawned over when he donned the cloak of Deputy Bass Reeves, nineteenth-century lawman. I scoured every article written about the "one master" comment and attended every public session where "Bass Reeves" was making an appearance. The upshot of this very public and highly racially charged event was articulated by *Times Record* and *City Wire* editorials on the matter. Each local media outlet emphasized that it was time for the city to quit looking so racist lest it scare away young professionals.[23] On cue, the issue disappeared from public view.

As a resident social anthropologist at the local university, I was alerted by the one-master episode that something far more complex was at work with Nkokheli's portrayal of Bass Reeves than simply bringing attention to a nineteenth-century African American deputy. In February 2011 Nkokheli gave two talks on the University of Arkansas–Fort Smith campus as part of Black Heritage Month events. The first was his standard Bass Reeves presentation, dressed in period clothes and discussing the life of Reeves from slave to runaway, from "riding for Parker" to becoming the Muskogee, Oklahoma, town constable.

The next day he came back as himself to explain precisely the derivation of his own unique full name: Tokunboh Baridi Nkokheli (he is known as Baridi in Fort Smith, and his signature is T. Baridi Nkokheli). I had heard whispered rumors of its origins and was extremely curious to find out the details. In this presentation he said he was given his Swahili name, which means "I was taken away on a slave ship but now I have returned to serve in the vanguard," by Maulana Karenga after Nkokheli's father, Sgt. Henry Wesley Kellough, was killed out of resentment by white colleagues in the Los Angeles Police Department on the day of President John F. Kennedy's funeral, November 25, 1963.[24] Hearing the explanation of his name set my mind reeling at the implications—when he performs as Bass Reeves, Nkokheli is reviving two dead lawmen. I suddenly saw several new applications of anthropological concepts and how I could deepen my interpretation of the frontier complex. However, what happened to me next was a totally unexpected experience of the uncanny.[25]

Nkokheli's presentation included a series of pictures of his father that reminded me a great deal of my own. Nearly contemporaries, both of our fathers served in the U.S. Air Force. It was impossible for me to look at these photos of Mr. Kellough and not think of my own father—walking the beach in uniform, standing relaxed and poised with such proud self-confidence next to his shiny new car, gazing lovingly at his beautiful bride as he took her hand to help cut the wedding cake, posed in his suit and tie—resembling my father's official school principal pictures. So, too, was it impossible for me to hold back the emotional torrent precipitated by the simple observations that my father has led a full life, and Nkokheli's father's was cut short. I grew up with my father and mother around, and Nkokheli never got to know his dad. I have lived a life of privileged position without concern for prejudicial discrimination, and Nkokheli has not.

To see such youthful energy, such joyous love, such sacredness of a human life shattered and stolen from a family, a family that resembled mine in nearly every way but one, to then be restored with such determined perseverance and grace by Baridi Nkokheli, to only be dragged back into the toxic muck of racist public discourse—all of this was, and still is, an abomination. The uncanny resemblance of my life to Nkokheli's made clearer to me the racial prejudices that permeate our social lives but that are so often veiled in the legacy of white privilege, mine in particular.

The realization that I was in a unique position to study and disclose the inequalities concealed within the frontier complex compelled me to interrogate and expose as many of its questionable alibis as possible. The thought of doing hundreds of hours of reading, research, and writing on topics such as murder, rape, hangings, and prostitution still turned my stomach. Now I could see not only the wider academic value of studying it but also the humanistic side of disclosing how the frontier complex contains contemporary and historical expressions of oppression by class, gender, and race. Because of my deeply felt motivation to understand and educate myself and others about systematically constructed inequalities in the United States, I put my prejudices against frontier tourist traps aside and dove wholeheartedly into the sordid lives of Fort Smith, Arkansas, inhabitants past and present.

Finally, a word about my position as a researcher within Fort Smith. I have been a professor at the University of Arkansas–Fort Smith since 1997, and many of the employees, volunteers, and even visitors at the sites of memory that constitute my field site are former students of mine. For five years, 1998–2003, I served on the board and then as director of the Fort Smith Multicultural Center, during which time I came to know many key figures in the city government and representatives of racial and ethnic groups in Fort Smith. A third avenue by which I am known in my field site comes from my community service. From 2008 to 2014 I served on the board of the Next Step Homeless Services, an agency that assists individuals to transition out of homelessness. Many homeless individuals circulate around the frontier complex, and some of the staff members at the sites, aware of my connection to Next Step, would often ask me questions regarding the homeless situation in Fort Smith.

From this perspective I realize that I have received responses in my fieldwork that are unique to the positions and relations that I have in the city and with the individuals I encounter in my field site. I feel fortunate to have had excellent rapport with all of these groups and with the employees at the historic sites. At times perhaps it has been too comfortable, as many of my former students have been very willing to share all they know with me; at times I have suspected they were simply telling me what they thought I wanted to hear. Other times this familiarity uncomfortably intruded on my observer status. In several instances when as a member of the audience I was asked to clarify historical facts during presentations at sites in the frontier complex. In some cases I knew the answer but refrained from answering so as to not change the narrative being presented.

In addition to the historic sites of memory, eight distinct reenactment groups were under observation for this research. Each has slightly different focus and by and large is made up of a distinct set of people. Some are associated with a particular locale, but most perform at various places throughout the Fort Smith frontier complex. All of the names used for reenactors herein are pseudonyms derived from mythic frontier characters except for Nkokheli's portrayal of Bass Reeves. Any name connected to an actual reenactor would be purely coincidental or due to a reenactor's changing of his or her handle without my awareness. Also, to further protect anonymity I have created the label of a composite group I call the Wild West Shooters to talk about a wide range of reenactment groups and skits that I have observed.

It was made apparent to me during the course of my research that I was insufficiently steeped in western lore and apparel, but such novice status led to several moments of candid instruction in frontier-complex performance like this one recorded in my field notes:

Inspired by my research into the Wild West I went out and bought myself a pair of cowboy boots. Well, honestly they aren't the real deal, full-out cowboy boots. They're those half-pint kind with a zipper on the side. Still, if your pants are covering them it's hard to tell they're pretend boots. I was on my way to the Wild West Shooters' monthly meeting at the local all-you-can-eat buffet, and decided to wear them to try to fit in, however minimally, with my subjects who were decked out in their "period correct" clothes, armed with their "period correct" knives and guns. I found Frisco Kid and Bat Masterson smoking and talking outside the restaurant and eagerly engaged them, hoping they might notice my new boots and feel akin to me. Within seconds I was being instructed on the proper way to break the boots in, to get them wet and let them set up to form around my feet, etc. Frisco Kid looked at me with a sympathetic yet mischievous smile and said, "I'd rather lick a skunk's ass than break in a new pair of boots!" The three of us burst into laughter. Masterson removed the half-toked cigar from his mouth, looked at me daringly, and said, "Write THAT down in your little notebook!"[26]

On the surface level much of my research did focus on material culture, on boots, buttons, bullets, and such. Much of the representation of the frontier, in reenactments, in museum exhibits, and in formal presentations focuses on being "authentic" and "period correct." However, it is my contention that these catch phrases are verbal feats of prestidigitation connected to the alibis embedded within the frontier complex. They direct our attention to the past that they are ostensibly representing, but they are concealing more than they are revealing, both past and present.

This thickly woven text that is the story of Fort Smith requires a thickly described narrative to tease out all the layers, all the contradictions and obfuscations, all the ideological assumptions of race and sex, and all the power-packed manipulations that have come to constitute the popular understanding and cultural memory of Fort Smith history. Ultimately the product of my research, this written document is a crafted object of the ethnographic process that constitutes my very subject, which is my academic interpretation of the frontier complex. I have endeavored to take the advice of both Mattie Ross and Clifford Geertz in my writing, and though this may be "too long" and "too discursive," my goal has been to make it an educational piece of faction.[27] Indeed, the findings of this research will be a surprise to many. What is about to unfold is not what is routinely said about Fort Smith. On the contrary, it is a significant counternarrative to the popular cultural memory. No doubt it will offend and shock the sensibilities of many of the people involved in the production of the Fort Smith frontier complex.

This research and my interpretation of it point out ways in which tourist narratives of the frontier complex are not true and at times not even historically honest or sensible to their consumers. When *True West* magazine declares Fort Smith to be the number one "True Western Town" of 2013, when people confuse the fictional novel and films of *True Grit* with historical lives, when it is declared in December 2012 that we will celebrate a "True Victorian Christmas" at the Fort Smith National Historic Site, then the question arises of what the word "true" means. In a classic Orwellian Ministry of Truth sort of way, all these sites of memory in the frontier complex and their accompanying stories perform a collective double-speak that dress them up to conceal many crucial aspects of oppressive social history. By focusing on a thin slice of the story and then adding a dose of aggrandizement, we leave the domain of historical fact and fully enter the domain of the mythic frontier complex.

So, in the words of anthropologist Edith Turner, "Let's Go!"[28] Come with me on a whirlwind tour of the Fort Smith frontier complex. Let's enter the complex the way a tourist would if arriving by plane. After disembarking in the Fort Smith Regional Airport we would be greeted with tourism guideposts for experiencing the Fort Smith frontier complex. The main exit from the airport features two large displays that attract our attention. We walk over and examine the contents: a vintage rifle, a pistol, an Indian peace pipe, and a photo of five young men shackled together overlaid with images of deputies brandishing their rifles. Intrigued, we read the greetings "Welcome to Fort Smith, a City Alive with History!" and "Judge Isaac C. Parker and the Fort Smith Outlaws." We learn that "the 'Hanging Judge' condemned great numbers of villains to die at the end of a stern rope" and that his "stern justice helped bring an end to the lawlessness of this early frontier's wild n' wooly days."

With our interest piqued we move to the next panel to closely examine the tourist map, pinpointing sites we dare not miss. We read that Miss Laura's is the only remaining brothel that was "one of a row of pleasure palaces along the riverfront." Down the hallway we wait for our luggage and are drawn to a framed scene of an audience gathered to watch a man about to hang from a gallows while a long-bearded fellow flanked by "LAW" books, the Holy Bible, and an American flag looks on. Four frontier-complex tourist sites are featured here. We learn that the Fort Smith National Historic Site is "perched on a bluff overlooking the Arkansas River at Belle Point, the First Fort was originally established to keep the peace among warring Indian Tribes." The "Gallows" are "a reproduction of the original gallows where 79 criminals met justice at the end of a rope." The "Barracks/Courthouse/Jail" tripled as "the historic barracks of troops stationed here in 1851, later home to Judge Parker's Courtroom and the jail known for miles around as 'Hell on the Border.'" The Fort Smith Museum of History displays "artifacts and memorabilia reflecting the colorful history of Fort Smith's frontier days." The City of Fort Smith's logo of an elevated block-house from a wooden stockade fort is underscored by the marketing brand "Where the New South Meets the Old West."

After picking up our luggage we see another invitation into the frontier complex—"Going Back in Time," with an image of a woman standing with arms crossed, gazing away from the scene of four men conversing on the porch of a cabin behind her. With no explanation of who this woman is (Belle Starr), we depart to find our rental car outside and head for Garrison Avenue. After navigating poorly signed one-way streets we are starting to feel a bit lost as we pass vacant buildings, electric power stations, refrig-eration warehouses, and a ramshackle freight-train yard. A few more feet down the road we see the sign for Miss Laura's Social Club.

We step into the restored brothel to find several enthusiastic docents waiting to give us a tour. Rooms are adorned with period furniture and pictures of suggestively posed women. We learn that "Miss Laura's girls had it pretty good" and that "on good nights there was Champagne in the bath tub." At the end of the tour we are treated to a reenacted hanging on a scaled-down gibbet as encouragement to visit Judge Parker's courtroom and gallows at the Fort Smith National Historic Site. Pressed for time, we purchase red souvenir garter belts and depart to learn more about Judge Parker.

As we walk onto the grounds we see six dangling ropes with nooses on the ends hanging from the life-size version of device we had just seen at Miss Laura's. It turns out we've arrived on an "execution anniversary day" and will be treated to a park ranger's talk on the grisly details of the mur-ders, trials, and hangings.[29] The sign on the stairs leading to the gallows platform reads, "Please keep off the gallows. Respect it as an instrument of justice." We pull out our cell phones and "like" the historic site's Facebook page and see a Judge Parker meme with his poised image hovering above the words "Keep calm and let no guilty man escape."

After touring the exhibits we walk to the adjacent Fort Smith Museum of History, where the Wild West Shooters are reenacting a bank rob-bery. Five deputies and six outlaws square off in a shootout that leaves all the robbers dead and all the lawmen standing. One of the bank robbers twitches and is shot again by a deputy for good measure. In the museum we read about the history of Fort Smith and take in the *In the Shadows of the Gallows* exhibit. On the way out of the museum we purchase a T-shirt adorned by a noose and inscribed with the slogan "Hang around Fort Smith awhile." As we stroll Garrison Avenue we make note of the Belle Starr Antique Mall and the Hanging City Body Modification piercing and tattoo parlor. We stop in at the Garrison Point convenience store to get some coffee, and we have a hard time choosing between the flavors— "The Rooster Cogburn Blend," "The Judge Parker Blend," "The Bass Reeves Blend," or the "Belle Starr Decaf Blend."

While driving past the Cheyenne Gentlemen's Club we hear on the radio, which is tuned to KFPW-AM 1230, dubbed "The Marshal," that the Choctaw Casino is right next to Fort Smith. On our way there we drive past On the Border Wine and Spirits, but we don't stop, as we don't want to be late for the Judge Parker band performance at the casino. On the casino door we see an advertisement for the Old Fort Days Rodeo, where "Legends with True Grit are made!" The frontier complex pervades our every move, and late in the evening we give some thought to permanently memorializing our trip to the Fort Smith frontier complex at True Grit Tattoo, but then we recall the quip that unlike love, a tattoo is forever. The next day we depart from the airport with Wild West frontier imagery floating through our minds.

3

////////////////////////

The Peacekeeper's Violence

This is the West, Sir. When legend becomes fact, print the legend.

Maxwell Scott, *The Man Who Shot Liberty Valence*

The Fort Smith National Historic Site is the flagship of the Fort Smith frontier complex. The nineteen-acre park is located downtown just off Garrison Avenue and at the foot of Rogers Avenue, along the Arkansas River, which is the border to Oklahoma, to Indian Territory. The site contains the remains of the original 1817–1824 fort, a second military fort of 1838–1871, the U.S. District Court for the Western District of Arkansas of 1871–1896, the so-called hell on the border basement jail as well as the modernized 1889 jail that replaced it, and a replica life-size gallows designed for hanging twelve individuals with the pull of one lever. The site was opened as a tourist attraction in 1957, became part of the National Park System in 1961, underwent major renovations of buildings and exhibits after the 1996 tornado, and reopened to the public in 2000. More than thirty-five thousand visitors entered the interpretive center in 2013.

It is from this single tourist site that Fort Smith has located itself within the frontier-complex imaginary. It was established in 1817 as one of the very first forts in the frontier complex era of removal (1804–1848) in the north-south chain of forts that served as a buffer between the "permanent Indian frontier" and white settlement, along with Forts Snelling, Atkinson, Leavenworth, Scott, Gibson, Towson, Washita, and Jessup.[1] The second military Fort Smith, which began construction in 1838 and was decommissioned in 1871, carried Fort Smith well into the frontier-complex era of restraint, 1848–1887. The focus here is how this military fort from 1817 to 1871 was part of the first two eras of the frontier complex and how those eras are represented in the redoubling era (1980–present) for cultural heritage tourism.

As is the routine at many such historical sites, visitors are shown an orientation video before touring the exhibits and grounds.[2] The video, *Peacekeeper of Indian Territory*, provides an example of how this border fort is treated in the Fort Smith frontier complex as sitting between the wild, savage, and lawless Indian Territory and the advent of law, order, and civilization.[3] Visitors step into the gift shop as they enter the site and find themselves instantly immersed in the frontier complex. Books, movie posters, and banners display immediately recognizable tropes of men in cowboy hats, pistols, nooses, defiant women, and tranquil homemakers. After checking in at the registration desk, tourists are often first ushered into a small, comfortable theater with soft seats and dimmed lights.

Several Hollywood images are used to quickly and firmly link historical Fort Smith to the frontier imaginary created in the recreation era (1920–1980). Six movie posters line the corridors, hung in marquee fashion and bordered with the words "Fort Smith in Fact *and* Fiction." Outside the theater, visitors see Clint Eastwood's image framed by six hanging nooses in a vintage poster promoting the 1968 film *Hang 'Em High*, with the cautionary words, "The hanging was the best show in town. But they made two mistakes. They hung the wrong man and they didn't finish the job." Pictures of John Wayne, Glen Campbell, and Kim Darby are framed to remind visitors that Rooster Cogburn, Mattie Ross, and Texas Ranger LaBoeuf met in Fort Smith before tracking down outlaw Tom Chaney across the river into Indian Territory in the 1969 Hollywood rendition of *True Grit*.

A third panel features covers Charles Portis' 1968 novel *True Grit* and a book by Douglas C. Jones titled *Winding Stair* with a picture of the Fort Smith gallows, as well as an advertisement for the film *When Daltons Rode*, described as a "frontier drama" about the "most reckless renegades in history." This panel offers some qualifying text to put the visitor on notice that what one reads in a novel or sees in a movie does not necessarily square with the facts: "Since the late 1800's, the characters who played out their lives in Fort Smith and the Indian Territory have inspired many books and novels. In the twentieth century, movies have also found them a gold mine for imaginative stories of harrowing adventure. Hollywood's vision of this region is gripping—but the real story of what happened here is just as fascinating!" There is an inherent contestation for knowledge in this conflation of Hollywood imagery and historical facts. The historic site is wagering that after the fantastic stories from popular culture have lured the visitors, historical facts will prevail.

Inside the theater there are three more, similarly framed movie posters. John Wayne has an eye patch on for the reprisal of his famous character with Katherine Hepburn in the 1975 *Rooster Cogburn (. . . and the Lady)*. This poster shows a drunken Cogburn on the ground holding up a bottle toward the scolding lady. Next is the poster for *Belle Starr: The Bandit Queen*. This 1941 film starring Randolph Scott and Gene Tierney failed to permanently affix Belle Starr into the national frontier imaginary, but it is used throughout the Fort Smith frontier complex to conjure images of a femme fatale version of a Scarlett O'Hara of Indian Territory. The final movie poster, promoting the 1950 film *The Daltons' Women*, features "Lash" LaRue snapping a long whip, the bearded "Fuzzy" St. John brandishing a pistol, and a poised woman in a classic dance-hall dress. Once primed with this heavy dose of frontier-complex mythology, the audience is ready for the ostensibly factual orientation video.

Mythic Removal

Chirping birds are heard before any image fills the screen.[4] Through a thicket of trees the Poteau River comes into focus. The audience begins the trip into the past hearing and seeing an image of unspoiled, pristine, and uninhabited wild nature. The narrator invites us to view the cutting edge of the frontier. The site is framed in the frontier complex with the first words, "Fort Smith, it's the window through which you see the history of the vast panorama of the west unfolding." The camera pans down the Poteau River to the confluence with the Arkansas River to expose a view westward into Indian Territory, into Oklahoma.

The background audio changes from sounds of nature to a low, foreboding, and suspenseful musical note. The music quickly turns into a frolicking tone that matches the exuberance with which the narration describes the frontier lying before the first settlers to the area. The narrator, former local TV news personality Bur Edson, tells us,

> This military outpost acted as a funnel, feeding into the wilderness soldiers, traders, explorers, emigrating Indians, and settlers. They came here first before heading out to their western destinations.[5]

The keyboard soundtrack builds to a playful flourish as the image of promise and new possibilities for this influx of people to the area is heralded. It is presented as a momentous precipice, full of adventuresome opportunities for everyone participating in it.

The narration moves quickly from this image of gleeful hopefulness to the seriousness of the role of law and order that the fort embodies:

And for nearly eighty years Fort Smith's presence served notice to the lawless that the full and complete authority of the United States government stood on the frontier.

With this central thesis of the orientation video established, the camera pans to a waving American flag flying over the remains of the 1817 fort to confirm its commanding presence. The screen transitions with the words "FORT SMITH: Peacekeeper of Indian Territory" overlaid on a halcyonic depiction of the fort. This is the overarching mythology of the frontier complex in Fort Smith—that it was initially built to keep the peace between the Indians on the edge of civilization and that it served that role for "nearly eighty years," from 1817 until 1896, when the Judge Parker era of the Western District Court of Arkansas ended, a span covering the frontier complex eras of removal, restraint, and reservation.

The facts of this peace and the chronology of the fort are, in actuality, not as smooth or tidy as the video suggests, but the viewer has no time to reflect on that. Suddenly we are standing on the Belle Point rock outcropping, looking up the Poteau River. We are told of the first troops' arrival from Little Rock who, in a matter of directional clarification, would have been seen looking down the Arkansas River, not up the Poteau. The camera cannot pan down the river because it would reveal a modern bridge carrying vehicles that would spoil the image of untouched nature. With that bit of visual misdirection, we are told,

Fort Smith's story begins on Christmas Day, 1817, when a keel boat heavy with troops and supplies landed at Belle Point on the Arkansas River. Major William Bradford and sixty-four men of the United States rifle regiment, under orders from General Thomas A. Smith, began constructing a small wooden stockade. This was the first Fort Smith.

This holiday arrival was not quite as maiden a landing as depicted. An advance contingent of soldiers who scouted out the location began setting up camp in November of that year and were at Belle Point awaiting the regiment's arrival.[6]

The video narrative presses the severity of the situation, as we see a drawing depicting the 1817 wooden stockade, complete with palisades and

Figure 3.1. Replica of the Thomas Jefferson peace medal. Akin to those carried on the Lewis and Clark expedition, the token ironically accents exhibits at the Fort Smith National Historic Site featuring the demise of Indian Territory. Photo by the author.

turrets, to confirm that the "escalating conflicts along the western frontier made this post necessary." In keeping with the premise that all tourism is local, the narrative leaves out the historical connection that Fort Smith had to the chain of forts built on the edge of the then far-western border of the United States. The absence of discussion about its role in the so-called permanent Indian frontier in the video or in interpretive exhibits is especially conspicuous compared to those at the Fort Scott National Historic Site two hundred miles straight north of Fort Smith. In Fort Scott's interpretive video and exhibits, the entire initial reason for its being was to be a buffer between the permanent Indian frontier and white settlement as with the rest of the north-south chain of forts.[7] The narrower concept of Fort Smith's frontier discourse creates neatly compartmentalized eras of military fort followed by the Parker federal court, which can then be conveniently packaged into touristic narratives emphasizing its relation to neighboring Indian Territory.

Fort Smith is presented as sitting on the frontier between the civilized East and the savage West. This positioning is reinforced:

The growing violence, however, was not between whites and Indians but between the Cherokee and the Osage.

This tribal warfare is explained:

For more than two hundred years Europeans had been moving inland from the Atlantic and Gulf coasts. This white expansion displaced many Indians who fled their native lands in the Southeast to preserve their way of life in unfamiliar territories.

At these words a map of the United States appears, and the original areas in the Southeast inhabited by the Chickasaws, Choctaws, Cherokees, Muscogees (Creeks), and Seminoles light up on the screen, each in a different color. As "unfamiliar territories" is spoken, the land acquired in the Louisiana Purchase is highlighted to show where these Indians "fled." While this was the conceived permanent Indian frontier, it is not labeled or discussed as such.

Instead, we are informed that "the clash between the Cherokee and Osage began this way." While there was indeed such a clash, the narrative firmly draws attention away from any hint that the violence was between whites and Indians. To the contrary, the video develops an 1808 land cession treaty with the Osage that "allowed President Thomas Jefferson to encourage more Cherokees to move into the area and settle permanently." A few significant points are omitted here in both the video and the site's exhibits. It was Quapaws, Tunicas, and Caddos more than Osages who lived in the region into which the Cherokee were being displaced, but they are not mentioned. Nor is it clear that it was the current state of Arkansas, then Missouri Territory (it became Arkansas Territory in 1819), not Oklahoma, where many Cherokee were settling. As early as 1780 Cherokees were moving into the then Spanish-controlled Arkansas River Valley. Before Indian removal began in earnest in 1830 and before Arkansas entered statehood in 1836, many Cherokees had well-established plantations complete with African slaves in the region.[8] Taking their own turn at othering their enemies, Cherokees argued that since they had slave-based agriculture they were more civilized than their savage Osage neighbors. In fact, the Osages were not the wild savages they are depicted as being; they had been trading with the Spanish and French for a century.[9] After Arkansas statehood, Cherokee settlement within the state's borders was wiped from official memory as quickly as Indians were removed from the state into the ever-shrinking

Indian Territory. The historical fact that many Cherokees initially lived in present-day Arkansas is very difficult to find mentioned anywhere in the Fort Smith frontier complex.

Meanwhile, the story line in the orientation video paints a strictly binary representation of very pale-skinned Cherokees who are shown in drawings dressed in European clothing, with their gaze focused on the viewer, juxtaposed to Osages, who are sienna and ochre in complexion, wearing animal-skin clothes and feather adornments, with their gaze looking defiantly away from the European way of life and decidedly past the viewer. We next learn from the narrator,

> As the number of Cherokees increased on what was once Osage land, outbreaks of violence became more frequent, and the two tribes were on the verge of open warfare. U.S. officials hoped the establishment of Fort Smith would ease tensions and make the area safe for future white and Indian settlement.

While the chaotic complexity of the situation is presented in this simplified narrative, delivered by a trained and soothing voice, it draws attention away from the most immediate concern at the time, which was to make what was then Arkansas Territory a secure place to relocate Indians from farther east.[10]

Instead, a scene of armed troops and officers standing in commanding composure appears with this narration:

> After several [five] years of struggle the military began to see results. In 1822 the Cherokee and Osage agreed to a peace treaty.

At this point the narrative begins to drop hints as to the underlying reason for the fort's existence:

> Soldiers could then concentrate on building roads, patrolling frontier boundaries, and regulating trade and travel through Indian country. Their success prompted a local newspaper editor to declare Fort Smith essential to western defenses of the nation.

The trajectory of the narrative suddenly shifts:

> By 1824 [two years later], however, the situation had changed. Military commanders realized that in order to maintain control of the frontier they needed to relocate the fort farther west. Troops abandoned Fort

Smith and moved seventy miles up the Arkansas River, where they built Fort Gibson.

This is largely how the establishment of the fort is framed. A park brochure reads, "First Fort Smith was built in 1817 to keep peace in the Arkansas River Valley between the native Osage and newly arriving Cherokee. . . . Trying to be more effective in maintaining the peace, the Army abandoned the fort in 1824 and moved farther west."[11] Thus, Fort Smith was abandoned for the first but not the last time in its long history of jilted relations with the federal government.

Removing Myth

Let's push pause on the video for a moment. We are three minutes and sixteen seconds into the fifteen-minute orientation video. Already, the simplified premise of the mythic frontier has been superimposed upon a complex set of historical facts. The peace that is consistently indicated is between Indian groups, not between Indians and whites or the U.S. government. In the larger scheme of national expansion, it was pursuit of the latter, not the former, peace that led to the establishment and perpetuation of Fort Smith. The small fort was part of a larger military strategy of establishing an entire string of forts along the western border of the expanding and encroaching political state. This point is clarified in a book commissioned by and sold at the Fort Smith National Historic Site gift shop. In *Fort Smith: Vanguard of Western Frontier History Southwest*, Billy Higgins notes that the fort was just one in "a chain of fortifications along the length of the western frontier of the United States, each one of them garrisoned by a single company of the U.S. Army's Rifle Regiment. These frontier posts formed the young nation's line of defense on its western borders and stretched from Green Bay on the Fox River in Wisconsin to Fort Claiborne on the Red River."[12] In a point that will become a recurring theme, though this historical context is readily available in books sold at the site, it remains unincorporated in its exhibits and interpretation.

In *Fort Smith: Little Gibraltar on the Arkansas*, by Edwin Bearss and Arrell Gibson, also sold in the site's bookstore, the first sentences declare that Fort Smith exists because "the United States Army was a primary force in opening the Southwestern wilderness. By 1817, a pattern of military settlement had developed which was repeated with increasing regularity." It continues, "When the area was safe for pioneer farmers and townsmen the soldiers moved on to open new frontiers."[13] Rather than protecting Indians, Bearss and Gibson emphasize, "the most obvious duty was military—guarding the United States when the Southwest was shared with Spain and Mexico." As a side effect, "an extension of the military role was pacifying the Indian tribes upon whose hunting range the military settlement intruded."[14] Though counterfactual knowledge is widely available, the rationale of keeping the peace between Indian groups dominates the frontier tourist narrative in Fort Smith.

Even if one entertains this trope it does not withstand historical investigation. Higgins notes that there is scant evidence that the military was used to encroach into Indian-versus-Indian affairs. On the contrary, "[Major] Bradford never ordered his rifle company into the field to head off or to punish the Cherokee or Osage raiders in Arkansas or in the territories to the west."[15] With a clear eye toward the west, it was in the best interest of the United States to allow Indians to war among themselves, thus making the path to the Pacific that much more open. Consequently, "Bradford was content to allow those bitter enemies their chances to settle scores directly with each other, which they continued to do."[16] Moreover, in this frontier complex era of removal the military stationed at Fort Smith lacked governmental authorization to use force. Even Colonel Matthew Arbuckle was surprised to learn this in 1822. The goal here was to oversee the border between the permanent Indian frontier and white settlement. Unable to turn the power of Belle Point on the Cherokee and Osage, Arbuckle was forced to shift to plan B, diplomacy.[17]

An even larger context can be drawn from Kathleen DuVal's *Native Ground: Indians and Colonists in the Heart of the Continent*, which is specifically about the North American Indians who inhabited the Arkansas River Valley, through Oklahoma, Arkansas, and into northern Louisiana, and how they actively negotiated their relations to the political states of Spain, France, Britain, and eventually the United States. DuVal argues that groups including the Caddo, Quapaw, Osage, and Tunica had the upper hand during the seventeenth and eighteenth centuries so long as they had the four contesting political states to play off one another. The Louisiana Purchase and the War of 1812 radically altered this strong position. DuVal observes, "The Osages had preferred white settlers to Cherokees, but soon white settlers would define all Indians as the enemy and push them all to the margin, establishing the region as their own exclusive native ground."[18] Suddenly there was only one political state to deal with, and it was narrowing its focus toward viewing all Indians as one conglomerate entity that had to be uniformly treated.

Indians as well as veterans were encouraged to migrate into the newly acquired land of the United States after it became free and clear. The population quickly began shifting, DuVal notes: "The defeat of Tecumseh's forces and the conclusion of the War of 1812 had decreased fears of Indian uprisings. As a result, the number of non-Indian settlers rose from fewer than 400 in 1803 to over 14,000 in 1820, making them the most populous group in the Arkansas region . . . reaching 30,000 by 1830."[19] The white migrants soon found themselves crosswise with the plans of the federal government to relocate Choctaw and Cherokee into the Arkansas Territory; these maneuverings led to clashes between Indian groups, especially the Cherokee and Osage.

The emerging role of the federal government was not one of protector or peacekeeper, even though requests to keep the peace came directly from the Cherokee and the Osage. This point was driven home when "in 1821, [Osage] Chief Clermont II told Major William Bradford, the commanding officer of Fort Smith: 'you tell us the president looks on all the Red People as a Father looks on his Children' and 'you tell us he is sorry to hear that the Cherokees & us are killing each other.'"[20] The Osage and Cherokee chiefs' arguments amounted to this: "If the United States insisted on sending Indians west, the chief held the United States responsible for compelling those Indians to respect the rights of those already there."[21] Despite the pleas to establish peace between the Cherokee and the Osage, "federal policy avoided direct involvement in Indian-Indian violence."[22] Higgins asserts the same: "Bradford's actions cast doubt on the standard historical interpretation that Fort Smith was founded for the purpose of keeping peace between the Indians. That does not seem to be the role that the commanding officer understood for himself and his garrison once it was established. Bradford intended to use force against Indians only when they attacked whites on non-Indian territories."[23]

When the Osage could not get a response from Washington, they reached out to their religious friends. "In 1821 . . . their missionary William Vaill was surprised to learn of Bradford's lack of authority to intervene," DuVal explains. "Vaill noted that 'we expected that the design of the garrison was to keep peace among the Indians. We find, however, that they are not to oppose the Indians in their wars with each other.'" On a more practical level, the idea of federal troops keeping the peace is fanciful: "Bradford's garrison of fewer than 100 men was no match for thousands of Cherokees and Osages."[24] The basic math of being so outnumbered makes the often-repeated narrative that the fort was put there to keep the peace between the Indians absurd. Regardless, the discourse that I observed during my fieldwork at the National Historic Site perpetuates this frontier complex myth.

In this light the narrative of white-Indian affairs and the military strategy for the existence of Fort Smith becomes clearer: "Federal officials had no qualms about intervening when Indian warfare endangered whites. . . . Official policy on the Osage-Cherokee war stated that 'the U. States will take no part in their quarrel; but if, in carrying on the War, either party commit outrages upon the persons or property of our citizens,' Major Bradford's troops should act."[25] In response to spreading rumors that Osage and Cherokee were about to cause violence to whites, Bradford, quoted in Du-Val, promptly and sternly laid down the power of the federal government: "'if you shed one single drop of a White man's blood I will exterminate the Nation that does it,' leaving 'not a Cherokee or Osage alive on this Side of the Mississippi.'"[26] The peace was thus kept by allowing Indians to kill each other and by threatening to kill any Indians who interfered with white intrusion into the region.

Why was the first fort built? At minimum it is clear that it was not to keep the peace between Indians but rather to create a stable place to relocate Indians from the Southeast in order to open up more agricultural land for whites in Georgia, Alabama, and Mississippi. At this time, Indian Territory consisted of the present-day states of Arkansas and Oklahoma, which means the first Fort Smith was in the heart of lands designated for removed Indians and surrounded by the Osage and the recently relocated Cherokee and Choctaw. From 1817 to 1828 the Cherokee lands included the northwest corner of present-day Arkansas, and from 1820 to 1825 the Choctaw lands included the far-southwest corner.[27]

The rolling frontier border was in reality a front line of removal, a destination for Indians in the way of white western advancement. White settlement came slowly but steadily, stretching hundreds of miles to the east in the wake of the earlier westward-moving settlers.

Savaging the Civilized

Resuming the video at the 3:16 mark, the military has moved upriver in 1824 to establish Fort Gibson, and we learn in the following minute and twenty-three seconds of the role that the frontier, and specifically Fort Smith, played in "civilizing" Indians:

> The soldiers, however, left behind a civilian settlement which eventually grew into a bustling trading center. Although no soldiers were permanently stationed here for the fourteen years between 1824 and 1838, the government viewed Fort Smith as an important part of its emerging policy of Indian removal.

This is a vague period in the history of the fort, as it is routinely said that it was both abandoned and had active troops. It also is emphasized that it was a key site in the supply chain for Indian removal during the 1830s, though little may have been there but a supply depot. Regardless, in the second life of the fort we can observe that it is once again complicit in the project to sequester Indians for the purpose of allowing and encouraging white settlement east of the Mississippi.

Instead of keeping the peace between the Indians, now the fort played the supporting role of assisting Indians in their transformation from savagery to civilization:

> For years, the federal government had promoted a policy of transforming the Indians into its image of a civilized people. However, the desire of land-hungry Americans often interfered with this process. It was hoped that the relocation of the Indians to the West would give them a chance to complete their conversion into Christians and farmers.

With no sense of irony the narrator reinforces the collective amnesia that Indians were not "civilized," and that they were unfamiliar with farming and missionaries despite centuries of evidence to the contrary. Because so many economic, political, and social practices were held in common, differences rooted in race had to be constructed and reinforced in order to legitimate the unfolding inequalities between the two groups.

The process of othering the peoples of North America into naturalized racial categories had been in process for decades. Ever since Thomas Jefferson outlined the intellectual capacities of the "three races" in his 1785 *Notes on Virginia*, Indians were favored with the ability to learn the ways of civilization, if just "given the proper chance." Africans fared far worse in Jefferson's estimation, as incapable of the cognition demanded for civilization and thus enslaved by whites and Indians of the Southeast: "I believe the

Indian, then, to be, in body and mind, equal to the white man. I have supposed the black man, in his present state, might not be so."[28] With this one little sentence Jefferson provided the impetus for more than a century of so-called race science and government policy that systematically privileged whiteness.

Meanwhile, the orientation video implies, in the Southeast and in early tribal migration into Indian Territory, the fruits of the Jeffersonian civilizing process were showing:

> Tribes like the Cherokee, Chickasaw, Choctaw, Muscogee, and Seminole in the Southeast farmed, built mills and plantations, and sent their children to missionary schools where they learned to read and write. Some of the Indians even owned black slaves. It's understandable, then, that they had no desire to give up their lands.

Indeed, slavery served as an overcard for the Five Tribes' entrée into civilized status and for identifying with whiteness. The video narrative insinuates a passive-aggressive way for contemporary whites to rationalize Indian resistance to removal. Further evidence shows that the Five Tribes were "civilized" well before their forced removal: Sequoyah's syllabary and its use in the publication of the *Cherokee Phoenix* newspaper beginning in 1828, the quick adoption of constitutional governments, and the rule of law in their own supreme court systems, not to mention the fact that they were farming prior to European contact.

While Jefferson's paternalistic and essentialized notions of race were highly flawed, Andrew Jackson's were shrewd and apparently above contempt. We are told in the next two minutes of our orientation about his approach to managing Indian relations:

> Although the Supreme Court eventually confirmed the sovereignty of Indian tribes, President Andrew Jackson would have none of it. He refused to enforce the Supreme Court's decision, and he ignored scores of treaties with various Indian nations which stipulated that the US government was to protect Indian lands from being overrun by white settlers.

The façade of keeping the peace between Indians crumbles during this policy-driven period of removal, and essentialized notions of savage and civilized are used as diplomatic chips as Cherokee, Osage, and white settlers all jockey for position in the frontier landscape. DuVal indicates the complexity of these categories as early as 1812: "Downplaying their ties to the past, Cherokee leaders used their 'civilized' reputation to attract United States support. Chief Tolluntuskee wrote Eastern Cherokee Agent Return J. Meigs that the Osages were 'savage,' 'barbarous,' 'uncultivated,' 'wild Indians.' Cherokees argued that they were implementing United States Indian policy while the Osages were impeding it."[29]

The military hero of New Orleans, Andrew Jackson, continued in his presidency the westward movement that his accomplishments in the War of 1812 had helped begin. He had a very clear vision of how to use newly acquired western lands, the orientation video explains:

> Jackson's administration was also responsible for the Indian Removal Act of 1830. It gave government officials the right to negotiate treaties with Indian tribes exchanging their eastern territory for land west of the Mississippi. These treaties were often signed by an unauthorized minority of the tribe because they supported removal, but the majority of Indians were reluctant to leave their homelands; however, they soon had little choice.

What had been rhetorically voluntary up to that point now became mandatory:

> By the mid-1830s, the Army was involved in removing some Indians from their lands, even though this violated recent treaties.

No matter how much civilization the Indians may have acquired, equality was an ever-moving goal post for them.

Nevertheless, Indian removal is said to have given Fort Smith its second life as a frontier border agent for the federal government:

> Fort Smith served as the primary supply depot for those Indians who managed to make it to Indian Territory. Between 1830 and 1834, soldiers dispensed blankets, axes, blacksmith tools, spinning wheels, and other goods that they had been promised by treaty. These goods were to help the Indians rebuild their shattered lives. When the distribution center moved farther west, Fort Smith's buildings fell into disrepair.

Fort Smith had been abandoned in 1824 when troops moved to Fort Gibson and was not garrisoned again until April 1831. The troops stayed until

June 1834, when they abandoned Fort Smith yet again and established Fort Coffee not far across the river in Indian Territory.[30]

What we are not told in the video or any of the exhibits at the site is that in the three years the fort was assisting in Indian removal, the military was dependent on local Cherokee farmers for supplies. Captain John B. Clark "hoped to secure several thousand bushels from Cherokee farmers."[31] This reveals the key point that many Indians from the Southeast had been living on productive farms in present-day Arkansas and Oklahoma for several decades prior to the mass removal to Indian Territory. This fact is consistently silenced across the Fort Smith frontier complex. Regardless, these "old settlers" were well established and clearly illustrating earmarks of "civilization" in that they were producing thousands of surplus bushels of crops. Captain John Stuart described the Cherokee as "very little behind the [white] people of Arkansas Territory" and "infinitely a better and more orderly people."[32]

At this juncture, the role of Fort Smith in the frontier complex was in serious jeopardy. The time between 1824 and 1838, when construction of the second Fort Smith would be decided, reveals the economic stakes of growing a country and how the local civilian population came to benefit from and exploit such growth. Why was Fort Smith given a third life when nearly all military personnel were opposed to it? One answer could be that businessmen in the area used their political savvy to garner the construction of a second Fort Smith, which infused more than $300,000 into the local economy.[33] The historical details of this period are important because they reveal the ulterior motives for the fort's existence and the way in which the savage/civilized binary was used on the border to exploit the situation for local economic gain. The second fort was built to satisfy the desires of these local business leaders, who contended that it would be an economic engine for the region. If American Indians had to be thrown under the wagon to do so, from John Rogers' point of view, so be it.

The cultural memory of this period is given a mythic gloss in the orientation video at the National Historic Site. At the 6:40 mark, the narrator explains how the second fort came into existence:

In 1838 the War Department ordered the construction of a new Fort Smith. It was a decision based largely on the Arkansas congressional delegation's argument that violent feuding within the Cherokee nation would spill over into the white settlements. Military leaders like future US president Colonel Zachary Taylor thought this unlikely and objected to the expense of the second fort.

Two significant points here need development. First, to say that Colonel Taylor and the military in general were "opposed" to the fort is a vast understatement. And second, we are given a clue here of how essentialized, binary notions of savage versus civilized were being used for political ends.

John Rogers, Fort Smith Lobbyist

Rogers had significant personal reasons for wanting Fort Smith rebuilt. He had been investing in and developing hundreds of acres surrounding the first fort for nearly two decades. Ultimately he incorporated the city in 1842, earning him the title of town "father." The main east-west bisecting road through Fort Smith today bears his name. He first moved to the area in 1821, when he operated a tavern and sutler store at Belle Point. A civilian population slowly grew to service the needs of the soldiers. The civilian clout, business acumen, and at times downright belligerent attitude that John Rogers wielded over the military presence is impressive.[34] After the military Fort Smith closed in 1824, Rogers actively lobbied any political party he could to persuade them to return the military installation to near the Belle Point settlement. He had made an investment in the area and he wanted to see a return on it. He had supply lines, goods, and a great deal of whiskey to sell to soldiers, and he could illegally profit from its sale to Indians as well. Fort Gibson was developed seventy miles farther upriver in 1824, and the smaller Fort Coffee was built about five miles up the Arkansas River from Fort Smith practically on top of the Mississippian Period remains of Spiro Mounds. Fort Coffee and this period are essentially omitted from the frontier narrative presented in the Fort Smith frontier complex, making for a smoother, simpler story.

The Fort Coffee site was widely believed by military personnel to be a superior location over Fort Smith for several reasons. Mainly the location afforded a much better view of the river and thus a greater opportunity to catch those trafficking illegal whiskey up the Arkansas River to be sold in Indian Territory. Captain Stuart was in charge of the troops at Fort Coffee and was concerned that townspeople at Belle Point settlement were taking advantage of their proximity to Fort Smith. John Rogers and his business partner, John Nicks, benefited from a previous military association from the War of 1812 that Nicks had with Colonel Arbuckle, who oversaw the military presence in the Fort Smith region. Rogers and Nicks thus took liberties in many places that irritated others such as Officer William McClellan. After the troops vacated Fort Smith and moved to Fort Coffee, Bearss and Gibson report, "McClellan said that it was startling to learn that the firm of Nicks and Rogers held a federal license to trade with the Indians at Fort Smith." Beyond that, the business partners were selling them whiskey, no less: "Nicks and Rogers had friends in high places, as was evidenced by the openness with which they flouted their operations at Fort Smith."[35] Such was the nature of the frontier political economy.

The relationship between John Rogers and Captain Stuart grew steadily more contentious, Higgins asserts: "When John Rogers began to lobby Arkansas congressmen and the secretary of war for rebuilding Fort Smith on a grander scale, Captain Stuart wrote stinging letters about the nefarious conduct of Rogers and other real estate speculators. Stuart suspected Rogers, the largest property holder in the town, of acting to further his own 'pecuniary interest' in seeking to restore the building and fortifications at Fort Smith."[36] This military oversight of the local economic gaming of the fort's presence is a recurring theme with Rogers, but he was a skilled negotiator.

Just as the Cherokee had done before him, Rogers used the narrative of the mythic frontier as a border between savages and the civilized as a political tool. Rogers was "having petitions circulated to persuade the War Department to expand the garrison at Fort Smith to six companies or to remove Stuart's company. Stuart's informants said that Rogers had employed three men to obtain petition signatures and paid them a set fee for each signature they obtained, including those of children and of persons no longer living." And then more pointedly, Bearss and Gibson note, "the purported grounds for calling in additional troops was that Indians were 'committing depredations upon the Property of the Whites.'"[37] Thus, Rogers played the savage card to "other" the Indians and incite fear in hopes of garnering the economic boom of the construction and presence of a second fort. More important, all Indians regardless of methods of food production or religious faith were now being put in the "other" category. Where differences used to be recognized between groups, say, the Osage and the Cherokee, now they were just all Indians. Though this may look like only a generalized American Indian identity was being constructed, the notion of what constitutes whiteness was also being solidified in the same process as the alternate position to the "savage slot."[38]

John Rogers' friend Major Mathew Arbuckle contributed to this savage othering: "Arbuckle warned, if the tribes resolved their differences and directed their energies to a war against the settlers, a 'strong work' at Belle Point" was the best defense.[39] The fort was now "needed" to protect whites from Indians, not to keep the peace between Indians. Captain Stuart roundly rejected Rogers' essentialized depiction and instead described the local Indians as "perfectly quiet, and [who] are on the most perfect terms of friendship with the whites, and have never manifested the least appearance of having any feeling to the Contrary."[40] Stuart is calling Rogers out on his use of what Richard Flores notes in the mythologizing of the Alamo as a "feigned frontier imagery."[41] Captain Stuart declared pointedly, "Pecuniary interest, and not fear of Indians, is the Sole Cause of Wanting a large body of Troops at this place."[42]

Most members of the military but Arbuckle contended that Fort Coffee, not Fort Smith, was where the troops should be positioned. Furthermore, Bearss and Gibson continue, Stuart "described Rogers' tract as 'generally poor and unfit for Cultivation.'"[43] It is clear from the record that Captain Stuart was dumbfounded by this entire process as he "searchingly questioned War Department officials on the issue of restoring and enlarging Fort Smith. He asked why the government should pay Rogers 40 dollars an acre for poor, denuded land, expose troops to taverns and loose women, and contribute to the moral deterioration of his men when the War Department could find much better military sites farther west."[44] Stuart even had the surgeon general look into the matter. Stuart's health concerns were well founded on a long record of ill health at Fort Smith. One Charles B. Welch, a surgeon from Washington, D.C., blamed inhabitants' poor health on the Poteau River's tendency to get backed up when the Arkansas River water level was high. The result was a stagnant breeding ground for illness, according to his report.[45]

For his part, Rogers did all he could to sway opinions in Washington back to Fort Smith. He "carried on an aggressive private campaign"; "he advertised in the *Arkansas Gazette* and in several Eastern newspapers plans to convert 160 acres of his Belle Point holdings into town lots"; he "revealed that he would be willing to sell any of his land in the area in question to the government at a fair and reasonable price" and would "hold in abeyance his plan to divide his land into lots if the government would give him some indication of interest."[46] On April 4, 1838, "Congress passed a joint resolution authorizing 'the Secretary of War to purchase a site for a fort at or near the western boundary of Arkansas." This was in direct contradiction to the established military policy of constantly pushing the army posts west with the advancing frontier" as well as "against the advice of leading military thinkers" who had previously "contended that there was not the slightest military reason for a fort in or near Arkansas."[47] Regardless, John Rogers' economic engine was revving.

While military officials exercised their disbelief, John Rogers made quick work of directing Washington officials to his property. Rogers owned 640 acres that he had purchased from the federal government for $450 in 1834. Four years later, he wanted the "fair and reasonable" price of $30,000 for that same property. Captain Stuart had estimated it was worth $1,300 at the most. Just eight days after the resolution passed to build the second fort, an agreement was reached with Rogers on April 12: "For fifteen thousand dollars, Rogers agreed to convey to the United States 'clear of all liens of encumbrances 296 acres of land adjoining the public reservation at Fort Smith.'"[48] Though half the acreage, Rogers got his asking price.

The birth of the second fort, a breach birth at that from the military point of view, came in fits and stops, but in the frontier complex narrative, these fourteen years of bitter contestation are smoothed to this lithe description in the orientation video:

Despite this opposition, building began on the new garrison slightly east of the original stockade. The second Fort Smith held quarters and barracks for approximately four companies of men and was enclosed by a stone wall twelve feet high and three feet thick. Over the next thirty years Fort Smith was essential to military operations in the Southwest. Goods from its commissary and quartermasters' storehouses supplied military outposts throughout Indian Territory.

The scale of constructing the second fort of rock and brick required skilled laborers to be imported from the Northeast. Costs of the second fort mounted.

The amount of government money flowing into Fort Smith did not escape the attention of the man who would become the twelfth president of the United States, Zachary Taylor. He resided in Fort Smith between 1842 and 1845 while commander of the Western Military District. From his vantage point, according to Higgins, "Taylor could imagine that a few promoters of Fort Smith were riding the government's coat tails not for the good of protecting the frontier, but for amassing personal fortunes."[49]

Wanting no part of Fort Smith, Bearss and Gibson relay, "Taylor established his headquarters at Cantonment Belknap [about a mile east of the
fort] . . . and was thus close to the Fort Smith situation and could observe
it at first hand. Taylor . . . was shocked at what he regarded useless expenditure of public funds at Fort Smith." He said that "when finished it would
'serve as a lasting monument to the folly of those who planned [it], as well
as him who executed [it].'"[50] In a personal letter Bearss and Gibson found
that Taylor's opinion of the second fort was unambiguous: "The plan . . . is
highly objectionable. . . . A more useless expenditure of money & labor was
never made by this or any other people. . . . The sooner it is arrested the
better."[51]

It is no wonder that a 2003 effort to raise a bronze statue of Taylor
on horseback in Fort Smith failed.[52] While there is some mythic frontier
imagery of Taylor in the city, it was not convincing enough to supply the
imagination needed to bring this monument to life. A 1936 plaque at the
end of Garrison Avenue in front of the Sisters of Mercy convent claims
to mark the location of Taylor's dwelling during his time in Fort Smith.
Though this has not been supported by historical and archaeological explo-
ration, the myth continues to be a social fact in Fort Smith. The Arkansas
Archeological Survey found evidence the dwelling belonged to immigrat-
ing Irish nuns in the 1850s, not Taylor. Thus, by highlighting Taylor at the
site an important history of women educators on the frontier is effectively
silenced.[53] Mistaken military history trumps complex ethnic immigration
in the mythic Fort Smith frontier imaginary.

Zachary Taylor would subsequently leave Fort Smith to help direct the
United States' military invasion of Mexico in 1846 that would in the end
add another expansive territory to the United States as did the Louisiana
Purchase, bringing to a close the frontier era of removal and beginning the
era of restraint. It was the westward expansion that Taylor himself was mil-
itarily orchestrating that ultimately secured the funds for the construction
of the very fort that he so opposed. The barracks at the newly constructed
Fort Smith were first occupied in 1846, just in time to help Taylor on his
way to Buena Vista in northern Mexico. It was speculated that it took eight
long years to construct the fort due to the lackluster attitude the military
had toward it.

While the fort was not decommissioned until 1871 and while it did have
a boom during the California gold rush, it was actually killed one more
time on the eve of its most prosperous decade. Zachary Taylor, the recently

departed and disgruntled denizen of Fort Smith and decorated war hero, was elected to the presidency in 1848, and he was not averse to settling old scores with his newly acquired power. Taylor took decisive action against Fort Smith: "General Order 19, issued May 31, 1850, directed the commandant of the 7th Military Department to dispose of the military stores and garrison at Fort Smith and to abandon the post."[54] Thus, a fort that took eight years to construct was abandoned after four years of occupation. With the tables turned, townsfolk and Arbuckle rallied to write the War Department to point out the error of its ways. As the order was issued by the president, all of their contorted objections were for naught. "On July 2, 1850, Captain Caleb C. Sibley formed Company E and took passage for Fort Gibson," effectively ending the military presence in Fort Smith.[55] One person stayed behind: "Captain Montgomery remained in charge of the building and remaining stores with no men to assist him."[56] The fate of Fort Smith looked bleak.

On July 9, 1850, one short week after the final evacuation of the second Fort Smith, President Zachary Taylor died. The necessary political machinations were promptly greased, and seven months later Taylor's order was reversed: "On February 12, 1851, the adjutant general directed Colonel Arbuckle to reoccupy Fort Smith by withdrawing Company E of the 5th Infantry from Fort Gibson."[57] Born again on the whims of mortality, Fort Smith lived to see another day and finally take its first long breath. The second fort and city alike "settled down to nearly eleven years of uninterrupted existence as a frontier military station."[58] The motivation for and continued existence of Fort Smith is full of ambiguity, ambivalence, and acrimony, but these characteristics are not included in the cultural memory of the Fort Smith frontier complex.

The National Historic Site orientation video sums it up this way:

> Forts Washita, Wayne, Gibson, Towson, Arbuckle, and Cobb all received a steady supply of troops, equipment, and orders from Fort Smith. As a result, all the military roads, stage routes, mail service, and telegraph lines extending across the frontier radiated from Fort Smith, which also acted as the distribution point for food, farming supplies, and federal funds for those Indians migrating west.

This list of forts, all located another step westward, reveals markers in the advancing frontier and the role of the forts left behind to facilitate white settlement and the political economy of the nation. Most remarkably, the narrative puts Fort Smith in the center of the action, disconnected from the larger national movement westward going on to the north and the south of it. All tourist narratives must be local.

Frontier Exceptionalism

At this point we are firmly in the frontier complex era of restraint, and this is reflected in how the period is discussed in policies and in action. It is still a curiosity to some as to why the second military Fort Smith was built along the lines of a coastal fortification. Nevertheless, its thick rock walls earned it the Bearss and Gibson book's subtitle *Little Gibraltar on the Arkansas*. The qualifier "little" may still not downsize it enough for the comparison to the Rock of Gibraltar, but it reveals how the history of Fort Smith is framed in cultural memory. The titles of two chapters covering this era quite grandly depict the role Fort Smith played in the 1850s: "Portals of Croesus" and "Mother Post for the Southwest." The authors estimate that five thousand travelers passed through it in that decade seeking their fortunes in the West. Military escorts would see them all the way to Santa Fe.[59] The scant amount of tourist discourse on this period focuses on the role Fort Smith played as a jumping-off point to the West. Little attention is paid to the social life of Fort Smith at the time or to the significant shift in Indian policy.

Fort Smith is far from the frontier by this point, functioning as a supply center for migrants and the military detachments that were protecting them hundreds of miles westward. The route to Santa Fe from Fort Smith followed the southern bank of the Canadian River. In the late 1850s the flow of white traffic through the Chickasaw Nation, in south-central present-day Oklahoma, led to battles with Indians. There was no question by now what the role of the military was. Fort Smith dutifully supplied Major William Emory at Fort Arbuckle with supplies to "sustain a cavalry campaign against the Comanches."[60]

Elsewhere, the U.S. military was busy protecting white travelers on the Santa Fe and Oregon Trails as well as during the Dakota Wars, and in the south, Fort Davis protected travelers heading west out of San Antonio, Texas.

Strategic military positions that once oversaw a place for Indians to be "permanently" removed to were now well positioned to restrain Indians as white Anglo-Americans felt empowered to take and use the land they had secured by war, treaty, and purchase. A Fort Scott National Historic Site orientation video is quite frank and succinct about this shift from the frontier era of removal to that of restraint: "As the frontier extended further westward, the idea of a 'permanent' Indian territory died a quick death and the army abandoned Fort Scott in 1853."[61]

Archival material that would add depth and nuance to the historical and touristic narratives of Fort Smith remain underused. The overreliance on famous men and military conflicts inherently skews the narrative toward reinforcing both white male hegemony and the legitimation of state violence. A history of Fort Smith that awaits telling will develop the greater complexities of social life in the town. The DuVal family records are available in archives and contain a wealth of insights seldom shared from this prominent family who first settled in Fort Smith in 1822. In the collection is the diary that Catherine DuVal Rector kept from 1850 to 1853. In it we are given a glimpse into what people in Fort Smith were thinking and feeling during this vaunted era of Fort Smith being the mother post and gateway to gold. We can glimpse the reality of parenting from Catherine DuVal Rector as she declares, "Oh what a responsibility to raise children." On being a wife during the gold rush era, she writes, "As the time approaches for Major Rector starting to California I feel dreadful." She shares with her diary her fears and concerns in this three-year period, over a third of which her husband, Elias, was gone on the gold trails to California.[62]

Leading up to her husband's departure Mrs. Rector confides on Friday, March 22, 1850, "Oh California, the thought of thee makes me sad, all the gold in the mines cannot prevent me from having sad forboding, will I ever see Major Rector again?" After his departure on Wednesday, April 3, she writes, "Major Rector started this morning, how utterly wretched I felt in biding my dear Husband goodbye for two years." Meanwhile, she goes about life in Fort Smith. On Monday, April 29, she playfully reports, "A beautiful sunshinery day. Made preparation for white-washing. Commenced planting corn. Had a difficulty with John today, what a difficult thing it is to manage children." On Saturday, May 18, she shares thoughts on a letter from her husband written while in Fort Scott, Kansas, where he had stopped en route to the Santa Fe Trail. She begins, "How wretched I do feel about him. He does not write in very good spirits, he says he expects to see more suffering on the road than he has ever seen in all his life. He says that it appears that the whole world was going to California on that road." The next day she concedes, "I do not feel very well today. I did not sleep, I could not but think of my dear Husband, if he was only at home again how happy I would be."

Over a year into her husband's absence she reports on Friday, April 4, 1851, "Mrs. Dillard was kind enough to come over and read her son letter to me, he spoke of Major Rector as broken very much in appearance and from the tone of his letter unfortunate. Oh miserable California, I wish you never had been heard of. William and his wife came out and staid until after dinner. Quite a storm this evening." Major Rector returned Sunday, April 20, 1851, and she records, "Rained a little this morning, my beloved husband arrived at his home about 12 o'clock, oh delighted we were to see him, he was completely overcome. Oh my heart was full. He looks better than I expected to see him. A year absence makes a great many changes."

One year after his return Catherine DuVal Rector expresses concern about her husband's business ventures and fears he is being led astray. Her fears turn out to be warranted when a hoped-for appointment at the Creek Agency does not pan out. Tensions over the typical marital issue of economic survival have clearly surfaced when on Sunday, June 20, 1852, she pens, "Major Rector returned last night, he is very well but very cross as usual. Bro. Ben and Ellen were here this morning. This afternoon Col. Rutherford called. I feel unhappy this evening I know I was bound for domestic happiness, but I have little of it." The diary alone deserves a lengthy analysis, but the point here is easily gleaned that the "portals of Croesus" were not accessible to all. Catherine's brother Benjamin DuVal would conduct a congressional investigation of corruption at the Fort Smith federal court and give a keynote address at the Sixth Annual Western Arkansas Fair in 1885. Records from the DuVal family are not used within the Fort Smith frontier complex, though they are readily accessible and would provide deeper perspective on the city's social history.

Yes, Fort Smith did benefit greatly as the nation grew westward, and some individuals did so far more than others. The California gold rush and further white settlement were facilitated during the 1850s by the military infrastructure. Locally, Bearss and Gibson explain, "Fort Smith's role as communications center for the Southwest was broadened by technological developments and expanding stage, steamboat, and mail enterprises. The system of military roads radiating from Fort Smith carried an ever increasing flow of traffic."[63] With the arrival of the Missouri River and Western

Telegraph Company in 1858, Fort Smith was suddenly within a few hours' reach from Washington. A description from the era regales the developments of the region: "Fort Smith is a thriving town of about 2,500 inhabitants, and they boast that every house is full."[64] Every house may have been full, but how well those people were living and what fates awaited them is not shared in historical or tourist discourses of the town. The prosperity of the town was directly contingent on its relation to federal monies invested in the region to support westward expansion.

As for John Rogers, he can truly be counted among those exceptional men who managed to make a profit on the frontier complex. The 1860 U.S. Census for Fort Smith lists a seventy-six-year-old John Rogers as having $100,000 of value in real estate and $25,000 of value in his personal estate; the 1850 census listed him with $60,000 in real estate. He is surpassed on the 1860 census only by a forty-eight-year-old man born in Ireland, Mitchell Sparks, listed as a merchant with $114,000 in real estate and $65,500 in his personal estate. Retired merchant G. S. Bernie had $52,000 in real estate and $58,500 in personal estate, merchant W. B. Sutton held $40,000 in real estate and $10,000 in personal estate, physician J. H. F. Main held $38,040 in real estate and $30,000 in personal estate, and hotel keeper W. W. Flemming had $20,000 in real estate and $12,545 in personal estate. A few other merchants approached the tens of thousands in wealth, but most citizens are listed with hundreds of dollars in worth or nothing at all.[65] Migration westward was profitable in Fort Smith, then, for a few businessmen, doctors, and hotel keeps.

At this point in the discourse of the frontier complex, the role of the mythic border between savagery and civilization is momentarily interrupted. The Civil War era in Fort Smith is summarized in twenty-five seconds in the orientation video:

> The Civil War brought an abrupt halt to these activities. In April of 1861, Confederate sympathizers known as the Arkansas Volunteers seized control of Fort Smith. The post's location and its reserves of food, clothing, and ammunition made it a plump prize worth fighting for. But within two years, Union forces reoccupied the fort and held it until the end of the Civil War.

In fact there was no fight at Fort Smith.[66] Exhibits and living history events feature the Civil War at the National Historic Site far more than is represented in the video. However, the brevity in the video is indicative of the emphasis on the frontier narrative before and after the Civil War in the contemporary Fort Smith frontier complex.

Thus, the mythic narratives of military Fort Smith's role in the frontier complex eras of removal and restraint camouflage the extent to which Native Americans were mistreated and women's points of view muted, let alone the near-total absence of the role of African Americans, free or slave. Here again there is a notable scholarly exception that has not been incorporated into the Fort Smith frontier complex. The life of Peter Caulder, a free black soldier who was stationed in Fort Smith, is told in great detail by local history professor Billy Higgins in *A Stranger and a Sojourner*.[67] Caulder was in Fort Smith during the first fort era of 1817–1824. He came to the region by way of his stint as a rifleman in the War of 1812 and a scout who accompanied Stephen H. Long on his trip to Belle Point, the Red River, and St. Louis. Caulder settled in north-central Arkansas to farm, but ultimately he fled the state to escape enslavement upon passage of the Negro Expulsion Act of 1859.[68] This richly told and well-documented story can be purchased in the bookstore at both the Fort Smith National Historic Site and the Fort Smith Museum of History, but Caulder's story has not broken through the lock that white male hegemony has on the frontier complex narrative.[69]

Frontier Interrupted

The prosperous decade of the 1850s in Fort Smith made it an ideal location for secessionists to secure heading into the Civil War. It continued to be amply stocked through 1860 and into 1861. For that reason, Bearss and Gibson point out, "Arkansas state troops seized Fort Smith several weeks before the Little Rock convention adopted an ordinance of secession."[70] The Confederacy occupied the fort from 1861 to the summer of 1863, and the Union occupied it from then to 1865. There were no battles at the actual site, only a few skirmishes more peripherally to the city. Notably for the frontier complex, the infamous Confederate guerilla warfare leader William Quantrill and one of his followers and subsequent bank and train robber Cole Younger were said to be in Fort Smith in 1862 and 1863, respectively. These two figures and their subsequent depredations become rich fodder for the imaginations of contemporary reenactors.

During the Civil War, Fort Smith found itself split but still used as a major supply line for each side in turn. Higgins maintains that "despite the two years of Confederate dominance and southern feeling from flag waving to patriotic speeches, Fort Smith was a town of divided loyalties. While some citizens fled, those who held Unionist views, a good portion of the population, stayed put after Blunt's Federal forces retook the town."[71] Although casualties and devastation were minimal in Fort Smith, the Civil War was not kind to it. One result of Arkansas' secession was the loss of the hub for the transcontinental railroad. Prior to the war, Fort Smith was being seriously considered for a more southerly route to the Pacific. The geography of a Fort Smith terminus would have been more easily traversed than that out of Kansas City, completed in 1869.

Another significant historical event that took place in Fort Smith in the post–Civil War but pre–federal court era was the Council of 1865. The gathering was intended to negotiate treaties with the Five Nations in Indian Territory that had fought in the Civil War regardless of whether they had sided with the Union or the Confederacy. They "were faced with redefining their relationship with the U.S. government. Some tribal leaders were optimistic about restored relations, but others feared harsh retributions from federal policy makers."[72] It had been quite a mixed bag between and within the different Indian groups in terms of Union or Confederate sympathies during the war. Regardless of which side they had taken, the results of this council would affect all the Indians equally.

The council struggled, so "provisions were made for a follow-up council but it was never called. Blacks were released from bondage, but only among the Seminoles did freedmen achieve full tribal membership. Nothing was set aside for them, nor was any reparation ever made to ex-slaves by the Indian tribes." The net result of the council was confusion, as Higgins describes: "Instead of unity, the Indian Territory seethed with claims, conflict, and resentments. Not only were the tribes divided, a situation that often convinced residents to take law into their own hands, but non-white emigrants were streaming into the territory, many of whom disregarded any authority beyond their own interests."[73] The Council of 1865 resulted in treaties signed in Washington in 1866.[74]

In the larger picture, the outcome of the council reflected the ongoing national strategy to fulfill manifest destiny. In Robert Utley's description, "Here Commissioner of Indian Affairs, Dennis N. Cooley and other commissioners spoke harshly to the 'Great Father's erring children' and spelled out the principles on which the treaties restoring peace would be based: surrender of western lands, abolition of slavery, granting of railroad rights-of-way, establishment of US military posts, and measures directed toward a territorial government for the Indian Territory."[75] Indians like Chief John Ross of the Cherokee were presciently opposed to many aspects of the treaty. Ross "recognized that the move toward territorial government [was] aimed at liquidating the tribal self-government . . . [and] that railroad agents and Kansas land sharpers . . . had rushed to Fort Smith" to take advantage of the Indians' situation.[76] The fate of Indian Territory was clear to see. Juliet Galonska, a former National Historic Site historian, has assessed the outcome: "Ultimately, the Fort Smith Council provided the foundation for the 1866 treaties which significantly altered conditions in Indian Territory and paved the way for Oklahoma statehood."[77] Only statehood would be satisfactory in the national project of acquiring the West.

The story of the 57th United States Colored Troops is another interesting episode from this period that is not interpreted in the Fort Smith frontier complex. Stationed at the fort from July 1865 to June 1866, they would have been witnesses to the Fort Smith Council of 1865. A Fort Smith newspaper reported of the colored troops that residents "were surprised to learn that one-third of the enlisted personnel could read."[78] What concerned the officers of the fort more was the refusal of the colored troops to obey an order to march to New Mexico. Upon hearing the news, "they became mutinous and refused to go."[79] After being surrounded and disarmed by the 3rd Cavalry, the mutinous troops were sent to Little Rock, where they were promptly sent back to Fort Smith with it being made clear that if any such rebellious activity should happen again the results would be quite serious. No doubt there is an interesting back story to this event, but it has yet to be found in the frontier complex. Complex counternarratives that challenge traditional touristic accounts are virtually absent in Fort Smith.

Uniting Whiteness

In the post–Civil War era, the narrative explanation for the existence of the military Fort Smith changes. We learn from a brochure that "after the Civil War (1861–1865) the military permanently closed the little-needed fort in 1871."[80] Why was it "little-needed" in 1871? Indian Territory was still present just across the river and full of more Indians and a growing number of illegally present whites. Saying that it was little needed in 1871 reveals precisely why it *was* originally needed in 1817—to advance the political state westward, not to protect the Indians. With that task accomplished the military could move on.

Figure 3.2. Reconciliation Park, Mankato, Minnesota. At this site thirty-eight Dakota Indians were hanged on December 26, 1862. The text on the bench reads, "Forgive Everyone Everything." Photo by the author.

The West provided a canvas for the nation to paint a unified image of whites who had just spent four years savagely othering each other during the Civil War. In *Never One Nation: Freaks, Savages, and Whiteness in U.S. Popular Culture, 1850–1877,* Linda Frost points out that even before Buffalo Bill Cody's Wild West show began to take form in 1873, P. T. Barnum was entertaining Americans with fanciful images of the savage and the civilized as early as 1863. Barnum's depiction of Native Americans as savages was especially problematic with the Union and the Confederacy literally and figuratively savaging each other during this same time.

Objectifying the enemy is common practice in all wars, but in this case doing so complicated efforts to savage all Indians while claiming whites to be uniformly civilized. Frost observes, "If the Union was itself an actualization of civilization, then those who had taken a stand against it could only be uncivilized."[81] Newspapers of the time ran articles and cartoons that portrayed white Northerners or white Southerners as the other, as savages. In tandem, "the Northern press . . . racializes as alien the Confederate soldier by grafting onto him a popular image of Indian savagery; just as the 'savage tribes' use their enemies' body parts for trophies or leave them 'to decay in the open air,' so the Southern male—*white* male—has similarly used those of his Yankee opponent."[82]

The boundaries of the savage/civilized argument were gerrymandered at will when it involved whites and Indians but held firm when it came to African Americans. Despite the savage narratives spread by Northerners about the South, they would not touch the barbarous nature of slavery as evidence of their adversaries' savageness. Rather, Frost has found, "Confederates in these instances are typically savage *not* because they perpetuate the enslavement and debasement of other human beings, but because they threaten the life and dignity of the Union soldier, a figure obviously metonymic for the Union itself."[83] The post–Civil War era necessitated a method for uniting all whites and making whiteness and civilization pristine and synonymous. As the nation turned its gaze to the West it was able to collapse North versus South into the same category, of "East." This restored whiteness and once again allowed the full force of savaging to be applied to Indians. The presumed frontier unified a wounded and divided nation. The same logic was at work as the Northern, Yankee, Radical Republican, carpetbagger Isaac C. Parker became absorbed into the frontier myth to become the singular watchman of frontier justice—not Northern or Southern, but western justice.

The social construction of whiteness is omnipresent throughout the Fort Smith frontier complex but seldom directly stated. In 1936, as the recreation era of the frontier complex was ascending, the Noon Civics Club members thought the presence of whiteness so important they erected a rock monument and plaque to mark the place and date of the first white birth: "First White Child. Here Was Born Sarah Ann Tichnell In 1826. The First White Child Born in Fort Smith. Erected as a Public Service by the Noon Civics Club, 1936."[84] This civic-minded organization put up several other monuments in 1936, the centennial of Arkansas statehood. Time and development have overtaken this "first white child" monument, which now sits out of view between a levee and a warehouse. Though it is literally within a stone's throw of the National Historic Site grounds, only the most committed or the lost will find this monument today.

Beyond the question of who has membership in the "white" category, what the monument inscribes on the frontier complex is whiteness, the arrival of civilization, and the assertion that only white women can be the bearers of white civilization. To be clear, the intent of this marker is to indicate the place where a white woman gave birth to a child of a white man. The previous instances of white men fathering children with female slaves, free black women, or Indian women, whether by rape or consent, would not have qualified for this distinction.[85] Making it safe for white families to ultimately settle in the region was the real mission of the 1817 military Fort Smith.

4

///////////////////////////////

The Hanging Judge's Injustices

Judge Parker knows. He is an old carpetbagger but he knows his rats.
We had a good court here till the pettifogging lawyers moved in on
it. . . . Now they have got the judge down on me, and the marshal too.
The rat-catcher is too hard on the rats. That is what they say. *Let up on
them rats! Give them rats a fair show!*

Rooster Cogburn, *True Grit*

The end of the Civil War necessitated restoring "civilization" to include all white Anglos, thus restoring and extending the privileges of whiteness to classes of Americans who had been brought under question during the war. Yankee and rebel alike were now subsumed under the banner of civilized people regardless of ethnic and cultural diversity or raging animosity against parties within the white category. As such, the charge of spreading white civilization across the continent could be resumed in full force, with Native Americans and African Americans bearing the brunt of it.

With the era of removal over and the era of restraint well under way, the jurisdiction of Indian Territory (at this point in time consisting of present-day Oklahoma less its Panhandle and Greer County, which belonged to Texas until 1907) fell to the U.S. District Court for the Western District of Arkansas from 1851 to 1896. In the Fort Smith frontier complex the often-used quip describing this era, "There is no law west of Saint Louis, and no God west of Fort Smith," is repeated with nostalgic pride today. The phrase locates the city within nineteenth-century frontier discourses by specifically connecting it to Judge Isaac C. Parker's campaign to bring law, order, and civilization to the otherwise lawless borderland of Indian Territory. The incessant incantation of these tropes has been used to excite the frontier imaginary.

The western frontier complex provided a traumatized white population living mostly east of the Mississippi a domain to freely "other" and "savage" social minorities. The very act of westward migration enacted a therapeutic and solidarity-building function for whiteness while it rationalized and legitimated manifest destiny. The popular narratives that sprang up around westward migration bolstered the process. This may explain why the civilizing trope can be found to describe many frontier towns as each lays claim to the same unique identity of being on the leading edge of the rolling frontier wave as it made its way toward the Pacific. In the 1939 film *Dodge City* we hear, "West of Chicago there was no law! West of Dodge City there was no God!"

By the 1970 film *Chisum,* the phrase has been moved farther west: "There's no law west of Dodge and no God west of the Pecos." Judge Roy Bean of Texas is said to have framed it, "West of the Pecos there is no law; west of El Paso there is no God." In the 1936 film *The Plainsman* these words are put into Wild Bill Hickok's mouth: "There's no Sunday west of Junction City, no law west of Hayes City, and no God west of Carson City."[1] So, no, Fort Smith is not exceptional in this regard and rather just one more iteration of the national frontier-complex narrative, but that does not make good copy for those marketing cities for frontier tourism.

Law and Order on the Border

The courtroom of Judge Parker sat directly on the border of Indian Territory. The Choctaw Nation boundary was literally two hundred yards from Parker's bench. This positioned him as an ideal symbol of American civilization on the cutting edge of the frontier complex.[2] In contrast, Indian Territory is characterized as replete with savage Indians and overrun with white criminals hiding out from the jurisdiction of other states. Images of frontier justice arose alongside these quintessential tropes of lawlessness, savagery, and abandon to match or surpass them with symbols of civilization and law and order. In cultural memory, Judge Parker has come to represent the archetypal superhero who came to save the day, who sat steadfast on the border for twenty-one years on the federal court bench, who unflinchingly and unwaveringly imposed civilization, law, order, and justice onto Indian Territory. A close examination of the historical record reveals a far more complex Judge Parker, one who fiercely imposed his concept of justice, one who came to believe that he above all others knew what was best for Indian Territory, and one who, because of his resolute constitution, compounded frontier injustices.

The tale of justice begins in Fort Smith in 1871 when the U.S. District

Court for the Western District of Arkansas moved to town from neighboring Van Buren. Though the military fort period of 1817 to 1871 is a primary reason the National Park Service incorporated Fort Smith into its system, it is the Parker era of hangings, deputies, and outlaws in Indian Territory that gets the most attention in the city. The Fort Smith Museum of History, Miss Laura's Visitor Center, the Clayton House, and the Bass Reeves story all derive their central historical and tourism narratives from the career of Judge Parker. For that reason I systematically look at how his story is told and locate the popular narrative in historical context to demythologize it.[3]

We resume the Fort Smith National Historic Site orientation video as a convenient benchmark. The video describes the transition from military fort to federal court thus:

> After fifty-four years of intermittent occupation, the Army permanently closed Fort Smith. But the site was not abandoned for long. In November of 1872, the federal district court of Western Arkansas, which was responsible for maintaining the peace in Indian Territory, moved into Fort Smith's former soldiers' barracks.[4]

The discrepancy in year of occupation stems from the court's being initially located in the Rogers Building when it was first moved to Fort Smith until it was destroyed by fire. The court then was moved to the abandoned fort.[5]

The federal court's two decades in nearby Van Buren, from 1851 to 1871, are seldom mentioned in either Fort Smith or Van Buren today. There are virtually no accounts of judges and deputies taking civilization to Indian Territory from its position in Van Buren. Memory of that phase has been eclipsed by the Parker era of the court. Despite the inconsistent military occupations and the transition to a federal court, the long-used justification of keeping the peace between Indians is extended to the entire Parker era. The very title of the orientation video, *Peacekeeper of Indian Territory*, subsumes the full seventy-nine-year range of federal presence at Fort Smith from 1817 to 1896. Parker's reign on the federal bench is presented as a continuation of the same overarching mission the military had there since its inception. But Judge Parker had an exceptionally corrupt predecessor.

Higgins notes that "on May 8, 1871, Judge William Story gaveled the first session to order in the new federal courtroom temporarily housed in the Rogers Building."[6] Many people were in attendance that day to witness the historic occasion of the court's first session in Fort Smith. A local newspaper reported that "the town is jammed with strangers from all parts, some in office, some hunting for office, and a vast number that have been in, and now out, and some who do not want pap, though they are scarce; altogether the U.S. Court adds considerably to the life of the city."[7] In lieu of a military fort, the federal court system then became the extension of the nation for marshaling civilization into Indian Territory.[8] As this newspaper account of the day indicates, local business once again became the direct benefactor of federal monies, so-called pap, and the traffic they created in the city. These direct economic benefits from federal money to the city are largely left out of the cultural memory of the site, in which all the focus is facing firmly westward at the civilizing process. The frontier complex era of restraint created economic opportunities for some Fort Smithians and even more for those willing to trespass into Indian Territory and take advantage of the situation.

The explanation for the lawlessness in Indian Territory sets up the supposed peacekeeper mission of Fort Smith in the orientation video:

In the aftermath of the Civil War, tribal governments were overwhelmed by the task of rebuilding their communities. Intertribal feuding and an influx of fugitives and outlaws who were not subject to tribal law made it impossible for the Indian nations to restore order. The federal government also seemed powerless to remove these intruders, and soon lawless men and women of every creed and color were moving into the 70,000 square miles of Indian Territory, where they roamed free, robbing and killing at will. The violence and lawlessness of the frontier gave rise to the saying "There is no Sunday west of Saint Louis, no god west of Fort Smith."

While routinely described as lawless and uncivilized, each of the Five Civilized Tribes had a functioning supreme court and its own lawmen, referred to as lighthorse police. The Five Nations were fully organized by the social institutions of law and jurisprudence. However, they were also coping with white criminals and illegally present entrepreneurs within arm's reach but still beyond their jurisdiction, as the Indian courts were not allowed to try whites.

Noteworthy too, early in the narrative of the Parker era, is how Indian Territory is described as being far larger in size than it actually was. By 1861 the boundaries of Indian Territory were that of the current state of Oklahoma minus what was claimed by Texas until Oklahoma statehood, which

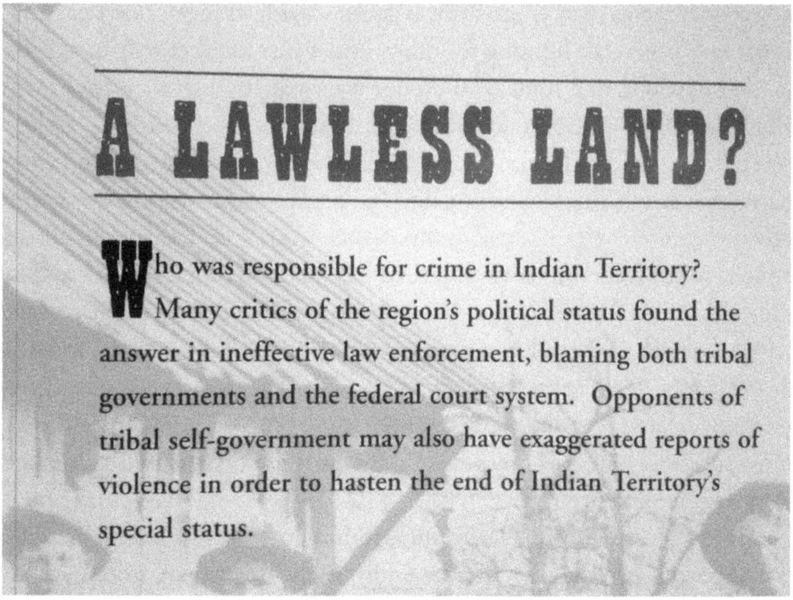

A LAWLESS LAND?

Who was responsible for crime in Indian Territory? Many critics of the region's political status found the answer in ineffective law enforcement, blaming both tribal governments and the federal court system. Opponents of tribal self-government may also have exaggerated reports of violence in order to hasten the end of Indian Territory's special status.

Figure 4.1. Interpretive sign, Fort Smith National Historic Site. Exhibits like this leave hints as to why Indian Territory was so "lawless"—the federal court system itself and "exaggerated reports of violence." Photo by the author.

would have made it approximately 62,000 square miles. Furthermore, the jurisdiction within Indian Territory of the federal court shrank in stages to half that size by 1883 and down to one-fourth of its original size by 1889 before going down to zero in 1896.[9] Despite this diminishing jurisdiction, the figure of seventy or even 74,000 square miles is routinely applied to Indian Territory for the entirety of Judge Parker's twenty-one-year career in Fort Smith and by extension to the tales about "his" deputies and the wantonness of roaming criminals.

The first few years of the federal court in Fort Smith got off to a rough start and are summed up in the orientation video in one sentence:

> The graft and corruption that plagued the federal court system in Fort Smith only contributed to the problem.

Not only was Indian Territory lawless, but so too was the federal court. Besides artificially inflaming relations within Indian Territory, Judge William Story and Marshal Logan H. Roots embezzled and extorted tens of thousands of dollars from their positions. Called to Washington to account for his part in the scandal, Story turned in his resignation to escape impeachment. Roots was found to have extorted more than $55,000 from the court while using the equivalent amount of money to become a founding shareholder in the First National Bank of Fort Smith.[10]

Corruption nearly cost the city of Fort Smith another closing of the federal funds spigot, Bearss and Gibson note, when it was "recommended that Congress abolish the court at Fort Smith, to assure that 'every door to fraud will be closed, and the administration of justice can be more successfully maintained.'"[11] This was not an idle threat, and "in the spring of 1874, a bill was introduced in Congress to abolish the federal court at Fort Smith."[12] With Story and Roots ousted from the court to freely pursue their enterprises in the private sector, interim Judge Henry J. Caldwell held the seat until Judge Parker arrived in Fort Smith on May 2, 1875.

Judge Isaac C. Parker's arrival on the border signals a shift to mythic order on the border, as told in the official video:

> It wasn't until President Ulysses S. Grant named Isaac C. Parker to the bench that some degree of order began to appear. Parker was appointed judge of the Western District of Arkansas in 1875 and for the next twenty-one years dispensed efficient and effective justice.

Parker indeed took swift action. After juries handed down several death sentences, the first executions under his watch took place on September 3, 1875, when six men were hanged at one time. The local newspaper reported a crowd of more than five thousand gathered to witness the event and ran headlines such as "Six Men Atone for Crime," "The Crime Committed in the Indian Country," "Arkansas Not Responsible," "Bad Men Will Be Punished, Good Men Will Punish Them," "Justice Is Slow, Justice Is Sure!"[13] Five were hanged at once in Parker's second execution day, April 21, 1876, and then four more on September 8, 1876. Condemning to death a total of fifteen men (19 percent of his total) on three occasions within his first year on the bench, Parker definitely made a statement about law and order on the border.

His very dramatic arrival contributed to the "Hanging Judge" reputation attached to Parker, but after this first run, hangings became less frequent, and more typically one or two individuals were hanged at a time. It was more than two full years before another execution would occur, on December 20, 1878. Parker did hand down death sentences in this two-year period, but due to community reaction to his first fifteen, all of those sentences were commuted. Roger Tuller documents the public response: "Fort Smith lawyers and residents reacted to the executions of fifteen men in just over a year by joining forces to ameliorate the severity of Parker's sentences. . . . Hundreds of residents from Fort Smith and Indian Territory—often including the jurors who had convicted the condemned—signed petitions supporting commutations or pardons."[14] In the end, nearly half of the death sentences Parker handed down were commuted. Sentiments about the arrival of his brand of justice on the border were clearly mixed.

Other instances of multiple hangings in a single day dominate the public imagination of Parker and his form of justice. Five were hanged on September 9, 1881; four were hanged on January 14, 1887; six were hanged on January 16, 1890; and five were hanged on July 1, 1896. These seven multiple-execution days account for 44 percent of all the executions carried out during Parker's term. If hangings of three at a time are included, then 59 percent of all of Parker's executions over his twenty-one-year stint happened on eleven days.[15] Parker heard a total of 13,490 cases. In the 344 cases he heard for capital crimes, he issued 160 death sentences, meaning he found 53 percent of capital defendants not guilty. Parker is best known for the 79 death warrants he issued that were ultimately carried out. In perspective, 0.012 percent of all the cases he heard resulted in the death penalty, and 0.006 percent resulted in hangings. These are the statistics that garnered Parker his posthumous yet fiercely unshakable moniker of "the Hanging Judge." From a national perspective, the United States was a "Hanging Nation" in the late nineteenth century. In the three-year period of 1890–1892 there were 332 executions conducted under legal auspices and at least 557 acts of lynching.[16] With an average of 300 hangings per year across the country, it is a wonder Parker gained particular notoriety.

The myth of justice in the frontier complex of a peacekeeper of law and order on the border does not stem simply from Parker. The federal court employed deputies to cover what the orientation video deems the 70,000 square miles of its jurisdiction:

The government's most urgent priority was to stop the lawlessness in Indian Territory, and to do this, it hired two hundred deputy marshals to track down the criminals and bring them to trial in Fort Smith. The deputy corps was made up of every racial group on the frontier. And men like Bass Reeves, Heck Thomas, Zeke Proctor, and Sam Sixkiller were among its most prominent members.

Though the video and other sources cite the two hundred deputies figure, the actual number of deputies at any one given time was more likely to be thirty-five to forty. Each federal district court has one U.S. marshal; the remainder are deputy marshals serving under him or her. U.S. marshals are political appointees, as is the funding to support the deputies. As a result, there is a good deal of fluctuation in numbers. Despite the far lower average numbers, the large number of deputies is routinely cited in the tourism narrative, as is the exaggerated size of Indian Territory, which is frequently emphasized to account for the rampant lawlessness. However, the actual number of deputies at any one time and the size of the Western District of Arkansas jurisdiction at different stages of its existence are never clearly stated in the Fort Smith frontier complex.

In addition to the 62,000 square miles in Indian Territory in 1861, the Western District of Arkansas covered nineteen counties in the western half of the state that constituted 13,500 square miles for the entirety of Judge Parker's tenure in Fort Smith.[17] Perhaps because no death penalty cases came from it, the cultural memory of the Parker era omits the court's obligations in Arkansas entirely. This is true in the orientation video, exhibits at both the National Historic Site and the Fort Smith Museum of History, and most accounts of Parker's career. Harman's 1898 account gives one of the earliest citations of jurisdiction size. Speaking exclusively about Indian Territory, he declares, "For many years it was with the ruffians of an immense tract of country, 74,000 square miles, stretching away to the Colorado line, that Judge Parker had to cope."[18] Harman does not cite any source for that figure, yet it became the cited figure and remains the "social fact" for the Fort Smith frontier complex.

A case in point of this widespread misrepresentation is the entry for the "Western District Court of Arkansas" on the online *Encyclopedia of Arkansas History and Culture*: "The jurisdiction in Oklahoma alone was more than 74,000 square miles in area."[19] With the ubiquitous citation of this flawed number it is no surprise that my questioning of jurisdiction boundaries was routinely lost on many people I consulted during my fieldwork observations in the frontier complex, including individuals among the most familiar with Fort Smith history. This blind spot in the cultural memory reveals how powerfully the legacy of Judge Parker is entirely contingent on Indian Territory.

In actuality, it is the total jurisdiction figure of the court that existed for the first third of Parker's time in Fort Smith that is customarily cited as the square mileage of Indian Territory alone for his entire time on the bench. In 1875 it encompassed approximately 75,500 square miles including the nineteen western Arkansas counties, leaving 62,000 in the mainly rectangular region making up present-day Oklahoma.[20] In 1883 the jurisdiction of the court in Indian Territory was reduced to only the lands of the Five Nations, roughly the eastern half of the state, approximating 35,000 square miles. The Chickasaw Nation and the southern half of the Choctaw Nation were removed from its jurisdiction in 1889, reducing the terrain in Indian Territory under Parker's jurisdiction to 22,000 square miles for the final third of his career in Fort Smith. Thus, the long arm of the law was not nearly as long as is portrayed.

Lawless Indian Territory

An exhibit at the Fort Smith National Historic Site is actually entitled *The Long Arm of the Law*. The textual narrative reinforces the notion that Parker reigned over a vast expanse of Indian Territory during the entirety of his career: "The U.S. Court for the Western District of Arkansas, with its seat at Fort Smith, is unique in the history of federal tribunals. At the height of its influence, it held a vast jurisdiction—about seventy-four thousand square miles—over land that was home to thousands of American Indians and an increasing number of residents who were not tribal members." This increasing number of whites moving into the territory became concentrated in the later part of Parker's career, when the jurisdiction of only 22,000 square miles of Indian Territory afforded him a much shorter reach.

Regardless, discussion of the deputies' duties is tightly reined to the more expansive notion of Indian Territory. The orientation video depicts widespread violence:

> These lawmen led hazardous lives. They not only had to track down dangerous fugitives in a lawless wilderness, they had to bring them back alive. A deputy who killed a suspect who was resisting arrest had no hope of collecting his fee, and he even had to pay the dead man's burial expense to boot. It was a job that required enormous skill and

even more luck. Many didn't make it. During Parker's tenure on the bench, over one hundred deputies lost their lives in the line of duty.

The extent to which Indian Territory is described and imagined to be replete with savage, lawless wildness in the Fort Smith frontier complex cannot be overstated.

One of the most popular writers and public figures of Fort Smith history, Art Burton, describes it this way: "No part of the West was more of a legal and jurisdictional nightmare, or criminal's paradise, than Indian Territory. Without a doubt, the territory offered outlaws their safest refuge and their richest field for uninhibited plunder. At one time or another, the worst scoundrels in the West accepted the open invitation to visit Indian Territory. The Jesse James Gang vacationed there between holdups, and the Dalton, Doolin, and Cook gangs roamed there, robbing and killing at will."[21] The repetition of such accounts in the frontier complex makes it easy to lose sight of the fact that Indian Territory was meanwhile home to tens of thousands of Indians who had their own judicial systems. It was not the exclusive province of ne'er-do-wells.

While I concede that it was a violent time and place in American history, the extent to which it is exaggerated as universally lawless is nothing short of suspicious. Why must Indian Territory be described in such drastic terms to the exclusion of any alternative? I believe this is part of the mental function of the frontier complex. This fabled description of Indian Territory constitutes a frontier attic that functions as a mental space in which perceived fears and threats to one's social status can be worked out. Both the white invaders of Indian Territory in the past and those with neoliberal perspectives on race and immigration today are exonerated in this binary space. Conservative whites who feel surrounded by and doing battle with imminent threats of foreigners, outsiders, and freeloaders can identify with what it must have been like back in the day when a potential threat stood waiting at each turn. This frontier attic is created in such a way that it stores a mentality that legitimates western expansion in the past and mirrors contemporary fears of outsiders and others.

Despite the historical complexity of the situation, the mantra according to the frontier complex maintains a singular focus: Indian Territory was full of lawlessness, and the federal government had to apply civilization and its particular law and order to it. The myth reinforces the arrival of white civilization being taken to the Five Tribes when in fact law, order, and civilization were already present in Indian Territory. In Tahlequah the Cherokee Nation Supreme Court had been functioning since 1844. Little mention is made in Fort Smith's cultural memory of Indian Territory about the application of law by Indians. Rather, we are told,

> Suspects were brought back to Fort Smith to face a court appearance before Judge Parker. A person found guilty of rape or murder faced certain death. That was the law, and Judge Parker sentenced killers like Cherokee Bill and rapists like the Rufus Buck gang to the gallows. Those who committed lesser offenses, like horse thief Belle Starr, received less severe punishment.

Upholding the law by the Parker court is held up as evidence of the impartial legal process he represented on the frontier border. Moreover, this is an alibi espoused in the frontier-complex tourism narrative of Parker's stern justice, that the federal court was not systematically dismantling Indian Territory for white settlement; that's not what it was doing on the border. Rather, it was impartially applying the law.[22]

Parker contributed to this impartiality narrative with his routinely cited comment "I never hanged a man; it was the law." The orientation video shares more of his legal philosophy:

> Parker never once attended an execution in Fort Smith. In fact, he wrote, "I am in favor of abolishing the death penalty, provided there is a certainty of punishment, whatever the punishment may be. It is not the severity of the punishment, but the certainty of it that checks crime."

Parker's comments are quoted from an interview he granted to *St. Louis Republic* reporter Ada Patterson coinciding with the September 1, 1896, removal of the remaining 22,000 square miles of Indian Territory from the Western District of Arkansas jurisdiction.[23] It was just six weeks before Parker's death. With his health failing and his jurisdiction restricted to only western Arkansas, Parker was no doubt feeling the weight of history's judgment upon his career. What is routinely cited as proof of his total devotion to the law and a basis for the imagined visage of his pure justice was instead his *repulsa mea culpa*.

Contemporary analysis of Judge Parker's judicial career is revealing. Up until 1889 there had been no recourse of appeal for death sentences in Parker's court except to the president of the United States. It was only from

1889 to 1896, the last third of his time in Fort Smith, that Parker's death sentences could be appealed to the Supreme Court. While this change is often explained in the frontier complex as "fixing a clerical error," David Kopel suggests that "the congressional concerns about Judge Parker's arbitrariness" necessitated the statute.[24] From outside the Fort Smith frontier complex an objective review of Parker's actions does not support his image of having an objective devotion to justice. Kopel analyzed the death sentences that were appealed to the Supreme Court during this time frame and found that "the Supreme Court had reviewed forty-four of Parker's capital sentences, and reversed thirty-one of them."[25] Seventy percent of the appealed cases were overturned. At minimum, this reveals that Parker was not practicing law by the generally agreed upon standards of the time.

The U.S. Supreme Court was of the opinion that Parker intentionally led his juries to his foregone conclusions. Kopel surmises, "Judge Parker's zeal for hanging went too far, as he repeatedly forced juries to bring in guilty verdicts against people who were defending themselves against criminal attack."[26] In his Parker biography, Michael Brodhead arrives at the same conclusion: "The grounds for the reversals were many and varied, but mostly they involved Judge Parker's instructions to the juries. Often the justices found Parker's wording calculated to incline the jurors toward a guilty verdict."[27] Parker's zeal for administering justice exceeded the written parameters of his duties.

Jeffrey Burton agrees with this interpretation: "It had been maintained that Parker was careless with the law, unversed in its finer points. Reference to some of his charges to grand and petit juries and to his pronouncements out of court affords convincing evidence—at any rate, to a layman—that he was deeply read in the law but evinced a keener regard for what he felt to be the spirit of the law than what he knew to be its letter." More pointedly, Burton describes the need to "put a curb on the judge's arbitrary influence."[28] Concern over Parker's record had been present for some time. In 1889 he was twice offered federal judge positions elsewhere, one in St. Louis and one in Little Rock, where he could do less harm. He declined because, in Tuller's words, Parker was "convinced that no one else could preside as well over Indian Territory lawbreakers."[29]

In the course of my fieldwork in the frontier complex, I frequently heard explanations that the inordinately long directions Parker gave to his juries was to help them out because they were not educated and needed a bit of instruction on the process. Brodhead contends that the Supreme Court would differ with these contemporary tour guides' explanations: "Parker's lengthy instructions to juries—some ranging from 40 to 70 typewritten pages—contained much that was confusing and contradictory. Reading the opinions handed down by the Supreme Court reversing the Parker court, one cannot help suspecting that the justices' obligatory references to 'the learned judge' were heavy with sarcasm."[30] Sarcastic or not, repeated rebukes from the Supreme Court soil Parker's image of dispensing pure justice from his bench.

Many of Parker's instructions to the jury have been preserved. In one that Harman called "Judge Parker's best petit jury charge," Parker begins,

Gentlemen, a moment's reflection satisfies us that in every trial of this character, there is involved one of the gravest propositions upon which depends the social happiness of men, women and children living in a state of civilized society and under a civilized government. That proposition is whether the law of the land, that rule of action which prescribes the conduct of men, when in the hands of intelligent jurymen of the country, affords a sufficient safeguard for all the rights of the governed, and especially that highest of rights known as belonging to man—the right to life.[31]

The opening paragraph of Parker's instructions to the jury in this case goes on for two-and-a-half pages. An example of what the Supreme Court may have thought a digression may have included this bit of instruction to the jury:

For centuries, yes, for ages, if geology be true, the lightnings had played in the heavens and men were awed and terrified from their sight. Morse came with the capacity to read their laws, and he chained them, and taught them to carry our messages of affection, our messages of fortune and misfortune, to friends thousands of miles away. When nature is correctly read she never deceives. For centuries the blood had gone to the heart and returned again to the extremities. For centuries physicians had dissected the human frame and had failed to discover the great law of life, that the lungs received the oxygen from the air we breathe and transmit it to the blood; that the blood thus provided with new life was sent out to feed the most remote organ, it may be said by a mechanism more delicate than human genius has ever been able to construct. Harvey came, read nature's law aright, made the discovery, and it was no longer a mystery. And so it is with nature everywhere.[32]

Parker goes on to elucidate the process by which trees reproduce themselves before he arrives at the tangential point of his examples in relation to law: "These are nature's laws which always tell the truth. Nature's laws to govern the working of nature in their innocence, and that they may serve the purposes of man. Nature has a set of laws which apply to the criminal acts of men as well as to their innocent acts."[33] This particular jury instruction runs more than thirty full pages, and one must look hard to find clear directions to the jury.[34]

Aside from his all-consuming jury directions, Parker's record also was particularly truant in self-defense cases. In Kopel's investigation of capital cases appealed to the Supreme Court he found that "nine defendants from Parker's court raised appeals involving self-defense; eight of them won reversals."[35] Many visitors to Parker's courtroom today voice the opinion that he represents a contemporary notion of being tough on crime and giving criminals what they deserve and that we should bring back that sort of justice. Nearly all the historical reenactors who were part of my research are staunch supporters of gun rights, particularly for self-defense, and cite the image of Parker's frontier justice as a model of their beliefs. But Parker's decisions regarding self-defense do not square with that point of view, in Brodhead's assessment: "Clearly, the Supreme Court and Isaac Parker were in disagreement over what constituted self-defense. They also held different views on the related matter of the duty to retreat. We have seen that Parker stood by the old rule that a person, when threatened, must use every means, including flight, to avoid bloodshed. Other courts, including the nation's highest, were moving toward acceptance of 'no duty to retreat.'"[36] Parker was not a fan of the self-defense plea, and he flatly refused to uphold laws governing it.

Notably, in seven of the eight self-defense cases reversed by the Supreme Court, people of color or recent immigrants were involved. The same Supreme Court that gave us the decision in *Plessy v. Ferguson* protected the rights of nearly every minority in these Parker cases. Kopel notes how exceptional this was: "All of the defendants whose convictions were reversed had been carrying guns." This was important because "the United States in the 1890s had virtually no gun controls aimed at whites, but there were extensive controls aimed at people of color. Much of the South had gun licensing and registration statutes which were never enforced against whites, but were rigorously applied against blacks."[37] This raises important questions of Parker's application of the law when it comes to race. These examples demonstrate how out of step Judge Parker was with legal proceedings of the day.

The power and significance of the oft-repeated Parker quote "I never hanged a man; it was the law" should not be underestimated. The sentiment is even on the dust cover of Brodhead's book, in which he directly questions the legitimacy of that very explanation. Notably, Supreme Court Justice William Rehnquist was a fan of Parker who, Kopel observes, "cited Parker's expertise in Indian law, and . . . approvingly quoted the Hanging Judge's statement, 'I never hanged a man. It is the law.' But according to the Supreme Court of the 1890s, too much of what Judge Parker did was not the law—Parker infringed on the right to self-defense."[38] In one case, "the question was the validity of Judge Parker's instructions to the jury about the difference between premeditated murder and manslaughter. Judge Parker had told the jury that [the defendant's] carrying of a handgun could be considered evidence of premeditated intent to kill, even if the carrying was purely for self-defense."[39] In another case he told the jury that the defendant "was a bond-jumper, [so] he could not claim self-defense.[40] The Supreme Court justices did not agree with this overt manner of leading the jury.

One of the reversals was due in part to Parker's citing the biblical account of Cain and Abel to a jury that "the wicked flee when no man pursueth." Justice Edward White retorted that such words were "'tantamount to saying . . . that flight created a legal presumption of guilt, so strong and so conclusive, that it was the duty of the jury to act on it as an axiomatic truth.'"[41] Kopel says of yet another trial that "Judge Parker instructed the jury that they were free to conclude that [the defendant] had provoked the trouble, and therefore lost his right to self-defense."[42] And again, "Judge Parker told the jury that even if [the defendant] had the right to use self-defense against an attack by [the victims], [the defendant] could not defend himself if [he] had the ability to retreat safely."[43] Repeatedly Parker led juries away from self-defense pleas.

Near the end of his career Parker was lambasted in a public tiff with

Solicitor General Whitney for doing so, as Tuller describes: "Parker refused to accept instruction. Whitney conceded that the judge meant well, but was 'ignorant and careless' with the law, continuing to fill his jury charges 'with gross errors. . . . On account of his great desire to secure convictions' Whitney concluded, Judge Parker had become 'the best friend of the criminals, for he insures them reversals.'"[44] While clinging to antiquated legal concepts Parker unwittingly became complicit in reversals of his own decisions. In another case Brodhead notes, the justices made sweeping comments on Parker's judicial conduct: "Other instructions by Parker were 'clearly illegal. . . . The charge given . . . violates every rule thus announced. It was neither calm nor impartial. It put every deduction that could be drawn against the accused from the proof of concealment and flight and omitted or obscured the converse aspect.'"[45] These are but a few examples with which scholars including Kopel, Brodhead, and Tuller have critiqued the notion that the record of Judge Isaac Parker was above reproach. Kopel raises the next logical yet disconcerting thought: "One can only shudder at how many of the 7,419 criminal convictions in Judge Parker's court (only a few of which, as post-1889 capital sentences, were reviewed by the Supreme Court) were likewise erroneous."[46] Such an application of the Supreme Court's overruling logic awaits a retroactive study.

Tuller points out that Parker came to his extremely powerful position with more political savvy than legal experience: "Parker was a political appointee with enough legal background to satisfy the needs of the Grant administration in filling a judicial vacancy, not an insightful legal thinker or an honored jurist. At the time of his appointment, he possessed only a year and a half of judicial experience as a state circuit judge. He was a frontier attorney who had used the law as a means of political advancement."[47] Competent at best, Parker carved out his own niche of frontier justice. Parker learned on the job, worked hard, and ran an efficient court but failed to adapt with the changing legal standards of his time, instead choosing to publicly attack his detractors: "On his controversial courtroom conduct, he reiterated 'I have been accused of leading juries. I tell you a jury should be led . . . if they are guided they will render justice.' Parker asserted that his critics 'utterly forget the hardened character of the criminals I have to deal with.'"[48] In a manner reminiscent of Raskolnikov, his was a special case, so he argued. These remarks come from his September 1896 deathbed interview. This was Parker's last attempt at leading the jury of public opinion regarding the justness of his career. In the Fort Smith frontier complex today the presentation of Parker's justice in the court of cultural memory clearly comes down in his favor.

From the vantage point of contemporary research on the death penalty we know that at minimum there are wrongfully convicted individuals on death row today.[49] Some states have discontinued the death penalty because the chances of executing an innocent person are so high and because of significant racial disparities.[50] It is hard to imagine that the legal and judicial approach to capital cases was more efficient in Parker's era than it is today. From this comparative approach it is nearly certain that innocent individuals were hanged in Fort Smith. Perhaps this is why no such contemporary comparison is ever made in the frontier complex.

Supreme Justice?

The historical record reveals a different side of Parker, Tuller has found, one very reluctant to relinquish power or take any criticism without rebuttal: "When the U.S. Supreme Court attempted to correct this bias, Parker interpreted the reversal of his sentences as personal attacks and responded in his usual manner—he struck back with invective . . . [and] retaliated with rebuke that shifted the blame to his foes." In the end he "initiated a series of public tantrums against his superiors." Tuller concludes that Parker "had become convinced that only he fully understood the complexities of his jurisdiction." After two decades of presiding over a hotly contested border, his ego was transformed "into a brittle sense of rectitude and indispensability."[51] At best, methinks the judge did protest too much. At worst, these are the responses of a megalomaniac. It was Parker, not Lady Justice, who was blinded by his all-consuming mission of instilling justice in Indian Territory. This was seen in his overturned death-sentence cases and in his refusal to appoint commissioners to Indian Territory to assist him.

The high cost of running the federal court was a constant irritation to Washington, which never lowered its scrutiny over the U.S. District Court for the Western District of Arkansas. Parker had it within his power to reduce costs and extend justice farther into Indian Territory but refused to do so. He had the authority to appoint U.S. commissioners in Indian Territory but did so only twice. Some advocates requested commissioners in at least ten more towns. This would have eased the cost of justice significantly. In some instances, Jeffrey Burton has found, the court reportedly had to pay "$50 to $250 to pursue through the courts the thief who had robbed him of a horse worth $40" because of the long distances parties necessarily traveled to stand before Parker in Fort Smith.[52] Commissioners serving farther out would have reduced the time, distance, and money required for serving justice.

Contrary to the clear benefits of such action, "Judge Parker almost never appointed commissioners in the Territory, and on the very rare occasions that he did, it was with reluctance at the time and regret afterward. His main objection to the location of commissioners' courts in Indian Territory was that, being away from the eye of the district attorney and judge at Fort Smith, they could be neither advised nor supervised."[53] Jeffrey Burton gently posits, "Perhaps Parker, a man of prodigious stamina and no small vanity, merely thought it intolerable that important antejudicial proceedings in his district should be held out of his earshot."[54] Burton sums up Parker's career: "The statistics say little of his qualities, except his stamina. His worst fault appears to have been the stubbornness of pride not uncommon in those appointed to public office, particularly if they are unused to having their decisions questioned. On the whole, Parker was a much better servant than a bad system deserved; but when that system was improved, he rebelled against it."[55] This characterization of Judge Parker is absent in the Fort Smith frontier complex.

In Fort Smith the cultural memory of the Hanging Judge remains one of unsullied frontier justice that is inflated all the more with Parker's humanitarian contributions as enumerated in the orientation video:

Judge Parker earned his reputation on the bench, but his influence extended far beyond the courtroom. He supported education reform and women's suffrage, and he worked to improve the living conditions of prisoners in his jail.

Parker's service on the school board and other civic efforts is said to have earned him saintly stature, as in this 1933 account: "To the children of that day he was the very embodiment of that patron saint of childhood made famous by the 'Night Before Christmas.' White of hair and beard, with pink cheeks, and slightly rotund, he had a twinkle in his eye and a little contagious chuckle, which always made them think of Santa Claus."[56]

The orientation video drives home the narrative of Parker's full and total devotion to justice and community in this penultimate statement:

His doctor said, "He worked himself to death."

The final statement in the National Historic Site video weds the military fort era and the Parker era in a perfect union for procreating white civilization on the western frontier:

> Fort Smith's leading role as the seat of law and order in the Southwest ended with the new courts and the death of Judge Isaac Parker. For eighty years, Fort Smith struggled to bring peace to this region. From the earliest military attempts to end the war between the Cherokee and Osage to Judge Parker's strict enforcement of the law, this post tells the story of the military installations, legal institutions, and specific individuals who truly defined the West.

The video leaves no alternative view of Fort Smith, no question of the mythical frontier justice, no doubt that the federal government, military, and court were bringing civilization and peace to the region. In fairness, the video was produced for the reopening of the Fort Smith National Historic Site in June 2000. This was before the scholarship of David Kopel was published that summer and before the academic Parker biographies of Roger Tuller and Michael Brodhead were published in 2001 and 2003, respectively. Only Jeffrey Burton's critique would have been accessible, as it was published in 1995. The video depiction and the exhibits, which have changed little since the June 2000 reopening, stand as a time capsule of the hegemonic narrative of the frontier complex and how Fort Smith is situated within it.

The image of Judge Parker exonerates him of any complicity in the taking of Indian Territory as another piece of manifest destiny. Parker is frequently cited as being a friend to the Indians, but closer scrutiny by Tuller reveals a greater complexity: "Parker, although portraying himself as an unflagging defender of Indian rights, may ultimately have done the Five Civilized Tribes more harm than good with his mixed record on American Indian issues."[57] Brodhead concurs: "Parker maintained that . . . legislation would hasten the 'civilizing' of the territory's inhabitants by having them participate in the white man's governing processes."[58] Tuller finds Parker's approach to helping typical of the times:

> His advocacy was decidedly paternalistic, typical of nineteenth-century humanitarians who believed their duty was to aid American

Indians 'in their journey along the pathway of civilization.' Seldom given to self-doubt, Isaac Parker never appeared to question his belief in the inherent superiority of his own culture. Nor did he waver in his conviction of the ultimate dominion of the United States over the tribal governments of the Indian Territory. Time and again he ruled against the Five Civilized Tribes, declaring that they could not prevent the construction of railroads across their lands, denying their rights to extradite criminals or to try adopted citizens. In fact, Parker contributed to the diminution of tribal self-determination and hastened the territorial status that he stridently opposed by consistently undermining American Indian sovereignty.[59]

Parker enthusiastically supported taking civilization to the savages, Tuller observes: "Parker presumed that his duty was to help American Indians assimilate into a superior culture, not to preserve their traditions. . . . He approached his role as judge over Indian Territory . . . as a protector of a less evolved people. Although some of his ruling weakened tribal rights, he believed that such rulings at least prepared American Indians for the time when they would participate fully in white society."[60] From this vantage point, taking peace to the Indians was but a thinly veiled code for the social construction of whiteness.[61]

For his time, Parker's was a progressive and humanitarian approach to Indians. By comparison, "some Indian-hating westerners favored outright extermination."[62] Considering how "civilized" the Five Civilized Tribes had become begs the question of what more was wanted of them than their land. Thus, the mythic frontier narrative makes the supposed justice of Judge Parker complicit in the project of manifest destiny and of constructing whiteness across the continent. In historical fact, Parker and his fellow Republicans' goal was to bring citizenship to African Americans and Indians alike.

We can now see the transition in Fort Smith from the frontier complex era of restraint to that of reservation. In essentializing Indians, Parker was effectively assisting the Dawes Severalty Act in pushing the civilization agenda onto the Five Nations of Indian Territory. The 1898 Curtis Act robbed the Indian nations of self-governance, further ensuring their sequestration onto regulated land that could be overseen and purchased by whites in such ventures as the Oklahoma Territory land runs.

Touring Capital Punishment

A visit to the Fort Smith National Historic Site obscures historical facts and criticisms of Judge Parker's time on the bench. Walking onto the nineteen-acre grounds one is enveloped in a forest of frontier symbols. It is difficult to miss the imposing life-size replica gallows, complete with a working trap door for full authenticity, though secured for safety reasons. As we step into the gift shop, we are immediately surrounded with kitschy Parker items such as noose-emblazoned ball caps, miniature gavels, and four-paneled, multicolored postcards that have morphed Andy Warhol's image of Marilyn Monroe into Judge Parker's visage. The walls are covered with photos of Parker and Indians as well as Civil War hats, canteens, toy cannons and guns, handcuffs, flags, popular books and films including the novel and both film adaptations of *True Grit*, and posters of John Wayne and Clint Eastwood. This pastiche of frontier-complex imagery is legitimated by park rangers in uniform and volunteers in period costume.

After paying admission and watching the fifteen-minute orientation video, *Peacekeeper of Indian Territory*, the tourist is fully primed to interact with the exhibits at the site. Walking into Hell on the Border, the original jail used by Parker, one hears reenacted voices of life in the dank basement jail. Making their way upstairs to the second jail and courtroom, visitors square off with a larger-than-life photo of outlaw Cherokee Bill and are then overtaken by the imposing edifice of what was the 1889 modern jail. It is complete with walk-in cells flanked by exhibit panels featuring portraits of miscreants from Indian Territory that one must dodge as if they were real people in the way. Finally, visitors walk through a corridor to step into the quiet of the replica of Judge Isaac C. Parker's courtroom.

All this takes place in the same building Parker and the most infamous deputies and criminals trod. How can there be any doubt that this was the place where law and order stood, where justice was meted out? There is a clue left in the exhibits, but it is very hard to find. At the farthest recess of the courtroom, on an exhibit panel that is facing the back wall, the persistent and diligent tourist will find a hint at a greater complexity. Gazing upward to the top of the eight-foot-tall panel the visitor reads: "The Court of No Appeal." The biggest image on the display is at the bottom of the panel, a portrait of Lady Justice sitting blindfolded and holding her balanced scale. The panel sends a mixed message that a court of no appeal rendered blind and balanced justice. As a whole, the exhibit invokes conflated images of definitive frontier justice. In between this contradiction lies the explanation.

The heading for the textual narrative on the panel reads, "Verdicts Overturned." The panel asks and answers a question about the decisions: "How did the advent of the appeals process affect Judge Parker? In the 1890s, 44 death sentences he handed down were appealed. Of those, 31 (or 70 percent) were overturned by the U.S. Supreme Court. Often the reasons rested in Parker's tendency to allow inflammatory evidence and lead juries." In the next paragraph, Parker's position, that he was standing for justice, is affirmed: "While Judge Parker did not oppose the appeals process, he strongly objected to higher courts that overturned cases on what he considered technicalities. He publicly criticized both the Supreme Court and the Attorney General, declaring 'The greatest cause of the increase of crime is the action of the appellate courts. . . . They make the most strenuous efforts, as a rule, to see not when they can affirm but when they can reverse a case.'" This is the extent of the explanation. From it, Parker's image of fighting for frontier justice emerges untarnished. Here, as elsewhere in the exhibits, Parker is presented as dispensing even-handed justice.

Accompanying the text on court of no appeal are two small portraits, one of Chief Justice Melville Fuller, who presided over the Supreme Court's critique of Parker's cases, and the other of John Henry Rogers, not to be confused with Fort Smith "founding father" John Rogers. John Henry Rogers, who was practicing law in Fort Smith well before Parker arrived, as early as 1869, led the legislation to have the Supreme Court hear appeals from Parker's court. Perhaps most significantly, he was Parker's successor on the bench of the U.S. District Court for the Western District of Arkansas and served until his death in 1911. This is the only place in the frontier complex where any information on Judge Rogers can be found. I was more than two years into my research at the site before I discovered this; it was news to me that Parker even had a successor. Upon questioning them, I learned that it was also news to many of the park rangers at the site. The narrative of Parker's frontier justice is so strong that it makes one believe everything just stopped when he died, including the existence of the U.S. District Court for the Western District of Arkansas.

There is little explanation in the frontier complex of what happened after 1896. The frontier imagination ends in Fort Smith with Parker's passing. We do not learn much of the subsequent law and order in Indian Territory or of the 1898 Curtis Act that abolished the court systems of the

Indian nations and concentrated all legal questions into the hands of federal courts. Nor is there development of the land runs leading up to Oklahoma statehood. The glossing of all this underscores what the mission of the federal presence in Fort Smith truly was—facilitating white expansion into Indian Territory.

Jeffrey Burton contends that tribal sovereignty was lost after the elimination of Indian nations' courts; it was simply a matter of time before Indian Territory would be overrun with whites who overwhelmingly voted for Oklahoma statehood in 1907.[63] Once the wild and savage frontier was civilized with the institutions of the white government in Washington, the reason for the federal presence ceased, as did the frontier rhetoric that legitimated it. This sudden shift or complete absence of frontier narrative reveals two things. First is the hollowness of how eighty years of white intrusion is excused as keeping the peace. Second, we can see the alibi function of the mythic frontier and justice in the frontier complex as its purveyors present a history that distracts tourists from the machinations and presumptions of manifest destiny.

Origin Myth

The mythologizing of the Parker era began as soon as it concluded. Within two years of Parker's death, Samuel Harman published *Hell on the Border*.[64] The book set the tone for images of the Hanging Judge's frontier justice. Harman's title underscores the observation that the intended function of the book was to convey not the history but rather the mythology of Judge Parker and his deputies' exploits, ultimately for Harman to make a profit from the book. It was "a business venture from the start," according to David Turk, historian of the U.S. Marshals Service.[65] *Hell on the Border* was devastating to the historical record of the court and of Fort Smith. Scholars subsequently wrote about the Parker court, but after Harman the damage was done. It is Harman's account and its retellings, namely Homer Croy's *He Hanged Them High* (1952) and J. Gladston Emery's *Court of the Damned* (1959), that captured the public imagination and have served as the storytelling template for the Fort Smith frontier complex and the National Historic Site's orientation video and exhibits.

Harman's accounts read more like pulp western fiction than factual history. He describes criminals as "brutes, or rather demons, in human form, and their crimes were deliberately planned and fiendishly executed."[66] As for their judge, he writes, "A man less resolute than Judge Parker would have failed in the task set before him. Failure would have meant bloodshed and a fierce domination of the lawless class in the district. A great work was to be performed and a man equal to the emergency sat upon the bench, who was fearless amid disorders, powerful in his grand individuality."[67]

It was Harman who immortalized Parker's words "Do equal and exact justice, permit no innocent man to be punished, but let no guilty man escape."[68] The mystique of Parker is that he oozed justice from every pore of his body, that injustice was such an abomination to his sensibilities it could not have been in his sight without being struck down—or strung up, as the case may be. Harman mythologizes the moment the jurisdiction in Indian Territory was entirely removed from the purview of the U.S. District Court for the Western District of Arkansas, tying the removal of jurisdiction directly to Parker's death, naturalizing the infusion of justice pulsing through Parker's bloodstream:

> At last, Congress, with ruthless hand, took from the court its jurisdiction over the Indian country, passing a law, March 1, 1895, providing that such jurisdiction should cease after September 1, 1896. Congress, no doubt, had thought it had done wisely, but Judge Parker thought differently. That court was his idol; with its destruction his mission ended. It was impossible for so great a man to dwarf his magnificent proportions to the dimensions of a petty court. Belittled as it was, it was his no longer; nature revolted; and as the day grew near for the great catastrophe, it was reported for the first time—early in July, 1896—that Judge Parker was too sick to hold court. He had performed his duty nobly; he had fought a good fight for the enforcement of law and for the preservation of the lives and property of those within his jurisdiction. He had taught the lawless to respect the rights and property of peaceful citizens, and had assisted the Indians in the Territory to advance to a higher civilization.[69]

In this epitaph, not to the deceased judge but to his lost jurisdiction, we see the mythologization of Parker as judge of supreme justice. Harman also builds on Parker's reputation for being a friend to the Indians, and he dismisses the errors of the Supreme Court as a hindrance to Parker's will to impose frontier justice on the border.

Harman dedicates *Hell on the Border* to Parker thus: "To the memory of my loved and honored friend, Judge I. C. Parker, one of the noblest of men, whose keen sense of justice, made him a rigid disciplinarian and a stickler for right, yet left him a devoted lover of humanity and in full sympathy with its sorrows, do I dedicate this book."[70] According to Juliet Galonska's introduction to the Eastern National edition of the book, Harman was assisted by J. Warren Reed and C. P. Sterns, who "drew upon court records, newspaper accounts, and interviews in writing."[71] Reed was familiar with the court as a defense attorney. Galonska, who was the park historian at the Fort Smith National Historic Site, warns that *Hell on the Border* "should be read and used with caution" and that "inaccuracies are scattered throughout the book."[72] Though Harman lived in Bentonville, Arkansas, he would travel to and stay in Fort Smith while the federal court was in session. He was only a juror between 1888 and 1896. This was during the last third of Parker's career, when his verdicts could be appealed to the Supreme Court and the jurisdiction in Indian Territory was down to 22,000 square miles. After Parker's death, Harman saw an opportunity to cash in his cache with the court by selling its story. David Turk reports that Harman never realized that income, as he died the year after the book's publication.[73]

While making preparations for its publication, Harman, Reed, and Stearns attempted to purchase parts of the old gallows. Harman had wanted to use them in a publicity stunt he was arranging. He employed George Maledon, an actual hangman, to go on tour displaying artifacts from the old court and discussing hangings in gruesome detail. Oddly, Harman shares this strategy with his readers:

> [D]esiring to secure some expression of public opinion before giving the necessary time and expense to preparing the manuscript, of ascertaining to my own satisfaction how the people in general would regard such a work, I made arrangements with Mr. Maledon and, after securing for him some of the ropes and other gruesome relics of his late vocation, as well as numerous photographs of the most noted desperadoes with whom the court had dealt, made a summer's tour of some of the country towns and small cities within a radius of, perhaps, five hundred miles from Fort Smith, exhibiting the famous hangman and the instruments of his office, in a tent, pitched in convenient localities in the places visited.[74]

By this time, Buffalo Bill Cody had clearly demonstrated there was money to be made in such displays of the Wild West. Harman claimed his motive for producing the book and the tour was as a morality lesson akin to the Newgate Calendar.[75] He insisted it was to keep the lessons of justice learned from the court alive. In sharing these thoughts with his reader, Harman demonstrates how he mythologized the Parker court:

Again and again, during this tour, was I assured of the demand already existing for the book I had in view, and when I would address the listening hundreds upon the great moral lessons to be learned from a close scrutiny of the records of crimes and criminals punished by the court that stood at the head, in America, in the number of capital punishments it had administered, many were the gray-haired fathers and earnest spoken mothers, who grasped my hand and in thrilling accents bade me God-speed in the work I had in mind and which, in their belief, would be a mighty agent in saving the girls and the boys of our land.[76]

And so began the cultural memory and mythic image of justice embodied in Judge Isaac C. Parker.

The historical facts in Fort Smith regarding Harman's acquisition of the old gallows reveal a deep ambivalence the town had regarding the entire Parker era. When the city council learned of Harman's plans to acquire pieces of the gallows for his tour, the council had it burned down. Harman clearly wanted a monopoly on the Parker myth. After hearing a rumor that the town council might sell the gallows to another party, Harman describes how he

at once sought the leading newspaper offices of Fort Smith and caused them to believe that I was about to procure the old death trap and exhibit it about the country, and the press was suddenly stricken with a holy horror and, imbued with the idea that such an act would reflect great discredit upon Fort Smith, their columns teemed with denunciations of the proposed plan most bitterly, and a howl of opposition went up, so strong as to compel the city council . . . [so that] the gallows was ordered torn down and burned.[77]

Harman felt such a claim to his mythologizing of Judge Parker's career that he shares these admitted plans in Hell on the Border with no apparent sense of impropriety.

The book is full of questionable newspaper accounts of trials, outlaws, deputies, and the action that revolved around the proceedings of the court. The Fort Smith Elevator, a key source for many of the accounts, provided aggrandized stories that only grew in proportion to Harman's hyperbole of the court's history. Academic historians dismiss nearly every aspect of *Hell on the Border*. From an anthropological perspective, however, it is a time capsule of a creation story, the origin myth of the Hanging Judge, how it was embedded into the American cultural memory, and how it functions to cover up several otherwise unpleasant facts of the Parker court.

Behind the Parker Alibi

As we have seen, Parker's long arm of the law was not nearly so long as it is portrayed. The exaggerated size of the court's jurisdiction functions as an alibi that explains why there continued to be such supposed lawlessness in Indian Territory throughout Parker's career. The alibi says, "It was a monumental task to cover such a huge jurisdiction; it wasn't because increasing numbers of whites were illegally penetrating it." A closer look at the historical facts of the period diminish the justice that Parker and his deputies were dispensing. It is my contention that the figure of 74,000 square miles must be repeated over and over as a mantra for the Parker era in order to assert supreme justice in the place where many injustices were occurring.

Furthermore, the alibi directs our attention westward, turning our backs on the East, from which the train of manifest destiny was originating, and away from the still open wounds of North versus South in Parker's time and today. The frontier attic takes the space of the Confederate attic. After all, Judge Parker was what some on the frontier border would prefer to forget: a carpet-bagging Radical Republican Yankee from the North who was keen on imposing white civilization from the East on the savage West. He was not a "friend of the Indians" in today's view of that phrase. The popular narrative socially constructs whiteness on the frontier, diverts attention from the national fallout from the Civil War, more locally distracts from corruption in the Fort Smith court, and entirely silences the fact that Parker had jurisdiction over nineteen counties in Arkansas.

The history of the eastern segment of the U.S. District Court for the Western District of Arkansas is neglected in almost every narrative of the frontier complex. In some ways, this is not surprising because there is evidence that Parker neglected it, too. While there are occasional accounts of deputies riding out of Fort Smith to Eureka Springs, they are few and far between. Accounts of deputies riding into Indian Territory totally eclipse anything the court may have done in Arkansas proper. Admittedly, the bulk of the criminal cases heard in the court stemmed from Indian Territory. This does not mean, however, that federal laws were not being broken in

Figure 4.2. Visitor caution, Fort Smith National Historic Site. The sign leading to the platform of the reconstructed gallows unequivocally declares it an "instrument of justice." Photo by the author.

the Arkansas counties. Parker made deliberate choices on where to expend his limited funds. This point has significant ramifications when locating Parker's term as judge in a broader context. Higgins raises one: "Control over forestry practices did not exist at the time, but so great was the volume of timber cutting in northwestern Arkansas and what is now northeastern Oklahoma, that the Secretary of the Interior urged the federal court in Fort Smith to quell the plundering."[78] Local historian Bradley Kidder Sr. argues that Parker's passive supervision of the natural resources in Arkansas and his negligent application of the law hastened the railway's intrusion into Indian Territory. The trees being stolen from Arkansas forests were quickly converted to railroad ties.

Kidder connects railroad development to the civilizing project of Indian Territory that Judge Parker was actively marshaling: "The nation's mood changed during the 1880s from civilizing savages to a development of stable and protected economic markets in Indian Territory. Well-meaning reformers, who had long argued that Indians could and should be assimilated into American society, provided justification for economic expansion into Indian lands. They maintained that the Indians would relinquish their savage heritage if they had the responsibilities of property ownership."[79] Parker facilitated white encroachment by allowing the trees to be taken, expediting westward expansion of the nation. Railroad kingpins were aware of the significance of Fort Smith's rail lines, Higgins contends: "One of America's industrial captains, Jay Gould had a personal interest in the district and visited Fort Smith twice, the last time in 1891 when he dedicated the opening of a railroad bridge across the Arkansas River."[80] The Gould Bridge arched the Arkansas River at Belle Point not three hundred yards from Parker's old courtroom, near where John Rogers' sutler store stood in the 1820s.

Florence Hammersly, daughter of Judge Parker's court crier of the period, composed a poem that was read aloud at the grand opening of the Gould Bridge:

Long years we've been near together
Our city and the Indian land,
So near we could see each other,
That hand could most touch hand,
But there's been a barrier to commerce
Friendship's social queen
Tho so near, we've been distant
The Arkansas rolls between.
But today we are united
By this highway of steel and stone,
No longer will commerce be blighted
Nor friendships wanton alone.
Fort Smith and the Indian country
Henceforth will go hand in hand
Abreast with the tide of progress
Our own, our native land.
Now, while our native vintage mingles
With the waters that flow to the sea
We'll unfurl our grand old banner
And shout for the home of the free.[81]

The freedom that the railroad brought was the freedom for white migrants to invade and rampage across Indian Territory. The bridge opening coincided with the ever-quickening land runs in Oklahoma Territory; the reservation era of the frontier complex was now well under way in Fort Smith.

The complicit role the federal court played in this process was not lost on members of the Fort Smith Chamber of Commerce who toasted the opening of the Gould Bridge from midnight to 3 a.m. on May 27, 1891. The occasion was considered so momentous the "Speeches and Proceedings" were documented in a "Bridge Banquet" pamphlet.[82] Invited guests listed in the program included Arkansas Governor J. P. Eagle, as well as U.S. Indian Agent Leo Bennett, Pleasant Porter of the Creek Nation, and H. T. Jackman of the Choctaw Nation.

The greatest thrust of the speeches was on the main event, the wedding of Arkansas to Indian Territory by way of the Gould railroad bridge. While the tone was clearly intended to be conciliatory and celebratory of the economic benefits the bridge would bring, the speeches were dotted with sometimes subtle, sometimes flagrant comments that reveal the highly racialized reality of this frontier border that was being bridged by the railroad. Principal Chief J. B. Mayes of the Cherokee was unable to attend but sent a letter saying, "As this grand structure unites the two countries in business and pleasure, it is to be hoped that it will unite us in friendship and fair dealing in all our intercourse as citizens and officers of each Nation and State."[83] The toast entitled "The Cherokee Nation and Fort Smith—Their Interest Identical" was delivered by Pleasant Porter of the Creek Nation.

Toastmaster Col. J. H. Clendening introduced Porter by saying, "I am glad to be able to announce the assent of a gentleman from the Creek Nation to take the place of Gov. Mayes—a Creek Indian, a gentleman and a scholar—one who is a credit to his race, and a living refutation of the slander that the good Indians are all dead."[84] Mr. Porter's indignation may have been veiled only slightly in his initial remark, "I trust that I may be able to say something that will be appropriate." He goes on then to emphasize the truth he saw in the toast's title of how Fort Smith and the Indian Nations are identical. He adds, "The idea that persons generally have of the word civilization, is not generally correct. Civilization as a term, is purely comparative. And I will say this, that Fort Smith, with the advantages surrounding it, has not progressed any faster than we have; that is, starting from the vantage ground that they have over us. We have progressed equally with them, therefore we are identical in our progress."

Further into the speech Porter returns to this identical nature and says,

"We have identical hearts within our breasts. I say that because to-day I have talked with a great many people whom I have met here and I have never met with a people that seemed to me they thought and felt more like I did than the people of Fort Smith." To this comment there was "[Great applause]." Porter closes by encouraging railroad lines be developed along the Canadian, North Fork Grand, and Verdigris Rivers.

Indian Agent Leo Bennett's toast to "The Future of Indian Territory" was dominated by a plea for statehood. He noted how the people of Indian Territory looked to Fort Smith for guidance and implied that the bridge would expedite that. He said, "The people know they are upon the verge of a very important change to them. What that will be they are unable to fathom. They are seeking for information. They want the kindly, the friendly and fatherly advice; they want the advice of those who have traveled the road they must travel to reach statehood."

Bennett's paternalistic guidance ends by his emphatically declaring, "We do not want a territorial government. We do not want to go through the trials and troubles of a territory. The future now looked to by the thinking citizens of the Indian Territory is statehood, and an early statehood," remarks that likewise met with great applause. Railroad companies had sought greater access to Indian Territory ever since the Treaty of 1866 gave them entrée to do so. The combination of railroads and the Dawes Act were well on their way to making statehood inevitable for Indian Territory by 1891.

The Fort Smith frontier complex was a key player in this inevitability. The peace that Fort Smith was keeping at least rhetorically between 1817 and 1896 is borne out in the number of whites in Indian Territory census data. As early as 1890, the census revealed Indians to be the vastly outnumbered minority in their own lands. The Dawes Act and subsequent land commissions simply made de jure what was already de facto—the 1907 census recorded a total territorial population, including both Indian Territory and Oklahoma Territory, of which only 5.3 percent (75,012) were Indians. The 112,160 African Americans significantly outnumbered Indians, while the 1,226,930 whites comprised 86.8 percent of the population.[85] The territorial referendum for statehood in 1907 was 180,333 for and 73,059 against.[86] The overwhelmingly white majority allowed into the state by the graces of Fort Smith's peacekeeping made this result a foregone conclusion.

Exhibiting Justice

Regarding the depiction of Judge Isaac Parker in the Fort Smith frontier complex, it is my contention that his reputed justice must be held up as the epitome of judiciousness in order to match the degree necessary to conceal the injustices born of imperialism: relocating thousands of Native Americans; appropriating natural resources from their land, such as the forests for railroad ties and coal for locomotives; intruding on their land with cattle drives, railroads, squatters, and land runs; dismantling their governance structures; and replacing clan access to property with individual allotments.

However, none of the concealment is to say that sound historical facts cannot be found in the Fort Smith frontier complex. It is just that they are very hard to find and connect. Many exhibits at the Fort Smith National Historic Site are lacking critical pieces of information that would break down these assumptions. Many important points can be found in the exhibits, but linking them is like a connect-the-dots game that visitors need to draw to grasp the larger significance.

In my experience, one needs to be well versed in much of the regional nineteenth-century history to begin making serious connections between the various dots. Two of the main exhibit rooms at the National Historic Site are arranged in this disparate manner. In the cavernous room featuring a full-scale cutaway reconstruction of the three-story-tall 1889 reform jail, important material that had been tightly interrelated in the nineteenth century has been disentangled, separated, and posted on opposite walls out of view from each other.

When visitors enter the first exhibit room the imposing jail structure can capture their attention much like the reconstructed gallows does outside on the grounds. If they turn away from the jail edifice and look to the eastern wall they will see exhibit panels with such damning titles as "The Attack on Tribal Sovereignty," "The End of Indian Territory," "Economic Invasion of Indian Territory," "Reassigning Tribal Land," and "Breaking Apart the Indian Territory." The textual content on these panels discusses the impact of white intrusion into Indian Territory but does not link any causality of these events to Fort Smith. They are presented as events happening in history in which the military fort and federal court in Fort Smith were somehow not involved.

Dotting these panels that embody so much violence are so-called peace medals. They are the size of a large coin and depict a handshake between a soldier and an Indian. A hatchet and tobacco pipe cross at midpoint, adorned with the words "Peace and Friendship." As visitors walk to the other side of the room they must navigate through the jail display as they dodge exhibit panels about Zeke Proctor, Ned Christie, Belle Starr, and Judge Parker. Panel titles declare "The Long Arm of the Law," "Law, Order and Confusion," and "George Maledon Prince of Hangmen," with rifles, pistols, posses, and ropes on display. Upon reaching the other side of the room visitors find a row of exhibit panels that announce "Mayhem & Mischief," "Noteworthy Last Words," and "A Lawless Land?" One panel leads with "The Roots of Crime" and follows up with this explanation: "Residents and nonresidents of Indian Territory all searched for ways to explain the criminal activity that plagued the region. Just as in our own times, the answers were complex and varied."

This occasion is then used to reinforce the perception that Parker let no guilty man escape as it reinforces his rebuke of the Supreme Court Justices reversing his cases. The exhibit panel reads, "After twenty years on the bench in Fort Smith, Judge Isaac C. Parker had developed very specific ideas on the causes of crime. He blamed a court system that allowed offenders to escape on legal technicalities." The exhibit that would offer some context to this remark, that would be another dot to connect to this one, is placed two exhibit halls away, in the far corner of a room and facing the back wall. Without mentioning the Supreme Court by name or its reversals of 70 percent of the cases they heard from Parker's court, Judge Parker is depicted here as a stalwart of supreme justice. In the context of *True Grit*, Parker, just like Rooster Cogburn, felt the justices were being too hard on the "rat catcher." The exhibit hall represents historical facts in such a way that neither the military fort nor the Parker court was culpable for the lawlessness in Indian Territory. Impunity is granted under the cover of Parker's cloak of supreme justice.

5

///////////////////////////////////////

The Invincible Marshal's Oppression

I don't feel we did wrong in taking this great country away from them, if that's what you're asking. Our so-called stealing of this country from them was just a matter of survival. There were great numbers of people who needed new land, and the Indians were selfishly trying to keep it for themselves.

John Wayne

At a national level the frontier complex reinforces whiteness in each of its five eras. As we have seen with the Fort Smith military fort and federal court, in the eras of removal, restraint, and reservation, from 1804 to 1934, the movement of colored people was systematically restricted to enable white privilege. The tourist narratives developed in the recreation and redoubling eras reinforced the power of the state and white social institutions as they muted alternative voices and perspectives. When the mythologization of the nineteenth-century frontier was encapsulated in film during the first fifty years of the recreation era, John Wayne emerged as one of its principal icons. On and off the screen he was a staunch patriotic supporter of whiteness. The epigraph quoted from his infamous 1971 *Playboy* interview is a raw and candid statement of an ideology that was only slightly more veiled in roles he played on film such as in *The Searchers,* in which his vitriol for Native Americans is channeled through the character Ethan Edwards, former Confederate soldier warring against Indians in Texas.

In many ways the history of Indian Territory encapsulates the arbitrary nature in which race has been socially constructed in the United States. The interplay of white, Indian, and African American in this frontier space reveals the contradictions within and between those categories and how they have been used by some individuals to leverage the political economy. While the end of Indian Territory brought its folding into white institutions and white civilization, the historical facts of the complex and messy process of divesting Indians and African Americans of their political and economic positions in the frontier are silenced by images of race in the Fort Smith frontier complex and reconstituted in a cultural memory more palatable for the predominately white tourists consuming cultural heritage.[1]

Here we will focus on how the racial history of whites, Native Americans, and African Americans in the frontier is reconstituted as myth and embedded into the Fort Smith frontier complex. Just as the stories told today of the military fort and Judge Parker tell us more about present concepts of power in the social structure, the stories told today of Bass Reeves, Belle Starr, and Miss Laura are reflections of contemporary notions of race and gender imposed upon the past. We need to untangle these tropes from their piers to see what racial and gender ideologies they are harboring.

The discourse of keeping the peace in the frontier and the justice of Judge Parker serves as the foundation on which mythic race is built in Fort Smith. The alibi of white-Indian relations says, "White people weren't systematically dismantling Indian Territory and taking possession of it. That's not what they were doing. Judge Parker was nurturing Indians toward civilization." The alibi of white-black relations says, "Former slaves could be successful in the nineteenth-century frontier. Bass Reeves was not systematically discriminated against by slavery, segregation, and racism. That's not where he was. He was given a great opportunity by Judge Parker, worked really hard, followed all the rules, and overcame all manner of limitations to have a very successful career." Here I will contextualize these alibis within the historical facts of Indian Territory and explain how they conceal institutionalized racism within the cultural memory of the Wild West frontier.

Equal Justice?

Discussion and display of the races of individuals executed in Fort Smith serve as a fundamental example of how Parker's mythic justice is entangled with contemporary conceptions of race. It can be frequently heard in Fort Smith that Parker was an impartial judge when it came to race because the numbers of those hanged was nearly equivalent among three races: thirty-three whites, eighteen blacks, and thirty-six Indians. The occasional note surfaces that the low figure for blacks was a sign of Parker's leniency for that race. Of course, this assumption would only be close to accurate if the population that Parker was judging was roughly 33 percent of each of those categories, which was never the case. To date, no attempt at determining anything like a proportionate population rate has been attempted for Parker's record.

There are many obstacles to surmount for making even a halfway reasonable "guesstimate." Determining the precise racial composition of Indian Territory in the period is difficult for several reasons. Lack of census data in general and problematic categorization labels make it hard to develop a specific demographic profile. Deciding who exactly qualifies to be in the "white," "Indian," or "black" categories and what criteria are used is a highly variable and imprecise process, especially considering the number of mixed-race individuals in Indian Territory. Nevertheless, data exist in the Indian Territory census and execution records for the Judge Parker court using the flawed schema, and those calculations determine how the information is presented in exhibits and programs.

The racial composition of Indian Territory in 1871 was quite different from that in 1907, when it became part of the state of Oklahoma. The proportion of white people in the territories in 1870 was substantially smaller, perhaps 10–20 percent, depending on which Indian nation or district one lived in. A census taken in 1877 of Cherokee, Choctaw, Creek, Seminole, and Chickasaw Nations determined the region to be 63 percent Indian, 23 percent black, and 15 percent white.[2] By 1890 these figures were drastically different: the Indian population had dropped to 28.5 percent and the black population to 10.3 percent, while the white population rose to 61.2 percent. The 1900 census reported those numbers to be 9.1 percent Indian, 11.8 percent black, and 79.1 percent white. Based on what we know today about the highly racialized nature of the criminal justice system, I believe it is safe to extrapolate backward to Parker's era to conservatively estimate that Judge Parker's court was handing down death sentences skewed by race, not to mention the fact that every jury in this time was composed exclusively of white men.

A closer look at execution data reveals that the numbers reported in exhibits at the Fort Smith National Historic Site do not match more current research. In *Hanging Times in Fort Smith: A History of Executions in Judge Parker's Court*, Jerry Akins features a profile of each individual hanged in Fort Smith during the tenure of the federal court's jurisdiction in Indian Territory, 1871–1896.[3] A revised analysis reveals that forty Indians, seventeen blacks, and twenty-nine whites were hanged in Fort Smith. That is 46.5, 19.8, and 33.7 percent, respectively. These figures are safe to compare with the changing population data in the censuses from 1870 through 1900, as none of the offenses that resulted in these hangings happened farther west than the Five Nations region of Indian Territory.

When examined in this light, stark patterns begin to stand out. For example, 66 percent of all those hanged were men of color. A closer look shows the bulk of African American executions came in the middle era of the court's jurisdiction (1883–1889), when thirteen of the seventeen black men in total were hanged. This most likely reflects heightened racial tensions against African-descent individuals after the Civil War by whites and Native Americans alike. Deeper analysis of these data awaits further study. Regardless, Judge Parker, his court, his deputies, and his entire era are perpetually portrayed as paragons of equal and exact justice in frontier-complex tourism narratives, museum exhibits, and historic site presentations.

Not Quite White

Despite the varied demographic history of the Fort Smith region, which includes European immigrant groups such as German and Irish, indigenous groups like Caddos and Osages, displaced Indian groups such as Cherokees and Choctaws, and groups of African descent like black slaves and free blacks, essentialized notions of white, black, and Indian dominate the discourse in the frontier complex, while mention of Latin Americans and Asian Americans is absent.[4] A close examination of the interplay among these socially constructed racial categories in Indian Territory and Oklahoma Territory—together referred to as the territories—reveals an underlying racism that is today concealed in the Fort Smith frontier-complex mythology. This is based on examining white-Indian relations and revisiting the ideologically laden savage/civilized dichotomy, then African Americans—former slaves of Indians, freedmen, and free black emigrants—living in the territories. The latter study establishes a refractive mirror through which we can more clearly see the myth of the legendary black lawman Bass Reeves.

Another consideration is that when Native Americans are spoken of in Fort Smith it is in quite generalized terms. In my research it was rare to find anyone speaking about Indian Territory or the Five Civilized Tribes who had actually been to visit any of those nations or conveyed an understanding of the internal complexity within any particular nation. "Cherokee," for example, is used as a blanket category with the assumption that it covers a homogeneous group of people. There is no recognition of the divisions within the Cherokees rooted in different periods of removal to the area, let alone awareness of the complex freedman issue or the Eastern Band of Cherokees.

In Tahlequah, these long-standing divisions are still quite real and play out in contemporary social life. There are separate museums for the United Keetoowah Band of the Cherokee and the Cherokee Nation, the former being more closely aligned with the traditional Old Settlers, who were removed from the Southeast to the region in the early 1800s, and the latter with the Treaty Party, who were moved there in 1838.[5] Indian nations in Oklahoma are today actively working to construct their own identities. Joshua Gorman has examined how the Chickasaws have been using museums and cultural centers to actively constitute an identity for the Chickasaw people.[6] In 2010 the Chickasaw Nation opened a $40 million, 109-acre cultural center in Sulphur, Oklahoma.[7] Identity formation and maintenance are just as complex when looking from the inside of those "othered" people.

Fort Smith's relation to Indian Territory was always more nuanced than tourist narratives in the frontier complex reflect. In 1833, when Captain Stuart was doing battle with John Rogers over whether a second military Fort Smith should be constructed, he aired a candid and prescient comment regarding the Fort Smith–Indian Territory border:

> If Troops are ever Stationed in this Territory, for the avowed purpose of giving protection of the White inhabitants against the neighbouring Indians, difficulties and contentions will at once arise between the two parties. The depraved portion of the Whites, feeling themselves Protected by the Military will commence their Lawless outrages on the Indians, by Killing and Stealing their property and often molesting their person.[8]

Captain Stuart's thinking was still quite grounded in the frontier complex era of removal. He was conceptualizing the land that was at that time still Arkansas Territory as the permanent Indian frontier; Arkansas became a state in 1836, and Fort Smith was not incorporated until 1842. Sixty-five years later, Captain Stuart's concerns had played out, and the restraint era had given way to the reservation era. From this new vantage point the use of the frontier complex looked quite different from Stuart's view.

Speaking of the exact same land as Stuart, Samuel Harman voices the spirit of the reservation era in 1898 thus:

Thousands of men—and *women*—whose feet for years had itched to tread the "public domain" on whose broad acres their covetous eyes had lingered greedily, longing, waiting for the time when the "Cherokee Strip" should be opened to actual settlers, which actual settlers could and then would be citizens, not aliens nor "intruders" in the land in which rested their homes—were finally permitted to settle the wilderness in a day . . . [and have] at *last*, the right to stake a spot of God's green earth they could call their own.[9]

These were among the white people who needed the land for survival to whom John Wayne was referring. Looking at the relation between white narratives in Fort Smith and those created in Indian Territory reveals contradictions in popular historical and tourism narratives.

Tahlequah, Oklahoma, is an easy ninety-minute drive from Fort Smith, but it may as well be ninety hours as far as the presentation of cultural facts of white-Indian relations is concerned. Several museums there are designed to tell the Cherokees' story—and it is a quite different story than the one presented in Fort Smith. *The Trail of Tears Exhibit* in the Cherokee Heritage Center begins with a panel in which the first caption declares that the Cherokee were "playing by the rules."[10] The exhibit goes on to detail the ways the Cherokee took on the traits of western civilization. This is not a new observation, Murray Wickett asserts: "Lewis Downing, the Principal Chief of the Cherokees, noted in 1870 that the Five Civilized Tribes had accumulated property, adopted the Christian religion, had built churches and schools, and established printing presses and agricultural societies"; the tribes accomplished this "all without the interference of white authorities."[11] The Cherokees had long been playing the game of white civilization, and were well aware of the ever-moving goal post of attaining it—always within reach but never in grasp.

The Cherokees arrived in Indian Territory steeped in the classic earmarks of civilization, already identified as one of the Five Civilized Tribes prior to removal. Despite their high degree of assimilation, they were still held at bay by whites. In the territories and nationally, Indians continued to be othered in an essentialized blanket of white opinion. Buffalo Bill's Wild West shows contributed to the othering of Indians as savages while legitimating Anglos' right to westward expansion. Wickett observes, "All of the scenes which included Native Americans were battles between marauding savage Indians and resilient white pioneer settlers." Manifest destiny was

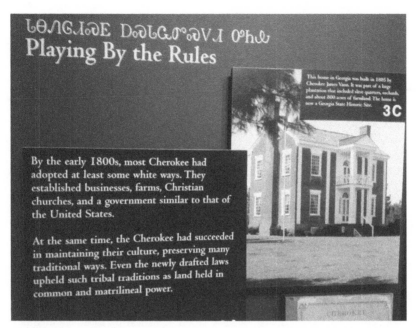

ᏝᎥᎮᎦᎸᎣᎬ ᎠᏬᏝᏓᎤᎲᎠᏉᎫ ᎣᎲhᏬ

Playing By the Rules

By the early 1800s, most Cherokee had adopted at least some white ways. They established businesses, farms, Christian churches, and a government similar to that of the United States.

At the same time, the Cherokee had succeeded in maintaining their culture, preserving many traditional ways. Even the newly drafted laws upheld such tribal traditions as land held in common and matrilineal power.

This house in Georgia was built in 1805 by Cherokee James Vann. It was part of a large plantation that included slave quarters, orchards, and about 800 acres of farmland. The house is now a Georgia State Historic Site.

3C

Figure 5.1. *The Trail of Tears Exhibit* in the Cherokee Heritage Center, Tahlequah, Oklahoma. The sign declares, "By the early 1800s, most Cherokee were . . . Playing by the Rules" of white civilization. Photo by the author. By permission of the Cherokee National Historical Society Inc.

reinforced: "By glorifying white violence against Native Americans as noble and just, Wild West shows gave cultural sanction to the prevailing racial ideology advanced by many white settlers and officials."[12]

Indians and African Americans alike were construed as immoral degenerates. In the frontier, "many agents complained that Native Americans were more intent upon drinking, gambling, horse racing, and dancing than undertaking any form of gainful employment. One Indian inspector noted that Indians seemed to have adopted many aspects of the white man, but that it was 'usually his vices, seldom any of his virtues.'"[13] This selective perception went across the board, as "many white reformers felt African Americans, like Native Americans, needed a strict moral guidance of a kind of authority figure."[14] Wickett notes that minstrel shows that reinforced this view were quite popular in Indian Territory as early as 1878.[15]

The colonizing whites had to continue to construct difference between races in order to legitimate the inequitable social structure of the United States. In the reinforcement of the "other," whiteness is constituted just as assuredly. John Hartigan has described whiteness in *Odd Tribes* as "the operations of racial privilege and advantage that structure the lives, attitudes, and actions of white people" and in an earlier journal article as "the coherence of privileges that white people, generically, have developed."[16] Whiteness is an essentialized mirror of the "othered," in this case Native Americans and African Americans, with the key difference being that whites have held the keys to the political economy.

Homi Bhabha posits that "colonial mimicry is the desire for a reformed, recognizable Other, as *a subject of a difference that is almost the same but not quite.*"[17] African Americans and Indians are simultaneously told to aspire to whiteness and that they will never attain it. This is why the nations must always be called the Five Civilized Tribes—they are not quite white; in effect, they are civilized savages allowed to come close to whiteness but ultimately turned away and deprived full access. The label "Five Civilized Tribes" discursively forms a principal racial ideology that legitimated Indian removal, relocation, and manifest destiny's claim to their lands. To avoid contributing to this subtle yet virulent justification for racial inequality, I will refer to the Cherokees, Choctaws, Creeks, Chickasaws, and Seminoles collectively as the Five Nations.

Convenient Marriages

Though each of the Five Nations functioned through political and legal institutions that mirrored those of the United States, these facts are silenced within the mythic frontier narrative. To allow them voice would be to expose the alibis of keeping the peace and taking civilization to the savages for what they are—subterfuge for exonerating America from the ills of imperialism and erasing the culpability of the federal fort and court that facilitated the overrunning and dismantling of Indian Territory by whites. Certainly the situation in Indian Territory was complex. Not all Indians were opposed to railroads and allotment nor all whites in favor of them. Many wealthy landowning Indians welcomed these changes as they increased their coffers and benefited from the encroaching masses of poor whites who quickly displaced freedmen as tenant farmers. The great range of opinions within as much as between racial groups holds true for the porosity of the so-called biological categories of race, too. The discursive formation of these categories and their shifting parameters becomes manifest when it is politically expedient to alter them.

In the frontier-complex eras of restraint and reservation one strategy used by some white men to acquire Indian land in the territories was to marry Indian women. Wickett notes, "The degree of intermarriage between white settlers and members of the Five Civilized Tribes was truly astounding."[18] What is even more remarkable is the apparent lack of self-awareness among whites who failed to see the contradiction in the racialized logic of its being acceptable for a white man to marry an Indian woman but not vice versa; when it is a white woman and Indian man, the narrative is invariably one of capture, and it was anathema and against the law after 1896 for whites and blacks to marry. Intermarriage of whites and Indians was initially explained by the lopsided ratio of white men to white women in the frontier but was intentionally used to gain access to Indian property and political processes. Such a marriage gave the white husband full citizenship rights in the tribes. Intermarriage, coupled with the Dawes Allotment Act, railroad intrusion, and mass white and black emigration into the territories, brought so-called peace and civilization to them, making a vote for statehood a foregone conclusion.

The life of James Jackson McAlester demonstrates the benefits of white privilege emanating from the Fort Smith frontier-complex border. Born in Fort Smith in the year of its incorporation, 1842, McAlester joined the Confederacy as a young man and returned home after the war. He boarded with Oliver Weldon, "a former engineer who had surveyed Indian Territory" and quite importantly "gave McAlester his memorandum book that detailed vast coal fields at the Cross Road area in Indian Territory."[19] The rich deposits in much of Indian Territory of coal, gas, and oil are scarcely if ever mentioned in the contemporary Fort Smith frontier narrative.[20] Development of this point would not only put the supposed lawlessness of Indian Territory in greater context but also expose the power play that was at work in the process. McAlester took full advantage of his position. He moved to the Choctaw Nation in 1866 and in 1872 married Rebecca Burney, a member of the Chickasaw Nation. This marriage gave him citizenship in both the Chickasaw and Choctaw Nations and thus access to mineral rights.

He wasted no time in staking claim to several coal deposits, and his business ventures prospered. The offense of McAlester's behavior toward the Choctaws is obvious when one learns that he and three of his associates were tried, found guilty by Chief Coleman of laying illegal railroad tracks to his coal mines, and sentenced to death by shooting. They only escaped death because the Choctaw Lighthorse law officer guarding them was reportedly sympathetic to their cause.[21] McAlester went on to serve a term as U.S. Marshal in 1893 and then as lieutenant governor of Oklahoma in 1911. McAlester joined John Rogers in the list of Frederick Jackson Turner's exceptional men who profited from the frontier complex.

Illegal cattle grazing and timber theft were two other significant ways in which economic advantage accrued to white privilege. Though Indian Territory belonged to the Five Nations, it was routinely exploited by whites when it came to railroads, coal, timber, and grazing rights. These acts of theft and exploitation by whites are given scant air time as reasons for Judge Parker having to deal with so much lawlessness. A trip into Indian Territory today to the tourist sites of memory constructed by the Five Nations, their exhibits, and available reading material offers a stark counternarrative to that found in Fort Smith.

The practice of intermarriage that garnered many white men access to their Indian wives' property was mimicked in political theater on the day these two territories merged into one state, November 16, 1907. The marriage between "Mr. Oklahoma Territory" and "Miss Indian Territory" symbolically assimilated Indians into full whiteness only at the exact moment that it no longer mattered. With tribal sovereignty effectively neutralized by allotment of land and abolishment of the courts, whites had reduced Indians to a numerical and social minority in their own homes, thus making the political theater of miscegenation of whites and Indians safe.

It is important to scrutinize what kind of marriage was enacted at Oklahoma statehood and dramatized in the wedding vows between Mr. Oklahoma and Miss Indian. A comparison of the event that day to how it is remembered reinforces the savage/civilized mythology. Guthrie, Oklahoma, the first capital of the state, was the location of this wedding. The site of the wedding later became that of the Oklahoma Territorial Museum. Today a statue commemorating the marriage stands outside the building. It depicts Mr. Oklahoma Territory dressed as a rancher with his pants tucked into his spurred boots marrying Miss Indian Territory, depicted as an Indian woman with two long braids of hair and wearing a tattered dress. She holds her left braid in one hand, while her right hand is taken by that of her husband. One hand holds savage tradition and the other is taken by civilization. The statue was erected in 1976 as part of the national bicentennial commemoration. It projects an image of a unified state and country

Figure 5.2. Mr. Oklahoma Territory marrying Ms. Indian Territory. The sculpture is at the Oklahoma Territorial Museum in Guthrie, near where the figurative marriage was enacted in 1907. Photo by the author.

created out of a diverse set of peoples. In fact, leading up to statehood there had been serious consideration of creating two states, one from Oklahoma Territory, essentially the western half of the state, and one from Indian Territory, whose proposed name was Sequoyah.

In actuality, Muriel Wright describes the clothing at the 1907 mock wedding as quite modern:

> The part of Miss Indian Territory, the bride in the memorial wedding ceremony, was taken by Mrs. Leo Bennett of Muskogee, a beautiful young woman of Cherokee descent, with dark hair and eyes. She wore for this occasion a lavender satin dress made in the latest fashion of the time, floor length princess style with long sleeves and high collar; and a large picture hat and gloves, carrying one large, mauve colored chrysanthemum. The part of Mr. Oklahoma, the bridegroom, was taken by Mr. C. G. Jones of Oklahoma City, a well-known leader and business man in the history of the city. He was tall, fair haired, and— noted for his punctilious appearance—wore for the wedding the best in striped trousers and black coat suitable for such an occasion.[22]

Wright then goes on to further correct the stereotype:

> Directors and writers of present day pageantry generally have Miss
> Indian Territory shown as an Indian girl wearing her hair in two
> braids, a feather headdress and a buckskin, beaded dress and moc-
> casins; Mr. Oklahoma always in a cowboy outfit, not in keeping with
> fact.[23]

In 1907 the marriage proposal was made by C. G. Jones. He described
the bridegroom as "only 18 years old, but . . . capable of assuming all the
matrimonial responsibilities of a stalwart youth." William Durant presided
over the marriage and presented the bride to the groom:

> I present the hand and fortune of Miss Indian Territory, convinced
> by his 18 years of wooing [the duration that Oklahoma Territory had
> existed] that his love is genuine, his suit sincere and his purpose hon-
> orable. . . . Despite the unhappy circumstance of her youth, which
> have cast a shadow of sorrow over a face by nature only intended to
> give back only warm smiles of God's pure sunshine, this beauteous
> maiden comes to him as the last descendant of the proudest race that
> ever trod foot on American soil. . . . Although an orphan, Miss Indian
> Territory brings her spouse a dower that, in fertile fields, productive
> mines and sterling and upright citizenship, equals the fortune of her
> wooer.[24]

Oklahoma Territory is depicted as a respectable, innocent, and sincere
suitor rescuing the orphaned and naturalized savage. If Miss Indian Territory was an orphan, it was only because Mr. Oklahoma Territory's parents
had murdered hers. This depiction once again contributes to effectively silencing the advanced features of civilization practiced by the Five Nations.

Performing Indian-ness

In Fort Smith, Indians are largely absent from frontier-complex tourism
aside from two exhibits at the National Historic Site, one dedicated to
Indian removal and the other to the Trail of Tears, but the information is
decontextualized from the active role that Fort Smith played in the process. Fort Smith is portrayed merely as a supply store along the path from
the Southeast to Indian Territory, with no details of what was happening
locally or that Cherokees had been established in the regions for decades.

In some ways Judge Isaac Parker set the tone for how contemporary Fort Smith would approach Indian Territory. Devon Mihesuah reports that in 1885 Parker openly "admitted that he had never been to Indian Territory, had never sat in on any tribal court proceedings, and had no knowledge of how the tribal courts functioned."[25] There is no evidence that he ever did acquire any of this knowledge or witness one of his seventy-nine authorized hangings.

Today the origins and destinations of Indian removal are presented in the abstract without grounding them locally. There is no deeper discussion of the Five Nations that still reside so close to Fort Smith and offer detailed interpretations of their history. Furthermore, Indians are seldom seen in living-history performances or reenactments; literally I have observed one individual representing an Indian in Fort Smith in my five years of fieldwork. When Native Americans are represented at events such as the Fort Smith Heritage Festival, they are seldom individuals from any of the neighboring Five Nations.

Fort Smith has not always been so reluctant to have Native Americans represented in the city. Judge Parker himself played a key role in the dramatization of the civilized/savage dichotomy as performed at the Western Arkansas Fair, first organized in Fort Smith in 1880. In his opening address at the 1885 fair, Benjamin DuVal, the oldest of six siblings of this influential Fort Smith family, declares of the city, "After the financial crash caused by the collapse of the banks, the town made little progress, and it has only been within the last five years that we have felt assured of its permanency. The birth of this Fair is contemporaneous with the beginning of the splendid growth and prosperity of the city and country."[26] DuVal elucidates the history of animal husbandry in the region and of the rise and popularity of fairs around the world. He cites the 1798 Paris industrial exhibition, the 1851 London World's Fair, the New York Fair in 1853, and the centennial fair in Philadelphia, which, he boasted, 9,910,966 people attended. While he acknowledged that the Fort Smith fair is not on this scale, the point he was machining is that the fair was the embodiment of the latest advancements in civilization, a lesson that was prominently featured eight years later at the 1893 Columbian Exposition in Chicago.

Perhaps it was to heighten the contrast of industrial advancements that in 1882 Parker initiated what Roger Tuller has called "an unusual request" of the commissioner of Indian Affairs: "We want to have some Osage Indians, say twenty," for an attraction at the annual fair. Parker "promised to 'take good care' of the Osages and argued that their 'visit' would 'have a good effect on the Indians.'"[27] Though Parker would not travel to them, he had no compunction against asking them to come entertain Fort Smithians. The attraction must have been a success, as newspapers report it as a regular feature of the fair for years afterward. In 1883 the *Arkansas Gazette* ran the headline "FORT SMITH FAIR. Twenty Osage Indians to be on Exhibition—A Great Attraction." The paper reported, "Among the company are a number of the leading men of the tribe. The fair association has gone to considerable expense and trouble to secure the attendance of a number of a 'WILD TRIBE OF INDIANS.'"[28]

The attraction was so popular that the next year the "Fair association of western Arkansas and Indian territory" made arrangements to take it to Little Rock. Leading up to the 1884 fair the *Gazette* headline read, "The Pawnee Braves to Exhibit at the Coming State Fair." In the promotional article we learn that the fair association planned to "have a band of Pawnee Indians here during the fair, who will exhibit some of their peculiar Indian games, war dances, etc., every day. This will be a very attractive feature; as the Pawnees are among the most noted of the wild tribes." Whether Osage or Pawnee, the Indian performers are framed in Arkansas as other, wild, savage, definitely not civilized. And yet, the *Gazette* reported later, "They [Pawnees] are looked upon by the government as the best and most trusty scouts to be had, and have been employed as such in nearly every expedition that has been sent out after Indians of other tribes since the war."[29]

The internal contradiction of the frontier complex that Indians are simultaneously savage and civilized is showcased in these reports. Regardless, the crowds did not seem to ponder that, as the newspaper describes the attraction: "The Pawnee Indians gave another exciting exhibition today, similar to that of yesterday, and some of the wildest and most daring and reckless riding ever witnessed was indulged in."[30] Thus titillated, the civilized spectators had their whiteness reaffirmed by the contrived performance of the savage other.

From Reservation to Segregation

A wider view of Oklahoma history situates what was going on in Fort Smith during the federal government presence of the military fort and then district court. Furthermore, it reveals the underlying canvas on which contemporary notions of race are painted during the reservation era of the frontier complex. As American Indians were being effectively neutralized in Indian Territory, African Americans were held out a false hope of equality in America. Carved out of Indian Territory in 1890, Oklahoma Territory comprised roughly the western half of present-day Oklahoma. White and black pioneers alike traveled through Indian Territory by train, wagon, horse, and foot on their way to stake claims, all of which contributed to the inevitability of statehood.[31] Land runs are still reenacted today just as is the marriage of Oklahoma.[32]

The land cessions gave whites and blacks alike access to "free" land, just as slavery had given whites and the Five Nations "free" labor. The consequences of allotment were the subsidization of white wealth, the overall impoverishment of Indians, and the disenfranchisement of freedmen and "state negroes," free blacks from the South who had migrated to the territory.[33] As the advancement of white civilization quickened, many recently freed African Americans also sought their dreams in the frontier.

While Indians of the territories were disenfranchised, then characterized as wild savages before and noble savages after statehood, African Americans fared no better as they went from slavery to emancipation to Jim Crow and were then all but scrubbed from the cultural memory of the frontier. At the very moment that Indians were being assimilated in symbolic marriage, African Americans were being legislatively separated: the very first law enacted in the State of Oklahoma was Jim Crow. Such contradictions in racial ideology—marrying one and forbidding contact with the other—reveal the economic and political motivations behind the socially constructed nature of race in the United States.

The rush toward white settlement of Oklahoma Territory was hastened by movements by many African Americans to make Oklahoma a predominately black state. There was a brief moment when it looked to many like this could be a reality. Several all-black towns were created in both territories, and advertisements were posted throughout the South encouraging former slaves to head west for opportunity and self-governance denied them in the South. Oklahoma Territory was especially successful from 1891 to 1894 at attracting large numbers of former slaves, with thousands participating in the initial land runs.[34] All-black towns were formed, but the migrants fought a double battle in their new homes—their presence was often met with violence by whites and disdain by freedmen. The freed slaves of the Five Nations referred to these former slaves from the South as "Watchina—the white man's negro" or as "state negroes."[35]

This particular place and time experienced an inside-out othering process of almost all racialized categories. In this frontier space we can see the working out of the American social structure of racial categories: full-bloods of the Five Nations were distancing themselves from black freedmen, while freedmen and so-called state negroes were contesting with one another for allotments. The blanket category of whiteness came to prevail over all those considered black or red. In actuality, all these people were living under a very similar umbrella of social institutions in the territories. What was at stake here was economic and political power, control of the emerging state, and its increasing oil and gas discoveries: when Oklahoma entered the Union it did so as the leading oil-producing state.[36] In that contest, whites threw down the "othering" gauntlet, blinded themselves to seeing Indians or African Americans as civilized, and were thus the heirs apparent to that economic and political power. Today that inheritance includes a number five ranking for Oklahoma as "most oil-rich state," and the sudden rise of fracking and earthquakes is becoming daily news for Oklahomans.[37]

In the 1890s there was an overtly racialized contest for political control. Edward McCabe, a leader in the all-black-town movement, carefully encouraged people to live in places that would benefit them politically, as Littlefield and Underhill describe: "He advocated a plan of dispossessing whites of political power by organizing colonies of blacks so that a majority of black voters could be situated in each representative and senatorial district."[38] Several all-black towns flourished and at face value could have served as evidence that African Americans were just as competent and capable as their white counterparts. But this was not to be, as Wickett notes, because "no white Americans were willing to admit that the success of the black towns undermined the racial stereotype of African Americans as childlike, lazy, and lacking in moral and intellectual capacity." In other cases, "those whites who recognized the contradiction explained it away by claiming the people who resided in the black towns were atypical of the race in general, or they simply refused to comment on the success of the black towns whatsoever."[39]

By 1895 McCabe's plan had run its course. Between white resistance to it and the harsh conditions migrants faced once they arrived, the reality of Jim Crow began to emerge, and enthusiasm for black emigration waned. If any lingering questions remained about how Oklahomans regarded successful, prospering African American communities, the Tulsa race riots of 1921 ended them.

Figure 5.3. *Unconquered.* American Indian figures stand and kneel in front of the Oklahoma History Center in Oklahoma City, their gazes forever fixed on oil derricks, oncoming traffic, and flags. Photo by the author.

In the Fort Smith frontier complex, all this racialized complexity is expunged by the myths of frontier justice of the federal fort and court keeping the peace between and taking civilization to the Indians. The record of African Americans in the territories is essentially absent from the frontier complex. Fort Smith has its own racial past to conceal. In 1912 Sanford Lewis was lynched at the corner of Sixth Street and Garrison Avenue. A lynch mob broke him out of jail after he was arrested for an altercation in which a police officer named Carr was killed. Evidence from the case shows that it was the gun of another police officer, John B. Williams, that killed Officer Carr when it went off while Williams was pistol-whipping Lewis.

Several police officers and citizens were arrested and tried for this lynching, as featured in a *Southwest Times* retrospective article. "Within a matter of weeks, the court found the policemen guilty and fined them $100 each," while the other defendants were acquitted after a long trial. "Frustrated by these failures, the prosecutor dropped all remaining criminal charges relating to the lynching of Sanford Lewis."[40] The article ran with an accompanying photograph of the lynching that showed the full length of Lewis' body strung up to a trolley pole. For such a heinous act to be done with impunity belies a deep-seated and vicious racism just beneath the thin veneer of sociality. A different photo that is seldom seen shows the prison cell that held Lewis when the angry mob attacked. The train rail used to pry the bars off the window can be seen in the debris, bent by the fierce leverage of racial hysteria. This is a grave and ironic injustice in a city that builds its tourist industry on Hanging Judge Parker's words "Let no guilty man escape justice."

Varied Visages of Bass Reeves

One hundred years after Lewis was murdered, another black man, Bass Reeves, was elevated in Fort Smith in a very different manner. In May 2012 a statue honoring this African American lawman, who died in 1910 at the age of seventy-two, was dedicated near the foot of the Garrison Avenue Bridge. Bass Reeves has recently emerged as a transcendent figure who evaded all levels of systematic discrimination to have a remarkably successful career as a lawman. Though the details vary or are absent, the general story told is that Reeves was born into slavery in 1838 and that sometime during his late teenage years he was involved in an altercation with his owner. Escaping to Indian Territory as a runaway slave, he resided there learning Indian languages and the lay of the land until the Civil War's end. By 1875 his reputation earned him a position as a deputy U.S. marshal. His story is held up as a testimony to the postracial, color-blind, racist ideologies that purport that black people can easily succeed if they just play by the rules and try hard enough. While this is not the effect Reeves' biggest proponents intended, I contend that this is how his story is embedded in the frontier complex.

The story of Bass Reeves is a recent addition to the Fort Smith frontier complex. His record as a lawman was first reconstructed from court records and newspaper accounts by a few historians in the 1970s.[41] There is little to no mention of him in the primary sources discussing the Parker court. Reeves made his first appearance in the popular press in 1976, when Charles Mooney wrote about him for the magazine *Real West: True Tales of the American Frontier*. Mooney pulled no punches in his estimation of Reeves in this popular-press monthly and set the tone for what was to come: "Bass Reeves, the invincible black Deputy U.S. Marshal, carved his reputation as a lawman second to none."[42] Reeves is introduced to frontier history enthusiasts in superhero terms: "More than once his belt was shot in two, buttons were shot off, and the bridle reins, held in his hands, were cut by a bullet ... not to mention the holes in his hat, shirt and trousers."[43] While this brief article reads fanciful and is playful with facts, the description is routinely repeated about Bass Reeves in the frontier complex.

Not until Art Burton and the publication of *Black, Red, and Deadly* did the story of Reeves begin to be incorporated into the cultural memory of Fort Smith. As the title implies, Burton's book features African Americans and Native Americans who were either outlaws or lawmen in Indian Territory. The title of the chapter that features Reeves seems to take its cue from Mooney's imagery—"Bass Reeves: The Invincible Marshal."[44] While purportedly rooted in historical facts, Burton's commentary on Reeves is frequently difficult to distinguish from historical fiction. Burton contends that "Reeves was the most outstanding peace officer of his era ... [and that] the man was a phenomenon ... one of the greatest frontier heroes this country has ever produced."[45]

That same year, Burton published a short piece on Reeves in *True West* magazine.[46] In it Burton describes a shootout that Reeves had with an outlaw: "Webb's first shot grazed Reeves' saddle horn, the second cut a button off his coat, and the third shot tore the reins out of his hand, causing Reeves to lose control of his horse. Reeves jumped off the animal pulling his Winchester from its scabbard in the same motion. Just as Reeves landed on his feet Webb's fourth shot clipped the brim of his hat!"[47] The invincible deputy got his man in the end. Reeves' reputation began to grow as a handful of authors picked up his story. Kareem Abdul-Jabbar features Reeves in his 1996 *Black Profiles in Courage* in a chapter entitled "Respect" that was clearly inspired by Burton's work. More recently the Travel Channel ran an episode of *Monumental Mysteries* that featured a reenactment of the above shootout between Reeves and Webb precisely as Burton described it. The segment is entitled "The Invincible Lawman."[48]

In 2005 momentum for Bass Reeves' story began to pick up. Paul L. Brady, a judge from Atlanta and a descendant of Reeves, published *The Black Badge: Deputy United States Marshal Bass Reeves, from Slave to Heroic Lawman*. The next year Burton published his full-length book on Reeves, *Black Gun, Silver Star: The Life and Legend of Frontier Marshal Bass Reeves*. A young-adult fiction book by Gary Paulsen also came out, *The Legend of Bass Reeves: Being the True and Fictional Account of the Most Valiant Marshal in the West*. With this burst of publicity for Reeves, Art Burton began making regular public appearances and lectures in Fort Smith. Both Burton and

Reeves quickly became minor celebrities among local history enthusiasts, and they particularly caught the attention of circuit court judge Jim Spears. He had been in search of a historic figure from Fort Smith's past to turn into a statue as a way of creating public art and promoting the frontier history of the city.

Spears initially proposed a statue of Zachary Taylor on horseback, but that concept never gained much traction, given that former president's outright disdain for Fort Smith. A 2012 newspaper account reports that Spears "then had a conversation with Bill Black, the superintendent of the Fort Smith National Historic Site, who mentioned Bass Reeves."[49] At this same time the City of Fort Smith had just hired Baridi Nkokheli to be the director of the Department of Sanitation. Spears immediately noted that Nkokheli bore a close resemblance to Bass Reeves. By May 2007, Nkokheli was making regular public appearances dressed as Reeves, promoting awareness of him, and raising funds for a monument to the deputy that was ultimately erected in May 2012.

Over that five-year period, there was a Bass Reeves blitz in Fort Smith. The Bass Reeves Legacy Initiative was formed; Nkokheli made hundreds of public appearances at schools, libraries, and civic groups to raise awareness and money for the monument; and the Clayton House, the restored home of William Henry Harrison Clayton, attorney general in the Parker era, promoted Reeves with a reading program in local schools of Vaunda Micheaux Nelson's *Bad News for Outlaws: The Remarkable Life of Bass Reeves, Deputy U.S. Marshal*. With a positive public reception of Reeves' story, famous western sculptor Harold T. Holden was commissioned to create the monument to him. The arrival and dedication of the monument, entitled "Into the Territories," was full of fanfare and programs to celebrate and educate the public about Reeves. Today, Reeves is such a powerful frontier trope that even books whose primary subject has nothing to do with him feature full pages of photos of him.[50]

My fieldwork for this entire project was initially inspired by Nkokheli's performance of Reeves. I first observed him at a presentation he gave for a noontime program at the Fort Smith Public Library in 2009. What struck me most about the event was seeing the audience, primarily white women over age fifty, apparently smitten with the story of Reeves and Nkokheli's portrayal of him. Any racial barriers that might have otherwise been present between these same people in ordinary street clothes walking down the sidewalk were completely absent. Seeing how Nkokheli's Reeves was a "safe black man" who broke down racial barriers and stereotypes between the two groups convinced me that further investigation was necessary to uncover the meaning behind all of this. The narrative of Bass Reeves is inextricably bound to the mythic frontier and justice. As such, the underlying narrative of Reeves, while intended to give praise to a noteworthy African American, is etiolated by wider American racial ideologies that turn Reeves' story into a poster boy for neoliberal, color-blind racism.

To unpack the mythological Bass Reeves and its underlying meanings, we will analyze key tropes of his story that must be repeated nearly every time he is mentioned, conspicuously so: Reeves patrolled 74,000 square miles; Reeves served more than three thousand writs; Reeves was illiterate; Reeves fiercely followed the letter of the law as exemplified by arresting his own minister and his own son; and Reeves was the basis for the Lone Ranger. Art Burton attaches the story of Reeves to the exaggerated claim of Judge Parker's jurisdiction and in the process inflates the grandeur of Reeves' reputation. In *True West* magazine Burton writes, "Judge Isaac Parker hired 200 deputy U.S. marshals to patrol the 75,000 square miles in the region, and possibly the most feared of them was a black lawman named Bass Reeves." A slight change in jurisdiction size appears in Burton's book on Reeves the same year, 1991, where "two hundred deputies were a mere handful to cover an area of 74,000 square miles, where the outlaws knew every trail and hideout and the deputies had little protection other than their own discretion and skill in serving these processes of law."[51] In the online *Oklahoma Encyclopedia of History and Culture* Burton repeats this mantra with the larger number: "When Reeves began riding for Judge Parker, the jurisdiction covered more than seventy-five thousand square miles." Burton is also the author for the "Bass Reeves" entry in the online *Encyclopedia of Arkansas History and Culture.*[52] Art Burton has a near-monopoly on the Reeves narrative today.

The ubiquity of the square-mileage figure acts as testament to Reeves' prowess as a lawman. Not only is it repeated in most newspaper articles and popular presentations on Reeves, it is found on signs of business establishments in Fort Smith. In 2012 real estate developers Richard and Rick Griffin opened Garrison Pointe, a gas station and convenience and liquor store at the corner of Garrison Avenue and North Fifth Street. On the side of the building, there are large signs that give tribute to Judge Parker and Bass Reeves. Of Parker, we read, "His jurisdiction covered 74,000 square miles of the Indian Territory." The poster of Reeves dovetails off the grandiose image of Parker's jurisdiction. In a sweeping generalization, it declares that Reeves was "recruited in 1875 to serve as Deputy U.S. Marshal under Judge Isaac Parker. When Reeves retired from Federal service in 1907 he had arrested over 3000 felons, killing 14 in the line of duty."

As established earlier, Parker's jurisdiction in Indian Territory was never larger than 62,000 square miles, and that was reduced to 35,000 miles in 1883 and to 22,000 in 1889. Furthermore, Reeves did not work for the federal court in Fort Smith for his entire career. He did from 1875 to 1889 and then continued to work as a deputy for other courts out of Paris, Texas, and Muskogee until he was prohibited from doing so in 1907 with Oklahoma statehood and the enactment of Jim Crow. He worked for two more years in law enforcement for the Muskogee city police. Less than half of his thirty-two-year career was spent bringing criminals to trial in Fort Smith.[53]

While there is evidence that early in his career Reeves traveled as far west as Fort Sill, Fort Reno, and Anadarko, each about 260 miles from Fort Smith, Littlefield and Underhill have found that more often his "duties were generally confined to the areas occupied by the Five Civilized Tribes—the Cherokees, Choctaws, Creeks, Chickasaws, and Seminoles"—which consisted of 35,000 square miles.[54] This issue of jurisdiction area might seem superficial, but when the entire narrative of Judge Parker and subsequently Bass Reeves depends upon this claim and it is incessantly repeated in the frontier complex, it becomes a significant element in the analysis of the frontier mythology. Simply put, Reeves was not personally covering 75,000 square miles for thirty-two years, and to imply that he did makes him larger than life.

It is widely repeated in the frontier complex that Bass Reeves served more than three thousand writs. This widely stated claim is based on a newspaper article from the *Chickasaw Enterprise* of November 28, 1901. Burton refers to this article's author as a "Pauls Valley" reporter to whom Reeves allegedly claimed to have served that many warrants.[55] I have not seen the article directly quoted, but I acquired a copy of it. In it we learn that Reeves "claims that he has been a deputy for twenty-seven years; that during that time he has arrested more than three thousand men and women."[56] This is the extent of the documentation I have found to verify the number of arrests made by Reeves. In other words, it is not a documented fact, which could be gleaned only through investigation of the court documents. Until that research is done, that figure stands as an exaggeration.

In the frontier complex, one cannot say "Judge Parker" without saying

"Hanging" first, and one cannot talk about Bass Reeves without saying that he was illiterate. This descriptive trait of Reeves is stated in the same breath as saying that he memorized all three thousand writs and never got one wrong. He is widely discussed as being exceptionally smart—yes, anyone to have survived thirty-two years of law enforcement in Indian Territory would have to be. His intelligence is reinforced by claims that he knew "multiple Indian languages" and frequently outwitted outlaws. Yet access to literacy is a sharply drawn line that Reeves is just as universally said not to have crossed.

To reinforce this point, we can examine a presentation given for the Bass Reeves monument unveiling day, May 26, 2012. "Warrants Memorized, Warrants Delivered" was performed at the historic Clayton House. In the skit, Judge Isaac Parker and prosecuting attorney William Henry Harrison Clayton are discussing the remarkable ability that Reeves allegedly had for memorizing writs. Dave Ross, the author of the skit, first explained to the audience, "The year is 1882 and the Clayton house has just been completed." Bass Reeves is not present for the occasion, just the two prominent white men talking about him.

Clayton says to Parker with amazement, "I hear Reeves brought in sixteen prisoners at one time." Judge Parker replies, "He may be the only black deputy in the entire country, but he's worth more than two dozen deputies." In actuality, Reeves was not even the only black deputy at that time in Parker's jurisdiction.[57] Clayton says, "Tell me more about Reeves. You interviewed him before he was hired. I've talked to him about these cases at great length, but he's a man of few words, and I'm not at all familiar with his past." Parker fills in the details:

What's absolutely incredible about the man is he never learned to read or write. As I heard it told, the young Reeves wanted to learn, but the slave master said no. Despite the lack of any kind of formal education, he worked the farm in Texas and grew to love animals as well as ride and shoot. He served in the Union Army in Indian Territory during the Civil War. Got in some kind of argument with his owner and escaped into Indian Territory. That was where he learned to become an excellent scout and tracker. I hired him there as a Deputy Marshal in 1875.

This is the popular genealogical narrative that is often repeated for Reeves in Fort Smith.

Clayton then introduces the topic that is the crux of the skit:

Life is paradoxical at times, isn't it? An illiterate former slave has the initiative to become one of the best marshals in our entire country. In watching him I kind of wonder what kind of man he might have become had he not been denied a full education, when I think of the thousands of extra hours Reeves must have spent in learning the simple task of connecting subpoenas and other legal documents to the suspects in question.

As an audience member, my mind began to wonder at this point how many hours it takes a person to learn to read and to what extent Reeves was simply passing for illiterate. Following the logic of the skit, if he spent "thousands of extra hours" memorizing writs, perhaps he might have developed some minimal literacy skills? Apparently Parker had no such doubts, as he replies, "It must be some system he has worked out that helps him coordinate the sounds of words and letters with the way they appear on the written page." Clayton says, "It's fascinating."

For a moment, the men become self-conscious of speaking for so long in the absence of their wives' company. They glance in the direction of the parlor and chide, "Mary and Florence may run out of things to talk about." The punch line of the "joke" here is that the men are smoking cigars and drinking brandy away from the "pesky conversation of ladies' fashions." As they debate whether to continue their sequestered repose, Clayton's daughter Maggie comes out to announce, "The ladies in the parlor are wondering if you're ready to be a little more sociable." This is another joke that is met with some polite laughter from the audience, but overall it falls flat. Clayton forces the joke even further: "Tell them we'll come out after we finish one more cigar." Maggie sarcastically replies, "One more cigar, I'll tell 'em that." Men indulging themselves at the expense of attending to their wives is presented as humorous.

Then, as if there is no question that the illiterate Reeves miraculously memorized three thousand writs, the men return to the question of just how he did it. Clayton shakes off the interruption with "Now where were we?" Parker replies, "Talking about Reeves and that almost uncanny ability to memorize case documents without knowing how to read or write." And then Clayton takes a stab at how Reeves might have accomplished such an amazing feat: "It must be some sort of incredible memory force he has. It's like he can study something and take a projection of it in his mind. He has the procedure down to some kind of science. It needs more study, maybe for future generations." I look around at faces in the audience for signs of incredulity but detect none.

Parker then picks up this thread: "Once he was fairly sure of the name, Reeves had someone read the document to him over and over until he had it committed to memory. Our clerk, Jorgenson, says he has seen Reeves repeat the procedure two or three hundred times. And it still fascinates him how Reeves has never been wrong in linking a suspect with the subpoena." Though the process they are describing resembles the act of reading, there is no mention of it. "Reading it to him?" Clayton asks. Parker responds, "Some of the marshals say that Bass often has to ride many, many miles before he can find someone who can read it to him or to write something for him. Here in Fort Smith we take reading for granted, but in Indian Territory the percentage of illiterates remains very high." Mary Parker and Florence Clayton are in the house discussing the development of a library for Fort Smith while their husbands marvel at the genius of a supposedly illiterate man.

Many familiar faces are in the audience. I have seen them at several other events such as this at the Clayton House, the Fort Smith Museum, or the National Historic Site. What is being presented, as outlandishly unbelievable as I think it is, is the sort of narrative about Reeves that people in the audience are accustomed to hearing. The skit ends with a strong-armed attempt to paint Fort Smith as a city that is "in the know" of the modern era. Clayton asks, "How 'bout another cigar, Your Honor?" The judge replies, "Splendid idea! Havanas, I assume?" Clayton responds with a grand gesture meant to convey affluence but that comes off as arrogant pomposity: "Of course."

Practically all sources on Reeves claim he was illiterate but cite no evidence to support that. His illiteracy has become a social "fact" at this point. However, in the same literature one can find references to Reeves sending telegrams, keeping books, and filling out forms. It is not always clear if someone was assisting him with that. Furthermore, if what is said about Reeves' repeated exposure to warrants and the legal verbiage they contain is even half true, then I posit that Bass Reeves was functionally literate. It requires too great a degree of suspended disbelief to think that he never recognized a single word. I believe Bass Reeves could read. Reviewing descriptions of Reeves with this in mind makes it seem obvious.

Burton relays a firsthand description from police Judge Walrond in

1909: "While Reeves could neither read nor write . . . he had a faculty of telling what warrants to serve on any one and never made a mistake. Reeves carried a batch of warrants in his pocket and when his superior officers asked him to produce it the old man would run through them and never fail to pick out the one desired."[58] As a black man in the late nineteenth-century United States, Reeves would have known full well that it was in his best interest to not let on that he knew how to read; he was "passing for black."

But I am not going to pretend to know the interworking of Bass Reeves' thoughts, and I doubt the historical record will reveal the truth of the matter. I will, however, venture an anthropological argument for why we must insist that he was illiterate today: his illiteracy legitimates and reinforces neoliberal racial ideology; it is proof that if a black man just works hard enough then he can succeed, no matter if he was a former slave, a black man who endured discrimination, and an illiterate to boot. I believe that Art Burton unwittingly contributes material for perpetuating this racial ideology.

In his efforts to elevate African American history, Burton fosters a widespread view that lowers the overall estimation of blacks. Burton states, "Reeves rose above his humble beginnings as a slave and preserved and excelled as a federal lawman even though he was illiterate."[59] This is the alibi of the mythical Bass Reeves. It omits the facts that at the very time frame this skit is set, thousands of freedmen and "state negroes" were systematically disenfranchised from the political economy being opened as "free land" to so many whites. It silences the fact that Reeves and thousands of other African Americans were institutionally discriminated against with the signing of Jim Crow laws at Oklahoma statehood.

The insistence of Reeves' illiteracy is equaled in measure with the claim that he was a consummate follower of the letter of the law. It is consistently repeated that he "always got his man" and "never got the wrong man," which is then underscored with the disclaimer "despite his illiteracy." The primary example used to drive home this point is that he arrested his own son for murder. In this and virtually all other instances, Reeves is projected in the same light of mythic justice as is Judge Parker—a universal emblem of pure justice to whom anything less is an abomination. Burton declares, "Not only did Bass Reeves arrest one of his sons for murder, he arrested the minister who baptized him. It is evident that Reeves was quite determined to uphold the law no matter the relationship he had with the offender."[60]

A closer comparison of the claim of Reeves' pure justice to the historical record reveals that he was human after all.

Benjamin Reeves, one of Bass Reeves' children, murdered his own wife. This fabled event is used to illustrate Bass' dedication to duty. Burton's chapter on this episode of Reeves' life is entitled "Devotion to Duty."[61] Paul Brady, in *The Black Badge*, recounts the story in much the same way in a chapter with the exact same title, "Devotion to Duty."[62] Art Burton dramatically sets up his chapter: "The incident that resonates most with many who follow the life and career of Deputy U.S. Marshal Bass Reeves is the time he had to arrest his own son for murder."[63] Burton quotes as the source an oral history interview with Reeves' daughter Alice Spahn as cited in an unpublished seminar paper written in 1960 by Richard Fronterhouse.[64] The theme of staunch dedication to the law is reinforced: "Bass and his deep-seated belief in the law are legendary. Nothing could deter him when he was forced to make a decision where the law was concerned. As proof of this, consider the time he arrested his own son for murder."[65]

The key part of this story that is uniformly presented in the frontier complex is that when Reeves heard a warrant was out for his son's arrest he insisted on being given the writ. His obedience to the law is emphasized while the charge that his son murdered his wife is minimized. This moment is recounted in an obituary of Reeves from 1910: "With a devotion of duty equaling that of the old Roman, Brutus, whose greatest claim on fame has been that the love for his son could not sway him from justice, he said, 'Give me the writ,' and went out and arrested his son."[66] The story that he would not allow anyone else to bring his son to justice is offered as demonstrable proof of the tenacity with which Reeves cleaved to justice.

The part of the story that is not heard in the frontier complex is that Benjamin Reeves, referred to as Benny most often but as Bill in quotations from Fronterhouse, murdered his wife because of her suspected adultery. Furthermore, the story according to the Fronterhouse paper is that Bass Reeves himself counseled his son to take such action. Allegedly, Benny had caught his wife in an adulterous situation once before but worked through that episode without violence. Sometime after that, he confided to his father what had transpired. Burton quotes Reeves from the Fronterhouse interview with his daughter as giving this fatherly advice to his son: "I'd have shot the hell out of the man and whipped the living God out of her." Soon after this conversation, "Bill came home from work and found his wife again with another man. In the melee that followed, the man Bill had caught in his place escaped, bloody and beaten, but otherwise unharmed. However, in his hysterical rage, he killed his wife."[67]

Not only is this unpleasant facet of Reeves' character left out of the Fort Smith frontier complex, but Burton also revised the story for another account. In his *True West* account of this event, Burton says, "His son had had a domestic fight with his wife and accidentally killed her."[68] There should be no confusion over the facts of this case. In one of the first academic articles on Bass Reeves, that of Littlefield and Underhill in 1971, we learn that Reeves' son "had brutally murdered his wife."[69] Burton and many others who have spread the "gospel of Bass," as it has been called, have been aware of this detail. Omitting this fact of what happened assists the myth of Reeves' "pure justice" to continue unquestioned.

In addition to basic fact checking of statements that have become part of the Bass Reeves cultural memory canon, I have found many other facts in the historical record that are selectively ignored. Historian Nudie Williams paints a more complex picture of Reeves. Williams notes that Reeves' contemporaries described him as "neatly dressed," "polite," "courteous," "well respected," "fearless and capable," and "the most feared U.S. Marshal that was ever heard of in . . . [Indian] country."[70] But then Williams includes damning information from records and opinions such as, "many times he never brought in all of the criminals but would kill some of them [because] he did not want to spend . . . much time in chasing down the man who resisted arrest, [so] he would shoot him down in his tracks."[71]

The *Fort Smith Elevator*, a daily newspaper full of sensational stories and many advertisements, ran from 1878 to 1907. While it is often cited in praise of Bass Reeves, it also ran articles that call his character into question. One of them, Williams notes, "reported that United States Marshal Thomas Boles dismissed Reeves in 1884 because 'he had the habit of letting a prisoner escape when more could be made than by holding him.'"[72] Williams further observes, "Reeves's contemporaries openly questioned the various methods he used in carrying out his duties. They accused him of being selective in whom he arrested. His personal honesty was debated in the local press." Williams then contextualizes the news reporting of the time as intended "to be sure every move was subject to close public scrutiny. Racism played an important role in Reeves' career and much of the criticism against him stemmed from prevailing racial prejudices among Southerners who resisted placing blacks in positions of authority over whites."[73]

The portrait that Nudie Williams paints of Reeves is one of complexity and ambiguity; the historical record supports this assessment. The popular myth of Bass Reeves has selectively chosen elements from this record to emphasize the heroic and the positive while omitting, glossing over, and overlooking the negative and contradictory pieces of his life. Reeves is said to have killed fourteen men in the line of duty and to have been investigated and exonerated for each one of them. Art Burton takes this as evidence of his prowess as a lawman and marksman. He compares Reeves' record to a gunfighter ranking created by Bill O'Neal: "The top three persons on O'Neal's chart are murderers, the highest ranked individual with twelve killings. The top peace officer is (Wild) Bill Hickock [sic], with seven killings. If we take the word of Reeves and the local Indian Territory press that he killed fourteen men, he would have to rank very high on O'Neal's chart."[74] The popular imagination of contemporary Wild West shootouts is captured by Reeves' dramatic record, and Art Burton glorifies it. Nudie Williams points out another side to that record: "By being involved in so many killings, his reputation was somewhat tarnished by the association."[75] On balance, Reeves' record is not so glowing. Fund-raising of more than $300,000 for the Bass Reeves monument on a more nuanced picture of his career would have been challenging.

Not only potentially incriminating historical facts but even the very race of Bass Reeves is concealed in the frontier complex. In four significant ways, Reeves' African American identity is elided: he is associated with whiteness in his 1910 obituary; he is equated with the Lone Ranger; a white mannequin is used for his depiction at Three Rivers Museum in Muskogee, Oklahoma; and the monument erected to him in Fort Smith does not bear his or a phenotypical African American's resemblance.

While Reeves was on his deathbed in November 1909, the *Muskogee Times-Democrat* published an article reflecting on his career and service. Beyond the usual accolades, that Reeves was a staunch defender of the law who brought numerous fugitives back from Indian Territory, it was also reported that "he was honest, fearless, and a terror to the bootleggers. He was as polite as an old-time slave to the white people and most loyal to his superiors."[76] In other words, Reeves was a model for other African Americans to follow.

After his death on January 10, 1910, the newspaper used his life as a model for whiteness. Reeves was "black-skinned, illiterate, offspring of slaves whose ancestors were savages, this simple old man's life stands white and pure alongside some of our present-day officials in charge of affairs since the advent of statehood." Contrary to the corrupt white politicians in Oklahoma, "Bass Reeves would not have served under such a regime. Black though he was, he was too white for that. His simple, honest faith in the righteousness of the law would brook no disrespect for its mandates." Reeves' devotion to the law is then again held up as a model of whiteness: "It is lamentable that we as white people must go to this poor, simple old negro to learn a lesson in courage, honesty and faithfulness to official duty."[77]

Through the lens of "color-blind" racism, Reeves was not "black" because no black person could follow the law as truly as he did. Just like the "Civilized Tribes" in the territories before him, Reeves as an African American was brought to the cusp of whiteness, but to his last breath he was denied it. His slave-to-accomplished-lawman life story is held up as a fabled testament of how racism is not an obstacle to having a successful career. On the heels of newly passed Jim Crow laws in Oklahoma and heavy-handed treatment of African Americans, Reeves in his death was held up as evidence that whiteness was attainable for blacks.

While the realities of institutionalized racism would make attaining whiteness nearly impossible for African Americans for decades to come, in the domain of myth, whiteness was more easily attained. Art Burton has successfully perpetuated the notion that Bass Reeves was the model for the Lone Ranger. The construction of this mythic element can be traced from its inception in *Black Badge, Silver Star* to its repetition in the frontier complex. Innocently enough, Burton introduces this idea as a "folktale," a "story." He reflects, "After I finished writing *Black, Red, and Deadly*, I thought about the uncanny similarities between Bass Reeves and the TV and radio character, the 'Lone Ranger.'" Burton then lines up a set of features that finds parallels between Reeves and the Ranger: Reeves was often called "The Black Marshal," and that rings a bell with "The Lone Ranger"; Reeves was known to pay for things with silver dollars, which equates to the Lone Ranger's silver bullets; they both rode white horses; they both associated with Indians, Reeves in Indian Territory and the Lone Ranger with Tonto; and the black mask embodies Reeves' black skin.[78]

Burton then attempts to draw a straight line between Reeves and the creation of *The Lone Ranger* radio program. Many prisoners from the federal court in Fort Smith were taken to the Detroit House of Corrections, and *The Lone Ranger* first aired in Detroit in 1933.[79] Burton ends his comparison with a qualified caveat: "I doubt we would be able to prove conclusively that Reeves is the inspiration for the Lone Ranger. We can, however, say unequivocally that Bass Reeves is the closest real person to resemble the fictional Lone Ranger on the American western frontier of the nineteenth century."[80] In public presentations on Reeves in Fort Smith, Burton routinely pushes the boundary of what he has called a folktale. In a presentation I attended, Burton said that he "talked with a living relative of the creator of *The Lone Ranger*, and they believe this to be plausible."[81]

This seed of suggestion has been sufficient for this claim to take root in the frontier complex. Other local Reeves promoters have picked up and repeated this tacit connection to the point that now it is stated as fact. An end-of-the-year article on the May 2012 dedication of the monument to Reeves states unequivocally, "Experts think that Bass Reeves was the person producers based the Lone Ranger character from . . . Bass Reeves had an Indian sidekick, he knew Indian languages, and he used disguises when he went after people to arrest them."[82]

Outside of Fort Smith, Henry Louis Gates Jr. has picked up Art Burton's thread and perpetuated this connection, and it was featured on the Travel Channel's 2014 *Monumental Mysteries* "Invincible Lawman" episode on Reeves. After repeating all the tropes of a lawless land, three thousand arrests, and an invincible marshal, the episode closes with the presumed link to the Lone Ranger: "Contemporary experts even believe that this legendary crime fighter may have inspired the beloved comic book and television hero the Lone Ranger." During this narration an image of Clayton Moore's Lone Ranger appears on the screen, then a clip of Moore as the Lone Ranger on his horse Silver rearing up. The *Monumental Mysteries* episode ends with an interesting comparison of the Lone Ranger to Reeves: "Like Reeves, the masked vigilante was an expert marksman who often dressed in disguise to track down countless outlaws in the Indian Territory."[83] The "experts" claiming this link between Bass Reeves and the Lone Ranger would be Art Burton and those whom he has convinced of this story.

The image of an authority figure with a minority sidekick has been around for some time. In James Fenimore Cooper's frontier, it was Natty Bumppo and his Mohican companion Chingachgook. While I concede that Art Burton has succeeded in turning the Bass Reeves–Lone Ranger connection into a social fact, a more plausible source for the actual character might be rooted in Zane Grey's 1915 novel *The Lone Star Ranger*; after all, the Lone Ranger was a Texas Ranger, not a Deputy U.S. Marshal. Grey dedicated that book to Captain John Reynolds Hughes, who himself was a Texas Ranger.[84] Even more likely, *The Lone Ranger* radio program that began in 1933 was a copycat of the popular Zorro story brought to life by Douglas Fairbanks in *The Mark of Zorro* in 1920.

Regardless of the veracity of the connection of Reeves to the Lone Ranger, the link fundamentally transforms Reeves from a black African American into a white man. The image of Bass Reeves is also whitened at Three Rivers Museum in Muskogee. As the last home of Reeves, the city has incorporated him into their museum and annual heritage festival. In 2011 and 2012, part of that festival was a Bass Reeves walking tour. There is not just one person portraying Reeves but an entire cast of characters who are members of the Bass Reeves Troupe of Muskogee. The ensemble includes a middle-age wife of Reeves, a young daughter of Reeves, and an old Bass Reeves as well as local characters with whom Reeves is said to have associated. The tour takes place along the path that Reeves once walked as a police officer where it is repeatedly said that "not a single crime was committed on his watch." His lawman superpowers were not diminished by shifting from federal deputy to town constable.

Three Rivers Museum has a shrine of artifacts dedicated to Reeves, complete with a tombstone—an actual headstone, although the exact resting place of Reeves is unknown. The heritage festival walking tour ends in the room with an exhibit in homage to Reeves. As part of this display, there is a mannequin dressed up to depict Reeves. While in this context it is immediately recognizable as Reeves—sporting his very distinct moustache—on closer inspection, it does not resemble Reeves at all. In actually it does not look like an African American in any way, not in features or skin color. Moreover, it does not even look like a male mannequin; it is in fact a white female mannequin. The thin facial structure, long and thin nose, high cheek bones, stylized eyebrows, and alluring, gazing eyes all point to this mannequin having modeled women's clothing in its previous life. Remove the moustache and it is not hard to imagine the mannequin sporting lingerie.

While the museum may use this mannequin due to lack of money to purchase one with greater resemblance to Reeves, it is interesting that this clearly observable and evident discrepancy is never mentioned. To the contrary, excited comments such as "Take my picture with Bass!" can be heard when visiting the museum. On one occasion, I was there with Baridi Nkokheli, who portrays Bass Reeves in Fort Smith. A gentleman who portrays Reeves in Muskogee was also present. As soon as people realized that the two most prominent Bass Reeves reenactors were present, they all started saying, "Let's get a picture with the three Basses." The third Bass being referred to was the mannequin. The ease with which this unintentional twist of tranvestism and of white passing for black is accepted underscores the flexibility, malleability, and socially constructed and performed character of race and gender. How is it that visitors are so willing to suspend their disbelief and see a black man instead of a white woman when they look at this mannequin? Are a thick black moustache and a wide-brimmed hat all that it takes?

Thus, in obituary, in heroic legend, and in mannequin representation, the popular image of Bass Reeves' African American identity is attenuated, etiolated, and then articulated to whiteness.[85] In the final act of misrepresenting his race, we will note the appearance of the monument raised to him in Pendergraft Park in Fort Smith at the foot of the Garrison Avenue bridge in May 2012. The sculpture of Reeves does not immediately strike a resemblance to Reeves, nor does it appear to be phenotypically African American. It does, however, favor Harold Holden, the white sculptor. In these examples, the mythic race of Bass Reeves functions to reinforce whiteness with postracial ideologies of neoliberalism and color-blind racism. It also creates a narrative more readily digestible for the predominantly white audience consuming it as tourism in the frontier complex.

Not everyone in Fort Smith has bought into this narrative of Bass Reeves. Public reception of the attention to Reeves and the arrival of the monument have been mixed. In the course of my fieldwork, I heard resentment toward it before, during, and after its raising. While local history enthusiasts warmed up to Art Burton and to the promotion of the city and its frontier history that the monument was bringing, there was frequently an undertone to comments that the attention Reeves was being given was misplaced. Many people would point to the so-called Three Guardsmen—Bill Tilghman, Chris Madsen, and Heck Thomas—as deputies more deserving of the attention. One person told me, "It's just a brush fire. Art has everyone excited about Bass, but it will soon pass."

More overt racial tones to these comments could be heard when the monument was within sight, traveling across the bridge into Fort Smith, as a line from *Blazing Saddles*, "The sheriff is a n——," was repeated under the breath of one individual in the awaiting crowd. In the weeks and months since the monument was dedicated, some have reported hearing other racist jokes about it, and still others are hostile to the monument, calling it racist to go "out of the way to pay attention to him just because he was a black man." One African American calls the monument a "white man's statue." I suggest these comments about the Reeves monument belie broader racialized sentiments and tensions present throughout the town today.

Trash Talkin'

A case in point concerns the public discussion that took place in the local media outlets after city board of director Bill Maddox told director Baridi Nkokheli of the Department of Sanitation that he could only serve one master during a 2009 city board meeting. This example is important as it involved Nkokheli during the time in which he was portraying Bass Reeves to assist in the fund-raising for a monument to him. It relates to cultural heritage tourism, as ultimately Fort Smith media admonished Bill Maddox for the racial dialogue because it made the city look bad. It also involved the only African American on the city board of directors at the time, Andre Good, who spoke up at the meeting to clarify that "Director Nkokheli serves one municipality, not one master."

While the general public reaction to the comment was that Maddox "misspoke" and that "he's just an old white guy who doesn't know better," I would argue that Nkokheli's and Good's responses illustrate racial perspectives deeply rooted not only in Fort Smith but in the United States. W.E.B. Du Bois' double consciousness framed much of the public discourse.[86] Nkokheli said of Maddox' remark and apology, "I told him it was not my default response to take offense, that I actually understood what he intended. Although I would have thought someone as intelligent as Director Maddox, living in a former Confederate state and addressing the city's only black department head, would have been more aware of how the word 'master' would come across . . . The first thought in my mind was, 'Did he just call me a slave?'"[87] Director Good responded, "I don't think he owes the public an apology . . . but the constituents could demand it."[88] Each man stated a sense of offense through the veil of double consciousness and then unequivocally accepted Maddox' apology. The matter appeared to be finished at that point.

A month later, Maddox reignited the furor when he distributed a racially inflammatory e-mail from one of his constituents at a city meeting where Nkokheli and Good were both present, setting off another month of news stories. The e-mail's author defended Maddox' previous "one master" comment:

> You used the term "master" in a manner that has been correct English for hundreds of years and if blacks take umbrage at it, they are revealing their ignorance of the language. Everyone who works for a salary or wage has a master! All salary/wage earners are modern-day slaves to the all mighty dollar, so the blacks need to grow up and enter the 21st Century. I, for one, have never owned a slave nor do I want one. They are too expensive to maintain and machines do the job faster and better than they would.[89]

This time Maddox' intentions were more closely scrutinized, but still no public officials condemned his words, let alone asked for his resignation. Maddox defended his actions:

> I was not raised up that way (racist). I didn't go to school with them (blacks) until college. I served in the Army with them, and absolutely no ill feelings toward them. . . . I hear people talk about the blacks in a derogatory way and I know white people and people of just about any color who are just as bad, you know, whatever they may say. So I do not have that feeling at all about the colored people, as I grew up knowing them, or with the blacks or Afro Americans, or whatever they want to be called today.[90]

Nkokheli and Good expressed taking offense to Maddox' remarks more forcefully this time but were given little to no support by elected officials or the community.

Quite tellingly, Nkokheli and Good spoke in the veiled language of double consciousness again, and both apparently felt like they needed to attach a caveat to their reactions that because of them they should not be put in the "angry black man" category. Quoted in *City Wire*, Good stated, "The fact that Director Maddox made an unfortunate remark—one that even he regrets—does not make him a racist. Also, Director Maddox did not write the email he referenced at today's study session. And the fact that I spoke out should not secure my place in the 'angry black man' category."[91] In the *Times Record* article Nkokheli responded to the initial "one master" comment in a similar way: "I would hope it doesn't put me in the light that suggests I have to be defended, or that my feelings were hurt, or that I'm an angry black man because I'm not."[92]

The reaction to this event by Good and Nkokheli, other city directors, and local media outlets reveals contradictory and paradoxical racial ideologies in Fort Smith. The same Fort Smith that lauded and fawned over Baridi Nkokheli's efforts toward reviving the memory of Bass Reeves simultaneously allowed such racial insults to be publicly put upon him and Good. In the lived social reality of Fort Smith, the mythic image of a subservient black man in a white world prevailed.

While ultimately taking a stand against Maddox' comments, both the *Times Record* and *City Wire* argued that such highly charged public discourse on race needed to stop because it was bad for business.[93] The *Times Record* ran an editorial in which it declared, "Diversity training may or may not be the answer here, but something needs to be said or done to address both diversity and unity in the city. Right now Fort Smith doesn't look like the model city we need to be marketing if we want sustained economic development."[94]

The *City Wire* similarly stated, "There is no doubt that socio-economic success is more likely and broad in communities and metro areas that do the best job of squashing prejudice based on race, gender, sexual preference, disability and religion. If we don't have a solid public position against such lapses in judgment, we risk losing the types of creative and entrepreneurial minds that come from all categories of humans."[95] The consensus view by Fort Smith's leadership was to keep up proper public appearances in order to prosper economically despite underlying racism. The current redoubling era of the frontier complex in Fort Smith was requiring the city to work overtime to reinforce its frontier brand for tourists and the frontier attic for public discourse. On this occasion the Confederate attic was more evident than was comfortable.

This embarrassing and most likely typical small-town political racial scuffle is related to the frontier complex because it reveals how leaders and other inhabitants of the city of Fort Smith talk about it; the conflict is part of the narrative a local society tells itself. These responses to Maddox' inflammatory actions are reminiscent of the mentality embodied in the notion of the New South. Historians like C. Vann Woodward and W. J. Cash describe a rebranding of the Old South, with all of its connotations of the Confederacy, to the New South that had allegedly turned over a new leaf in shifting from agriculture to industry. The new economy, Cash contends, looked much like the old as "the Southern factory almost invariably was:

a plantation, essentially indistinguishable in organization from the familiar plantation of the cotton fields."[96]

Atlanta newspaperman Henry Grady coined the "New South" phrase during Reconstruction as a call to action, as a method for revisiting the Civil War and defeating the North. Cash observes, "The New South meant and boasted of was mainly a South which would be new in this: that it would be so rich and powerful that it might rest serene in its ancient positions, forever impregnable."[97] The citizen's e-mail that Maddox distributed articulates this New South sentiment—agricultural slaves are too expensive, industrial machines can do the job more effectively, and blacks need to get over it.

Fort Smith has a history of inscribing Civil War imagery on its social landscape. In 1922, when the first automobile bridge spanned the Arkansas River from downtown Fort Smith to Oklahoma, it was named the Albert Pike Free Bridge. Pike is considered a Confederate war hero in the region. The main road that bisects the town north and south, Rogers Avenue, doubles as State Highway 22, which the Arkansas Legislature named the Jefferson Davis Memorial Highway in 1925. The monument stands today at the very point where Garrison Avenue and Rogers Avenue intersect. After the Fort Smith School District lost a lawsuit filed against it in 1964, the district's schools were desegregated. Lincoln High School, the African American school, closed, and two high schools were created—Northside and Southside. Southside was built in the more affluent and white part of town, continuing de facto segregation. The school mascot was Johnny Rebel and "Dixie" the school fight song until 2015.

Interestingly, the Fort Smith Convention and Visitors Bureau's branding slogan for the city is "Fort Smith, Where the New South Meets the Old West."[98] In the example of Mr. Nkokheli in his role as director of the Sanitation Department, we can see how the New South ideology has been used in reaction to real and overt racism, ironically directed at a person who has been instrumental in promoting the Old West in his portrayal of Bass Reeves. It is my contention that in Fort Smith, this New South has intersected with the mythic Old West to collude in silencing racism of both the past and the present.

6

///////////////////////////////////

The Hello Bordello and Brave Men Matrix

> There is some mix-up here. I am Mattie Ross of near Dardanelle, Arkansas. My family has property and I don't know why I am being treated like this.
>
> Mattie Ross, *True Grit*

The mythology of the Fort Smith frontier complex is highly gendered. The two main male figures—Judge Isaac Parker and Deputy Bass Reeves—are both held up as models of righteous men, models of "what to do." They are presented as role models of the highest ethical order to be emulated. As we have seen, the historical facts of these figures do not necessarily square with this frontier-complex tourist narrative. Furthermore, most of the figures featured at the National Historic Site and the Fort Smith Museum of History for the nineteenth century are men, namely, deputies and outlaws. Similarly, the reenactment groups in Fort Smith largely emphasize the roles that men purportedly played in the nineteenth century.

In contrast, the principal women discussed in the frontier complex, Laura Zeigler and Belle Starr, are held up as models of "what not to do," as models of immoral, decadent, reproachable behavior. Miss Laura ran a brothel, and she and her "girls" are playfully talked about in Fort Smith as the colorful side of the frontier. Belle Starr is depicted as a wild, sex-crazed, Amazon bandit queen who met a brutal end. The fact that otherwise respectable men were clients at the brothels in Fort Smith is made to be part of the joke in tourist discourses.

Tourist narratives of Zeigler and Starr are used in the frontier complex, just as we have seen with Parker and Reeves, as mythic alibis. In this case they disguise the exploits of white men in the frontier, reinforce female domesticity, conceal facts such as men flocking to Oklahoma Territory for easy divorces, and hide the history of soldiers stationed next to Fort Smith at Camp Chaffee from 1941 to 1961 frequenting brothels in downtown Fort Smith, not to mention that soldiers at the military fort from 1817 to 1871 were carousing the town for "comfort women" too.

Gender is a malleable social construct, bent by historical context and ideology to suit social purposes and otherwise poetically performed by individuals with motives ranging from capitulation to subversion of the social structure.[1] Judith Butler observes, "Gender ought not to be construed as a stable identity or locus of agency from which various acts follow; rather, gender is an identity tenuously constituted in time, instituted in an exterior space through a *stylized repetition of acts.*"[2] In the frontier complex, women as well as male deputies and outlaws are routinely portrayed in formulaic fashion. In each case, historical facts compared to the tourist discourse illuminate what the alibis of these gender myths selectively omit and conceal. In this context, power, class, race, and gender can be synthesized to show that the primary task of the frontier complex is to inscribe whiteness, manliness, and civilization onto this tourism imaginary.

We have already seen above how civilization is equated with whiteness in the Fort Smith frontier-complex narrative by the federal fort and court taking civilization to the savages, the erection of the First White Child monument, the disenfranchisement of African Americans in the territories, and the marital assimilation of Indians into the family of statehood. Gail Bederman, in *Manliness and Civilization,* details how "civilization" in the nineteenth century was construed as synonymous with "manliness." The 1893 Columbian Exposition demonstrated this unilinear notion of progress with "authentic live savages," while Frederick Jackson Turner delivered his frontier thesis. The removal and restraint eras of the frontier complex were being legitimated by this imagery at the very moment that the reservation era of the frontier complex was being consummated. We will now turn our attention to how representations of "manliness" and "womanliness" found in the Fort Smith frontier complex fit into this national frontier matrix of domination.

Brave Men?

The video *It Took Brave Men* is shown to tourists at the Fort Smith National Historic Site as part of the permanent exhibit.[3] It runs on a continuous loop on the second floor of the 1889 reform jail exhibit and is available on the National Historic Site's YouTube channel. This video complements the *Peacekeeper of Indian Territory* orientation film shown at the visitor center. The mythical imagery of deputies and outlaws is neatly laced in *It Took Brave Men* over that of the frontier justice of Judge Parker. The video begins with a dramatic introduction to the frontier that squarely locates the courage and bravery of the men who served as deputies in Judge Parker's jurisdiction. The sun sits low on the horizon, distant mountains come into view, and then Judge Parker appears on the bench as the narrator intones:

> The western edge of Arkansas.
> The border of the United States and Indian Territory.
> The seat of the federal court for the Western District of Arkansas, Judge Isaac C. Parker presiding.
> Having jurisdiction over Indian Territory, the court sees some of the most wicked, nasty, and despicable characters of the West. The court records chronicle their deeds—assault, larceny, theft, rape, manslaughter, and murder. The warrants issued by the court initiate the long arduous process of serving justice.

The exaggerated size of Parker's jurisdiction as described by the narrator is then cited as evidence of the difficult task faced by the deputies:

> Unlike their invincible counterparts in Hollywood, these real law men had the perilous task of enforcing federal law in Indian Territory. They patrolled the vast area stretching beyond the wide Arkansas River.

The narrator's voice slows down to stretch out the word "vast" and then draws the word "wide" out even further to convey to the viewer just how impossibly huge the jurisdiction was and by association how tenacious the deputies had to be to venture there.

The danger of the jurisdiction is repeatedly emphasized:

> The US Attorney General estimated in 1888 that of the twenty thousand white persons residing in Indian Territory, only five thousand are law-abiding. Out of every eleven men convicted in Parker's court, seven are white, three are black, and one is Indian. Packs of outlaws roam freely.

A scene begins to unfold as three outlaws approach an Indian farm, sexually harassing the wife, and stealing horses from the husband. But then something happens. Judge Parker arrives in Fort Smith. The narrator continues,

"What had seemed an outlaw paradise slowly begins to change. Ranging out of Fort Smith, a stalwart force of deputy U.S. marshals ride in the line of duty." The historical facts are contrary to this narrative. The crime rates did not go down in Indian Territory and Parker's workload did not decline despite his ever-shrinking jurisdiction.

The video depicts deputies arriving at the scene and then tracking the horse thieves. Their manliness is lauded:

There is a stoic toughness about them. As if cut from the same mold, they accept this hard life on the edge. They are noted for determination on the trail.

Then a supposed recollection from a retired deputy is inserted to legitimate the unfolding story:

Dress up the stories of those early days all you like, add anything hair-raising that you may think of, and still, you will not overexaggerate them. The outlaws we dealt with knew neither fear nor honor. We realize that we rode with our lives in our hands all the time, and we lived and thrived on the excitement.

This characterization of the Judge Parker era with the deputies and Indian Territory and outlaws is the standard depiction found in the Fort Smith frontier complex; the day is saved by the arrival of white civilization.

Another point frequently reinforced is how many deputies died in and near Fort Smith:

The cost of policing Indian territory is high. At least sixty-five deputy US marshals are killed in the line of duty during Parker's twenty-one-year tenure on the bench. Time and again, new men of courage and self-reliance must be recruited for this dangerous job.

There is no question here of their manliness or how it contributed to justice on the frontier. Judge Parker's words are used to validate this: "Without these men, I could not hold court a single day."

I do not take issue with the claim that it was a dangerous place and time. However, a close examination of the historical record reveals that not all the men were brave and true and that some of them may have died due to incompetence and nefarious plots from within rather than at the hands of dastardly outlaws. Historian Jeffrey Burton suggests that what was going on in Indian Territory and the character of the deputies were far more complex than what is heard in Fort Smith tourist narratives. Burton has analyzed the reports of Samuel Galpin, a clerk from the Office of Indian Affairs who viewed the action from Indian Territory. From his vantage point, Galpin paints a very different image. Of the deputies he writes, "Many of them . . . appear to devote their whole attention and arbitrary power to the arrest and lodgement in Fort Smith of any person, white man or Indian, who is charged, often by perjury, with a petty and technical violation of the Internal Revenue laws, they are no terror to evil-doers or protection to the law-abiding citizen, and are the least valuable members of the body politic."[4] Serving a writ on the more dangerous outlaws required a larger posse to assist them. However, "by working, instead, in ones and twos, the officers might make many more arrests, but they would go in greater hazard of their lives—or be tempted to let the most desperate criminals escape."[5]

Brave as they may have been, if they were not getting paid and supported properly, the deputies inclined toward easier quarry. Motives for becoming a deputy surely varied, but fundamentally it was a job. As such, Littlefield and Underhill note, "by cutting expenses, an enterprising marshal could make large amounts of money under this system. But his profit depended on him bringing in prisoners, and he sometimes did not bother to consider whether or not he had jurisdiction in a case."[6] Profit motive, not supreme justice, was a key variable in the calculus of serving writs. Galpin ends his report, cited by Jeffrey Burton, with a point that is at times laughingly cited in the frontier complex. Among the deputies, "some of the present officers of justice, clothed with the full authority and majesty of the law, are well known as formerly horse thieves."[7] On one hand, the deputies are uniformly presented as brave and courageous, and on the other hand, the fact that several of them crossed back and forth between the categories of lawman and outlaw can be cited in the frontier complex as just another example of the wild nature of Indian Territory.

Ultimately, Jeffrey Burton concludes of the federal court that its "difficulties were insuperable: it had too much to do, in too large a territory, through officers of variable character and quality, upon too slender a body of cohesive criminal law, and against too much economic and constitutional constraint."[8] In other words, criminality and lawlessness were inevitable. At worst, Parker's refusal to appoint commissioners farther out of Fort Smith into Indian Territory compounded these issues and made the deputy's work more dangerous than necessary. At best, the federal court in Fort

Smith was holding a plug in the dam preventing an outright flood of white intrusion into the territories. The narratives of mythic justice and mythic gender blend here to conceal this situation.

One of the most touted examples used to illustrate the dangers of Indian Territory to deputy U.S. marshals is the so-called Going Snake Massacre. The incident in which eight deputies were killed happened in the spring of 1872, three years before Parker's arrival. It is routinely cited by the Fort Smith National Historic Site, the Fort Smith Museum of History, and the U.S. Marshals Museum as unimpeachable testimony to the dangers that Indian Territory represented and the bravery exhibited by deputy U.S. marshals. The gist of the precipitating event is that Ezekial Proctor, a Cherokee, inadvertently killed Polly Beck, an Indian woman who jumped in front of his intended target, a white man named James Kesterson, who by some accounts was said to have been married to Proctor's sister, Susan. Kesterson had abandoned Proctor's sister and was allegedly having an affair with the accidental victim of the shooting, Polly Beck. After the shooting, Proctor turned himself in to the Cherokee law official, the Going Snake District sheriff, for the murder of the Indian woman, Polly Beck.

This brief, three-sentence summary of the initial shooting already contains several live rounds of explosive assumptions contained in the popular telling of the story. Two key points need explanation in order to demythologize this incident: the question of legal jurisdiction and the conduct of the marshal at the U.S. District Court for the Western District of Arkansas at the time, Logan H. Roots. First, while the motives for Kesterson marrying a Cherokee woman are unknown, what is documented is that at this time many white men were intentionally marrying Indian women to get their hands on her economic assets, which would be automatically conferred to him upon becoming an adopted member of the wife's Indian Nation.[9] Thus, as an adopted Cherokee citizen Kesterson gained access to the political and economic benefits offered by his wife's clan. Also, under the Treaty of 1866, which stemmed from the 1865 Fort Smith Council, since all parties of the incident were Cherokee by blood or adoption the jurisdiction of this case fell legally in the lap of the Indian court, not the district court in Fort Smith. As Jeffrey Burton puts it, "If words have meaning, all jurisdiction in the Proctor-Kesterson case rested with the Cherokee Nation."[10] Following the law, Proctor turned himself in to the Going Snake District sheriff and was put on trial for the murder of Polly Beck by the Cherokee court system.

Dissatisfied with this course of events, James Kesterson overlooked his submission to Cherokee law by virtue of his adoptive marital process, traveled to Fort Smith, and roused enough sympathy at the federal court to garner a warrant and a posse of deputies to attend Proctor's legally sanctioned trial and to arrest him in the event he was acquitted by the Indian court regardless of jurisdiction rights and submission to his adopted nation's laws aside. The writ executed by U.S. Commissioner James Churchill and given to U.S. Marshal Logan H. Roots was for the attempted murder of a white man, James Kesterson, by a Cherokee, Zeke Proctor, a case that would have fallen to the federal court in Fort Smith, less Kesterson's adopted citizenship. Thus, Marshal Roots sent a posse of deputies accompanied by Kesterson's kinfolk to Proctor's Cherokee trial in anticipation of a miscarriage of white justice.

The second key element that must be defused before proceeding with the story is the conduct of Marshal Roots. He was marshal for the court during Judge William Story's notoriously corrupt and brief tenure on the bench. Judge Story and Marshal Roots embezzled and extorted tens of thousands of dollars in their positions in the court. Called to Washington to account for his part in the scandal, Story turned in his resignation to escape impeachment. Roots was found in Benjamin DuVal's congressional investigation to have extorted more than $55,000 from deputies and the court in less than two years.[11] Notably, Roots used the equivalent amount of money to become a founding shareholder in the First National Bank of Fort Smith.[12] Though removed from office in June 1872, he went on to a successful banking career with impunity and had a military fort named after him in Little Rock in 1897.

The conduct of U.S. Marshal Roots and the quality of deputy he was recruiting were far from brave and far from just, but none of this is disclosed in the frontier-complex narrative. An investigation and congressional report on the court's corruption is quite revealing. Regarding the services of deputies, the DuVal report states, "On his accession to the office, Roots appointed a large number of [deputies]. They were selected with regard to their energy, enterprise, and capacity to 'work up business.' These deputies, with their posse, made a large army, and were sent out in the Indian Territory with instructions to hunt up all offenders and make arrests, no matter how trivial the offense."[13] This was the quality of deputy and behavior at the time of the Going Snake District trial of Zeke Proctor. This small amount of social and historical context drastically changes the complexion of the story of the Going Snake incident.

We can now resume the story at the point where Deputy U.S. Marshals Jacob Owens and Joseph Peavy were escorting their posse to the Cherokee trial of Proctor. Kesterson himself, as well as kin of the slain Polly Beck, were members of this posse, given "special deputy" status for the occasion. The deadly affray that lay on the horizon was so telegraphed that the Cherokee moved the Proctor case from the usual courthouse to the Whitmire schoolhouse precisely because it was more defensible. In other words, the shootout was predictable, if not inevitable, before the trial even started. The shootout began almost upon arrival of the Fort Smith posse. Up to eleven men are reported to have been killed—eight from Fort Smith, three in the Cherokee courtroom—and Proctor was wounded. Discrepancies in accounts aside, clearly both sides were prepared more for a battle than a trial.

On the part of the Fort Smith posse, this is hardly a model of conduct of professional officers of the law. The unqualified, overzealous posse of deputies from Fort Smith did not allow the Cherokee justice system to run its course. When we consider that three of the deputized men killed that day had the last name Beck and were kin to the deceased woman, the posse begins to resemble a lynch mob more than a unit of law officers. We will never know if a more subtle, tactful approach to this situation would have been less fatal. However, we do know the context leading up to this hapless event and how both sides in the dispute subsequently used it to reinforce their positions. Marshal Roots cited it as evidence for why more money and support should be given for dampening the lawless unrest of Indian Territory, and the Cherokee pointed to it as yet another example of the United States violating a treaty.

The U.S. Marshals Service webpage describes this event, but the larger historical context is not explained, no question of jurisdiction, no mention of Polly Beck, no names of the suspect posse members. The subheadings of "Ambushed" and "Dangerous Duty" appear accompanying a narrative of brave lawmen.[14] In November 2013, at the dedication of the Marshals Museum cornerstone, Marshals Service Director Stacia Hylton addressed the crowd at the Fort Smith riverfront. She cited the high number of deputy marshal casualties in this region as creating a "sacred ground"—and as further evidence of how the Marshals Service "fights evil." She went on to say, "Those that died at the start of the nation's journey and those that have fallen since in the line of duty are why we're here and why we continue to move this project forward."[15] This language functions to reinforce a narration of the nation, of the "homeland," while it elides historical facts and context. The injustices perpetrated by whites in the frontier-complex era of restraint are veiled by mythic narratives in the current frontier-complex era of redoubling.

Clearly, the issue of law and order on the border is not as black and white as it is often depicted in popular cultural memory or the narrative of our nation. The mythic gendered alibi of justice says deputies died because they were brave and because Indian Territory was so dangerous, not because they were incompetent or looking for trouble. These gendered images of male deputies and outlaws are highly essentialized and leave little room for variation in how men are thought to have performed gender in the nineteenth century. Women likewise are portrayed in the Fort Smith frontier complex in narrowly defined gender roles.

Businesswomen?

We are told by a local historian in *200 Years of Grit*, a promotional video made by the City of Fort Smith to attract the U.S. Marshals Museum, that Fort Smith in the late nineteenth century was a place of "equal opportunity in the Old West."[16] It is stated in a manner reminiscent of Frederick Jackson Turner's frontier thesis that the nature of the frontier environment made the rule of employment somehow exceptional or different, offering equal employment opportunities to social minorities ahead of the rest of the country:

> It wasn't one aspect of society that was employed by the Marshal Service. We know for a fact that in addition to African American deputy marshals there were Native American marshals and there were some women employed by the Federal Court in various capacities. That, at a time when those things weren't happening in other segments of society, in other parts of the country, probably had a little bit to do with Fort Smith's location on the edge of Indian Territory, on the edge of this border situation. You know, this unsettled area is an area that needed some special people to go in there and be able to operate and do that kind of work.[17]

With this contemporary manner in which the skewed social structure of the nineteenth century is described in Fort Smith, we can critically examine discourses surrounding the roles of women in the frontier complex. While

Figure 6.1. A well-dressed guest in the parlor at Miss Laura's. He is holding a token with which to compensate a "daughter of joy." Photo by the author.

it took brave men taking peace and civilization into Indian Territory, the frontier complex maintains that the Wild West spilled into Fort Smith and lined Garrison Avenue with prostitutes and taverns. Claims of bars and brothels lining downtown Fort Smith are legion and used today as evidence that Fort Smith was on the border between unbridled savagery and staid civilization. Women are essentialized as either good wives and homemakers or some extreme deviation from heterosexual normativity such as prostitutes or wild women. For example, at a presentation given at the National Historic Site by members of the United Daughters of the Confederacy in 2012 concerning women's clothing from the nineteenth century, the audience was told quite matter-of-factly that when a woman was widowed she could either learn to make hats or become a prostitute.[18]

Three women who are shown conforming to the rules of heterosexual normativity are Mary Rogers, wife of town developer John Rogers, and her contemporaries Florence Clayton and Mary Parker, wives of prosecuting attorney William Henry Harrison Clayton and Judge Isaac Parker, respectively. These women are not used to exemplify any sort of active role in the frontier, but they are routinely cited as embodying the latest styles and accoutrements of civilized life. Mary Rogers' portrait hangs at the Fort Smith Museum of History. The caption next to it tells us "this oil on canvas [was] made at New Orleans before Mary came to Fort Smith to join her husband." Her portrait hangs between John Rogers' sideboard and a four-poster bed. With severely pursed lips she is framed in domesticity for perpetuity. Of her husband's chest of drawers we are told, "The marble top and fancy woodwork on this large sideboard announce John Rogers' ability to acquire wealth and power in Fort Smith. According to family history, John bought the piece in New Orleans, the city where his wife, Mary, grew up."[19] We are not told much else about Mary Rogers, but in a short space she twice mimetically attaches frontier Fort Smith to New Orleans, the closest, most accessible port of civilization in her time. She sits as a portrait of a domesticated white woman amid the otherwise savage frontier.

In the skit about Bass Reeves performed in the frontier complex during my fieldwork, the wives of Clayton and Parker are only referenced and do not actually appear in it. The year is 1882, and the Clayton House has just been completed. We are told that Florence and Mary adjourned to the "poshly decorated parlor where they will talk about the latest East Coast fashions. They will also talk about ideas of starting a public library in Fort Smith." Mary Parker and Florence Clayton were active members of the Fort Smith Fortnightly Club. While their husbands were imposing whiteness in Indian Territory, their wives were representing it in Fort Smith. Thus, the elite white women of the nineteenth century are used in today's frontier complex to equate the arrival of whiteness with the arrival of the more refined traits of civilization.

In contrast, the theme of prostitution in the Wild West is featured in the frontier complex with nearly equal prominence to Judge Parker's gallows. Miss Laura's and Judge Parker's histories are commingled by the miniature gallows overseen by a portrait of Parker in the restored brothel. The official Fort Smith Visitor Center is housed in Miss Laura's Social Club, a nineteenth-century "Victorian home" that allegedly was built and functioned as a brothel at the turn of the twentieth century. The building was put on the National Register of Historic Places in 1973, was restored in 1983, and has served as the official visitors center since 1992.[20] There, free maps and brochures about the area's attractions are dispensed, and tours of the brothel are conducted. In 2012, the guest register at Miss Laura's Social Club was signed by 12,718 visitors.

Figure 6.2. Miss Laura's Social Club building. The top of the visitors center can be seen beyond the Fort Smith Railroad yard. Photo by the author.

Originally called the Riverfront Commercial Hotel, the dilapidated building was saved from demolition by the Donrey Media Group in 1963. It took two full decades before it was opened as the restaurant Miss Laura's Social Club, and then it was closed within a decade. Don Reynolds Jr. recounts this venture in his book, *Crackerjack Positioning: Niche Marketing Strategy for the Entrepreneur*.[21] The Donrey Media Group made several attempts at leasing the building to be managed as a restaurant. After those failures it took on that role itself. Despite becoming a "Fort Smith landmark and tourist attraction," it was not a financial success.[22] After conducting some research Reynolds concluded that the restaurant was considered a tourist attraction or a venue for special occasions but not appealing for return trips from locals. He adds that "the structure was located in an industrial area next to a railroad track and rendering plant. A switch engine was usually parked on the track, not far from the restaurant. The switch engine's diesel engine was noisily running most of the time."[23] Similarly inhospitable conditions continue there today.

Despite its rivaling the popularity of the Hanging Judge Isaac C. Parker's Courtroom, the existing tourism trade was insufficient to make the restaurant a going concern. Reynolds notes in his 1993 publication, "The Fort Smith tourist market was shrinking. Visitor count at the Fort Smith National Historic Site of Old Fort Smith was steadily declining." He specifically notes the loss in the popular frontier-complex imagination: "It had been a long time since John Wayne rode out of Fort Smith as Rooster Cogburn in *True Grit.*" Then, citing the increasing competition in the tourist trade, Reynolds concludes, "Fort Smith is not the unique historical attraction it once was."[24] Unable to cultivate a consistent, competent, and committed business, Donrey "purchased a large padlock and closed the restaurant."[25] Within a year of its failing as a for-profit business venture, the city of Fort Smith took it over in 1992. Since then women have been dressing in costume to portray the more colorful side of the frontier complex for tourists.

Tourist materials in Fort Smith describe the brothels from Miss Laura's day as a row of "pleasure palaces," and the brochure for Miss Laura's Hello Bordello coyly teases, "Our brothel still takes care of visitors!" Tour guides at Miss Laura's routinely tell visitors, "Miss Laura's girls had it pretty good. They got three dollars instead of one, like at the other houses on the row." Guests are enthusiastically told, "Miss Laura encouraged her girls to go see the theater when it was showing in town." The idea that this was most likely a way to advertise for business is not mentioned. Rather, the good life that prostitutes had in the establishment is emphasized.

The brochure for Miss Laura's begins by sharing some background. Though operated as a hotel between 1896 and 1963, the first line locates Miss Laura's squarely in the mythic frontier: "At the turn of the century, Fort Smith, Arkansas was a raucous border town perched on the edge of a yet untamed Oklahoma, which was known then as Indian Territory." Oklahoma is described as untamed although by the early 1900s there was no part of it that had not been "civilized" by railroads and federal courts. The brochure narrative then taps into the mythic character of the kind of people entering the territories: "Cowboys, outlaws, outcasts, as well as God-fearing pioneers, all streamed through this wild little city. Each sought different adventures, different pleasures. An eager-to-please Fort Smith accommodated all requests."

In the frontier complex, prostitution is never depicted as a demeaning or dangerous line of work for women. No mention is made of syphilis, violence against women, suicide, destitution, unsafe abortion, shame, or women's displacement from their homes and communities. The brochure touts that "houses of ill fame catered to one of many vices that were practiced, and enjoyed, openly." The "fun" of nineteenth-century prostitution is evidenced by the kitschy items that tourists can consume at Miss Laura's, such as red garter belts and replica tokens. On the tour of Miss Laura's, we learn that the women used these tokens instead of money so their customers could not rob them, nor could the girls rob Miss Laura. I was informed by tour guides on several occasions that "replica tokens are especially popular around Christmastime for wives to put in their husbands' stockings."

On a wall of the gift shop parlor are several photos of women that the tour guides point out: "These photos were found in the attic, but we do not know for certain if they were all Miss Laura's girls." In one photo, a young woman in a short dress stands on a swing as two older men pose in front of it for the picture. In another photo, a woman in a full-length dress with sleeves down to the wrists stands holding a tree branch. Still another image has five women sharing a swing, smiling and laughing. In one picture, three women wear short skirts and sun bonnets and shade themselves with a parasol. They lie on a hillside interlaced with each other in coquettish fashion. Their shoes are fastened by straps that crisscross up to their knees. On one tour, a couple visiting from Chicago was taking in these photos when the woman pointed at the shoes and gleefully declared, "Oh, look at those cute shoes! Aren't they just soooo cute!"

At the end of each tour, women are presented with replicas of a "Certificate of Clean Health," while men are given tin deputy badges that have "Live the History" printed on them. We learn on the tour that "Miss Laura's girls had monthly health inspections and had to pass them in order to work." The words "Inmate House of Prostitution" are stamped across each certificate. When I inquired what that meant, I was told that "the women were inmates. They were not free to just go around town whenever or wherever they wanted—they might run into one of their customers on the sidewalk with his wife, and that just wouldn't do." But still, "Miss Laura's girls had it pretty good."

The adulterous behavior of the men in the story is not questioned, while the sequestered and behaved manners of the inmates are reinforced. This is heard on tours repeatedly and seen in the brochure that brags how Miss Laura's "ladies were known to be the most refined and the healthiest of Fort Smith's 'daughters of joy.' Miss Laura herself was a poised and attractive lady who was known to have occasionally confronted a rowdy customer with a loaded .45." The image projected is that Miss Laura's was a respectable place, replete with good times,

> filled with song, dance, gambling, and, of course, other pleasures. During a good business month, champagne was chilled in an upstairs bathtub and served at no charge to appreciative customers. Fort Smith's first player piano banged out popular tunes there while patrons of all classes mingled with the ladies. Many prominent local figures also were known to frequent the flourishing bordello, and Miss Laura reaped the profits.[26]

The key elements of champagne in the tub and the player piano were worked into every one of the more than ten tours I took over the course of my fieldwork. Everyone, including the prostitutes, is presented as having an enjoyable, pleasurable, and profitable time. On the Miss Laura's Social Club brochure, the letter "i" in the spelling of "Miss" is dotted with the shape of a heart, obfuscating the sex industry under the guise of love.

The fact that Laura Zeigler paid off her bank note on the building within two years is seldom skipped. It is claimed in the brochure and on tours of the brothel that Zeigler turned a handsome profit on its sale in 1911 for $47,000. Research has revealed, however, that the actual figure on the title of sale was substantially less, $5,450.[27] The cumulative effects of repeating these mythic elements are that structural gender inequalities are elided and neoliberal gender ideologies are reinforced with the success of the individual female entrepreneur's capitalist venture.

Miss Laura's brothel was the featured cover story in the August 2012 issue of 2NJOY magazine. In the article, Carolyn Joyce explains how the former brothel was part of the Wild West on the edge of Indian Territory, which was full of violence and bandits.[28] The champagne in the tub is mentioned, and Joyce maintains that "Miss Laura's 'girls' were well trained— never seen on the first floor unless fully clothed." And "rather than permitting the girls to walk the streets and shop, merchants brought goods to the house for them to purchase." On the occasions when they went to the theater, Joyce says, "they sat in the balcony as targets for hostile stares from wives seated below; I imagine many men slouched down and stayed face forward in their seats."[29] On tours of the bordello, which is "still furnished much as it would have been on its busiest evening," one hears "a delightful story of the early days of the frontier." As the delightful frontier drew to a close, so too, goes the narrative, did the good times at Miss Laura's.

The story of Miss Laura's in the cultural memory of the frontier complex begins to fade shortly after 1910. By then, we read in the visitor center brochure, "the golden days had passed" and the "community had tired of the frontier permissiveness." In 1911, Laura Zeigler sold her business to Bertha Gale Dean, who operated the hotel until she died in 1948. Soon after Dean purchased it we are told, "business slowed and the neighborhood declined to slum status.... During her ownership, the property became an informal haven for drifters, drunks and gamblers." This important shift in the story line leads us to believe that prostitution was curtailed soon after 1910 and was a behavior that was contained within the frontier era, not something that lingered into the twentieth century, let alone the twenty-first. The re-enactment character of Miss Laura was invented by Carolyn Joyce in 1992 for marketing Fort Smith's frontier past.[30] After more than twenty years of performing the character, she playfully quips, "Miss Laura's story has not changed from 1903 to today. Miss Laura has always taught us that 'It's a business doin' pleasure with ya!'"[31] This mythical projection of highly gendered behavior into the frontier complex does not align with historical facts about prostitution in Fort Smith.

Though Laura Zeigler opened her hotel in 1903, Miss Laura's girls are routinely depicted as overlapping the late nineteenth-century Parker era. In some skits, Judge Parker is actually put in the same time frame, though he died in 1896. In the frontier complex, decades of difference are conflated to project a unified myth of the wild western frontier. Just as with Judge Parker and Bass Reeves, I do not doubt the veracity of every detail of their stories, but some are clearly mythic. Fort Smith was indeed the home to much prostitution. Unlike the stories of Parker and Reeves in which I believe their exploits are exaggerated beyond historical fact, the mythic alibi of Laura Zeigler actually minimizes and conceals an even greater and longer-running business of prostitution in Fort Smith. The alibi of Miss Laura says prostitution was confined to the frontier time frame, and as soon as the frontier ended, so too did prostitution. In fact, it may have been just getting started at frontier's close.

Fort Smith has a checkered and corrupt past when it comes to prostitution. In April 1895, for example, the chief of police was caught using city money to purchase items including a stove, wallpaper, and paint for a "bawdy house." Chief Henry Surratt resigned in apparent embarrassment, but the city council turned immediately around and reinstated him.[32] A survey of the Fort Smith City Police docket from 1895 reveals that at the start of every month, twenty to thirty women were found guilty of being "inmate[s] of a house of ill favor," charged five dollars, then released by the police until the start of the next month, when police would bring them in again to collect the same fine from the same women.[33] On May 4, 1904, fifty-one women were arrested and found guilty. Among the names listed in the police docket were Laura Zeigler (spelled Zegeler in the docket) and Bertha Gale Dean. Their names recurred in the docket for several years before and after the opening of Miss Laura's.

What is usually excluded from the narrative of the frontier complex is that Fort Smith experimented with legalized prostitution between 1907 and 1924.[34] After 1907 the city made essentially the same amount of money as from the fines collected at the start of each month when prostitution was illegal. Individual women had to pay for their certificates of clean health. "Similarly, all keepers of the houses of prostitution were required to purchase licenses for engaging in prostitution within the district. Both of these groups made monthly payments to the city of the exact same amounts that they had been paying monthly in the way of fines."[35]

The ordinance legalizing prostitution in 1907 states, "All prostitution in the City of Fort Smith, Arkansas, shall be confined to the district embraced between North 'C' Street on the North; the alley in Blocks No.s 2 and 3, City of Fort Smith, on the East; North 'A' Street on the South; and Arkansas River on the West, and there only." This neighborhood is essentially the first few blocks on the immediate northwestern side of Garrison Avenue, one block from Judge Parker's old courtroom. Ben Boulden, who has written extensively for a local newspaper on the history of Fort Smith, notes, "The most significant innovation was the introduction of the bimonthly health inspections by a city health officer. According to the ordinance he was to inspect both inmates and keepers and to revoke their licenses if they were found to be sick and to withhold their licenses until they were restored to health." In effect the city functioned as a pimp. The law was revoked in 1924, Boulden explains: "Amidst a wave of law-and-order vigilantism and the resurgence of the Ku Klux Klan statewide and locally in the 1920s, the city board of commissioners acted to repeal the 1907 ordinance. With sweeping words, the new city law established a fine of $25 to $100 for use of any place or thing for 'illicit sexual intercourse, fornication or adultery, or as a place of assignation.'"[36] Obviously, this did not bring prostitution to an end in Fort Smith, and I suggest its peak had not yet been reached.

Bertha Gale Dean's (formerly Laura Zeigler's) brothel continued to function into the 1960s; writer Kay Dishner notes that "the occupation of the roomers did not change, but the auspices under which they operated did."[37] Local history and personal interviews attest to at least five motels in downtown Fort Smith that effectively functioned as known brothels up until the late 1970s: the Como, Palace, Saint Charles, Ozark, and Rex Rooms. None of these is mentioned in the frontier complex, and their existence is muted in the city's history in general. Widespread oral accounts attest to prostitution and gambling in Moffett, Oklahoma, during this time frame. Moffett is just across the bridge from downtown Fort Smith. Today it consists of very few residences and a few very large, well-supplied junk yards. But anyone who has lived in Fort Smith more than forty years might recall hearing that back in the day, all military personnel were banned from entering Moffett and that the town was full of dangerous establishments replete with drinking, gambling, and whoring. To date I have found no written record of this military ban despite the preponderance of tall tales that abound about it in Fort Smith.

In these legends of Moffett lies the clue to the flourishing prostitution in Fort Smith proper: military personnel stationed at Camp Chaffee, adjacent to the eastern border of Fort Smith. This connection is directly stated in Dishner's *Insight 2000* article: "The Row, along with surrounding saloons and boarding houses, was torn down in the 1920s to make room for a growing furniture industry. Yet, Bertha Gale's rooming house survived the wrecking crew and business continued as usual, right up to and through the next heyday for prostitution, when Camp Chaffee was opened in the 1940s."[38] The claims of Moffett's wildness deflects the cultural memory away from Fort Smith and away from the men stationed at Camp Chaffee from 1941 to 1961 who frequently paid for sex in downtown Fort Smith. Another article by Dishner in the likewise links prostitution in Fort Smith of the 1940s to World War II: "The jewel of Bordello Row, known today as Miss Laura's, had one last flourish of vigorous business during the 1940s when Camp Chaffee became the training center for thousands of soldiers being inducted into the U.S. Army. Garrison Avenue was flooded with soldiers looking for a good time whenever they could get a pass to come into town, and Bertha's Place once again became a place for a good time."[39]

C. Calvin Smith reveals that a near-epidemic of syphilis broke out at that time: "In Fort Smith, the growth in reported cases was so alarming that Circuit Judge Sam Woods called for a grand jury investigation."[40] Dishner reports a sordid detail about this particular impact the war had locally: "Of the total number of cases there were more girls in the 14-year-old bracket than any other. The 'Victory Girls'—those young girls who performed 'patriotic' sexual favors for men in uniform—had arrived in Arkansas."[41] The power of the mythic narrative that Miss Laura's girls had it pretty good conceals all of this.

I believe we can minimally conclude that prostitution is not as fun or safe as it is depicted and that the tourist narrative in Fort Smith selectively sequesters prostitution to a narrow time in its history. There are a few newspaper accounts from the Miss Laura era of prostitutes committing suicide, but these are not mentioned in the frontier complex. Distinguishing the facts of prostitution from the mythic gender projections of Miss Laura's girls is quite easy but very rarely done in Fort Smith, with one notable exception. A former employee of the Fort Smith Convention and Visitors Bureau told me, "Miss Laura's is all about marketing. Many facts of prostitution are not exactly 'family friendly.' When they moved Miss Laura's they found fetus bones in the walls." The actual building was moved about sixty feet when it was remodeled for the Visitor Center. While the claim of finding fetus bones may be as suspect as that of Miss Laura's girls having fun, this reference to a consequence of the sex industry was a rare moment of candor about the ugly nature upon which Fort Smith has built its tourism industry.

The myth of Miss Laura's brothel reflects an attempt to sequester prostitution in a distant time and place, to convince us that prostitution has been left in the past. Not only was prostitution stimulated during Camp Chaffee's heyday, but the Fort Smith Police Department still regularly makes arrests for it. In January 2013, a former city director was caught in a sting for soliciting prostitution online at Backpage.com, and a local hotel was busted for renting rooms by the hour for selling sex.[42] The outlandish nature in which nineteenth-century prostitution is playfully discussed in the frontier complex becomes apparent when contextualized in its contemporary surroundings. Two establishments catering to the sex industry have operated within very short distances to Miss Laura's. The Cheyenne Gentlemen's Club, a strip club, is five minutes down the road, and Pleasures by Kasey, a sex-toy shop with pole-dancing classes, was located in the 500 block of Garrison Avenue. I conducted very brief fieldwork in both of these establishments in order to bring some basic perspective to the otherwise lighthearted treatment of prostitution in the frontier complex.

The Cheyenne Gentlemen's Club is euphemistically referred to as the "Oklahoma Ballet" in Fort Smith and jokingly known as such by many people. The venue is one big, wide-open room with a bar along one side, a large stage with a stripper pole along the front wall, and a second pole and stage on the other side. Near this second stage is an entrance to the VIP Room, a.k.a. the Champagne Room, to which one can gain access with one of the employed dancers by buying her a $35 drink. In my one visit to the club I tried my best to sit inconspicuously along a wall and observe the entire scene. There were at least fifteen to twenty employed women working the room. It was early in the evening, before the bars in downtown Fort Smith had closed, so the place was only about half full, with seventy-five to eighty men. Many of the patrons had strippers at their tables, while others were watching the dancers on the stages; all seemed to be in their own internalized worlds. Several women led men into the VIP Room. Nudity, sexual touching, and mimicked sex were on full display.

As I sat there taking in what I found to be a horrific scene, the phrase "Miss Laura's girls had it pretty good" began to ring in my ears. With that pithy quip juxtaposed to the events transpiring in front of me, my stomach turned in revolt at the romanticized narrative at Miss Laura's as much as at the unfolding scene in the Cheyenne. I could not help but wonder how visitors to Miss Laura's Visitor Center would feel about coming to the Cheyenne. Would they find the employees' outfits "just sooo cute"? Though less than five minutes from Judge Parker's courtroom, the Cheyenne Gentlemen's Club is "othered." It is a different sort of manifestation of the present redoubling era of the frontier complex where Fort Smithians go for strip clubs and gambling, with the Choctaw Casino and the Cherokee Casino adjacent to the Fort Smith–Oklahoma border.

Pleasures by Kasey was an adult-oriented store with a pole-dancing studio. It had been in Fort Smith for a few years, but when it moved to Garrison Avenue in March 2012, it caused a minor uproar, including the city board reviewing its policies of sexually oriented businesses. In the end, it was found that Pleasures by Kasey was not a sexually oriented business because less than 10 percent of its merchandise was directly sexually oriented.[43] The few times I entered the store it had no other customers and little merchandise to browse. The storefront operated for about six months but then closed while the business offered pole-dancing classes for a few months before finally closing altogether. Though a minor flap to be sure, this incident revealed that while Fort Smith can build its tourism industry around making light of women who engaged in prostitution in the past—even declaring, "It's a business doin' pleasure with ya!"—but commercial efforts to provide people with sexual pleasure today are not found so colorful or business-worthy. Women giving men pleasure for hire in the past is romanticized, while women giving themselves pleasure in the present is vilified. As we take up the case of Belle Starr, we will see how this rule applies even in the past.

Victim of Circumstance

A cursory glance at the literature on Myra Maybelle Shirley, famously known as Belle Starr, reveals her long list of dramatic titles: "A Cleopatra," "The Bandit Queen," "The Female Jesse James," "The Dashing Female Highwayman," "A Daring Amazon," "King Philip," "Tecumseh," "Powhatan," "Sitting Bull," "Geronnymo!!" "The Petticoat Terror of the Plains," "The Prairie Amazon," and "Queen of the Outlaws," just to name a few.[44] From these labels, she was attributed with being "braver than Joan of Arc" as well as "excessively erotic, [but] weak in maternal feeling . . . [having] an excessive desire for revenge, cunning, cruelty, love of dress, and untruthfulness, forming a combination of evil tendencies which often results in a type of extraordinary wickedness," while possessing "superior intelligence," and deriving "wild pleasure of the chase."[45]

It is said that the name Belle Starr "struck terror to the hearts of the timid and caused brave men to buckle an extra holster about their loins before setting out through the territory of her operations." Apparently, men could not resist her. A man named Middleton "had loved Bella [from the time] he had first laid eyes on her, and determined to win her if it were in his power."[46] One observer ventured, "To sum up her character in one trite paragraph, I will simply state that Belle was a maroon Diana in the chase, a Venus in beauty, a Minerva in wisdom, a thief, a robber, a murderer and a generous friend."[47] Reflecting on this list of labels and characteristics of the person originally known as Myra Maybelle Shirley, it is clear that we have left the domain of historical fact but also of ordinary language and have entered the domain of myth.

The historical veracity of these tall tales has been debunked by Glenn Shirley in *Belle Starr and Her Times*, in which he separates historical wheat from mythical chaff. He observes that at the time of her death, to most, "the woman's name meant nothing. The *Vinita Chieftain*, in Indian Territory, gave her ambush murder only a paragraph."[48] Rather, the entire dramatic story behind her was fabricated through the network of Richard K. Fox, who ran the *National Police Gazette* out of New York as well a lucrative business in dime novels. Fox "perceived Belle Starr as a circulation builder and dispatched Alton B. Meyers . . . to Fort Smith."[49] From there the legend of Belle Starr was born and soon perpetuated as subsequent authors elaborated on the initial fiction.[50]

Knowing that the wild stories about her are fiction makes the rapacious energy with which they are told all the more fascinating. In a presentation given in 2012 in the Fort Smith frontier complex, Belle Starr was introduced in high mythic fashion:

> This is something you may not know, but Belle Starr attempted to assassinate Clayton at the Sebastian County Fair. Belle Starr was friends with Jesse James and the Youngers. She was outlawing and bootlegging. In the Starr gang she was the brains of the gang and would plan the robberies. When she was tried by Parker for stealing horses, Clayton did not call Belle Starr to the stand because she was too smart, but Sam Starr was dumb and he could confound him. Well, Fort Smith is known as Hell on the Border because of the terrible prison conditions, so Parker looked for a more humane place to send them. Belle Starr served nine months at the Detroit House of Corrections and then immediately went back to her old ways. She was almost as feared as Jesse James! Men feared her. She shot first and asked questions later. When she was shot dead, people were not upset about her death. The townspeople could [not] have cared less.[51]

Such hyperbole so readily consumed by the popular imagination and firmly embedded in the cultural memory of Fort Smith demands academic attention. The only question that must be asked about Belle Starr is Why? Why must she be described in such exaggerated terms? These wild claims were fabricated for a reason, and they still resonate today for a reason. It is my contention that the story of Belle Starr is another mythic alibi of the frontier complex. In the case of Belle Starr, I suggest the alibi goes something like, "I wasn't an intelligent, free-thinking woman in the late nineteenth century. I was a gun-toting, sex-crazed, wild woman. That's why I was gunned down."

To see what the myth surrounding Belle Starr is covering up, it is useful to look at what historical facts we do know about her. We know she was born and raised in Carthage, Missouri, and was well educated. Her biographer Glenn Shirley notes that at the Carthage school, "Myra Shirley was one of the first to master its curriculum of reading, spelling, grammar, arithmetic, deportment, Greek, Latin, Hebrew, and music, and she learned to play the piano."[52] We also know that she was arrested twice for horse theft, went before Judge Parker both times, was found guilty one of those times, and spent six months in the Detroit House of Corrections. We know that she had a series of husbands who had a habit of breaking the law. Clearly, she did not associate with the most genteel of men.

On February 3, 1889, while riding her horse sidesaddle near the Canadian River, she was shot in the back with large buckshot from a shotgun and then again with smaller shot on the side of her face and neck; she subsequently died from these wounds.[53] None of these basic facts fully explains the manner in which the character of Belle Starr became so wildly exaggerated after her death. There is more here than meets the eye and far more than meets the historical facts of the matter. To get to the bottom of this, we need to travel from Younger's Bend near Eufaula in the Choctaw Nation to ancient Greece.

There is a Greek myth of the Amazons, powerful women who lived alone on an island, who had pearls and gold, and who only admitted men into their domain for reproductive purposes. This myth led some explorers to search for these exotic, eroticized women and their fabled treasures. European explorers were well acquainted with the myth. Virginia Bouvier, in her *Women and the Conquest of California 1542–1840*, asserts that the myth was serialized in popular literature and read widely by sailors and explorers in the New World. In these stories, the violent tendencies of the Amazons who live on the island of California are tamed by white, male, European Christians.[54] The names of the Amazon River and the state of California are thus derived. More significant, this pervaded Europeans gendered and racialized consciousness of people in the New World, legitimating conquest in the process.

In this Greek myth, the Amazon women lived as warriors and as steely, reserved women who only needed men for sex. When European explorers made contact with the New World they mistakenly believed they had found this lost tribe of Amazons. The mythic narrative established a highly gendered dichotomy. A tribe of "strong, independent women who fiercely defended a kind of female utopia, the Amazons taunted a population of male conquerors from afar."[55] Bouvier argues that in the conquest of California the Amazon myth constructed a "basic gendered hierarchy of power."[56] The fundamental paradigm it created was one of "conquest as a male venture enacted upon a 'feminized' population."[57] This is paralleled in the story of Belle Starr, who while holed up at Younger's Bend taunted the lawmen in nearby Fort Smith. Turning Belle Starr into an Amazon not only policed the boundaries of heterosexual normativity, it also assisted in transforming Indian Territory into grounds upon which the mythic justice of Judge Parker and his deputies were imposed. White peace and civilization were being taken to the savages.

Amy Kaplan, in *The Anarchy of Empire*, argues that the encroachment of the imperial United States created border friction that systematically called into question the safety of the hearth, the home, and whiteness and subsequently fostered the fear of miscegenation. The response to this fear was to shore up the boundaries of domesticity in tandem with manifest destiny to create what Kaplan calls "manifest domesticity."[58] The murder of Belle Starr, an intelligent, capable woman living on the frontier, called into question the safety of the domestic sphere at a time when the U.S. populace was being encouraged to migrate west and fill the "great void." The murder of a white woman in the frontier era of reservation necessitated a cover-up, an alibi, to sustain the illusion that westward expansion was safe for white women and families, but it also reinforced the importance of conforming to the hegemonic rules of heterosexual normativity.

The mythologization of Belle Starr as an Amazon and femme fatale establishes an excuse for why this white woman was killed in Indian Territory. The alibi says Belle Starr was not killed because she was living in a dangerous environment; that is not where she was. Rather, Belle Starr was killed because she was a crazy Amazon woman who dominated men and used them for wanton and lustful purposes. Given that her murderer was never found, the myth is a way to conceal the fact that an educated white woman was murdered on the frontier. This was not tolerable to the mission of manifest destiny. It was not tolerable to have bald facts expose that it was a dangerous place for women. The reason the myth is so exaggerated and so often repeated in the frontier complex is to rationalize her murder. She was killed because her persona was too far removed from the boundaries of normal domesticity that was being reinforced at this very moment in U.S. history.

Belle Starr can now be placed among the pantheon of deities in the frontier-complex mythosphere with Judge Parker, deputies and outlaws, Bass Reeves, and Miss Laura" Together the set of alibis, embedded in popular tourist narratives in the Fort Smith frontier complex, function to distract us from observing the significant, harmful, debilitating, and irreparable harm done to entire populations in achieving the goal of manifest destiny in the nineteenth century and the global ambitions of the United States in the twentieth. The overarching myth of the frontier serves as a container of impunity for all the misdeeds perpetrated in the name of westward expansion of the political state. When it comes to gender, the frontier complex creates essentialized images of men and women in stark, binary terms.

Civilization and Its Discontents

Mythic images of the Wild West in novels and film are drawn from the time frame 1871–1907, when Judge Parker, Bass Reeves, Laura Zeigler, and Belle Starr lived, from placement of the federal court in Fort Smith to Oklahoma statehood. This is the end of the restraint era and the start of the reservation era of the frontier complex. It is from these eras that the collective set of Wild West images are drawn that burst into television westerns and Hollywood films from 1940 to 1960, in the middle of the recreation era of the frontier complex. Film and TV westerns exploited the already hyperbolic accounts from the late nineteenth century, and it is from those westerns that the contemporary reenactors in the current redoubling era retrieve mythic images from the frontier attic with which to conjure their performances for tourists today. What this means is that frontier reenactors are copying the westerns on which they grew up, which were copies of late nineteenth-century pulp fiction promoted by the frontier club that had no counterpart in reality. It is the copy of a copy of a fiction.

The late nineteenth century was a contested time in gender and sexual relations. Though homage is paid to Sigmund Freud in the subhead here, Michel Foucault is more helpful for seeing that in Freud's time sexuality was simultaneously muted and excessively discussed as the boundaries of heterosexual domesticity were being created and policed.[59] The mythic frontier, and subsequently the frontier complex, provided a vast environment in which to explore the poetics and performativity of gender.[60] The nation was expanding its boundaries across the continent and beyond while also shifting from an agrarian to an industrial, from a rural to an urban, and from a producing to a consuming society. Industrialization provided the tools for making manifest destiny and global imperialism a reality; it also created an environment in which individuals anxiously negotiated their gender performances.

At this moment, many East Coast urbanites suddenly found themselves wracked with the pangs of neurasthenia. George Beard and S. Weir Mitchell, late nineteenth-century physicians, described and diagnosed this ailment as early as 1881.[61] Sometimes it was called sexual neurasthenia, or more often it was simply called "hysterics," the "vapors," or "brain sprain" in the popular press. Just as the grandeur of taking civilization to the savages was nearly complete in Indian Territory, Beard claimed that same civilizing force to be a debilitating one for urban white people. He argued, in Michael Kimmel's description, that neurasthenia "was the result of 'overcivilization'—changes such as steam power, the periodical press, the telegraph, and the sciences had so speeded up the pace of social life that people simply couldn't keep up despite their tireless efforts."[62]

The result was a set of a maladies including "insomnia, dyspepsia, hysteria, hypochondria, asthma, headache, skin rashes, hay fever, baldness, inebriety, hot flashes, cold flashes, nervous exhaustion, and brain collapse."[63] Men and women who found themselves living in large cities in small homes and working office jobs that no longer required strenuous physical activity were particularly prone to contract these afflictions. In Kimmel's *Manhood in America* he assesses an underlying cause among men of the times: "The question was how to participate in the business world, find their rung upon the ladder, and still maintain a sense of their manhood."[64] What the disorder fundamentally amounted to, in Beard's opinion, was a case of too much civilization. Total immersion in the modern milieu, he maintained, was making men and women alike forget their traditional gender roles, lose their moorings, and experience a plethora of emerging diseases.

Men no longer knew how to be men, and women no longer knew how to be women. The simple remedy laid out by the likes of Beard and Mitchell was for each sex to return to the purported womb of its gender, to bathe and be reborn refreshed and clarified in thought and action, recalibrated to proper gender specifications. Women of the late nineteenth century were given the "rest cure" of sitting at home to meditate upon the domesticity of their position, while men were sent west to dude ranches to take on the role of cowboy and acquaint themselves with guns and horses or recover their primal urges by playing Indian.[65] Charlotte Perkins Gilman chronicled the remedies for neurasthenia in *The Yellow Wallpaper*. She was told by Dr.

Mitchell to "live as domestic a life as possible. Have your child with you all the time. Lie down an hour after each meal. Have but two hours intellectual life a day. And never touch a pen, brush, or pencil as long as you live."[66] Fortunately, she did not take her doctor's advice but instead picked up the pen to champion the cause of women confined to the home, to the domestic sphere.

For men, coming into contact with the great outdoors became a cure for just about everything. This was the era of the *Frontier Club* described by Christine Bold, when the white men who were the captains of the political economy were fashioning popular fictional narratives that lionized the very actions that made them prosper. Michael Kimmel also chronicled how Theodore Roosevelt, George Bird Grinnell, and William Kent belonged to groups for men like the "Boone and Crockett Club to encourage big game hunting." Philip Deloria expands this portrait of turn-of-the-century gender negotiations to include how children were sent to Camp Minnewawa, Camp Mirimichi, Camp Pokanoket, and other such settings to play Indian and be restored by nature's healing forces. The Boy Scouts and Camp Fire Girls were born out of this same presumably felt need to retreat from excessive civilization, to escape from what some described at the time as being "imperiled by an effeminate, postfrontier urbanism."[67]

Three famous men who suffered from neurasthenia and reclaimed their health by traveling to the frontier were Owen Wister, Frederic Remington, and Max Weber. German sociologist Weber was in such ill health with the hysterics that he had to resign his professorship from 1897 to 1904. It was ultimately his 1904 trip to the United States, where he delivered a paper at the St. Louis World's Fair, and his subsequent foray into Indian Territory to Guthrie and then for a week in Muskogee, that propelled Weber out of his dark period and invigorated his writing until the time of his death in 1920.[68]

Weber was cured by the leisure activity of traveling by train to the frontier, which his white-collar position afforded him. In that very same moment he formulated his critique of the Protestant work ethic, which he argued led to a value system that increased the wealth of its adherents in direct proportion to sucking them dry of their manhood; they became, in Weber's words, "specialists without spirit, sensualists without heart." Modernity had supplied the ailment and the cure: buying tourist experiences on the open frontier that might restore the manhood taken from them in the urban office space.[69]

Owen Wister created icons of western frontier imagery in fiction and Frederic Remington in painting after being inspired by the West themselves. As was Max Weber, they were complicit in constituting the cure as they partook of it. Wister was a banker before he made his fateful trip and realized his masculine potential at a dude ranch in Wyoming. At the ranch, Kimmel notes, Wister "slept outdoors in a tent, bathed in an icy creek each morning, spent hours in the saddle, hunted, fished, worked in the roundup, and helped to brand calves, castrate bulls, and deliver foals." Within a very short time of being there Wister wrote, "I am beginning to be able to feel I'm something of an animal and not a stinking brain alone."[70] With health restored, in 1902 he wrote *The Virginian*, which sold more than three hundred thousand copies from 1903 to 1907.

After decades of taking civilization to the savage Indians in the West, suddenly white men wanted to go out and experience nature to regain contact with their inner savage-selves. Here is the point where we can see race and gender being embedded in the frontier-complex narratives. It is not African Americans, Indians, or women, but rather it is fictitious depictions of white men on the frontier embedded in tourist narratives that veil the injustices of their imperialist, capitalist, racist, and sexist vices. By the time Wister arrived in the West, it was a highly modernized one. To him "the West was 'manly, egalitarian, self-reliant, and Aryan.'" It was very important to Wister that the West was where whiteness was possible: "To catch the deeper meaning of our life, one's path must be toward that Western verge of the continent where all white men are American born."[71]

Frederic Remington's story is similar. He was the son of a newspaperman and himself an aspiring journalist at an East Coast college before he was directed out west to cure his neurasthenia. His paintings of the West, of cowboys, of the rugged living of the frontier are among the most popular of that genre today. Remington actively rejected the urbane East as "he rejected effete conceptions of beauty, of the 'cards and custards' of the eastern establishment, and he hated Europe with its 'collars, cuffs and foreign languages.'" While Wister's campaign of whiteness was subtle, Remington's was blatant. With vitriol, he declared "Jews, Injuns, Chinamen, Italians, Huns—the rubbish of the earth I hate. I've got some Winchesters and when the massacring begins, I can get my share of 'em, and what's more, I will." Of African Americans, he lamented that in the Civil War, "so many Americans had to be killed to free a lot of damn niggers who are better off under the yoke."[72] Wister and Remington, following in Buffalo Bill Cody's

Figure 6.3. *Coming thru the Rye*, Old Cowtown Museum, Wichita, Kansas. Visitors are welcomed by the boisterous image of the Wild West in Frederic Remington's statue. Photo by the author.

footsteps, projected highly racialized mythical images of the western frontier into the American psyche, up into the frontier attic.

Ironically, it was not until railroads and reservations had tamed the "Wild West" that it could be constituted as such. As early as 1880, most cattle ranches were downsizing or put out of business entirely.[73] Barbed-wire fences and railroads quickly closed the open range as beef production was industrialized. As the cowhand was being displaced, the cowboy was invented. There had been cattlemen, ranchers, and steer drivers, but there had never been the co-opted, commoditized, mythologized image of a cowboy. It is truly mythic because the activity to which the word "cowboy" was originally attached no longer existed. The mythic frontier was created as a substitute for the historical reality.

In 1882, Buffalo Bill Cody took his Wild West show on the road, and in 1883 the first rodeo was held. The cattle hands who had been put out of work as their occupations were overtaken by technology could find employment in the burgeoning field of western tourism. Cattle ranches that had gone bankrupt from the closing frontier reopened as health spas for city folks who had just been diagnosed with the disease of civilization, or neurasthenia, and needed to go out West to fill their prescriptions. Only after "civilization had been taken to the savages" could urbanites escape civilization by traveling to the West.

Wister freely admits in the preface to *The Virginian* that it is a "colonial romance" set in Wyoming between 1874 and 1890—a simulacrum, at best. He suggests, "Had you left New York or San Francisco at ten o'clock this morning, by noon the day after to-morrow you could step out at Cheyenne. There you would stand at the heart of the world that is the subject of my picture, yet you would look around you in vain for the reality. It is a vanished world."[74] Though a different part of the frontier from Indian Territory, that process holds true and the mythologizing carries throughout the West: the West is conflated, again. To paraphrase Trouillot, the "American frontier west" is not a place, it is a project.[75]

As the national scene of gender jockeying unfolded, the newly created Oklahoma Territory, split from Indian Territory in 1890, became a haven for renegotiating marital contracts. Besides the abundant advertisements designed to lure recently freed African Americans from the South to Oklahoma Territory, a separate advertising campaign was aimed at men and women on the East Coast who were looking for easy divorces. The allure of divorce described by Littlefield and Underhill adds complexity to the narratives of land runs and criminality and reveals another concealed facet of what the frontier offered.[76]

Just as relationships between husbands and wives were strained and waning from neurasthenia, New York urbanites were being shown a way out of unpleasant relationships. They could read advertisements of a far-off land that provided another kind of cure for what afflicted them. Circulars were distributed in the city that "extolled the virtues of Oklahoma's divorce laws, emphasizing particularly the ninety-day residency requirement and inviting the unhappy and distressed to come west."[77] Thus, the brave and courageous deputies and the violent criminals were joined by men and women who lacked courage to end their relationships back East.

North and South Dakota openly competed for these divorce emigrants, but their six-month residency requirement and harsher climates made ninety days in Oklahoma's milder climate far more appealing. The town of Guthrie not only was the starting point of land runs but also promoted as "an ideal resort for divorce seekers. It was scenic and friendly, legal fees were reasonable, and court appearances often unnecessary."[78] Divorce emigrants were drawn from the West Coast too, with deceptive advertisements in papers that "reported that a man could get a divorce in Oklahoma, then move out of the territory within thirty days, without his wife knowing about it."[79]

Opponents of easy divorce actively worked to curtail this lucrative business. As public sentiment and changes in the law were bringing the era of easy divorce to a close, people rushed to Oklahoma to file. The scene was so intense in some district clerks' offices that "the editor of the El Reno News compared the situation with the 'runs for homestead filings at the land office at the opening of an Indian reservation.'"[80] It was not until 1906 when the U.S. Supreme Court ruled that out-of-state divorces did not adequately notify defendants, extending it to one full year of residency required, that the divorce mill in Oklahoma closed. Within a year, this divorce haven would use a mock wedding to symbolize its creation. The courtship between Mr. Oklahoma Territory and Ms. Indian Territory effectively granted a divorce to the United States from its entailments with Indian Nations.

The net result of this mythic representation of frontier gender is the creation of a starkly binary past when men knew how to be men and women knew how to be women. Some cling to this fictionalized account of gender in the frontier era as a talisman to ward off fears and anxieties over contemporary gender trouble. The projected myth of men and women knowing their place provides assurances to some that their contemporary ideas of narrow gender roles have a basis in history. In my five years of fieldwork, I heard this sentiment expressed many times by the more enthusiastic reenactors. Several told me they felt they were just born in the wrong time. By clinging to an imagined past, they can comfort themselves from their unease of the perceived confusion of gender roles, race relations, and government intrusion of today, when in fact the past was fluid, malleable, and oppressive.

All of this mythic projection of gender conceals the reality of men profiteering off industrial advancement and stealing land from Indians and African Americans while they sought easy divorces and other escapes from unsatisfactory marriages in a heartless age of iron horses and what Max Weber called "iron cages." These facts must be covered up with romantic images of self-assured men claiming what is rightfully theirs, defending the sanctity of heterosexual normativity, and protecting whiteness. This is why the military fort must be keeping the peace, why Isaac Parker must be the Hanging Judge, why Bass Reeves must be a rule-abiding illiterate, why Miss Laura's girls must be enjoying themselves, and why Belle Starr must be a Bandit Queen.

7

/////////////////////////

Performing "Frontier in the Attic"

Buffalo Bill Cody smiled—a tired smile though. How to explain to these
men [Doc Holliday and Wyatt Earp], who didn't even seem to be gunmen, that a show had to be real and yet not real at the same time?

Larry McMurtry, *The Last Kind Words Saloon*

For the past sixty years, Fort Smith has intentionally used its nineteenth-
century frontier history to promote cultural heritage tourism. When the
Fort Smith Museum of History opened its doors in 1910 as the Commissary Museum, its exhibits were shaped by amateur curators and largely
featured the history of the military forts and the role Fort Smith played
in the Civil War. Founded by several local women's groups including the
Daughters of the American Revolution and the United Daughters of the
Confederacy, the museum was housed the 1838 commissary building on
the grounds of the second military Fort Smith and intended to champion
the story of the Lost Cause and the New South. The Parker era and the
frontier eras of restraint and reservation were still recent history in 1910.
Two score and five years later the recreation era of the frontier complex was
in full swing, and the way in which Fort Smith remembered its past was
about to jump onto that chuck wagon.

In *Devil's Bargains*, Hal Rothman suggests that tourism and the West
are inseparable: "Western tourism stands at the heart of the American
drama precisely because it occurs on the same stage as the national drama
of self-affirmation. To Americans the West is their refuge . . . [and] home
to the mythic landscapes where Americans become whole again in the
aftermath of personal or national cataclysm."[1] Though Arkansas is not a
western state and Fort Smith is not a western town, the national popularity
in the recreation era of the frontier complex—of reaching into the western
frontier bag of myths that reconcile contemporary political, gender, and

racial ideologies—most likely contributed to the city's risking its reputation on the gallows in exchange for tourist dollars. By 1955, it was ready to make that devil's bargain.

Perhaps the seed for the Fort Smith frontier tourism was planted by Homer Croy's *He Hanged Them High*. Croy claims that while in Fort Smith gathering materials for his 1952 book, he "told the Chamber of Commerce that the only thing the town was known for was the court, and that the gallows was the most dramatic part of the court, and suggested that it should be rebuilt as a tourist attraction."[2] Apparently the Chamber of Commerce had not yet embraced this idea, as Croy declares, "I was frowned into the street. Fort Smith is still sensitive about the death machine."[3] Within a few short years, however, the gallows would be rebuilt and Parker's courtroom reopened for tourists.

Whether it was Homer Croy's suggestion that triggered the quick turnaround may never be known, but in January 1955, Mayor H. R. "Happy" Hestand appointed Circuit Judge Paul Wolfe to head a commission for the rejuvenation of the Parker courtroom and gallows as a way to promote tourism. Documents from the Paul Wolfe Collection at the Fort Smith Museum of History clearly reveal that tourism was a primary goal of resurrecting Judge Parker's courtroom and gallows.[4] In a newspaper clipping in the Wolfe Collection, the writer of a December 24, 1954, letter to the editor declares, "The best idea that's come along in a long time is the plan to recreate some of the landmarks here, like Judge Parker's court etc. I'd go a step further and say it would be a good thing to rebuild the old gallows. I think tourists would flock to see it." Commission members expressed high hopes in the early months of meetings. One member reported that "plans to restore the court of Judge Parker indicated the city was becoming more 'hospitality minded' and that the restoration would bring 'millions of dollars' of tourist trade into the city." Dollar signs were featured in the enthusiasm for the project: "If every tourist who comes through can be encouraged to stay over one day . . . the restoration would be worthwhile."[5]

"Relive the Heritage, Restore the Pride"

On May 26, 1957, Public Historical Restorations Inc. opened the "Historical Federal Court of Judge Isaac Charles Parker" for business.[6] The program for the occasion reflects a few speeches made by dignitaries and several religious and patriotic songs performed by the Fort Chaffee Army

Chorus, including "Oklahoma," "Soon Ah Will Be Done," "Battle Hymn of the Republic," "God Bless America," and "The Stars and Stripes Forever." There was no divided nation in the imagery being invoked at this event. Divisive Civil War history was traded in for that of a united nation amid the imminent Cold War communist threats of the 1950s.

The initial brochure advertising the tourist site features photographs of a young Judge Parker and the restored courtroom and gallows. Textual narrative is overlaid with watermarks of spurs, a pistol, and an Indian counting coup stick, traditionally used for touching but not harming one's enemy. One panel of the brochure is factually incorrect and then particularly candid on the contributions of the court. Under the heading "Law and Order Established" we are told that "as the trials went on through 21 years, as the gallows took its toll, the impact was felt on the lawless and they either retreated further west out of the jurisdiction of the court or, out of regard for the hard won authority of the law, checked their depredations." This account is among the first of the mythical exaggerations heaped upon Parker's court.

The narrative is framed by two line drawings. At the bottom is a stagecoach pulled by six horses with a silhouette of the driver waving as they pass a home. Above the text a portrait of nuclear-family domesticity is drawn as a husband, son, daughter, and wife walking hand in hand in front of their new home on the settled frontier. The text continues, "Thus law and order was established and the Indian Territory made safe. The lone traveler could traverse the land safely, the cattle could be driven north to the market without being preyed upon, the trail to the west was open for the pioneer, and the settler could homestead the land without fear to his family and possessions." The unvarnished truth is spoken; the objective of Judge Parker's court was to make Indian Territory safe for white economic practices and settlement.

The text of the brochure boasts, "The Indian Territory became the great state of Oklahoma in 1907, and it may safely be asserted that if it had not been for this great and unique court, its courageous judge, jurors, deputy marshals, and its gallows, that the mantle of statehood would have been much later in falling on this part of our country." Such direct claims to white privilege have since been softened to keeping the peace and taking civilization to the Five Nations.[7]

The Hanging Judge was fully ready to receive the tourists from the recreation era of the frontier complex who had been primed by Hollywood

westerns. The next step in developing it as a tourist destination and applying for National Park Service status was the removal of a squatter town
that had developed on top of the site of the original 1817 fort. Through
1958–1959 the Chamber of Commerce systematically negotiated with the
residents of Coke Hill, sometimes called West Fort Smith, to purchase
their land and remove them.[8] This process entailed othering the people
and the place of Coke Hill as questionable residents living in a dilapidated
slum. The removal was framed as urban renewal. Stories swirled of what
a horrendous place it was to live despite evidence that people led content
lives there and that if there was trouble, it was most often attributable to
outsiders such as soldiers stationed at Camp Chaffee.[9]

Photographs of the eviction of residents reveal the power of the gaze in
constructing otherness. R. K. Rodgers, chairman of the Coke Hill Clear-
ance Committee, can be seen in several photos from the time, but he does
not look at the camera.[10] Rodgers became very active in town politics after
making a fortune in the Fort Smith area in Checker cabs, a bus line, stock-
yards, coal, and natural gas.[11] Always wearing a pressed white shirt and a
tie, Rodgers stands in stark opposition to his bricolage surroundings, as out
of place and scrutinizing as Bronislaw Malinowski among the Trobriand
Islanders. In one picture, he stands before a home put together with clap-
board siding and other wood remnants; he is holding a jug at arm's length
as if it were a wild animal about to bite him. The image directs viewers to
look at how these "backward" people were living.

Another photo in front of a home shows a mother and her son. The
young boy stands next to his wagon, proudly smiling into the camera, with
his dog in his arms. Rodgers gazes scowlingly at the dog as if it were a
rabid varmint. The mother gazes straight into the camera in front of her
happy home, clothes drying on the line behind them, and a rocker and sofa
on an inviting front porch. In a different photo a man in overalls stands
with his hands squarely placed on his hips, elbows flared outward, looking
straight into the camera with a determined if not defiant gaze. Rodgers
stands poised, disarmed with his hands behind his back, staring directly
at the man, as if to declare this man here in overalls is the one standing in
the way of urban renewal. By early 1959 all the residents were gone, and an
amateur archaeology team led by Clyde Dollar revealed the foundation of
the 1817 fort. That discovery, coupled with the removal of the Coke Hill
"eyesore," paved the way for applying for National Park status.

President Kennedy signed that legislation on September 13, 1961; a month and a half later, on October 29, he had the deed to the property handed to him during a brief speech at the Fort Smith airport en route to a campaign event in Oklahoma. Kennedy is said to have responded, "I don't know exactly what part of Fort Smith this entitles me to, but I'm sure it's a good part."[12] The president had no idea then, nor do the people who visit the park know today, since the story of Coke Hill is not part of the interpretation.

The Fort Smith–based Public Historical Restorations transferred ownership of the Parker site to the National Park Service in an August 14, 1963, ceremony. The event was marked with a theatrical embodiment of the courtroom itself addressing the audience: "Nobody knows the trouble I've seen—and I mean it. Many, many people have come to me when they are in trouble—very serious trouble. Usually that trouble was Murder; Oh! I beg your pardon; I haven't introduced myself. I am Judge Isaac C. Parker's courtroom." At this key moment of Fort Smith frontier tourism the central mythic theme was invoked: "Judge Parker and I reigned undisputed in Fort Smith over the area from the Arkansas River on the east to Colorado on the west. For 16 years the Supreme Court of the United States could not intervene. I have seen the most desperate outlaws of the West tried."[13] Between May 26, 1957, and August 14, 1963, the period in which the site was locally operated, 61,985 people visited it.[14] In other words, the initial wager on frontier tourism resulted in an average of ten thousand visitors per year. Lady Bird Johnson dedicated the site as a national park with a speech on October 27, 1964.

What is important to note here is that Fort Smith officials had the gallows burned down in 1897; the first fort had been completely abandoned and its location largely forgotten until a later generation of city leaders had to justify moving a small town of 250 inhabitants in order to find it again. The Fort Smith of 1955 was neither a "western" town nor a "frontier" town. Just as Dodge City, Deadwood, and Tombstone had done in the 1920s, Fort Smith had to exhume its past in order to breathe tourist life into it.[15] Once the skeletal remains of its nineteenth-century history had been unearthed, the archetypal mythic images of the Wild West that were flourishing in the popular media of the 1950s could be readily fleshed out to constitute and perform the frontier complex.

This particular performance of the frontier was designed with a very specific audience in mind—tourists. As such, what is constituted is created for the biggest possible draw, not the most historically accurate. The steps that Fort Smith leaders took in this constituting of the frontier complex can be found in primary sources left behind from the process. Newspaper articles, photos, and handwritten notes in the Paul Wolfe archives provide a record of performing the frontier complex into existence between 1954 and 1964.

The performance consists in part of the repetition of key mythical elements of the frontier military fort and the Parker court. They repeat the same inaccuracies and platitudes found in Samuel W. Harman's 1898 *Hell on the Border* and what Homer Croy reworked from that source for his 1952 book. Statements including the exaggerated jurisdiction of "74,000 square miles," of "keeping the peace between the Indians," of "lawless Indian Territory," of "Parker never hanged a man, it was the law," and of "88 men hanged on the gallows" are restated over and over in the articles and speeches from this formative decade. This repetitive rhetorical pattern is a key aspect of a performance that is not conveying historical facts but rather constituting the mythical frontier complex as a cultural fact.

Note cards from the Wolfe Collection outline a sales pitch given to the audience about the development of the National Historic Site. Images from 1950s TV and film westerns are dramatically invoked as Judge Wolfe declares, "This important event is worth telling—and because it pertains to Indians, the Wild West and outlaws, the young people may enjoy it too. (Don't we all)." By 1964, the Wild West enjoyed by all was one fabricated for movies based on mythic fabrications from the late nineteenth century. What was being sold to tourists was a spirit or a mood, a frontier ethos, not a tangible commodity. Rothman suggests of pitching tourism, "The exchange is more complicated and ambiguous than a typical material sales transaction. A feeling is transmitted and perhaps shared; a way of living is expressed. A mode of behavior, be it the ethos of skiing, the appreciation of the Mona Lisa, or the way to hold your cards at the Blackjack table, is offered and recognized if not always understood."[16] The feeling of the Wild West was thus being embedded onto the Fort Smith frontier complex through an oral performance given to civic groups.

The handwritten note cards end the speech with a new identity for the city: "We folks here in F. S. may not have a pedigree—but we have a historical heritage to which we can point with pride to the entire nation." The underscored words in the notes connect the self-consciousness of a New South under siege with civil rights protests taking refuge and a new pride in the imagined myth of the Old West. Another set of handwritten notes for a public speech end with "Pride in not letting past go to waste, <u>PRIDE OF ANCESTRY</u>. Tourist attraction of 1st magnitude. (History first). A reason to stop over in Ft. S."[17] This is not a simple description of the historical past; it is a performance of frontier tourism that was crafting a new identity for the city while turning its past into a commodity so as to not waste it.

This new identity and commoditized past came with a price. What Fort Smith residents waded into was a devil's bargain, in Rothman's terms, in that "the embrace of tourism triggers a contest for the soul of a place" and that "in this new form of exchange, an entity meaningful but intangible, typically the identity, way of life, or feel of a place and its people seems to be offered up for a price."[18] Whether this bargain was worth the price became an open though seldom asked question in Fort Smith. The next significant shift in frontier tourism came twenty-eight years later.

Constructing "Miss Laura"

In 1992, the former Riverfront Commercial Hotel became the official visitor's center for Fort Smith and rebranded as Miss Laura's Social Club. In the performance of frontier tourism, the old hotel's Victorian era style is repeatedly emphasized in all printed materials, tours, and references to Miss Laura's. This is a performative act that conjures the nineteenth century ethos for contemporary frontier tourism in Fort Smith. This construction is sustained by volunteers and employees dressing in elaborate and colorful dresses reminiscent of Hollywood film depictions of late nineteenth-century prostitutes, only more flamboyant than even Miss Kitty's best on *Gunsmoke*. This tourist model of the frontier itself becomes a cultural fact while it perpetuates the myth that prostitution in Fort Smith was relegated to the nineteenth century. At Miss Laura's Social Club, we can see a seamless fusion of elements for performing frontier tourism.

As tour and travel sales director of the Fort Smith Convention and Visitors Bureau, Carolyn Joyce created the persona of Miss Laura in 1992 to "promote Fort Smith to motorcoach groups." *Group Tour Magazine*, an industry publication, has dubbed her the city's "first lady of tourism" and describes how "in the role of Miss Laura and dressed in a costume true to the frontier period, Joyce welcomes tour groups and keeps alive part of Fort Smith's colorful history."[19] Asked about the inspiration for Miss Laura, Joyce replies, "To entice motorcoaches off the interstate I decided I would create the character of Miss Laura as a marketing tool. So I would tell the operators at the different marketplaces that if they would bring

Figure 7.1. One of "Miss Laura's girls" welcoming a customer into her room. A portrait of Carolyn Joyce as Miss Laura hangs on the wall. Photo by the author.

their motorcoaches into Fort Smith, I would be in costume to greet their group, give the tour and make it a fun stop for them."[20] The ills of nineteenth-century prostitution are thus constituted as fun and a pleasure in the performance of frontier tourism.

Carolyn Joyce quickly realized that to keep the tour buses in town, more entertainment had to be provided. All the offerings at the National Historic Site and the Fort Smith Museum of History was apparently insufficient for tourist desires to stay in town, so Joyce developed a musical, "The Medicine Show on Hangin' Day," to be performed by Miss Laura's Players.

The show is described in 2NJOY magazine as "a musical comedy exaggerating the public draw that Judge Parker's hangings had on the area. Back then people would come by wagon from miles around to see the hanging, often bring their dinner with them. In the play, Miss Laura brings two or three girls to the public gathering and entertains along with a Huckster hawking his elixir assured to cure most any ailment a body might have."[21] Which part of that description is the exaggeration can be hard to discern. The part that appears most stated as fact, of people coming to town for hanging day, is as exaggerated as the other elements. In fact, the erection of the walled fence around the gallows and the intentional scheduling of hangings on weekdays all cut down the fanfare in the 1870s.

When asked for *Group Tour Magazine* why Miss Laura's show is so popular, Joyce replies, "It's that wild west flair. And of course, we have so much western heritage in our area. When you crossed the river behind Miss Laura's, you were in Indian Territory. The lawless of all of that. Fort Smith has such a rich western heritage along with Judge Isaac Parker and everything we have encased in our national historic site. And of course this was part of the red-light district. It was part of our history."[22] While these quotations from Carolyn Joyce are essentially infomercials, as they appear in tour and travel literature, they illustrate how Fort Smith performs the frontier myth for tourism by repeating formulaic elements that inextricably conflate fiction and historical fact. In the above quote, Joyce hits these performative marks as her comments travel from "Wild West," "western heritage," and "lawless," to "Judge Parker," "historic site," and "history."

Bus tours to Fort Smith are advertised on the Group Travel Leader website with the frontier complex featured in a "Hats, Boots, and Spurs" themed package that takes in Dodge City, Oklahoma City, Fort Smith, and Branson. The article "Fort Smith: Scoundrels Welcome" pitches the tour stop to tourists by declaring, "You might think that a town would shy away from a rough past that included murderers and other assorted lawbreakers, the Trail of Tears, a notorious jail dubbed 'Hell on the Border,' a judge known as the 'hanging judge,' a gallows where more than 80 men were hanged, 66 saloons on the town's main street and seven houses of ill repute."[23] The tourist is invited to an attitude, a persona, and an ethos, to become a "scoundrel" and walk where those earlier figures walked.

Some individuals employed in the Fort Smith frontier complex who are aware of the greater complexity and subtlety of the site often voiced their frustration to me at being hamstrung in their presentations by the tourist pitch that visitors have come to expect. They bemoaned the tourist emphasis on the Hanging Judge and more recently what they saw as the exaggerated claims and enthusiasm about Bass Reeves. Todd Barnes, one of the park rangers, one day insisted on showing me the Arkansas travel map that labeled the Fort Smith National Historic Site not as such but rather as "Judge Parker's Court." The complexity the site has to offer is attenuated into commercial sound bites. The short time visitors spend at the site confounds efforts to convey more nuanced interpretations.

At the end of tours of Miss Laura's, the final performance of frontier tourism takes place at the miniature gallows where hanging little gingerbread-like men are reduced to tourist fun. An example of this act can be viewed in a very brief YouTube video entitled "Fort Smith 'Hangin' Judge' Gallows Demonstration."[24] A young woman is preparing to pull the lever when another woman, off camera and presumably the videographer, inquires as to why people were hanged in the past. A man's voice off camera answers, "Killers, horse thieves, really anything." The woman on screen fills in, "So, stealing, thieves?" With that factually incorrect description, she pulls the lever, the gingerbread men Weeble-Wobble, the off-camera woman declares, "Hooray," and the executioner smiles for the camera. Performing executions is not about justice; it is about constituting Fort Smith's frontier ethos that can be consumed by people of all ages.

Long Gallows Shadow

Fort Smith is not without a critical audience. One of the most hypnotic displays of the "Hanging Judge" mantra is an exhibit of artifacts and illustrations at the Fort Smith Museum of History that originally called out the question of performing the frontier for tourism. *In the Shadow of the Gallows* was constructed and put on display at the museum in 1998.[25] It was on display for three years before being taken down and was then reinstalled as an exhibit in 2009 in a slightly different manner than the original. While this exhibit was a direct attempt at critiquing the use of gallows, nooses, and the Hanging Judge theme for tourism, I argue that in its strenuous effort to debunk the frontier tourism performance, it actually performs it better than anything else. Throughout the small exhibit are no fewer representations than forty nooses and thirty gallows.

The exhibit is on the second floor of the museum. Upon stepping off the elevator, visitors are greeted by an easel holding an exhibit placard for *In the Shadow of the Gallows*. An image of a noose artfully frames the title

Figure 7.2. Judge Parker's birthday cake. The occasion is celebrated at the Fort Smith Museum of History, where the noose motif is associated with his face even on the cake. Photo by the author.

as if it were a corsage. A whiskey barrel and bottle are the first material artifacts on display, but they have no explanation as to the role they play in the exhibit. Next to the barrel is an enclosed case that features a small doll of Parker standing in a coffee cup that also bears his likeness. A similar doll figure of Belle Starr, once convicted of horse theft by Parker, accompanies him in the cabinet, which is lined with postcards featuring a photo of the replica gallows and other memorabilia not from Parker's era, but from the tourist kitsch used by Fort Smith to market memories of him.

The first placard to frame the exhibit asks the question "What do dolls, t-shirts, metal badges, postcards, and mugs have in common? All have been used to popularize Fort Smith's modern image as a 'Wild West' tourist destination. Such memorabilia highlights the transformation of the city's historic past into a part of its present commercial life." This initial placard encapsulates the central paradox of the mythic frontier in Fort Smith. The frontier complex simultaneously purports to be historically accurate and a contrived marketing scheme. Next to this cabinet is a T-shirt that has an image of a noose dangling between the words "Fort" and "Smith."

The exhibit interprets the item by explaining that "many of these items feature the noose or gallows. Why? Because it is *this* story—the story of 86 men executed by the U.S. Court in Fort Smith for crimes committed in Indian Territory—that people come here to see." The italics of "*this*" reveals it is not "this story," as in the record of the nineteenth-century history of the U.S. District Court for the Western District of Arkansas, 1851–1896, that people have come to see. Rather, it is "*this* story," the story of the touristic Wild West frontier that has been exaggerated and fabricated into grandiose, legendary, and mythic proportions since 1955 and that this exhibit in front of them is embodying for the visitors. This is the story of performing the Wild West frontier for tourists in the recreation and redoubling eras of the frontier complex, from 1920 to the present.

Leaving no room for doubt, the exhibit drives home this point in a placard entitled "Never Forgotten." It reads in part, "Sixty years after Fort Smith burned the gallows, however, the city reopened a new one in 1957 as part of the restored Parker courtroom. The story that emerged as a tourist draw was not quite the same history that nineteenth century residents of Fort Smith experienced firsthand. This exhibit is about both stories." On one hand, *In the Shadow of the Gallows* directly reveals the contrived nature of how Fort Smith and the Parker court are remembered. Quite pointedly, it declares that "ever since Judge Parker's court was restored in the 1950's people have been coming to Fort Smith in search of the 'Wild West.' Attracted today by images of stagecoaches, guns, badges, and handcuffs, tourists explore Parker's courtroom, watch a 'Medicine Show on Hanging Day,' or stop at a visitor's center named after a notorious frontier madam."

In the very same moment the exhibit displays Fort Smith's actual frontier past, it becomes complicit in the heist of historical facts for tourism; the exhibit's very existence constitutes that which it apparently is intended to question. Or in the words Larry McMurtry put into Buffalo Bill Cody's mouth in speaking to Wyatt Earp and Doc Holliday before their first Wild West performance, "A show had to be real and yet not real at the same time."[26]

By the end of the exhibit, gallows and hangings are reduced to entertainment and children's playthings. In one display cabinet, a wooden picnic basket sits with a rope coming out of it ending in a hangman's knot and noose.[27] There is no explanation of these items. Nor are they contextualized in relation to facts previously stated in the exhibit that measures were consistently taken to reduce the amount of fanfare and public picnic atmosphere, such as a wall being erected to conceal the gallows and scheduling weekday hangings instead of weekend events that made it harder for people to attend. Once again the exhibit plays the gibbet both ways, saying "there was" and "there was not" a festive atmosphere at hangings.

Among the thirty representations of gallows including photographs and illustrations are two miniature gallows on display in the exhibit. One of them is presented as a carved piece of art made in 1984 entitled "Hanging Around." It is introduced as a "whimsical version of the gallows story." This small gallows accommodates two people to be hanged at a time, but in this depiction, only one person has been hanged. The victim has fallen, his body dangling halfway through the trap, black hood over his head with a contourless face, his arms bound around his waist, and his hands clutching at the air. The hangman stands with another noose in his left hand. Tall and thin, wearing a broad-brimmed hat that casts a shadow over his bug-eyed stare, with a beaked nose and thick moustache, he looks at the visitor as if to say, "Watch it, buddy, or you'll be next." This mini-gallows sits atop the donation box. One can see dollar bills lining the glass case below the gallows and a sign that reads "Donations Are Greatly Appreciated." The proximity of a pretend hanging to a request for money to keep the tourist attraction in operation reveals their intimate relation.

The other miniature gallows in the exhibit is encased in a Plexiglas box that is complemented with a copy of Samuel Harman's book (Harman's name is repeatedly misspelled "Harmon" throughout the exhibit)—*Hell on the Border*—with the textual heading of "The Story Lives On." This gallows stands about a foot and a half tall and wide. Five unpainted wood-block figures are hanging through the trap door at varying heights. Some dangle midway through the trap, while others' heads are barely visible, eternally hanging for their crimes. This same miniature gallows can be seen in an undated black-and-white photo pinned next to some other pictures in the exhibit. It comes with no explanation at all.

In the photograph, this gallows has been arranged as if someone had been playing house with it. A set of stairs adjoins the scaffold, and a cardboard backdrop is made to look like the old brick wall of the fort, with a painting of a tree and the sky beyond the view of the wall. The old photo has an entire cast of characters on the gallows. Six people stand as one figure has been hanged. These are not wooden blocks but little lifelike dolls. One is clearly clergy, while others wear suits but have no discernible designation of office. The victim hangs a bit off kilter, with torso and head above the trap door, appearing almost mistakenly lodged midway through the execution.

Near the end of the exhibit, a placard asks "Why Rebuild the Gallows?" and then provides some possible answers such as these: "The image of the 'Hanging Judge' (a term rarely used in Parker's lifetime) made it difficult to separate the man from the punishment"; "The hangings attracted the general public to the story. It was *this* Fort Smith story that fit with the pop-culture 'Wild West' of the 1950s"; and "The character of the 'Hanging Judge'—one man bringing law to a 'lawless frontier' by way of the gallows—was a variation of an enduring western myth." Over and over this exhibit simultaneously deconstructs and creates the frontier mythos and accompanying ethos, featuring Judge Parker as the principal architect.

Within a year of Parker's death, the gallows were considered an embarrassing eyesore by the city and burned down. The *In The Shadow of the Gallows* exhibit includes an 1897 newspaper epitaph: "Fare thee well old Gallows! Whether thou hast been a necessity . . . or a lingering relic of darkness . . . remains to be decided." No longer having jurisdiction in any part of Indian Territory, the U.S. District Court for the Western District of Arkansas proceeded to conduct business in Fort Smith, but its proverbial bridge to the frontier had, quite literally, been burned.

Today it is difficult to miss the life-size replica gallows at the National Historic Site. Gallows are seen throughout the complex: the working miniature set at Miss Laura's and three other miniature but nonfunctioning gallows at the Fort Smith Museum of History. The Old Fort Gun Club also has a full-size gallows at its shooting range on the east side of town. When I inquired for what purpose the gun club needed a replica gallows, I was just stared at as if the answer should be self-evident. It was not, but I will now suggest that the omnipresence of gallows throughout Fort Smith is the principal method by which the politics of mythic frontier justice is performed and constituted. "Hanging Judge, Hanging Judge, Hanging Judge" must be repeated to sustain the illusion of justice throughout the frontier complex.

H. Bruce Franklin, in *Vietnam and Other American Fantasies*, describes this process as the "plausibility of denial," that is, continuing to believe "something is not true or does not exist despite convincing evidence to the contrary."[28] It functions as a cover-up, as an alibi. In this case, the repetition of "Hanging Judge" creates the plausibility of denial that the military fort was not put there as one small part of a systematic strategy for the nation to

advance across the continent, that Judge Parker did not methodically contribute to injustices in the territories, or that the frontier had not been for
the advancement of white male civilization. No, the performance of frontier justice persuasively maintains it was there to keep the peace between
and take law and order to the Indians. This is why nooses must swing back
and forth, back and forth, throughout the frontier complex.

True Grit Brand

In the Fort Smith Museum of History, a *True West Magazine* cover from
April 2011 depicting side by side the two Rooster Cogburns—Jeff Bridges
and John Wayne—has been blown up to movie-poster size and is pinned
below a display featuring one of the miniature gallows. Just a few feet from
this case is a life-size cardboard cutout of John Wayne as Rooster Cogburn
in the 1969 film. Another nearby placard indicates that the museum gave
pictures of nineteenth-century Fort Smith to Ethan and Joel Coen's set
team for the design of Fort Smith in their 2010 remake of the film. While
the story of *True Grit* is fictional, the museum boasts a factual, literal connection to it that entirely confuses the matter. The net result of this col-
lage is a hopeless conflation of fact and fiction inextricably bound with one
another. The curators' seeming assumption that facts will prevail once the
myth lures visitors to the site is wishful thinking.

The novel *True Grit* blends historical people and places with fictional
characters. In the first chapter, the made-up Deputy Marshal Rooster Cogburn is called to the stand to testify in a case in which he was involved
before the real Judge Parker. After inquiring for a deputy possessing "grit,"
the young Mattie Ross hires Cogburn to avenge the death of her father,
who was killed in the streets of Fort Smith at the hands of criminal Tom
Chaney. Joined by Texas Ranger LaBoeuf, the trio disembarks from Fort
Smith and crosses the Arkansas River into Indian Territory to track down
the killer. In other words, the frontier complex is the real-life stage setting for an imaginary story to play out, which it does in numerous ways.
I am told by my consultants at the National Historic Site that visitors
frequently claim ancestry to the fictional characters created by the novel's
author, Charles Portis. They say they are descended from LaBoeuf, from
Mattie Ross, or from Rooster Cogburn himself. Indeed, Brett Cogburn
asserts himself as the great-grandson of Rooster Cogburn from the novel
in his own book, *Rooster: The Life and Times of the Real Rooster Cogburn,
the Man Who Inspired* True Grit.

Figure 7.3. Movie posters at the National Historic Site. "Fort Smith in Fact and Fiction" is a theme at the theater where the site's orientation video is shown. Photo by the author.

Charles Portis has offered some counterpoints to the way his novel is performed in the frontier complex. He was extended an invitation to attend the grand reopening of the National Historic Site in 2000 after extensive renovations were made following the 1996 tornado. In lieu of attending, Portis replied in a letter to park Superintendent Bill Black.[29] A few important observations can be gleaned from this exchange. On the issue of fictive kinship, Portis unequivocally states, "No, Rooster Cogburn wasn't based on a specific person . . . he was just a representative figure of those hardy deputy marshals who worked for Judge Parker's court." A park ranger from the National Historic Site walked this letter over to Brett Cogburn on the day he was signing copies of his book at the Fort Smith Museum of History.

When presented with counterfactual evidence to his claim, he simply replied that he was descended from Rooster Cogburn and that he was not going to discuss it further. When I and others interviewed Brett Cogburn to get some information on this topic, he deployed various tactics of distraction and evasion that ultimately deterred the requests. He not so skillfully avoided answering the question while simultaneously received press and attention that further constituted the frontier complex as a place where fact and fiction reside side by side, often indistinguishably.

The city of Fort Smith readily embraced the news that Ethan and Joel Coen were releasing a remake of *True Grit* in December 2010. Two of the festivities were "True Gritapalooza," sponsored by the Fort Smith Convention and Visitors Bureau, and "Roosters by the Dozen," held at the National Historic Site on the eve of the film's debut. According to the event's Facebook announcement, the goal was to set a "world record for the most Rooster Cogburns in one place, and the only Rooster Cogburns at the actual site where True Grit would have occurred!"[30] Deputy badges and eyepatches were provided for all those who attended. The crowd, said to be more than five hundred, gathered in front of the replica gallows.

Through a bullhorn, mayor-elect Sandy Sanders read the lines of outlaw Lucky Ned Pepper to the assembled Roosters: "What's your intention? Do you think one on four is a dogfall?"[31] The Roosters replied, "I mean to kill you in one minute, Ned. Or see you hanged in Fort Smith at Judge Parker's convenience. Which will you have?" Ned Pepper responded, "I call that bold talk for a one-eyed fat man." Hundreds of Roosters responded in unison, "Fill your hand, you son of a bitch!"[32] This performance of mythic-fictional characters at "the actual site where True Grit would have occurred" with the backdrop of the replica gallows where Judge Parker would have sentenced Ned Pepper to be hanged continues the conflation between fact and fiction and once again constitutes the frontier complex in performance.

The academic year of the film's release, 2010–2011, the University of Arkansas–Fort Smith (UAFS) featured Portis' novel in the "Read This!" program, which required several freshman English II students to read it in the fall and spring semesters. Following that program, in September 2011 a group of English students, alumni, and professors from UAFS participated in the fiftieth-anniversary celebration at the National Historic Site by performing a dramatic reading of a scene from the novel in the replica of Judge Parker's courtroom. Professors played the roles of Cogburn, Parker, and the prosecuting attorney, while students and alumni rounded out the cast. Again the frontier complex is constituted by performing fiction in a facsimile of the place in which it supposedly happened.

In Fort Smith it has been hotly debated: Who was the real character with "true grit"? Was it Rooster Cogburn? Was it the Texas Ranger, La-Boeuf? This question carries over to actual deputies from the Parker court era. Was it Bass Reeves, or was it Bill Tilghman? Was it Chris Madsen, or was it Heck Thomas? For a program produced by the Smithsonian Channel, *The Real Story: The Facts behind the Fiction*, a crew came to Fort Smith to film an episode on this very question. The producers hired local reenactors to play various roles, and the film asked if it was Deputy Reeves or Madsen or Thomas who had true grit. There was great excitement and stir about the film. I was told by one of the reenactors, "When they said 'action' I was in the zone, I was right there, back in that time. I was hooked and told 'em I wanted more if they needed me for anything." This episode of *The Real Story* was widely referred to as a documentary by those in the frontier complex, but it resembles more of a reality show of the past.

When *The Real Story* episode aired, few of the local people who had been involved actually saw it.[33] Full of quick camera work that seldom focuses on one shot for very long, it does not answer the "Who had grit?" question in the end. The heavily edited show gave most of the local reenactors mere fractions of seconds on the screen, with one exception. A young man who portrayed a deputy for the show has his same short scenes repeated several times throughout the program. While he is playing a role of law enforcement, he is made to look like a cold-blooded murderer. One day as we discussed the veracity of the episode, he exasperatedly said, "They have it looking like I walk up behind this guy along a riverbank, shoot him in the back, and then hightail it out of there on my horse! They make me look like I'm the bad guy!"

The TV episode spurred speculation in the frontier complex over which deputy had more grit than the others. One alternative answer to this question is seldom suggested, but Charles Portis gives a clue to it in his letter to the park superintendent. Portis says of Mattie Ross that "she shows herself, unconsciously, perhaps, to be just as hard in her own way as these hard customers she disapproves of, and has to deal with." Though seldom in contention in the greatest-grit contest, Mattie Ross clearly demonstrates it. The highly gendered framework in the frontier complex disqualifies her from such consideration. In contrast, English department faculty report that in a classroom context many UAFS students concluded the true-grit award went to Mattie Ross.

A final element from *True Grit* to note is how many reenactors in the frontier complex use it as a template of their anti–government interference attitudes. The setting of the novel in the lawless Indian Territory is a place where government bureaucracy has yet to tread, where justice can prevail unfettered by the oversight of the Supreme Court, rule of law, or due process. Rooster Cogburn expresses his disconcertment with how the machinations of a bureaucratic, rational-legal system permits guilty men to go free. Cogburn says to Mattie Ross, "You can't serve papers on a rat, baby sister.... These shitepoke lawyers think you can but you can't. All you can do with a rat is kill him or let him be. They don't care nothing about papers."[34]

Cogburn's disdain for bureaucracy as well as John Wayne's abhorrence of big government come through again in the film when the character says to Mattie Ross: "Your Government marshals don't have time to be paying a lot of social calls. They are too busy trying to follow all the regulations laid down by Uncle Sam. That gentleman will have his fee sheets just and correct or he does not pay."[35] Cogburn's position exemplifies the frontier in the attic attitude of operating above the law, of opposing bureaucracy and government regulation. This stance is appealing to many frontier-complex reenactors who hold similar political views. In Judge Parker's staunch opposition to Supreme Court oversight of his court, he was down on those bureaucratic, regulatory rats, too.

It is Cogburn's association with the guerrilla-warfare Confederates William Quantrill and Bloody Bill Anderson who patrolled the Missouri-Kansas border that most excites the imaginations of reenactors who disdain government interference. In the novel, the local horse trader says, "Report has it that he [Cogburn] rode by the light of the moon with Quantrill and Bloody Bill Anderson. I would not trust him too much. I have heard too that he was *particeps criminis* in some road-agent work before he came here and attached himself to the courtroom."[36] By that simple reference, Cogburn carries a heightened antigovernment persona. Many local reenactors frequently drop the name Quantrill here and there in conspicuous ways. In the early months of my observations of their shootouts and interactions with them between shootouts, I would hear this name dropped, but I felt like I was missing something. Even after developing basic knowledge of who Quantrill was and what he did, I still felt a bit lost.

It was not until it occurred to me that the use of his name was part of the script in the frontier performance that it made sense to me. "Quantrill" is a trope; it does not refer to the person who led the historical paramilitary group against the Union, but rather in one short name it evokes an entire attitude and persona of defying government. I have found that the majority of members of frontier reenactment groups in Fort Smith hold conservative political views. In addition to conversations and comments that I have recorded, their postings on their Facebook pages of tea party material, of staunch gun rights, and so forth reveal their opposition to government interference. By aligning themselves with Rooster Cogburn and by intimating a connection to Quantrill, they take refuge in the frontier attic as they perform their political ideologies.

The frontier attic is thus a place of refuge in the current redoubling era of the frontier complex from the neoliberal economic policies, the deindustrialization of the American economy, and the no-holds-barred globalization of commerce that have harmed many working-class and middle-class American families. The perceived and felt challenge to one's social status can be defended with pride of heritage on the performative stage of the frontier complex.

Reenacting Frontier Heritage

In the Fort Smith frontier complex, there is a wide variety of reenactors and reenactment groups who purport to dress in period clothing to represent a part of life as it was in the late nineteenth century. Without exception, each group claims to be keeping history alive, and each group's name reflects its dispositions. Among these are the Lawbreakers and Peacemakers, Sons and Daughters of the Old West, Indian Territory Pistoliers, Clayton House Players, and Bass Reeves Troupe of Muskogee. Apart from these groups, Baridi Nkokheli portrays Bass Reeves as a stand-alone character, but in third person. His performance focuses on providing the history of Reeves rather than reenacting him.

The National Historic Site also conducts a Night Court quarterly in which specific court transcripts from Judge Parker's era are studied and then performed in period clothes and first-person dramatizations in the replica courtroom for a paying audience. After performing for eighteen years together, Miss Laura's Players performed their last show in December

2012. Carolyn Joyce continues to portray Miss Laura on occasion, and some of the volunteers at the visitor center dress in period clothing. Volunteers at the National Historic Site, too, can frequently be seen in costume. Many other reenactment groups use the grounds of the National Historic Site but are outside the frontier period of history and imagination on which I focus. Here I analyze just the reenactment groups who portray some aspect of the frontier era closely tied to Judge Parker's tenure of 1875 to 1896.

I spent many hours during three years conducting fieldwork among these reenactment groups. Here I use pseudonyms for all individuals and groups where distinction in a group is not key to the interpretation. I consolidate the data under the heading of the Wild West Shooters group name to make the description as anonymous as possible. Pseudonyms that reflect personas are challenging with these subjects, as most of the classic western names are already in use by the reenactors. One characteristic about which all of the frontier reenactment groups agree is that they are keeping the frontier past alive. In some way, members of all groups report feeling that what they are doing constitutes some aspect of life as it actually was back then. Conversely, it is my contention that the groups are instead constituting the frontier complex today. We will now examine a few skits that are typical of those presented in Fort Smith. The skits range from deputies chasing horse thieves to bank robberies to town drunks shooting guns all about town. Some skits are meant to amuse, while others end with carnage.

The Wild West Shooters perform at nearly all the local heritage festivals and at key historical sites and museums for special occasions. An often-repeated skit is the gag marksman bit featuring the legendary marksman Kit Carson. The skit begins when Wyatt Earp and Kit Carson stand about thirty yards away from a cluster of six other reenactors at the far other end of the street. One of the six is holding an inflated red balloon. The gag of the skit is that Kit Carson will demonstrate his prowess with firearms by using a mirror to shoot backward and pop the red balloon. This eventually happens, but not until two or three bystanders are wounded or killed and the man holding the balloon is hit several times.

Wyatt Earp uses a bullhorn to set up the skit for the audience and warns the crowd to move to the edges of the street. He announces, "Kit Carson has generously agreed to do a demonstration of his shooting prowess. Now, what Kit will do—can I have someone down there show the balloon? As you can see there is a man down there with a balloon." As directions are being given, a flurry of people suddenly scamper through the middle of

the skit, momentarily distracting the reenactors as they let down the balloon. Wyatt advises, "Back up, down there with the balloon, please." Carson
booms over the bullhorn, "Get out of the street!" to the spectators still encroaching on the stage. "That's good, that's good," say Wyatt and Kit. Earp
then says, "Now Kit, I have a mirror in my pocket, and if you will, will you
use the mirror?" In a very stern voice, Kit responds, "Yes I will, I will use the
mirror." Wyatt reaches into his duster for the mirror, which is about eight
inches in diameter, and he shouts, "All right, Kit has generously agreed to
use the mirror." Carson declares, "This is going to make it pretty difficult,
but I'm going to try to do it anyway."

"Kit is ready! Can I have the first holder of the balloon?" Wyatt gives
away what is about to happen when he says "first holder," but the audience
isn't meant to understand that at this point. Kit draws his pistol out and
gives a strong look down the street at the balloon holder, then turns his
back to him, holds the mirror up, places his gun over his left shoulder, and
takes aim at the balloon. "Hold up the balloon, we should only have one
shot here, ladies and gentlemen. This is the great Kit Carson," Wyatt says to
the crowd over the bullhorn. Kit takes aim and fires. There is a thunderous
blast, and smoke shoots from his pistol. He rocks back on his heels, then
spins around to survey the results. "You missed!" come the hollered-back
responses. He not only missed the balloon, but he also downed a bystander.

Why six men stand close together near the one holding the balloon is a
good question. Presumably they all have great confidence in the firing accuracy of Kit Carson and do not feel the need to move out of harm's way. The
men all holler back, "You missed, you missed. You hit 'im," as they point to
the man who has fallen dead to the ground. Wyatt Earp hollers back, "OK,
then hold the balloon farther to the right." They continue with the shootout
demonstration. The slowly developing joke is that Kit hits everything but
the balloon. The attempted humor generally falls flat or is lost altogether
on the perhaps wary and weary crowd.

"Second shot coming up," announces Wyatt. Carson again turns his
back and takes a broad stance, holding the mirror up again with his left
hand. He takes aim with his right hand as he reaches back over his left
shoulder. As he is taking aim, the men down by the balloon give him aim-
ing directions. "A little to the left," they yell, and "A little bit lower!" Carson
fires, and this time a man who was about ten feet away is hit and collapses
backward to the ground. Wyatt Earp yells, "A little more to the right, Kit."
This punch line garners one loud guffaw from the audience. "He's gone,

Kit!" the men yell, pointing to yet another corpse that has fallen victim to Kit's bad aim. Two minutes into the skit, two men are lying dead on the ground, legs splayed, hats placed over their faces. Few in the audience are laughing, but the skit marshals forward with Kit Carson now given even more direction on where to aim—not to stop, but to continue with the accidental murdering.

On the third shot, two men who were standing about eight feet apart fall down. They have not rehearsed, and the cue of which one is supposed to be the victim has gone awry. Wyatt Earp ad-libs, "You hit two of 'em, Kit! Well, that was a fantastic shot, Kit." I laugh heartily under my breath, but I hear not even a chuckle from the rest of the crowd. I think to myself, "Is nobody paying attention?" I search the faces in the crowd of about thirty for some clues but only find blank expressions. Back on the street, Carson is preparing for his fourth attempt.

A reenactor portraying the Frisco Kid has now taken the balloon as the original holder is dead on the ground. Frisco crouches low, reaching his hand with the balloon as high as he can go. "Easy now, Kit, he yells," wincing in concern over what fate awaits him. The shot is fired, and the Frisco Kid is hit in the left leg. He takes a knee, hollering that he's been shot. He reaches into a pocket and removes a planted prop. Frisco takes a white handkerchief that had been prepared with a fake blood stain to make the gunshot wound come to life. Kit hollers, "What's the matter?" at Frisco as if to say he's being a wimp for not sticking in there with the shooting demonstration.

They do the same routine until on the fifth attempt the balloon is punctured to create the illusion that it's been struck. There is virtually no crowd response. Kit Carson fires four more rounds into the air and then takes what seems an interminable length of time painfully prolonging the anguished conclusion to the skit. He then declares, "I'm Kit Carson, pistolier extraordinaire!" The final punch line signals a relief to the crowd, who had been maintaining a basic level of politeness throughout. They now take their cue and depart.

The emcee of the festival gets on the public address system and says, "Thank you so much for being here." Then with what seems like a wish that by repeating something over and over one can make it come true, she says to the reenactors, "We really, really, really, really, enjoyed your presentation." A few hours after the shootout, Bat Masterson, one of the reenactors, came up to me and asked, "How did that come off?" There was a hint of wonderment, perhaps even embarrassment in his voice. The shootout skit had not gone well; very few people laughed, and there was little response from the audience. I pointed out to Bat that "the weather put a damper on the event, and the football game interfered too." He took solace in that as he squinted off into the horizon as if looking for other clues.

Before and after the skits, there is occasionally some mingling of the re-enactors with the crowd, but more often the reenactors retreat to their enclave and visit among themselves. Surprisingly, they are not overly friendly or interactive with the crowds whom they are ostensibly there to entertain. Some picture taking and posing with the deputies goes on between skits, but most of the time the performers and audience are mutually stand-offish. Audiences do not demand more performance. It is more accurate to say the reenactors demand the attention of the audience. People do not intentionally drive to see these skits; rather, the performances are imposed on people already there.

Members of these reenactment groups say they are doing the performances to keep history alive because they love the past or wish they could have lived back then. They have all invested hundreds and some thousands of dollars in what they consider period-correct weapons and clothes. The considerable time, money, and energy expended for these performances raises the important question, For what? For a small number of adults to perform a vignette not up to the standards of the smallest of community theaters? While the balloon skit is done for fun, it begs the question of what the objective is, as it is preposterous to think this in any way, shape, or form resembles nineteenth-century life.

In all the reenactment groups I observed, I was told at some point, in various terms, "You know, what we do isn't *really* accurate. Back in the day someone would have just come up and shot someone in the back. It would have taken thirty seconds. That's not entertaining." Performance of frontier tourism is simultaneously contrived and considered historically accurate. As one skit was being set up, the audience was told, "We are here today to entertain you with the 'Old West', fictitious of course, but what the heck?"

"Fire in the hole!" yells Bloody Bill Anderson as he fires his double-barrel 12-gauge shotgun into the air. After the shot, he opens the gun and blows through the barrel to force smoke out the end. He tells me later, "Yeah, every time I shoot the shotgun the people just go 'ooh, ooh.' They love it, and then I do the thing where I open it up and I blow the smoke out of the end of the barrel, they love that." He cracks a wide grin and cocks his head in self-congratulatory adulation as he declares, "Theatrics!" This skit is tacitly rooted in a story about a gang of outlaws who have escaped from Fort Smith and are being tracked by a deputy and his posse. It does not reference a specific historical case.

The skit begins in a small town, literally a western town set. The reenactment group has constructed western town building façades resembling a movie set, though on a much smaller scale. There is a bank, a saloon, and a sheriff's office. The skit begins with a U.S. marshal speaking to the mayor and asking him if he's seen the outlaws in question. The mayor asks, "What are you going to do after you've found them guilty?" The marshal responds, "That's when we're going to have a neck-tie party. That's when we stretch their necks, you know, a neck-tie party." Besides the jab at due process, evidently this line is an attempt at humor, but the crowd, which is quite close, has no reaction. Often the skits are done in public spaces that make it extremely difficult to hear all the dialogue. In many cases, it is simply impossible for the crowd to hear all of the narrative and understand what is going on. Subsequently, what is left is the sight of a lot of shooting and people falling down dead. In bigger venues, wireless microphone headsets are deployed but more often than not fail in some capacity and do not make the voices clearly audible. At this particular shootout, however, every word can be easily heard by the audience.

In these shootouts, there are always good guys and bad guys. All the good guys survive, all the bad guys die, and all the loaded rounds get fired. Criminals are never apprehended, only killed. The women in the skits are scripted to end up huddled together off to the side. Occasionally one of them will fire a gun, but most of the time they play a passive, cowering role, waiting until the coast is clear to run out and poach items off the dead bad guys. During the skits, the men nearly always tell the women where to go, where to stand, to "get back" and "move over there." In one skit, I observed a woman reenactor who began to speak be told very quickly, "You don't do that there."

The shootout in this particular skit pits three good guys wearing badges against four bad guys. The deputies have caught up with the outlaws, and a standoff is framed by the street in front of the little town. "Put your guns down right now!" is the initial demand made by the marshal, and it is met with a defiant "Fiddledeedee!" and "You get *your* hands up!" from the outlaws. "No, you get 'em up" and "You get 'em up" is bantered back and forth several times before the shots begin to fly. One of the bad guys has two pistols, two of them have one pistol apiece, and one of them has a rifle and a pistol. The three good guys are also heavily armed, one with two pistols, one with a pistol and a shotgun, and the marshal with two pistols and a shotgun. As if those were not enough to hold onto, the marshal goes through the entire shootout with a tobacco pipe in his mouth. In the firefight that ensues, fifty rounds are fired in twenty seconds. None of the three good guys has been wounded, let alone killed. All four bad guys are on the ground, ostensibly dead. But the skit is not over.

There is no movement from any of the bad guys for more than a minute, yet some men and the womenfolk who have been witnessing the shootout bait the good guys to "Shoot 'em again" and call out, "He ain't dead yet!" "This one's still moving" and "It's not dead yet" can be heard. One of the good guys fires his shotgun at one of the dead outlaws and then flippantly justifies the pot shot with "I think he twitched." A minute and half after that, a final shot is taken at an unmoving bad guy lying prostrate with his back to the good guys. "What about that one over there?" They bend over in feigned inspection of the corpse, "I'll get 'em right here," hollers the marshal, who proceeds to blast the motionless outlaw in the back with a shotgun.

What does it mean for men portraying U.S. marshals to shoot and then continue to slaughter their victims? This is not an atypical conclusion to these skits. Is this justice? Does this resemble anything from the nineteenth century? What heinous act must these men have committed to be so objectified? The audience is told that the Johnson Gang was wanted for horse theft. In these shootouts, nobody screams in pain when they've been shot. All the bad guys fall down gallantly, shooting all the way down, firing on bent knee, now on the ground, shooting while rolling over toward death, somehow maintaining the resolve to continue fighting even after having been shot several times.

Nobody screams or cries at the loss of loved ones. The bad guys are never shown to have kin or women companions. Rather, they are looted for what items might be sold for profit. The shootout reenactments mute any of the real pain and anguish that would have been present in a shooting. Instead, they are performances of frontier tourism where reenactors can dwell in an imagined, dehistoricized past, as tourists experience a decontextualized yet potent ethos of a different era, the attic of the frontier complex.

Authentic Fissures

"Sit down and shut up!" yelled Jesse James from the back of the room. "Who are you?! Who are you to tell me what to do?!" came the screamed reply from Emmett Dalton. The two men, each armed with guns and knives, advanced on each other, and as their chests bumped they were drawn back by others in the room. This was not the performance of a skit but instead twenty minutes into the monthly meeting of the Wild West Shooters (WWS) when the conversation had taken a contentious turn. We had just spent the previous hour dining from an all-you-can-eat buffet in the meeting room while posturing for best place to observe this fight, for everyone knew it was going to take place.

Pressure had been building under the surface for several months over a breakaway reenactment group that I will call Quantrill's Raiders (QR), which was drawing membership from within the ranks of WWS. About ten individuals were simultaneously members of both groups, and QR had been getting paid shootout gigs that would have otherwise gone to the WWS. The members of WWS who were not invited to be in QR were feeling resentful for being overlooked as members but also because it meant that the more QR flourished, the more WWS would languish for lack of income from the paid events.

This fight had been telegraphed the day before in a melodramatic e-mail from the club president, Cole Younger, who said in that correspondence and repeated at the meeting that night that he would be resigning due to "the inability to work effectively in this environment." The details of "this environment" were never clearly articulated. Cole Younger was one of the members participating with both QR and WWS. In the two monthly meetings leading up to this one, Cole Younger had begun to lay a trail of contention to justify the behavior of QR. He had said at previous meetings, "We're [WWS] losing gigs because we're not period-correct enough." He cited author Brett Cogburn, who had recently given a book talk in Fort Smith, as an example of someone who refused to hire them for their lack of authentic appearance. He then chastised WWS for not rising to a higher degree of authenticity while also benefiting and profiting from this "fact" as a member of QR. Ironically, the WWS was not authentic enough for Brett Cogburn, the author who claimed direct descent from the fictional Rooster Cogburn.

On the surface, the explanation for why QR developed as a distinct group from WWS was one of a greater degree of "period correctness." QR originally joined the Reenactment Guild of America when it broke away from WWS and used its guild membership as a cloak of higher authenticity to legitimate the new group. However, guild turned out to be too period-correct for even the QR. In a conversation with Bloody Bill Anderson from QR, he matter-of-factly told me that the guild's "thread counting and button scrutinizing is bullshit." There was no suggestion of irony that standards of authenticity, which Cole Younger valued so much that he led his own posse to operate outside of the WWS, were in this case invalidated because they were too stringent. Degrees of authenticity among reenactment groups are finely split hairs. QR defines itself as somewhere between WWS and the guild, and yet to the novice, there is truly no evident difference between any of them.

An alternative explanation for why QR may no longer be guild-certified is because the members do not abide by the safety regulations clearly specified in the guild's rulebook. Certain distances must be kept, and shots must be taken from specified directions. I was told by a guild safety marshal that the QR as well as the WWS had "too many safety violations" by guild standards. The Reenactment Guild of America posts its rules and regulations on its website. "Weapons and Performance Ammunition" regulations state that all pistol shots must be taken from at least fifteen feet away from the target and all shotgun blasts from at least twenty-five feet. After reviewing my filmed footage of shootouts of all the observed groups, I can say that not one of the shootouts in Fort Smith met these safety standards. The guild also requires safety ropes or lines that clearly demarcate the performance space. This rule was also routinely broken at events I observed. What does this tell us about their performance?

In my many hours of fieldwork with these reenactment groups, I observed only one occasion in which a request was made from one reenactor to another to "watch where you're pointing that thing." On that occasion, the request was ignored the first time and had to be repeated. The offender reluctantly complied, sulking as if his gun-handling skills had somehow been challenged. I was slow to come around to observing exactly where guns were pointed. Between skits at one event, all the shooters were standing around reloading guns and talking. As we all huddled around visiting, I suddenly noticed that the end of a shotgun was absent-mindedly pointed straight at my head not less than a foot away. At that same event, I accidentally knocked a rifle to the floor that had been balanced on the seat of a chair. What does this tell us about their performance?

If neither QR nor WWS is period-correct, then what was the argument between QR and WWS all about? I suggest that period correctness is being used as a superficial excuse, an alibi, for the break. The skits that these groups perform usually have about five to ten men on either side—good guys and bad guys. In the larger WWS group, the numbers on both sides swell to more than ten, and the practical result of this is that fewer reenactors get to shoot their guns and be stars of the show. The stages, the venues in which these shootouts are performed can only hold so many shooters. It is my contention that the reason for the QR split comes down to stage time and shootout time—in other words, the time they get to be featured in the show. Comments from the reenactors reveal that they frame what they are doing in movielike terms. They frequently engage in excited banter about western films and television shows and cite favorite lines from them or strike familiar poses from them.

I suggest too that their lack of safety is directly related to the Quantrill's Raiders ethos that members of all the groups wish to affect: their distrust of government and of bureaucracy and their disdain for having to follow rules in general. At various times, individual reenactors or entire groups have been banned from coming onto the grounds of the National Historic Site for not abiding by gun rules. In some instances, they were invited to appear and asked to leave their guns at home but arrived armed anyway. On one occasion they were specifically told not to come dressed in period clothes. As they strolled onto the grounds dressed out, they caught sight of me and approached with mischief on their faces. As we greeted each other, they pulled their coats back to reveal their holstered pistols and their defiance of the National Park Service request as they performed their Quantrill trope.

Polyphonic Frontier

The frontier complex is a portable time-space continuum that permits multiple voices and views to be expressed within it.[37] We have now heard park rangers pleading for historical accuracy, a city tourism employee dressed as a madam flagging down charter buses, and centuries-old racial and gender ideologies being reinforced. The frontier complex is a platform for all of these perspectives and acts as well as a stage for other, competing voices.

Researching and writing this book has been, in part, my effort to discern meaning from this otherwise cacophonous chatter. One voice that needs more analysis in the context of performance is that of Art Burton. Since publication of his book on Bass Reeves in 2006, Burton has been instrumental in shaping a particular image of Bass Reeves that has come to be the universally repeated story of Reeves in Fort Smith and nationwide.

I suggest that Art Burton has performed the legend of Bass Reeves into existence. Burton has given talks on two separate occasions at the local university, made special appearances at the National Historic Site, one of them at the July 2011 "Hell, Grit, and Justice" conference. In January 2010 he was a featured speaker at the Fort Smith Museum of History for the one hundredth anniversary of Bass Reeves' death. He gave several special talks during the events leading up to the unveiling of the Bass Reeves monument in May 2012. He is a celebrated historian among enthusiasts of Fort Smith, and when people are quoted talking about Reeves, they are often reciting elements laid out by Burton. He has constructed a mythic narrative about Bass Reeves in Fort Smith that has come to be the accepted historical fact by the sheer force of his performance.

In May 2012 there was a series of events associated with the unveiling of the Bass Reeves monument.[38] Art Burton was on hand for the occasion as an honored guest and key speaker. On the last day of the events, the Fort Smith Public Library hosted a wrap-up session in which all the key players in the promotion of Bass Reeves in the frontier complex participated: Art Burton, Vaunda Nelson, Baridi Nkokheli, Jim Spears, and Harold T. Holden.

In one of his closing statements, Art Burton held forth on Reeves in his very familiar fashion:

> I can say emphatically, and I would challenge anybody to say that there was a better lawman on the western frontier, in that era, than Bass Reeves. And I think that it's great that Fort Smith has embraced him, and I think that there's just going to be a multitude of attention that's going to be given to Bass Reeves in the coming years. Because as more information comes out and more research is done I think that people are just gonna have to [pauses, feigns conceit] agree with me, that he was the best. [laughs] And you will not find a better statue of anybody, of [a] western character in the United States than what [Harold Holden] did on Bass Reeves. So, not only will the statue

stand up, Bass Reeves will stand up. I've told Baridi and I've told
Vaunda, I've told everybody, Bass is bigger than all of us. We're just a
conduit to get this information out, and I think it's divine interven-
tion really, and you know Bass was not perfect and I'm sure he had
some pit holes and stumbles along the way, but when we talk about
lawmen there was no better lawman than Bass Reeves in the Wild
West.[39]

Art Burton's enthusiasm for depicting Reeves in heroic terms is pal-
pable. In various speeches he has repeatedly said things such as "No man
is comparable," "Reeves is the greatest lawman in U.S. history," "Getting in
a gunfight with Bass was the equivalent of suicide," "The only time Belle
Starr voluntarily turned herself in was when Bass Reeves was serving the
writ," "Reeves is the greatest man in frontier history," and "Bass Reeves is
Bass Reeves." In the spirit and attitude with which Burton delivers these
comments, one would not be surprised to next hear that Reeves could float
like a butterfly and sting like a bee.

Burton's language is on a par with the legend of Davy Crockett as someone who could "run faster, jump higher, squat lower, dive deeper, stay under
longer, and come out drier than any man in the whole country."[40] One story
repeated by Burton and his surrogates is that Reeves could spit on a brick
and break it. At some point in his Reeves liturgy, Burton invariably delivers
in messianic tones the line that "Bass Reeves walked in the valley of death
for thirty-two years." It was with this sort of praise that Burton successfully lifted the discourse on Reeves into a biblical domain. A phrase that
emerged in the May 2012 presentations was "WWBD?" Instead of "What
would Jesus do?" it became "What would Bass do?"

When asked at one of these speaking engagements about the connection of Reeves to the Lone Ranger, Burton responded with his litany of
connections, including silver dollars, white horses, Indian companions, and
the link to Detroit. He concluded his speculation with a caveat of omis-
sion: "But! Even if you can't prove all of that, Bass Reeves is the closest real
individual that had characteristics like the Lone Ranger. There's nobody
else in reality that had characteristics like the Lone Ranger other than Bass
Reeves." And then again in a mixture of qualified statements he said, "I
would think personally that Bass Reeves was probably the inspiration for
the Lone Ranger."

Burton's personal website is largely designed for selling his books. The background image he uses throughout it is the iconic Monument Valley in northern Arizona. This is more than eight hundred miles from anywhere he writes about. The banner on his website reads: "ART BURTON'S WILD WEST." I believe this is an indication that the frontier complex is voicing yet another aspiration for Art Burton: his stated objective has become to get a major Hollywood movie made of Reeves' story. Burton is repeatedly asked and provides updates on the status of movie plans. Names such as Louis Gossett Jr., Morgan Freeman, and James Pickens Jr. are routinely dropped while discussing the possibilities. Burton tells stories of being personally called and courted by the handlers of these Hollywood stars.

At the end of a talk he gave in May 2012, an audience member asked, "Listen, all this information about Bass Reeves, is it not about time we get us a movie about this guy?" The applause generated by this question elicited the following response from Burton: "I've been talking to Hollywood since about '92, round '92, yeah. Suzanne de Passe had rights to my first book, she produced *Lonesome Dove*, and I said, 'Well, if this woman produced *Lonesome Dove* I'm sure they could do us a movie on Bass Reeves.'" Noteworthy is that he is claiming ownership of the Bass Reeves story. Burton continues, "I'm going to tell you what she said. Suzanne's people tried for about three years, but she told me, 'Hollywood is having a hard time with a black marshal even though this is not fiction, we know this is real history.'" Then, in a strange combination of disbelief and belief, he declared, "Hollywood made a West that didn't exist. It's a Hollywood creation, but I'm sure that a movie on Bass will be made." Burton has presented himself as the definitive authority on Reeves, and he basks in that role. Performing frontier tourism in Fort Smith has many meanings, indeed.

While Nkokheli recognizes the connection that the Bass Reeves story has to tourism, as of this writing he still performs the character of Bass Reeves based on Burton's account. Nkokheli apparently is operating under the assumption that all of what Art Burton has said about Reeves is historically accurate. In his presentations, Nkokheli routinely borrows a line from Burton: "Everything we know about Bass is true because it was read into the court record at Judge Parker's court." On the surface it may appear that Nkokheli is simply a mouthpiece for Art Burton. However, Nkokheli's story behind his portrayal of Bass Reeves is far more complex.

Shortly after moving to Fort Smith, Arkansas, in 2005 to become the director of the city Department of Sanitation, Nkokheli was approached by Circuit Judge Jim Spears about bringing the famous African American lawman Bass Reeves back to life because of his physical resemblance to Reeves. At that time Spears was unaware of Nkokheli's personal background. In February 2011, for the first time after four years of performing as Reeves in Fort Smith, Nkokheli publicly spoke on the University of Arkansas–Fort Smith campus of his father being murdered by fellow Los Angeles Police officers. He reflected on his performance as Bass Reeves:

> You understand that there is a power at work in this universe however you want to describe it. You know there is something that is greater and stronger than all of us and all of the little things that we do. For Judge Spears to see me and see the mustache and to say that he looks a little bit like the guy that we want to promote, but not to know that in my own personal history, my biography, that I also am the son of a lawman who had character equivalent to Bass Reeves. To get the chance to portray a real, true historic figure like Bass Reeves, a real life person is an honor that's beyond measure. I really don't have the words for what this opportunity has meant to me.[41]

Thus when Baridi Nkokheli performs Bass Reeves, he resurrects two deceased lawmen. Nkokheli has described his performance of Reeves in the frontier complex as one of a healing process for himself and for his entire family.

After his talk, I published an article about the story of his unusual name in the local history journal. Afterward, I anxiously awaited someone to comment or ask me questions about Nkokheli's story. Because of my research, I have been traveling in the circles of people who read that journal, but no questions were forthcoming. Nearly a year after its publication, I was finally approached about it by a local reenactor. He asked in a serious voice, "Can I ask you a question about that article you wrote about Baridi?" "Alright," I thought to myself, "finally." I excitedly replied yes to his request, and then he asked, "Why didn't you give the Wild West Shooters proper credit for supplying Baridi with his period-correct clothes?" Such are the polyphonic voices of the frontier complex.

While Nkokheli's personal story demonstrates the healing function of performance, it is ultimately lost on most people. What is left is an image of him wearing period clothing, striking a pose with his duster pulled back, his hand on his hip, pistol exposed, and rifle on display in mimic of the Bass Reeves monument. Nkokheli's portrayal has become synonymous with Bass Reeves. Without Nkokheli's efforts, it is likely the monument would not stand in downtown Fort Smith today. If it were not for Art Burton, Nkokheli would not have had a script to read for his presentations as Reeves, which are almost exclusively based on Burton's accounts.

As we have seen, frontier tourism is performed in Fort Smith not simply for economic profit in this redoubling era of the frontier complex but also for healing from personal and national traumas—including the racially motivated killing of Nkokheli's father, Sgt. Henry Wesley Kellough, LAPD. The myths of the fort—and of Parker, Reeves, Starr, and Zeigler—are particularly crafted for tourism in Fort Smith. They do not exist independently of each other, nor do tourism and history in general. In *Tourists of History*, Marita Sturken draws a clear connection between tourism and modernity and how Americans use tourism as a way of mediating various traumas caused by modernity and American imperialism. Sturken focuses on how tourism is performed in Oklahoma City and at Ground Zero in New York City; I believe the frontier complex functions similarly. Sturken argues, "American cultural responses to traumatic historical events enable naïve political responses to those events. They do this precisely because these cultural responses allow American history to be seen in isolation, as exceptional and unique, as if it were not part of the rest of world history and as if it were something simply to be consumed."[42]

The Fort Smith frontier complex is routinely presented as if it constitutes an exceptional time and place as it decontextualizes and dehistoricizes historical facts of the nineteenth century and repackages them in kitschy activities or commodities that can be consumed such as in the "fun" act of hanging little figures at miniature gallows or wearing a noose-adorned "Hang around Fort Smith" T-shirt. As we have seen, the military fort was not unique in its relationship to Indian Territory; it was just one small temporary link in a chain sweeping westward at a deliberate pace. The district court judge and the deputies who worked out of that court were not exceptional defenders of justice; their exploits are exaggerated and aggrandized to inflate their efforts and conceal their injustices; Indian Territory was not lawless, as each of the Five Nations had its own Supreme Court; Native Americans, African Americans, and women did not find the frontier to be an equal opportunity provider, as they were systematically discriminated against by individuals and institutions as white male privilege flourished. Performing frontier tourism conceals this vice in the veil of justice as the performance bends race and gender to reconcile and alleviate contemporary fears and anxieties of the othered while it exonerates the dominant group from complicity in the project of constructing whiteness.

This point is reinforced in sentiments often expressed by the reenactors during my fieldwork. Many of them shared with me their feelings of great admiration, fondness, and longing they have for the good old days. One reenactor, Hondo Lane, stated that his performances in the shootouts took him "out of time." When asked to elaborate on what he meant, Hondo told me, "Yeah, it takes me out of this time and puts me back where I'd like to be." Still unsure of what about the late nineteenth century was so alluring to him, I pushed the issue further. He told me the draw for him to that time was all about freedom:

> Freedom, freedom, yeah. You could go where you wanted to go and more or less do what you wanted to do. You had to . . . you had rough times. If you did the wrong thing you was in trouble, bad. And if you did good things then you had a chance to do what you wanted to do. Go where you wanted to. Didn't have to worry about income tax and doctors and all that stuff. It just seemed to be a . . . it was a bad time, but it was a cleaner and fresher time. You could trust people. They'd leave their doors open for you and everything else. That's kinda why I like it. I was raised on western movies anyway.

Though a popular sentiment, this world that Hondo describes simply did not exist. Who in the late nineteenth century was free to do what they wished or had the resources to be free to come and go? Big business and big government were firmly established in the late nineteenth century and meddling in the lives of people and in their freedom. Being a white man certainly made freedom easier, both then and now. Can you imagine an African American today wishing to go back to the nineteenth century to be free? Frolicking in the frontier complex becomes untenable from that perspective.

On December 14, 2012, I was in my office immersed in writing about Fort Smith's frontier reenactors. Upon hearing the horrific news from Sandy Hook Elementary School in Newtown, Connecticut, I had a dull, plaguing sense that somehow this senseless killing of young schoolchildren was related to my research. Is there a direct line between frontier reenactors and perpetrators of school shootings? No, absolutely not. Does the mythology of the frontier complex validate that sort of violence?

Richard Slotkin, perhaps the preeminent writer on frontier mythology, has shared his thoughts on this question.[43] In a 2013 interview with Bill Moyers, Slotkin addresses how the dark side of the mythic frontier complex could contribute to the impulse that might have triggered the Newtown massacre:

We produce the lone killer. That is to say the lone killer is trying to validate himself or herself in terms of the, I would call, the historical mythology of our society, wants to place himself in relation to meaningful events in the past that lead up to the present . . . and I've always felt that it has something to do, in many cases, with a sense of lost privilege, that men and white men in the society feel their position to be imperiled and their status called into question. And one way to deal with an attack on your status in our society is to strike out violently.[44]

It is hard to imagine how the frontier-complex mythology that conceals a legacy of so much actual violence and visually displays a gratuitous amount of egregious violence in film and fiction would not have an underlying basis that could facilitate real murderous behavior.

If related at all, school shootings are certainly an extreme manifestation of the frontier complex. Perhaps, though, we should bear in mind Kurt Vonnegut's admonition in the introduction to his novel, *Mother Night:* "We are what we pretend to be, so we must be careful about what we pretend to be."[45] Performing the frontier complex for tourism allows reenactors and tourists alike to tap into the mythic frontier West and reimagine their contemporary ideologies of class, race, and gender. The frontier attic is a space that allows for many different perspectives. The city of Fort Smith is designing a frontier complex for tourists to come and eat in restaurants, sleep in hotels, and fill their cars up with gas. Ultimately, cultural heritage tourism is an industry; it is about money.

8

////////////////////////////

Doubling Down on
the Wager of Frontier Tourism

Baby sister, I was born game and I intend to go out that way.

Rooster Cogburn, *True Grit*

The recreation era of the frontier complex, 1920–1980, established frontier tourism in Fort Smith with Judge Parker's courtroom, restored gallows, and refurbished military fort at the Fort Smith National Historic Site. But profits from the initial wager were not sustained and had to be supplemented with redoubled efforts such as we saw with the additions of Miss Laura's Social Club as a visitor center in 1992 and the Bass Reeves monument in 2012. Despite a lackluster performance, Fort Smith is now poised for doubling down on the wager of cultural heritage tourism in the frontier complex in its quest to build the U.S. Marshals Museum. The tourist economy in the current redoubling era is significantly different from that of the recreation era. This is a national trend that has been going on for decades, not isolated to the "great recession," and is particularly problematic for history museums.[1]

Today, the American landscape is strewn with struggling, bankrupt, and failed museums and cultural centers. Despite the impressiveness of the Great Platte River Road Archway, which stretches over Interstate 80 at Kearney, Nebraska, it has just emerged from bankruptcy, having been held afloat by city and county taxpayer support. In its first two years, 2000–2001, more than 200,000 visitors stopped annually, but it never approached or sustained its predicted attendance of 300,000 per year. By 2012 attendance was below 50,000. Building for tourism in the frontier complex is no sure bet, even if millions of people literally drive right underneath it.[2] In Fort Dodge, Iowa, the Fort Museum celebrated its fiftieth anniversary in 2014.

Figure 8.1. Tourist reenactment at the Great Platte River Road Archway in Kearney, Nebraska. Travelers of Interstate 80 can tour exhibits and see reenactments of traveling, this one with Jack Kerouac's *On the Road* on the seat beside the driver. Photo by the author.

With a completely reconstructed log stockade and adjacent frontier town, this small nonprofit struggles to survive despite its visual grandeur.

In Oklahoma City, the American Indian Cultural Center and Museum, originally conceived in 1994, has been under construction since 2006. Ninety-one million dollars later, the buildings and grounds stand empty and unfinished, stalled since 2012 awaiting millions more to complete and operate the facility. Incredibly, in the face of this dire predicament, great expectations for the museum are still assumed. Oklahoma State Representative David Dank declared in 2014, "It could be a real boon to this state. It is history, culture and heritage. It will draw thousands of people here every year and will pay for itself."[3] Implicit in this comment is an inherent faith that cultural heritage tourism will automatically result in profits for the facility and the community and that demand for such venues is nowhere near satiated.

A city considering building a new cultural center or museum would be well served to do its homework before investing any time, money, or energy in the project. Recent research has uncovered some significant cautionary trends that counter the adage "If you build it, they will come." First, the supply of museums and cultural arts centers has, at least for the moment, surpassed demand. Second, new building construction of this type exceeds estimated costs 80 percent of the time. A third significant finding is that hopes of continued donor support for keeping the doors open after construction often falls significantly short of expectations. These and other insightful observations were made in the 2012 *Set in Stone* report by the Cultural Policy Center at the University of Chicago. The extensive study examined construction of new museums, cultural centers, and arts centers ranging in cost from $4 million to $335 million begun between 1994 and 2008.[4]

This bumpy economic stretch in frontier-complex tourism and support for cultural heritage centers is frequently attributed to the economic recession of the late 2000s, but seldom is it put into the larger economic context of neoliberal policies that led to the deindustrialization of America beginning in the early 1980s.[5] The shift toward offshoring production of goods led to a direct change in the economy and a decline in wages and job security for millions of Americans. When it comes to spending money on domestic tourism of the frontier complex, it is just not the same environment as the post–World War II period. The 1950s and '60s saw job growth, affordable cars, cheap gas, new interstates, and televisions full of Wild West stories to stoke the imagination and compel families to head out on vacation.

Understanding museum attendance patterns is difficult because research on it is sparse and plagued by inconsistent standards on collecting and sharing data. Cary Carson notes, "The truth of the matter is that nobody knows for sure what's really going on. No national organization keeps statistics on museum attendance. . . . Nor is there an industry-wide formula for counting admissions."[6] This is problematic for a sector of the economy purported to be so valuable to the economy.

Reach Advisors, a New York–based museum industry research group, calls into question three assumptions frequently spoken by enthusiastic proponents of museums—that they are economic engines, that they educate people, and that they inspire people.[7] The president of the board of the U.S. Marshals Museum and other community leaders in Fort Smith consistently maintain that they are not just building a museum but that it will be an economic engine for the region. There simply is not the empirical

Figure 8.2. Chickasaw National Capitol Building in Tishomingo, Oklahoma. Indian nations' museums and cultural centers, coupled with gaming, represent stiff competition for the Fort Smith frontier complex. Photo by the author.

evidence necessary to support this assertion. If museums were truly the economic engines they are claimed to be, so many of them and their communities would not be suffering economic shortfalls to the extent that they are. Educating and inspiring people turn out to be platitudes that do not differentiate museums from other activities that do the same thing. Returning to a textbook approach to cultural heritage tourism, we can add to these the problematic waning of "pull factors" and the declining cultural "push factors."[8]

Mechanisms for pushing Americans into frontier complex tourism have changed significantly since 1980. The Soviet Union is gone, as is the plethora of westerns on television and in films. With the "tourismification" of the Wild West frontier completed during the recreation era, the process of "imagineering," of instilling the frontier ethos in the minds of the youth, has not kept pace in the redoubling era, leaving a disconnection between supply and demand. Different frontiers are being constructed to capture the imaginations of would-be tourists and entice them to spend their money. The rise of ecotourism and culture tourism have paralleled the globalization of the economy, while at home Indian gaming competes with and compounds the challenge of attracting tourists to the frontier complex.[9]

What television westerns, interstates, and affordable cars did for frontier tourism between 1950 and 1980, the Internet and income inequality have retracted. As the Fort Kearny State Park superintendent put it, "What took me thirty years to learn reading *Time-Life* magazine, you can now learn in two hours from Ken Burns."[10] The Wild West frontier complex attracted tourists in the past because the underlying infrastructure of the economy allowed it. Assuming that the same old strategies will work in today's economy is not only unrealistic, it qualifies as what Lauren Berlant calls "cruel optimism."[11] Though it may create a lot of excitement and enthusiasm and recollections of family vacations for some, it is not economically viable to continue increasing the supply of frontier tourism without an equivalent increase in demand. Regardless, in a postindustrial economy of vacant manufacturing buildings, cities turn to packaging and marketing whatever commodity they have on hand. As Fort Smith watched its manufacturing base shrink over the past thirty years, it more aggressively turned to cultural heritage tourism. With a dig at the Whirlpool Corporation, which closed its local plant in 2012, community leaders often quip, "You can't send our history to Mexico."

The "#1 True Western Town"?

While the city of Fort Smith has actively wagered on frontier tourism since 1955, beginning in 2003 the city went all-in with the hopes of drawing the U.S. Marshals Museum to Fort Smith and hitting the frontier tourist jackpot. However, what many in Fort Smith do not fully realize is that two other cities have failed in this same wager, making the current attempt a case study in the economic vicissitudes of frontier cultural heritage tourism. What follows is an analysis of how the first two cities lost their gambles and how the latest one is doubling down despite long odds. We will look at them in reverse chronological order and make note of how each time, each community's boosters believed it had the perfect location, how each city had great excitement and enthusiasm for the project, and then examine the ultimate results.

According to the Marshals Museum website, it was awarded to the city of Fort Smith because "Fort Smith was the natural choice to host the new Museum. Not only did the city leaders and the regional population lobby for its presence, Fort Smith is a place of true authenticity." The "natural" and the "authentic" are derived from the sixty-year-old mythic narratives firmly rooted at the Fort Smith National Historic Site and Miss Laura's Visitor Center. The explanation goes on to link the location of the museum to the lure of the imagineered frontier complex: "It was the gateway to the Old West, an era ingrained in the American Imagination." Fact and fiction blur as we read, "It was here that Judge Isaac C. Parker tried the fugitives arrested by the marshals. And who could forget it was here that the ficti-tious Rooster Cogburn began his search for the fictitious Tom Chaney in the popular movie True Grit."

The museum website goes on to repeat phrases of mythic justice in Fort Smith: "The U.S. Marshals Service was the only law enforcement agency with the jurisdiction to enter Indian Territory"; the deputies "patrolled the vast 74,000 square mile territory"; and "the danger of the job and the vio-lent criminals they faced resulted in the burial of more deputy marshals and special deputies in this region than anywhere else in the country."[12] The Marshals Museum immediately and seamlessly incorporated itself into the existing Fort Smith frontier complex, and vice versa—the Fort Smith fron-tier complex began to cannibalize the Marshals Museum.

In December 2012 the future looked bright for the Fort Smith frontier complex with the potential addition of the U.S. Marshals Museum—de-signed as a badge. It was announced then that Fort Smith had been chosen as the "#1 True Western Town of 2013" by True West Magazine. Elated by the news, Claude Legris, executive director of the Fort Smith Advertis-ing and Promotion Commission, proudly said in an interview, "We have 'branded' Fort Smith with our frontier heritage since the Convention and Visitors Bureau was established two decades ago. It's a 'natural' brand for Fort Smith because it's who and what we are."[13] The True West announce-ment was taken to be payout on the wager of frontier tourism.

What precisely this accolade meant, however, is debatable. True West is essentially a trade magazine intended to get people to travel to western states. Each year, it reveals a new "top ten Western town" list as a way of promoting tourism throughout the West writ large. All the winning towns invest in advertisements in the magazine, which features fantastic stories and pictures from the Wild West. These create the illusion that it is an ac-tual magazine with historical information about the West and not just one long advertisement for frontier-complex tourism. Regardless, the Adver-tising and Promotion Commission was pleased with the results. Arkansas

Business, a weekly business journal, repeated the mantra: "The two versions of the movie 'True Grit' and the naming of Fort Smith as the future home of the United States Marshals Service national museum did much to so-lidify and expand the Fort Smith tourism brand."[14] It is said that for these reasons the Convention and Visitors Bureau applied for and ultimately received the "#1 True Western Town of 2013" title.

On the morning of the announcement, December 12, 2012, news of the award spread like a prairie fire through the frontier complex. Blog, Face-book, and Twitter posts from the visitors bureau, the Fort Smith Museum of History, the National Historic Site, and the Clayton House all trum-peted it as great tourism news. The *Times Record* ran an editorial the next day espousing the benefits likely to accrue.[15] The editorial describes Fort Smith "both as Hell on the Border and the place that brought civiliza-tion to the West." The editorial continues with a conflation of fiction and facts: "Portis' well-known gallery of ruffians, rubes and rule-enforcers—Rooster Cogburn, Mattie Ross, Tom Chaney, LaBoeuf and Lucky Ned Pepper—have enough of the real to them that they live in our celebration of our town almost as much as the people we know walked here, Judge Isaac Parker, Deputy Marshal Bass Reeves, W.H.H. Clayton, Miss Laura and Belle Starr." The imagineering of the frontier complex was pervasive for the occasion.

The *True West* press release announcing the decision ties the fate of the tourism industry in Fort Smith directly to the gallows. It dramatically begins, "They called him the 'hanging judge.' Isaac Parker certainly threw a big rope around Fort Smith, Arkansas, during his 21 years on the federal bench. His courtroom and jail—restored to their 1880s appearances—are part of the reason nearly one million visitors came to town in 2012."[16] A bit of fact checking reveals that even with the most generous accounting of visitors to the frontier complex, not even 10 percent of that figure could be attributed to Judge Parker's big rope. Before proceeding to examine the fate of the Marshals Museum, it is instructive to look at the current state of frontier-complex tourism in Fort Smith.

The National Park Service's reported annual visitor numbers show the National Historic Site at 69,584 for 2013 and a five-year average of 75,062.[17] These figures actually represent twice as many people who en-tered the building and registered at the desk. The National Park Service officially doubles that number for its records, assuming that an equal num-ber of people come to use the grounds but do not go inside to pay the nominal admission fee, which is a deterrent to some potential visitors. The Fort Smith Museum of History reported an average of 20,000 visitors for 2012–2013, Miss Laura's had 12,718 sign its register in 2012, and the Clayton House estimated 6,500 people came through its doors.[18] In all likelihood, these attendance numbers do not represent unique visitors, as many tourists visit more than one of these sites. Schools bring busloads of children to these sites each year. Their numbers are counted in the total but obviously do not count as tourists who stay in local hotels, eat in restaurants, or fill up their gas tanks before leaving town.

As such, the overall National Historic Site attendance count would be a generous estimate for adult tourists making an economic impact in Fort Smith as a direct result of cultural heritage tourism. According to the 2013 "National Park Visitor Spending Effects," national parks brought 2.78 million visitors to Arkansas who spent $144 million. The nonlocal visit count specific to the Fort Smith National Historic Site was 58,451, with an estimated $3.7 million in nonlocal visitor spending.[19] While these figures appear large and are definitely better than nothing, they are quite small when compared with economic pressures working against Fort Smith.

A final document prepared by consultant Wallace Roberts and Todd for the Fort Smith Comprehensive Plan detailed that the local economy has a "leakage" of $812.9 million, with $272.9 million of it leaving for "general merchandise" and about $200 million each leaving for "foodservice & drinking places" and "food & beverage (grocery)." There was a retail surplus in "sporting goods, hobby, book, music," "big materials, garden equipment," and "electronics & appliance" totaling $278.9 million, resulting in a $533.9 million retail spending deficit.[20] The economic picture in Fort Smith would be drastically different if the people who live there would spend their money there. Still, it is hoped that the future Marshals Museum will ease this level of self-inflicted hemorrhaging.

The fact is that the Fort Smith frontier complex is not a huge tourist destination. It is not a Clinton Presidential Library in Little Rock or a Crystal Bridges Museum of American Art in Walmart's hometown of Bentonville, let alone a Tombstone or a Dodge City that can attract 200,000–400,000 visitors annually. With 87,000 residents, Fort Smith is technically the second-largest city in a state of barely 3 million.

Data from an economic report on 2012 tourism prepared by the Arkansas Department of Travel and Tourism puts tourism in the frontier complex into perspective. With $5 billion spent by travelers in the state that year, there is a definite share of tourist money to be sought. The state agency divides Arkansas into twelve tourism regions. Fort Smith, in Sebastian County, is in the Western Arkansas Mountain Frontier Region, which ranked fifth among the twelve regions for tourist expenditures in 2012. While five other counties are in the same region, Sebastian County, home to Fort Smith, took in 80 percent of its tourist revenues.[21]

In 2012, tourist expenditures totaled nearly $431 million garnered from almost 1.2 million total visitors to this five-county region. For comparison, the Northwest Arkansas Region, which includes Benton, Carroll, Madison, and Washington Counties, generated close to $744 million in tourist expenditures from more than 3.2 million visitors. The Heart of Arkansas Region, which includes Little Rock, led the state with nearly $1.8 billion in expenditures from almost 6.4 million visitors. The other two regions that drew more revenue and tourists than the Fort Smith region were the Diamond Lakes Region, which includes Garland County with Hot Springs and recreational lakes, and the Arkansas Delta Byways Region, which includes all the state's counties contiguous to the Mississippi River, with the lure of its gambling boats.[22]

Sebastian County itself is in the top five counties for tourist travel spending, with 6.0 percent of the pie. Garland and Pulaski are ahead of it with 10.4 percent and 28.0 percent, respectively. The contiguous counties of Washington and Benton come in fourth and fifth, but with their combined share of 9.8 percent, Sebastian County comes in last. Thus, Fort Smith is in serious competition with other regions and counties in the state. Perhaps the most pointed evidence that Fort Smith's frontier complex has not truly made it onto the tourist radar is that Sebastian County is not among the top ten counties listed as final destinations for tourists coming to the state. The piece of the frontier tourist pie becomes even smaller considering that of all the visitors to the state, only 26 percent include historic sites as "activities participated in."[23] Nevertheless, Fort Smith is annually recognized for tourism with awards by the state and by the local tourism industry.

Arkansas has long recognized the significance of the tourism industry to the state's economy and has held an annual Governor's Conference on Tourism since 1974. Awards for accomplishments in tourism are given each year and referred to as the Henry Awards. The "Henry" being referenced is Henri de Tonti, an eighteenth-century French explorer who eventually abandoned his plans for making money in the Arkansas River Valley and went back to France.[24] In 2014 the Fort Smith Convention and Visitors

Bureau won the Henry Award for Community Tourism Development specifically for the manner in which it promoted its *True West Magazine* designation as #1 True Western Town of 2013.[25] In April 2013 Fort Smith had two Henry Award nominations. Tokunboh Baridi Nkokheli was nominated in the Outstanding Volunteer Service Award category, and the Bass Reeves monument was up for the Natural State Award. While neither award was taken back to Fort Smith, the city's brand as a frontier town was reinforced.

Beginning in 2012 Fort Smith heightened its connection to frontier tourism when it began recognizing those who had made outstanding contributions to tourism in the city by taking nominations for and giving GRIT Awards, further entangling *True Grit* with tourism as "GRIT" stands for "Giving Recognition in Tourism." In 2014 the Fort Smith National Historic Site won Attraction Partner of the Year, and Floyd and Sue Robison won Hospitality Person of the Year for their portrayal of Isaac and Mary Parker.[26] Nominations for the April 2013 GRIT awards in the category of Attraction Partner of the Year included two elements from the Fort Smith frontier complex, the Bass Reeves Legacy Initiative, described at the event as a "classic example of a hospitality dream come true," and the Fort Smith Museum of History, which was framed as "Fort Smith's own version of the Smithsonian."[27]

Two couples who contributed to performing frontier tourism in Fort Smith were nominated for the Polly Crews Hospitality Person of the Year award. Baridi and then wife Tonya Nkokheli, who served on the Bass Reeves Legacy Initiative board, were jointly nominated, as were Floyd and Sue Robison. The museum and the Nkokhelis won their respective awards in 2013.[28] In 2012 the Clayton House won over the nominations of the Bass Reeves Legacy Initiative, the Fort Smith Museum of History, and the Fort Smith National Historic Site.[29] The frontier complex is thus inextricably bound to the tourism industry in Fort Smith, or more correctly, we can now see it is the other way around—cultural heritage tourism is entangled in the frontier complex.

The 2013 GRIT Award for Business Partner of the Year was awarded to downtown owner-developers Richard Griffin and his son, Rick Griffin. Accepting the award, Rick Griffin addressed the audience and earnestly advised, "I want you to all take a moment and look forward to the U.S. Marshals Museum, which *is* coming. Richard and I are personally working to help raise money for that project. When it does come, it is a game changer for downtown Fort Smith and for the region at large."[30] Under the grandiloquent fanfare surrounding the Marshals Museum, we can see the machinations of the local political economy at work, just as we did with the ploys of Fort Smith's founder, John Rogers, to have the second Fort Smith built in 1838 or as with R. K. Rodgers and the Chamber of Commerce in dismantling Coke Hill in the name of frontier tourism. Together, Rick and Richard Griffin own a substantial amount of real estate downtown and have renovated several buildings on Garrison Avenue to "historic" condition.[31]

Besides raising money for the Marshals Museum, between the two of them the Griffins sit on enough boards in town to create an interlocking directorate within their family that can directly influence development in the city. Richard Griffin is the current chairman of the Fort Smith Historic Downtown Preservation Association, the Central Business Improvement District Commission, and the Fort Smith Housing Authority. His son, Rick Griffin, serves on the board of the Marshals Museum. On the same day they won their GRIT Award, the local newspaper reported that the Central Business Improvement District Commission headed by Richard Griffin gave Rick Griffin of Griffin Properties permission to go ahead with plans to spend $3 million renovating the 400 block of Garrison Avenue. Rick Griffin "said the restoration will be done with attention to historic preservation, and efforts are being made to secure state and federal tax credits. He said the effort at preservation 'is the right thing to do for downtown,' given the city's goal of emphasizing its frontier heritage, a goal that is expected to intensify in the area as the U.S. Marshals Museum is developed on the Arkansas River front." Using the Marshals Museum as the basis for their business venture, he emphasized, "We want to start the ball rolling on that."[32]

The Griffin family is well positioned to see a profit from potential tourists they are making key decisions in attracting. Meanwhile, they are clearing the way to maximize their investment. As is not uncommon in cities' downtown areas, agencies that assist individuals experiencing homelessness are close to it; three are near the region that the Griffins plan to develop, and homeless camps dot the riverfront near the proposed location of the U.S. Marshals Museum.[33] At the time of this writing, Richard Griffin, the real estate developer, in his capacity as board president of the Fort Smith Housing Authority, was the boss of Ken Pyle, that agency's executive director. Pyle, in turn, was board president of the Old Fort Homeless

Coalition, which had been tasked with relocating all the agencies that work with homeless individuals, along with all the homeless camps along the river, to a centralized homeless campus.

The city Board of Directors has clearly defined the only location homeless agencies can expand as several blocks south of Garrison Avenue in a largely abandoned industrial park, away from Griffin properties and far from the gaze of frontier tourists.[34] Pyle argues in a *Times Record* opinion piece, "Economic common sense should tell us that downtown and riverfront development will not happen unless and until existing homeless services are consolidated to a 'social service campus' in the chosen area south of Garrison Avenue."[35] Homelessness thus becomes the scapegoat for the failure of downtown tourism and perhaps the Marshals Museum. Clearly, Fort Smith has pushed all its chips in on attracting tourists to its frontier complex and doubling down on its wager with the Marshals Museum, and it is willing to further marginalize individuals experiencing homelessness and the nonprofit agencies that assist them in the process.

Following Richard Flores' lead in his dismantling of the master symbol in *Remembering the Alamo*, I have striven to do the same here with the frontier complex in general, its iteration in Fort Smith in particular, and now with its wager with the Marshals Museum in particular. Flores argues, "A semiotics of place serves to anchor meaning in a foundational and thereby mythical past; a semiotics of project binds social actors in the present with a sense of historical subjectivity and attempts to silence the stories of those whose presence may unravel the tightly wound strands of meaning in the master symbol."[36] Regarding the emerging master symbol of the Marshals Museum in Fort Smith, more than a few stories that have not been heard do indeed unravel some key strands holding it together.

Fort Smith's Marshals Museum

It was in July 2003 that talk began to circulate in Fort Smith about putting in a bid for the U.S. Marshals Museum. Arkansas Congressman John Boozman initiated a meeting with Marshals Service Director Benigno Reyna "about placing the museum with the Fort Smith National Historic Site where U.S. District Judge Isaac Parker held court during the frontier days." Very little was said at the time regarding the Marshals Museum stint in Laramie, Wyoming, only that it had been there since 1991 and closed in 2002 "when the Marshals Service pulled its exhibits because they were not properly maintained and the security wasn't sufficient."[37] Sweeping imagery from the mythic frontier complex was used to present the public face of the transition of the Marshals Museum from Laramie to Fort Smith.

Local news media covered the story in hopeful terms from the start. A *Times Record* reporter notes, "Fort Smith officials are angling to lure the U.S. Marshals Museum to the city, saying the law-and-order legacy of Judge Isaac Parker makes it a natural candidate."[38] Senators Blanche Lincoln and Mark Pryor jumped on the bandwagon, suggesting the museum could be located in the vacant Frisco Station that had recently been renovated and is immediately adjacent to the Fort Smith National Historic Site.[39] Within three months of the newspaper's first article on the potential move, a *Times Record* editorial declared Fort Smith a "natural site" for a Marshals Museum.[40] What happened next is an important juncture in the chronology of the Marshals Museum.

What becomes manifestly obvious at this point is that the project becomes framed as an economic engine for the region. The public discourse about the museum is not primarily about having a facility to pay tribute to U.S. marshals and deputy marshals who have fallen in the line of duty, nor is it about recognizing the more than 225-year history of the U.S. Marshals Service upholding U.S. law. Rather, it is about bringing tourists to town; it is about revitalizing the local economy; it is about syphoning tourists away from their flow to Crystal Bridges and the Clinton Library.

The Fort Smith Convention and Visitors Bureau was quick to add enthusiasm to the project and escalate the expectations of what it could mean to the city. According to the *Times Record*, Executive Director Claude Legris said in 2004, "It would be a natural extension of Fort Smith's frontier history, and it would bring another major attraction to draw out-of-town tourism dollars to the area."[41] The proverbial chickens were being counted long before the roost was built, let alone any eggs laid.

The *Times Record* fueled the enthusiasm with more editorial titles including "Fort Smith a 'Natural' Museum Location" and more boldly, "City Deserves U.S. Marshal Museum." In the latter, a 2004 editorial, the writer confidently states that Fort Smith is "the 'natural' and best possible location for the U.S. Marshal Museum" and specifies the old depot as the logical site for it: "Fort Smith and Arkansas tourism promoters have all the right things to say about why the museum collection . . . should be moved to the old Frisco Depot at the foot of the bridge at Second Street and Garrison Avenue."[42] We will return to the point of the museum location momentarily; for now what is important to note is the widespread optimistic enthusiasm for the project.

The Fort Smith Advertising and Promotion Commission immediately began work on a promotional video to make its case for landing the museum in which all manner of mythic frontier justice was put on display. Scenes from John Wayne's portrayal of Rooster Cogburn in *True Grit* were interspersed with pictures of real-life deputies as then Arkansas governor Mike Huckabee delivers the pitch:

> The proud histories of America's oldest federal law enforcement agency, the frontier border town of Fort Smith, and the state of Arkansas are intertwined with romantic and adventuresome tales of lawbreakers and peacemakers. Fort Smith and Indian Territory were the setting for John Wayne's fictional portrayal of a deputy U.S. marshal in the movie *True Grit*; Rooster Cogburn always got his man, as did those who rode for Judge Isaac C. Parker. More than one hundred deputy marshals died in the line of duty between 1871 and 1896—a majority of whom are buried within fifty miles of Fort Smith.[43]

A local history enthusiast adds to the promotional video's mythic depictions: "Starting in 1871, Fort Smith was the granddaddy of all Marshal Services. There was [*sic*] more marshals here, spread over a larger part of the country; more people brought in; more marshals killed in the line of duty." This description of rugged characters is then reinforced by both the narrator and the images displayed on the screen.

The narrator says, "And in Fort Smith, Arkansas, the gallant men and women who brought law and order to the old west helped change the landscape of our great nation." With no context, explanation, identification, or sense of irony, the 1892 photo of the deceased Cherokee Senator Ned Christie tied to a door, propped up on the courthouse steps, and surrounded by the posse that had killed him is displayed on the screen as that line is spoken. The image reinforces stereotypical Hollywood depictions of binary cases of good and evil while glossing a case hotly contested between Fort Smith and the Cherokee Nation. The desired effect is that it will quickly attract the popular imagination of the viewer; it is not meant to explain the complex and nuanced history of the advancing nation displacing Native Americans, let alone the complex case and tragic death of Ned Christie.

The video was ready by the time officials from Washington, D.C., made their first visit to Fort Smith. The assistant director of the Marshals Service, Michael Pearson, and Marshals Service historian David Turk arrived for a four-day visit in November 2005. The *Times Record* declared, "It's show time!" By the time the officials departed they had toured potential sites for the museum, and within two weeks it was being reported that Fort Smith was on the short list of cities under consideration.[44] In 2006 the "Bring It Home" campaign was developed to actively create local community support for the project. That was its objective, as stated in a *Times Record* editorial: "The purpose of this campaign is to capture the enthusiasm of Fort Smith residents."[45]

In June 2006 two dozen community leaders traveled to Washington to sell that captured Fort Smith enthusiasm to the Marshals Service. There to assist them were state Senator Blanche Lincoln and Congressman John Boozman. Lincoln emphasized, "This is a community that engages itself and embraces its ideas and stops at nothing to put on an A-plus show." Boozman said, "Truly, I think Fort Smith makes all the sense in the world. The good thing is, I think they are buying it, but you just don't know until they decide."[46] The community support and political reinforcement seem to have been effective. On July 25, 2006, it was announced that Fort Smith was a finalist, competing with Staunton, Virginia.[47]

It was the image of the frontier and not the role of the Marshals Service that was emphasized by both applicants. The competitor's position was reported in the *Times Record*: "The frontier starts in Staunton, or so say the locals. Eighteenth-century settlers plodded westward through the Shenandoah Valley through Staunton, seat of a county that at one time stretched west to the Mississippi River and north to the Great Lakes."[48] The decision came down to which city could find greatest purchase in the frontier complex.

Fort Smithians made their final pitch in November 2006. Nine members of the Marshals Service site selection committee spent several days in the city gathering their final impressions. They were "given a special Murder and Mayhem Trolley tour" during which outlaws held up the trolley and the visitors were saved by deputy marshals. At another event, "more than 900 area residents showed their support for making Fort Smith the home of the National U.S. Marshals Museum." The visitors from Washington "were serenaded by members of the Southside High School Rebel Band playing the theme song from the 1960 western, *The Magnificent Seven*."[49]

The final plea was made in Judge Parker's reconstructed courtroom after the panel observed a night court reenactment of a Parker trial. In a brilliant move, Claude Legris pulled a reverse Johnny Cochran. Speaking before the panel seated in the courtroom, Legris introduced the acronym "FRESH . . . standing for Free-standing, Relevant to visitors today and in the future, Education, Self-sustaining and Historically inclusive—holding up another finger with each point. With all five fingers out, Legris then pulled out a black leather glove and said 'If you see a fit, then Fort Smith is it.'"[50] The good, the bad, and the ugly of Hollywood imagery and mythic frontier justice were the underlying script to the entire campaign, and it worked.

Three full years of lobbying resulted in the museum being awarded to Fort Smith in January 2007. Staunton came in second place; two earlier contenders—Cheyenne, Wyoming, and Hollywood, California—had been eliminated in the initial round. The announcement was trumpeted with much fanfare. Local, state, and national dignitaries praised Fort Smith as the best place for the museum, and optimism was running high: "Fundraising for a building expected to cost about $15 million and operation expenses of about $5 million will start immediately," the city administrator declared. While it was suggested by some that it might "take up to six years before the museum opens," others were confident that "money will be available and the site ready much sooner."[51] Richard O'Connell, U.S. marshal for the Western District of Arkansas, offered an optimistic time line: "We're hoping to turn the locks in 36 to 40 months."[52] In retrospect, these early projections of three or six years were nothing short of fanciful.

More encouragement was heaped on as many public figures held out promises of substantial monetary support. Senators Blanche Lincoln and Mark Pryor and Congressman John Boozman were joined by state Representatives Tracy Pennartz and Jim Medley in creating high expectations that the Marshals Museum would receive taxpayer monies. In the heady days following the announcement, figures of $10 million and $25 million of support were bravely proffered and bantered about with splashing headlines of potential federal funding and a state "surplus trough."[53] Such bold talk trebled museum fever.

Local business leaders including Bennie Westphal and Richard Griffin and their families were quick to throw in their support. The two families combined own a substantial portion of available real estate in downtown Fort Smith and thus had considerable profits to potentially reap, depending on where the museum landed. The Westphal family offered to donate two properties for the museum even before it had been awarded to the city. But support was strong for the vacant Frisco Station next to the Fort Smith National Historic Site, whose presence was a deciding factor for the committee awarding the museum. Partnering the Marshals Museum with existing tourist sites that would complement it was cited as an important variable in deciding the recipient city.[54]

In September 2007 the museum board voted nine for and three against placing the museum north of Garrison Avenue on the riverfront, away from Frisco Station and a short but inconvenient mile away from the National Historic Site. This decision moved the future museum farther from existing tourist sites and adjacent to property owned by the Griffins and the Westphals, and the museum would require new construction at the site. At this time Bennie Westphal was a voting member on the museum board and a member of the site selection committee that unanimously recommended to the board the location nearer existing tourist sites. An informal vote at the start of the meeting showed a six-to-six split on the measure. After discussion, only Jim Spears, Claude Legris, and Mike Blevins voted against moving to the entirely new site.[55]

The *Times Record* has been an active voice in building hopes and expectations of what the Marshals Museum might bring. Each step of the process has been trumpeted with optimistic headlines. One such article in May 2005, "Heritage Tourism Grows," connected the bid for the Marshals Museum to the local university's brand-new historical interpretation degree, which hypothetically would serve as a feeder of interns and future employees to the Marshals Museum and other historic sites in town.[56] The fate of that degree program is one indicator in a list of many that the hopes and dreams embodied by a few enthusiastic supporters and expressed in headlines veil the struggle for the Marshals Museum to become a reality in Fort Smith. The historical interpretation degree was discontinued within a few short years after it began.

The big-dollar support for the museum never materialized. A year after holding out hope for $25 million, Governor Mike Beebe delivered a $2 million check toward the museum fund as seed money. The City of Fort Smith eventually kicked in $100,000, and a few high-profile donations brought the total figure to about $3 million.[57] Barely more than two years into the venture, in April 2009 the price tag for the museum ballooned from an initial estimate of $15 million to $50 million as architectural plans were introduced for a badge-shaped building jutting over the banks of the Arkansas River; the design is said to be based on the scene at the end of *High Noon* when Gary Cooper takes his badge off and drops it in the dirt. Sandi Sanders, the museum project director at the time, said the estimated $50 million was a fund-raising goal, with $22 million of it going for construction, $15 million for exhibits, and $5 million in an endowment.[58]

In 2013 it was reported that the behemoth Walton Family Foundation was donating a slim $2 million toward the effort, though that is not reflected in the foundation's 2013 annual report.[59] The Marshals Museum financial reports claim to have raised $14 million as of June 2014, but this does not account for expenses of operating the endeavor for the previous seven years. Subtracting operating expenses and outside fees, including architectural designs, exhibit design consultants, and marketing firms, the figure of cash on hand is closer to $5 million.[60]

Between 2008 and 2012 reality set in that the Marshals Museum board would have the hard work of raising most of the $50 million without assistance from taxpayers.[61] A separate Marshals Museum Foundation was created to keep fund-raising and operating procedures distinct, and gestures were made to try to bring more nationally recognized names such as former Governor Huckabee into the project. New Market Tax Credits began to be discussed as a way to secure $10 million to $15 million, and the U.S. Mint "Marshals coin" created hope for acquiring another $5 million. While there was much talk of these initiatives, the bottom line did not fluctuate.

Despite a lackluster response, or perhaps because of it, the Marshals Museum held a dedication of the museum's cornerstone on November 9, 2013. This was done well in advance of the September 2014 groundbreaking for the facility and, curiously, in a different location than the planned site for the museum along the Arkansas River. A few months prior to the cornerstone dedication ceremony, the Marshals Museum board announced it would be locating the museum about a quarter-mile from its initial chosen location on the riverfront to better accommodate space to park the cars of the estimated 165,000 tourists each year. The assessment of parking needs was based on comparisons to accommodations at Crystal Bridges Museum of American Art in Bentonville and the Clinton Presidential Library in Little Rock, which both attract well over 200,000 visitors per year.[62]

The cornerstone dedication was attended by many high-ranking political officials, current and retired marshals, and community leaders. Headlining the event were Edwin Meese, attorney general during the Reagan administration; Howard Safir, one-time associate director of the U.S. Marshals Service and former New York City Police commissioner; and Stacia Hylton, current Marshals Service director. Rhetoric at the event reinforced the mythic imagination of frontier justice and inscribed it upon the contemporary landscape. During her speech, Hylton wistfully conceded that though she might be a Washington bureaucrat, she sometimes daydreamed of working on the frontier, arresting fugitives and returning them to Fort Smith to be tried in Judge Parker's courtroom. To punctuated applause, she declared, "So for us to be here in Fort Smith, a part of our dreams throughout our life and of growing up in law enforcement and the Marshals Service, I'm here to tell you that for a marshal standing here, for me standing here, to all of us, Fort Smith is like sacred ground."[63] The mythic frontier is still a warm refuge from Max Weber's icy iron-cage of bureaucracy.

Attorney General Meese delivered a much more direct conflation of fact and fiction to the crowd. The *Times Record* reported on Meese's remarks that "the history of the marshals parallels the history of the U.S. The exploits of the marshals, including well-known marshals Wyatt Earp and 'Wild Bill' Hickok, have served as the inspiration for many films and TV shows. 'Where would John Wayne have been without the material provided by the marshals?' Meese told the audience." The "sacred ground" comment by Hylton was reinforced by local news reporting and by museum president and CEO Jim Dunn. The *City Wire* reported that Dunn linked the future Marshals Museum to larger national memorials in stating that it "has the potential to become one of America's most sacred sites, much like the Vietnam War Memorial and the 9/11 Memorial in New York."[64] Such grand metonymic connections were also made on September 11, 2012, when the Marshals Museum unveiled a piece of steel I-beam recovered from the World Trade Centers that is to be put on display once the museum opens.[65]

The effort to create an effective sentimental connection between these national traumas is a marketing strategy the Marshals Museum promoters have used in other efforts. Rudy Giuliani is the featured speaker in the Marshals Museum's video "Your Marshal: Yesterday's Legends—Tomorrow's Heroes." The former New York mayor contributes to the sacralizing of the Fort Smith landscape:

> Well, if you know the history of the U.S. Marshals Service because of the spreading to the west and everything else that happened, that's

probably the place where more U.S. Marshals have given their lives, sacrificed their lives, than any place in the country. So, I think it's a place that has a great deal of the very glorious history of the U.S. Marshals Service kind of built into it.[66]

Each line is delivered in Giuliani's trademark confident fashion.

Throughout the video, Giuliani reinforces the righteousness of federal law enforcement in relation to an expanding country:

I mean it goes back to our days as a frontier country that was expanding. Towns that were lawless became towns ultimately that had some form of rule of law, then a really good rule of law. None of that would have been possible without the United States Marshals.

He then connects national history to the museum:

I think more people can learn about what the Marshals Service has done, and it can be a great study in the expression of the rule of law, a great study in how to take an organization and organize it correctly and give it the right kind of spirit.

While Giuliani's emphasis on the rule of law does not square with Rooster Cogburn–style marshaling, let alone that of a Bass Reeves or a Logan H. Roots, it does function to legitimate the power of the political state. Images and footage from September 11 interspersed throughout the video tap into the emotional trauma of that event while eliding more complex and nuanced perspectives of both September 11 and the frontier border in Fort Smith. It remains to be seen if such attempts at connecting the emotional memorialization of these traumatic events will result in financial support. The YouTube video was viewed just over four thousand times in three years.[67]

Offline, two other revenue sources for the Marshals Museum look troubled. Hypothetical figures of $10 million to $15 million in New Market Tax Credits and up to $5 million from marketing a U.S. Mint Marshals commemorative coin inflate the success of fund-raising efforts. Adhering to even the most exaggerated figures, $25 million to $30 million from these sources would be available toward a goal of $50 million. In reality, the Marshals Museum directors quietly announced at the June 2014 board meeting that the campaign failed to secure any New Market Tax Credits for that cycle, and while local newspapers routinely cite the $5 million from the

Marshals coin minted in 2015, that money must be earned by the Marshals Museum aggressively marketing it. Initial sales of commemorative coins have not been dependable, and even more problematic for opening the museum, it is stipulated that the revenues from the coin may not be used for construction.[68]

Besides sluggish monetary support for the Marshals Museum, the misspelling of Governor Mike Beebe's name as "Bebee" on the cornerstone is symptomatic of a series of foibles associated with the overall effort. On two occasions, Marshals Museum directors have had to backtrack on announcements that it had secured firearms associated with famous frontier figures. In one case, Marshals Service historian David Turk donated a gun he considered to have been used by the outlaw Frank James, a claim quickly disputed by the James estate. A few years later, board member and local real estate developer Rick Griffin assisted in securing a gun believed to once be held by George Maledon, the so-called Prince of Hangmen who worked as a deputy for the U.S. District Court for the Western District of Arkansas during Judge Parker's era. In this case, the receipt linking the rifle to Maledon turned out to be a forgery.[69] In June 2014 the Marshals Museum board revealed that the U.S. Corps of Engineers has an easement on the chosen building site beside the lock-and-dam-regulated Arkansas River. Though a threat to the planned museum's location, board members were calm and confident that the restriction would be changed, only conceding that it might "take some time."[70]

The easement issue had not been addressed by September 24, 2014, when a formal groundbreaking ceremony was held for the museum. The crowd of more than six hundred people included state representatives and congressmen, Governor Beebe, and nearly a hundred retired deputy U.S. marshals. The director of the museum board addressed the audience:

> Today's ceremony indicates how far we've come and marks the first phase of the museum's construction. In preparation for the beginning of the project we discovered an unrecorded easement, the Corp of Engineers has [long pause], and we're working on that, we're working with the Corp of Engineers, and a lot of people are working on our behalf to resolve that issue, and it will be resolved [long pause]. But, uh, you know, we've always said that we can only develop this museum, build this museum, as the money becomes available, but we're at a milestone. We raised some money. And I hope you saw the

announcement last week of the $5 million anonymous gift we got—
that's wonderful. That is wonderful, what a [applause]. We still have a
lot of work to do, but we're confident in the not too distant future the
U. S. Marshals Museum will stand right here on this spot.[71]

Six months later it was reported that the Army Corps of Engineers
would not give up the 100-yard-deep easement on the property. Further,
"The easement location may change where the museum is built or if it can
be built there at all, but the museum's directors said they don't know what it
means for the future of the project because they weren't aware of the Corps
of Engineers had been out there in the first place."[72]

No amount of goodwill and enthusiasm can totally compensate for being in over one's head. Creating a national museum from scratch requires
a great deal of expertise. While several firms have been contracted by the
Marshals Museum, the project has been led by people who have no experience in museums. Sandi Sanders was appointed as the first Marshals
Museum project director in April 2007, shortly after she was not offered
the position of chancellor at the University of Arkansas–Fort Smith, where
she had worked in administration for several years. With a background in
education, she did not bring any direct museum experience to the effort.
Jim Dunn, after thirty-six years as an attorney with the local law firm Warner, Smith, and Harris, replaced Sanders in June 2009. Within two years,
Warner, Smith, and Harris, a firm that had been around since 1887, closed
up shop.[73] In order to succeed at such undertakings, a researcher on the *Set
in Stone* study asserts, it is necessary to recruit strong and knowledgeable
leadership, not simply fill the slot with a local person looking for a lateral
move.[74]

Laramie's Marshals Museum

This hit-and-miss pattern of Fort Smith's Marshals Museum effort has
played out in two earlier failed attempts of cities to secure the elusive Marshals Museum. In 1988 Oklahoma City was off to a good start for landing the museum; by 1990 it had failed miserably due to alleged corruption
within the Marshals Service and the Marshals Memorial Foundation. By
1991 the Marshals Museum was heading to Laramie, where it would spend
a decade embedded within what was then called the Wyoming Territorial
Prison and Old West Park, locally often called the Wyoming Territorial
Park. By 2001 that joint venture had failed. Next we will look more closely

at what happened in Laramie and then turn our attention to the Oklahoma City attempt.

The *St. Louis Post-Dispatch* reported in late July 1990 that three cities were competing to be the permanent home of *America's Star*, the Smithsonian-created traveling exhibit featuring the legacy of the U.S. Marshals Service. The article reports that more than 400,000 people saw the exhibit in the two months it was temporarily displayed adjacent to that city's iconic Gateway Arch. U.S. Marshals Foundation member Herbert Bryant said that "the St. Louis area's central location would make it an excellent spot for the exhibit base."[75] Despite the success and accolades it received in St. Louis, the exhibit was on its way to Laramie a year later.

The arrival of the U.S. Marshals Service *America's Star* exhibit at the Wyoming Territorial Park was met with a ceremony to mark its official conveyance in August 1991. This new and intended permanent home for the exhibit was within "an historic theme park centered around the Wyoming Territorial Prison," which famously once held the outlaw Butch Cassidy. The exhibit was said to have been on tour for two and a half years and visited by more than 1.2 million people. Displays had titles such as "Lawmen for the Territory," "Lawmen and the Courts," "The Gunmen: Romance and Reality," and "Gunfight at the O.K. Corral" and artifacts including Al Capone's St. Valentine's Day Massacre machine gun, Wyatt Earp's shotgun, Jesse James' pistol, and warrants for other infamous criminals.[76] Promotional material for the Smithsonian-created traveling exhibit immediately began calling *America's Star* the National U.S. Marshals Museum.

Brochures listed key events interpreted in the exhibit, among them the Whiskey Rebellion, 1807 African Slave Trade Act, taming the frontier, Prohibition, desegregation, Wounded Knee, Anti-Hijacking and Counter-Terrorist Program, and drug enforcement.[77] Documents from its 1991 arrival in Laramie reflect a strong feeling on the part of Wyoming Territorial Park constituents that the Marshals Service had found the permanent home for its museum. It was billed "Where justice tamed the west." A letter to U.S. Senator Malcolm Wallop explains that "the Wyoming Territorial Park is modeled after the three well-known, east coast attractions—Old Sturbridge Village, Colonial Williamsburg and Plimoth Plantation. The Park is the creation of a legacy—a legacy linking us to the past and allowing our guests to learn about Wyoming's unique contribution to the development of the American spirit."[78] Promoters of this new union between Laramie and the Marshals Service were confident that it was a perfect marriage that would produce significant tourist numbers.

Newspaper articles from the time reinforce this perspective. In one, U.S. Marshals Foundation president Herbert Bryant, conveniently forgetting he had recently declared St. Louis an ideal location for the museum, now said, "It would have been inappropriate somewhere else. . . . It would have been out of place on Park Avenue in New York. You might get more visitors on Park Avenue, but it's not what they expect to see there." The manager of the Wyoming Territorial Park, Craig Post, agreed with him: "There is a certain integrity and a certain reputation the U.S. Marshals Service has and I think they were looking for a place where it would fit and give it all the surroundings necessary."[79] Just as some tourists might travel to Branson expecting to see hillbillies or in Hawaii a hula dancer, tourists going to a U.S. Marshals exhibit no doubt expect to see the mythically imagined setting of the nineteenth-century Wild West lawman.[80]

Laramie museum supporters expressed faith in having the right fit, a belief that tourists would pull off Interstate 80 to visit the site, and an expectation that the Marshals Foundation would keep the exhibit fresh with new artifacts and the collection rotating to keep those tourists coming back. The city of Laramie and the state of Wyoming put money and trust behind this effort. As early as 1987, more than $5 million was raised to restore the old territorial prison. The city of Laramie voted for sales-tax increases on two separate occasions, and the state of Wyoming made a $10 million loan for improving the land around the Wyoming Territorial Park.[81]

Four years later, in 1995, the enthusiastic folks in Laramie were still working on lining out a "vision plan" for constructing a stand-alone U.S. Marshals Museum within the Wyoming Territorial Park. Details included plans for a 25,000-square-foot building costing $5 million and another $7 million for "acquisition, preservation and maintenance of displays as well as the establishment of an operating endowment for the United States Marshals Museum."[82] The record from this plan reveals a great deal of discussion on how to gain active buy-in from a wider national audience and on which consultants and attorneys to hire at what point in the process: a cost consultant, a capital campaign firm, and a construction lawyer. Other sites used for comparison by the Marshals Museum were the Norton Museum of Art in West Palm Beach, Florida, and the Fort Lauderdale Art Museum, which was $9 million in debt at the time.

Several different tactics for fund-raising were discussed. One strategy, which has also been deployed in Fort Smith as Descendants Day, was the inception of an annual Marshals Day. In 1997 Laramie held its fifth such annual occasion. These events are used to form relations with potential donors, to gather stories related to the Marshals Service, and to attract donations of artifacts. Minutes from two separate meetings of the National U.S. Marshals Museum trustees reveal other fund-raising ventures as well as impending fissures in the Marshals Service relation to Laramie.

Live auctions, dinner-theater auctions, sales of prints of western-themed paintings, and the sale of raffle tickets for a Colt pistol had accrued a paltry balance-sheet total of less than $12,000 at the end of 1998.[83] Evidently there had been no takers for the 42-inch version of David Manuel's *Frontier Marshal* sculpture, which was available for $17,500. Manuel had been declared the "official sculptor for the United States Marshals Bicentennial." His 10-foot-tall version of the statue was unveiled at the 1989 Marshals Memorial in Oklahoma City.[84]

The minutes of the July 19, 1998, trustees meeting report a veiled comment about previous Marshals Museum blunders and a more direct comment about the growing disconnect between Laramie and Washington, D.C. In reference to the failed Marshals Museum attempt in Oklahoma City, an idea to develop a Friends of the U.S. Marshals Museum organization was rejected: "There is still some bitterness about a previous donation program that raised a large amount and the funds disappeared." Turning their attention to the *America's Star* exhibit, the trustees posed questions about what U.S. Marshals Service historian Ted Calhoun was doing to assist with maintaining the exhibit: "Can we negotiate with Ted Calhoun to handle all donations and to rotate displays; new exhibits each season? We need someone to ensure authenticity, etc. It was agreed that is [sic] was important to keep Ted and the U.S. Marshals Service involved." Discussion followed about a new exhibit on display at the U.S. Marshals headquarters that was not open to the public. The question arose as to whether the exhibit in Laramie should be declared a "satellite" museum. In the end, "All agreed that we needed more communication with the U.S. Marshals Service."[85]

By fall 2000 the imminent collapse of the Wyoming Territorial Park, and thus the U.S. Marshals Museum, was in public view. The *Sheridan Press* headline flashed, "Laramie Park Still in Midst of Financial Problems May Close." In response, the park's officials went all-in on the wager on frontier tourism. With only one year of operating monies remaining, they hired a marketing firm and had bright-colored billboards plastered along Interstates 80 and 25. Park Director Pam Malone said, "The way we looked at it was we could die of cancer or we could die of a heart attack."[86] Once hidden from public view, relations between the Wyoming Territorial Park and the Marshals Service were about to take a turn for the worse.

Jennifer Goodman, executive director of the Wyoming Territorial Park, addressed several concerns and rumors in a certified letter to Marshals Service Director Benigno G. Reyna on August 21, 2002. Chief among Goodman's concerns was the speculation that the Marshals Service was not going to keep the Marshals Museum in Laramie. She assured Reyna that the Wyoming Territorial Park would not be closing its doors and that its staff would accommodate any concerns regarding care of the *America's Star* exhibit. While Goodman conceded that the "USMS Museum deserved more attention and needs a dedicated effort to improve visibility, accessibility, and resources," she also was quite put out with the lack of communication from the Marshals Service: "Because no line of official communication exist [*sic*] between the WTPC and the USMS we have been left to speculate as to the issues that might have arisen concerning the care of the exhibit."[87] Clearly, this break had been quietly building for some time.

One week later the Wyoming Territorial Park was put on notice that the U.S. Marshals Service would be coming to Laramie in a matter of days to pack up the exhibit. In response, a lawyer for the Wyoming Territorial Park was directed to notify the Department of Justice that "the Park is asserting a lien over the artifacts in the amount of $55,000. This lien is asserted pursuant to Wyoming Statutes Section 29-7-102, et. seq. Under the terms of the statutes, the artifacts will not be released to the USMS until this lien has been satisfied." The September 4, 2002, letter notes that the "cooperative spirit" between the two agencies "has obviously ended."[88]

Two days later the *Laramie Boomerang* ran an article about the park's pending removal of the exhibit.[89] Park Director Goodman took the gloves off and pulled no punches in a flurry of cutting comments: "We've not gotten any new artifact for the last 10 years"; "We've tried to go out and support (the museum) without any assistance at all"; "People generally have a higher expectation of what the exhibit will be and are disappointed when they leave"; "They've had that (renewal request) on their desk since May and we have had no response from them"; "It sprang on us with no prior warning. I thought it was quite unprofessional." Notably, the term "Marshals

Museum" was never used in the article; it was quickly downgraded to only an "exhibit."

The departure of the *America's Star* exhibit was met with much concern about the money that had been put into the Wyoming Territorial Park, the impact the exhibit would have on tourism, and the dispirited contributors to the Marshals Museum cause. Museum trustee Jack Smith countered a month later, "The (exhibit) is being closed by people who have never been to the park, and know nothing about it. (They) don't care that we have a wall of honor where retired U.S. marshals paid $1,000 for a brick with their name on it."[90] A few of those contributors would get their money back, but it is doubtful that their confidence in such endeavors was left intact.[91]

For its part, the Marshals Service responded with a lawsuit of its own blocking the lien on the artifacts and putting the blame on the Wyoming Territorial Park. From the Marshals Service perspective, it had loaned the exhibit for years and not been compensated. Further, "the park did not make any efforts to return the Marshals Service artifacts; rather, the park continued to display them at the park and continued to use and publicize them to promote and/or benefit the park up to and through the end of this year's season on Sept. 30, 2002, and, in fact, beyond."[92]

Ultimately the lawsuits ended up in the Casper, Wyoming, circuit court, where it was reported that the judge in the case "told both parties . . . to stop bickering and 'act like adults.'" Goodman backed off her strong position, saying, "The park had threatened to auction the items in a desperate attempt to have problems resolved, but had no intention of carrying out the threat."[93] Eventually the Marshals Service did come and pack up *America's Star* and reportedly kept it in storage in Wyoming until it was shipped to Fort Smith in November 2007.[94] The Wyoming Territorial Park closed but was quickly reopened in 2004 as part of the Wyoming State Park system.[95] In Fort Smith, little is spoken in public or newspapers regarding the Laramie era of the Marshals Museum. At most, it is said that the Laramie site was having financial problems or was in a bad location and only had 40,000 visitors a year.[96] If people in Fort Smith know that the situation was far more complex, they have not publicly shared it.

Oklahoma City's Marshals Museum

Approaching the 1989 bicentennial of the creation of the U.S. Marshals Service, the U.S. Marshals Foundation was established in 1986 with a stated goal to "promote public understanding of the role and evolution of law and enforcement in America."[97] Stanley E. Morris, director of the U.S. Marshals Service, announced in May 1988 that after an eighteen-month search, Oklahoma City had been selected for a $6.5 million project to build the U.S. Marshals National Memorial and a 25,000-square-foot interpretive center that would include a museum on a 7.2-acre site. A host of accolades accompanied the announcement. Oklahoma Governor Henry Bellmon bragged, "There is not a more appropriate place in the country for this memorial than in Oklahoma next to the Cowboy Hall of Fame." The article concluded by saying, "Site selection for the memorial was based on [a] historical relationship to the U.S. marshals, demonstrated local support for the project and potential visitorship."[98] Oklahoma City was the ideal place for this project.

The scope of the project grew nearly immediately from simply a memorial to including a museum as the Marshals Foundation's optimism ran high. Aram Mardirosian, credited with designing the Museum of Westward Expansion beneath the St. Louis Arch, was employed to design the memorial. The mood of the moment was articulated in a September 1988 news article: "Everybody seems to agree the site is perfect." Phase 2 of the project would entail an interpretive center, a museum building, a library, an auditorium, archives, and a gift shop. An estimated 300,000 annual visitors were expected.[99]

In March 1989 the *America's Star* traveling exhibit visited Oklahoma City and was on display at the Cowboy Hall of Fame. This coincided with another significant centennial—that of the Oklahoma land run: the "exhibit's sponsors say it is appropriate for the display to come to Oklahoma City during April because a U.S. marshal fired the shot opening the Unassigned Lands to settlers in April 1889." Director Morris offered a further connection of the marshals to land acquisition in Oklahoma Territory: "The first Sooners were deputies. They used their badge to get across the line before the land run and picked up some nice pieces of property."[100]

The collective faith in the marshals memorial was high, but the project reached its zenith on November 8, 1989, and would fall to the ground just as quickly as it had risen. The dedication of the U.S. Marshals National Memorial on November 9, 1989, marked the completion of Phase 1. Dignitaries from Oklahoma and Washington, D.C., were on hand to participate and witness the unveiling of the 10-foot *Frontier Marshal* statue designed by Dave Manuel. Members of the Marshals Foundation board of directors included such prominent names as James Arness, Gene Autry, James Q. Wilson, and Winthrop Rockefeller. At the dedication Governor Bellmon proclaimed, "It seems only right that the U.S. Marshals National Memorial be formed from the red earth that has been stained by the blood of so many U.S. marshals. U.S. marshals paid a very high price for the taming of our state while it was a territory."[101]

The marshals were eulogized by the U.S. Marshals Foundation board chairman, G. T. Blankenship, in his closing remarks for the dedication as he reflected, "As I gaze across the sea of faces within the 190 foot replica of the five-pointed star, I can't help but believe there are more than 400 marshals who are here in spirit whose badges never shined brighter than they do today."[102] Within a year, visions of the memorial to those bright, shining badges were snuffed out with the bankruptcy of the U.S. Marshals Foundation and the selection of Laramie to become the permanent home of the *America's Star* exhibit and U.S. Marshals Museum.

While it is unclear exactly what transpired in Oklahoma City, construction on Phase 2 of the project came to a full stop in early 1990 when it became apparent there was no money to pay "about 55 creditors [who] held more than $600,000 in construction debts," the *Dallas Morning News* noted. "Mismanagement has been cited as a reason for the project's failure."[103] Much finger pointing and name calling ensued between Jack Mc-Crory, a former Marshals Service official, and Kenneth Collins, Marshals Foundation executive director at the time of the November 1989 dedication ceremony.

McCrory declared, "I was dismayed to see myself cast as the scapegoat for the memorial's debt problems," while Collins retorted, "There was a lot of enthusiasm and things were great, but the money just didn't come in as anticipated, and everything was stopped." Faced with these dire accusations, Collins optimistically said, "When you have leaders like Bryant, G.T. Blankenship and the rest of the board, things will turn around and be fantastic."[104] Things did not turn around, and the site was abandoned, with the property reverting to the city. The U.S. Marshals Foundation with Bryant still at the helm moved on to Laramie in 1991, carrying the debt along with it.[105]

While cursory mention of the Laramie failure is noted in Fort Smith, there is zero talk of the Oklahoma City episode. After four years of research on the topic I only found out about it accidentally. A common statement

Figure 8.3. Ruins of the Oklahoma City Marshals Memorial. A concrete replica of a marshal's badge crumbles at the site of the deteriorating 1989 memorial. Photo by the author.

in Fort Smith is that the Bass Reeves monument is the only memorial to a U.S. marshal. When I Googled around looking for other possible examples, I hit upon the U.S. Marshals Service website, which features a page with the *Frontier Marshal* statue.[106] As it is a generic, nonspecific, yet somehow archetypal white male marshal, it is not any named marshal, so the claim on the Bass Reeves statue may still stand. The larger point is that officials at the Marshals Service are aware of the long legacy of these failed attempts; whether they have shared them with people working on the museum in Fort Smith is unknown. The community of Fort Smith certainly has not heard the full extent of museum problems in Laramie and is largely unaware of the 1989 Oklahoma City attempt.

One can still visit the abandoned 1989 memorial site today. I walked the overgrown ruins in June 2014. I could see the concrete pad where the visitor's center and museum would have been. A short walk up into a clearing I found the outline of the marshal's badge overlaid with a smaller, 10-foot-wide badge with a round plinth at its center point. It was disheartening to see the remnants of so much time, money, and public trust decaying and crumbling away. Looking at the demise of two attempts at a U.S. Marshals memorial or museum, it is difficult not to look upon the present effort in Fort Smith and wonder what fate has in store for it.

Closing the Frontier Complex

Eight years into the U.S. Marshals Museum effort, the public still saw a brave face put on the endeavor. Occasionally, though, a bit of guard is let down. In January 2014 at the Sixth Annual Fort Smith History Conference, Marshals Museum board president Jim Spears participated in a session entitled "Marshals Museum Update." It was, in part, Judge Spears' success at leading the local effort of raising $300,000 for the Bass Reeves monument that landed him this new challenge. After reviewing a brief history on the project and discussing names and descriptions of exhibits to eventually be found in the museum, he grew more candid with his remarks: "We need fifty-three million [dollars]. We got about fifteen. We are hoping that some big foundation will come through." A few minutes later he became extremely frank: "We've got about five million in cash. . . . We've got to have some sugar daddy come forward with a fairly large contribution. When that happens I think the waters will start flowing." And then, with a combination of cocksureness and cruel optimism, he declared, "My assurance is that it's going to happen or you're going to step over my dead bloody body."[107] The anguish, torment, and concern in these remarks is inconsistent with a project that is so enthusiastically promoted as being a sure-fire economic engine.

Others have made public comments that throw light on the concern for how long it is taking to get the museum off the ground, not least of which came from Governor Beebe. While addressing members of the Chamber of Commerce on its 125th anniversary, he adamantly declared, "We're going to have a Marshals Museum. You can book it Danno. It didn't happen as fast as I wanted it to, but it's going to happen. It's going to create another tourist stop for our people."[108] At this point, asking why we need a Marshals Museum is not an exclusively academic question. Research supports a positive relation between having a clear need for such a facility and its having successful outcomes. If there is no strongly felt need for a museum, why would people come? Joanna Woronkowicz makes clear in the University of Chicago *Set in Stone* report on creating new museums that "the project manager needs to take into account both the demonstrated *need* for the project (and how real that is)."[109] Distinguishing enthusiasm from facts, in other words, would provide a more realistic assessment of the situation.

Let's assume for a moment that the Marshals Museum clears the numerous hurdles in its path and opens its doors in the near future. Will people come? Will it be the promised economic engine to the region? The frontier history of deputies in Indian Territory that it will interpret will not differ substantially from that found at existing frontier sites and will therefore not attract a new demographic. However, a new offering in the Marshals Museum plans will be interpretations of the role the Marshals Service played in key civil rights events such as enforcing the Fugitive Slave Law, escorting James Meredith into the University of Mississippi, and participating at Wounded Knee II. These are complex stories that do not always paint the Marshals Service in a flattering light. It remains to be seen if financial support for the museum from retired deputies will continue to flow if exhibits depict the service critically.

The question here is why tourists interested in civil rights history would come to the Marshals Museum in Fort Smith when they could just as easily go to nearby sites where major events actually happened and that offer a wide variety of additional amenities: to Little Rock Central High National Historic Site or to the National Civil Rights Museum in Memphis incorporated around the Lorraine Motel. The Marshals Museum will lack the gravitas necessary to pull tourists out of these primary civil rights tourism orbits.

From this vantage point, we can now see the frontier complex as a crafted cultural space, as a master symbol that can be unraveled to expose the underlying power structures behind it. The ground upon which the Fort Smith frontier complex sits has gone through many claims in the past two hundred years. From Osage and Caddo to the U.S. military to abandonment; from Indian Territory to the states of Arkansas and Oklahoma; from the U.S. District Court for the Western District of Arkansas to social service agencies; from the squatters village of Coke Hill to the National Historic Site; and today from homeless camps to the Marshals Museum.

At the national and local levels the frontier complex performs narratives of mythic justice, race, and gender that omit or elide the deleterious effects of manifest destiny and the injustices done to American Indians, African Americans, women, the disenfranchised, and the impoverished. Performances like those of Baridi Nkokheli complicate and even trouble such myth-making processes. Still, the mythic tropes of the Wild West loom large behind the marketing scheme and the "frontier" brand that the leadership in Fort Smith, Arkansas, has wagered will attract tourist dollars.

The only questions remaining are these: How long will the frontier complex stay open for business? Will the redoubling era of the frontier complex pay out and be rewarded with a more profitable era? Or has the era of the frontier complex closed?

Notes

Chapter 1. The Significance of the Frontier Complex in American History

1. Marx Toys began manufacturing Fort Apache in 1951; Marx Toy Museum, http://www.marxtoymuseum.com/western_items.html.

2. Salazar, "Imaged or Imagined?"

3. See Trouillot, *Silencing the Past*, and Salazar, "Imagineering Otherness."

4. Visitors to Fort Smith frontier tourism sites are routinely presented with narratives that jump between fictional and factual representations of the frontier without explanation. This is especially the case regarding the intersection of Judge Isaac C. Parker and Rooster Cogburn; "Fort Smith Historic Site Hosts 'True Grit' Event," *Times Record*, May 21, 2015; "True Grit: Based on a Real Place," Fort Smith Convention and Visitors Bureau, http:www.fortsmith.org/things-to-do/truegrit-fortsmith.aspx.

5. Lowenthal, *Heritage Crusade*, x.

6. For a discussion of performance theory see Bauman, *Verbal Art as Performance*, and Hymes, "Breakthrough to Performance."

7. Flores, *Remembering the Alamo*, xv.

8. Barthes, "Myth Today," in *Mythologies*, 104.

9. For analysis of a variety of frontier regions across the globe see Parker and Rodseth, *Untaming the Frontier*, and Michael Rosler and Tobias Wendl, *Frontiers and Borderlands: Anthropological Perspectives* (New York: Peter Lang International Academic). See Penny, *Kindred by Choice*, for the popularity of western novels penned in Germany by Karl May in the late nineteenth century and adapted to film in the 1960s. May's depiction of the American western frontier remains popular in Germany today.

10. See J. Hall, *Reconstructed Forts*.

11. See Frazer, *Forts of the West*; Hart, *Tour Guide*; and Utley, *Indian Frontier* and *Frontier Regulars*.

12. Frazer, *Forts of the West*, xii.

13. See Faiman-Silva, *Choctaws at the Crossroads*, 209–213, for a discussion on

how the Choctaw Nation adapted to gaming as a result of Reagan's "New Federalism" and deregulation.

14. Higgins, *Fort Smith*, 11–15.

15. See Willoughby, *Brothers Robidoux*, for a detailed account of early trade along the Santa Fe Trail between Mexico and the United States.

16. For discussion and maps of the military forts along the permanent Indian frontier see Utley, *Indian Frontier*, 38, and Oliva, *Fort Scott*, 3.

17. See DuVal, *Native Ground*, for a detailed discussion of the complex interactions between Spain, France, Britain, and the United States with Arkansas River Valley Indians.

18. See Wallis, *David Crockett*, 235, for a discussion of how Crockett was remembered in his lifetime and portrayed in James Paulding's 1831 play, *The Lion of the West*.

19. For a discussion of Pike and Long see Bearss and Gibson, *Fort Smith*, 33, and Hine and Faragher, *American West*, 160. For a map of Irving's route and an example of how his tour is remembered in Oklahoma see Thoburn, "Centennial of the Tour on the Prairies."

20. Barnes, *Forts of the Northern Plains*, 28.

21. The military fort is spelled Kearny, while the Nebraska town is spelled Kearney. A state name appears in parentheses if it was not yet a state at the time the military fort was established.

22. For a discussion of the use of the West for uniting the North and the South after the Civil War see Frost, *Never One Nation*.

23. Higgins, *Fort Smith*, 53–55.

24. See Gibson, *Chickasaws*, and Faiman-Silva, *Choctaws at the Crossroads*, for a development of the impact of cattle trails on Indian Territory.

25. Kansas Historical Society, "Home on the Range," *Kansapedia*, modified December 2014, http://www.kshs.org/portal_kansapedia.

26. Shaffer, *See America First*, 17–19.

27. Britz, "Long May Their Legend Survive."

28. Ibid., 14.

29. F. Turner, "Significance of the Frontier." See Etulain, *Does the Frontier Experience Make America Exceptional?*, also for contemporary critiques of Turner's original essay.

30. For a discussion of the role anthropology played in constructing this racialized landscape see Baker, *Anthropology and the Racial Politics of Culture*, and Visweswaran, *Un/common Cultures*.

31. Gruen, *Manifest Destinations*, 46–47.

32. In Pomeroy, *In Search of the Golden West*.

33. Shaffer, *See America First*, 20–25.

34. Kimmel, *Manhood in America*, and Bederman, *Manliness and Civilization*, offer excellent discussions of this topic.

35. Bold, *Frontier Club*, xviii.

36. See Brownlee, *1904 Anthropology Days*, 26, and Shaffer, *See America First*, 33.

37. Shaffer, *See America First*, 141–143.

38. Jakle, *The Tourist*, 152–168.

39. Hine and Faragher, *American West*, 543.

40. Ibid., 505.

41. Salazar, "Imaged or Imagined?"

42. Bodnar, *Remaking America*, 180–181.

43. Shaffer, *See America First*, 126.

44. Flores, *Remembering the Alamo*, 164.

45. Ibid., 119.

46. Sturken, *Tourists of History*.

47. See Souther and Bloom, *American Tourism*; Handley and Lewis, *True West*; and Shaffer, *See America First*.

48. Pomeroy, *In Search of the Golden West*, vii.

49. See Schnack and Wilson's 2013 documentary, *We Always Lie To Strangers*.

50. Rothman, *Devil's Bargains*.

51. For a variety of tourism studies see Bruner, *Culture on Tour*; Chambers, *Native Tours*; Desmond, *Staging Tourism*; Gmelch, *Tourists and Tourism*; MacCannell, *The Tourist*; Selwyn, *Tourist Image*; Sheller and Urry, *Tourism Mobilities*; Smith, *Hosts and Guests*; Wrobel and Long, *Seeing and Being Seen*.

52. Pomeroy, *In Search of the Golden West*, vi.

53. See Harvey, *Brief History of Neoliberalism*.

54. For examples of the globalizing trend see Bruner, *Culture on Tour*.

55. National Trust for Historic Preservation, "Heritage Tourism," 2014, http://www.preservationnation.org/information-center/economics-of-revitalization/heritage-tourism/#.U8hJr_ldUrc.

56. Berlant, *Cruel Optimism*.

57. Ritchie and Goeldner, *Travel, Tourism*.

58. Ibid., 236.

59. John Lovett, "CBID: Update Needed On Downtown Development Traffic Study," *Southwest Times Record* (Fort Smith, *Times Record*), July 15, 2014.

Chapter 2. The Frontier Complex in Fort Smith, Arkansas

Epigraph: Portis, *True Grit*, 39.

1. Lowenthal, *Heritage Crusade*, 4.

2. See DuVal, *Native Ground*, for a detailed history of Arkansas River Valley region.

3. Higgins, *Fort Smith*, 12.

4. For the contested nature of the city and the region see Bearss and Gibson, *Fort Smith*, and DuVal, *Native Ground*.

5. Ryan Saylor, "Cherokee Nation Unveils $80 Million Gaming Complex in Roland," *City Wire* (Fort Smith), April 29, 2014, http://www.thecitywire.com/node/32894#.U9FU__ldUrc; "Cherokee Nation to Build New Casino, Hotel in Roland," *City Wire*, April 21, 2014, http://www.thecitywire.com/node/32785#.U9F-fPldUrc.

6. Aric Mitchell, "New jobs come with $60 million casino expansion," *City Wire*, November 28, 2012, http://www.thecitywire.com/node/25331#.VaZrRflVhBc.

7. "Casino Amendment Qualifies for Ballot Signatures," *City Wire*, November 16, 2011, http://www.thecitywire.com/node/18852#.U9F_8_ldUrc; "Mayor Speaks against Gambling, Michael Ream," *Times Record*, October 4, 2000; Jeff Arnold, "Mayor Opposes Casino Plan," *Times Record*, July 7, 2006; Michael Tilley, "Riverfront Gaming Faces Big Hurdle," *Times Record*, July 13, 2007.

8. Ryan Saylor, "188th Has Last Mission with A-10s on 'Bittersweet' Training Day," May 16, 2014, *City Wire*, http://www.thecitywire.com/node/33156#.U85p8vldUrc.

9. Fort Smith Western Heritage Month, December 1, 2013, https://www.facebook.com/FSWHM.

10. Fort Smith Western Heritage Month, video, uploaded to YouTube, December 5, 2013, https://www.youtube.com/watch?v=-V_W4onTRDk.

11. Horwitz, *Confederates in the Attic*.

12. Salazar, "Imagineering Otherness."

13. For the use of mythic narratives functioning as alibis see Barthes, "Myth Today," in *Mythologies*; Franklin, *Vietnam and Other American Fantasies*; and Sturken, *Tourists of History* and *Tangled Memories*.

14. Harman, *Hell on the Border*.

15. On performance theory see Schieffelin, "Performance and the Cultural Construction of Reality"; and V. Turner, *Anthropology of Performance*.

16. Durkheim, "The Field of Sociology," in *Emile Durkheim: Selected Writings*, 51–68; Rabinow, "Representations Are Social Facts."

17. A. Burton, *Black Gun, Silver Star*, 11.

18. In Scott Smith, "Unveiling of Bass Reeves Statue Voted No. 6 Story of 2012," *Times Record*, December 26, 2012, http://swtimes.com/sections/news/unveiling-bass-reeves-statue-voted-no-6-story-2012.html.

19. Henry Louis Gates Jr., "Was the Lone Ranger Black?" *The Root*, http://www.theroot.com/articles/history/2013/12/was_the_lone_ranger_black.html?wpisrc=mostpopular.

20. Sturken, *Tourists of History*.

21. Nora, "Between Memory and History."

22. Karp and Lavine, *Exhibiting Cultures*; Kirshenblatt-Gimblett, *Destination Culture.*

23. Wanda Freeman, "City Director's Remark Stirs Racial Feelings," *Times Record*, August 8, 2009; "Latest Incident Creates Ugly Looking Pattern," *Times Record*, September 10, 2009; "Our Character Test," *City Wire* September 13, 2009, http://www.thecitywire.com/node/6049#.UYJNorWYZQU; "Racial Remarks Again Part of Fort Smith Board of Directors Meeting (Updated)," *City Wire*, August 8, 2009, http://www.thecitywire.com/node/5976#.UYJLBrWYZQU.

24. Maher, "Men behind the Badges"; Nkokheli, "Affirmation in the Face of Adversity," University of Arkansas–Fort Smith, February 22, 2011.

25. The uncanny is that which is quite familiar on one hand but on the other hand is unfamiliar at the same time. This rub draws attention to such events. Mark Auslander led sessions on applying Freud's notion of the uncanny in cultural anthropology at the 2010 and 2013 annual meetings of the American Anthropological Association; see Mark Auslander, "Holding on to Those Who Can't Be Held," *Southern Spaces*, November 8, 2010, http://www.southernspaces.org/2010/holding-those-who-cant-be-held-reenacting-lynching-moores-ford-georgia.

26. Author's field notes, Wild West Shooters monthly meeting, October 4, 2012, Fort Smith.

27. Geertz, *Works and Lives*, 141.

28. E. Turner, "Interview with Edith Turner," 845.

29. At the close of preparing the manuscript I was informed that a decision was made at the Fort Smith National Historic Site to discontinue the display of hanging nooses on execution anniversaries. An October 9, 2014, Facebook post explained, "We have just recently stopped placing nooses on the gallows on execution anniversaries. However, we have not stopped using them in interpretive and educational programs. We are now using the noose as an interpretive prop during ranger programs. This is just one of the ways we are expanding the interpretation of our park's story and helping our visitors connect with the historical objects we use to tell that story."

Chapter 3. The Peacekeeper's Violence

Epigraph: In Ford, *Man Who Shot Liberty Valance.*

1. Coleman, "Quartermaster," 8.

2. Michael Paskowsky's *Peacekeeper of Indian Territory* video has been shown at the site since it reopened in 2000 after being remodeled from the 1996 tornado. Quotes from the video are my transcription.

3. I model my analysis after Richard Flores' treatment of the orientation video shown to visitors at the Alamo, in *Remembering the Alamo.*

4. The background audio is only heard in the video when the closed captions are turned off. It can be heard on the National Historic Site's YouTube channel at https://www.youtube.com/watch?v=MJ5Cpq4gsA4.

5. Much of the phrasing of this video is derived from *Fort Smith: Little Gibraltar on the Arkansas*, written in 1969 by Edwin Bearss and Arrell Gibson, both of whom went on to become major contributors to interpreting American history. Bearss was chief historian of the National Park Service from 1981 to 1994 and remained an actively sought-out interpreter of American history.

6. Higgins, *Fort Smith*, 12.

7. "History and Culture Orientation," video, Fort Scott National Historic Site, Kansas, http://www.nps.gov/fosc/historyculture/index.htm.

8. DuVal, *Native Ground*, 196–226.

9. Ibid., 172.

10. For more historical perspective on Arkansas see Bolton, *Arkansas, 1800–1860*.

11. "Fort Smith National Historic Site," brochure, National Park Service, 2012.

12. Higgins, *Fort Smith*, 15.

13. Bearss and Gibson, *Fort Smith*, 3.

14. Ibid.

15. Higgins, *Fort Smith*, 15.

16. Ibid.

17. Bearss and Gibson, *Fort Smith*, 61–62.

18. DuVal, *Native Ground*, 227.

19. Ibid., 228.

20. Ibid., 221–222.

21. Ibid., 222.

22. Ibid., 225.

23. Higgins, *Fort Smith*, 103.

24. DuVal, *Native Ground*, 225.

25. Ibid.

26. Ibid., 226.

27. Bolton *Arkansas, 1800–1860*, 71.

28. Jefferson, *Notes on the State of Virginia*, 268.

29. DuVal, *Native Ground*, 218.

30. Bearss and Gibson, *Fort Smith*, 113, 136.

31. Ibid., 113.

32. In ibid., 122.

33. Higgins, *Fort Smith*, 37.

34. John Rogers was largely responsible for having both Captain Thomas and Captain Stuart removed from Fort Smith, and he spearheaded the argument against the military's interest in locating a second iteration of Fort Smith near the site of the first one; Bearss and Gibson, *Fort Smith*, 130.

35. Ibid., 102–103.

36. Higgins, *Fort Smith*, 34.

37. Bearss and Gibson, *Fort Smith*, 130.

38. Trouillot, "Anthropology and the Savage Slot."

39. Bearss and Gibson, *Fort Smith*, 139.

40. Ibid., 130.

41. Flores, *Remembering the Alamo*, 164.

42. Bearss and Gibson, *Fort Smith*, 131.

43. Ibid., 132.

44. Ibid., 139.

45. Ibid., 140.

46. Ibid., 149.

47. Ibid., 150–151.

48. Ibid., 152.

49. Higgins, *Fort Smith*, 39.

50. Bearss and Gibson, *Fort Smith*, 168.

51. Ibid., 168–169.

52. Jordan Grummer, "Bass Reeves: Statue Project Saw Starts, Stops on Path to Unveiling," *Times Record*, May 23, 2012.

53. Brandon and Hilliard, "Zachary Taylor and the Sisters of Mercy."

54. Bearss and Gibson, *Fort Smith*, 209.

55. Ibid., 212–213.

56. Ibid., 213.

57. Ibid.

58. Ibid., 214.

59. Ibid., 208.

60. Ibid., 231.

61. "History and Culture Orientation," author's transcription, Fort Scott National Historic Site.

62. Catherine Du Val Rector, diary, 1850–1853, Benjamin T. Du Val Family Papers, 1816–1957, MC 1212, Series 2, box 1, file 12, Special Collections, University of Arkansas Libraries, Fayetteville (hereafter cited as Du Val Family Papers).

63. Bearss and Gibson, *Fort Smith*, 216.

64. Ibid., 217.

65. U.S. Census 1860, Schedule 1, Free Inhabitants in the City of Fort Smith, Genealogy room, Fort Smith Public Library.

66. Higgins, *Fort Smith*, 49.

67. Billy Higgins is an associate professor of history at the University of Arkansas–Fort Smith. He has published books and articles on Fort Smith and is editor of the *Journal of the Fort Smith Historical Society*.

68. Ibid., 159.

69. We will see that despite the enormous publicity of African American Deputy U.S. Marshal Bass Reeves, much of his story is based on poorly documented sources and highly skewed racial narratives.

70. Bearss and Gibson, *Fort Smith*, 237.

71. Higgins, *Fort Smith*, 49.

72. Ibid., 54.

73. Ibid., 55.

74. For more detail on how Indian Nations were affected by the 1866 treaty see Gibson, *Chickasaws*, 274–277; Debo, *Rise and Fall of the Choctaw*, 85–90; and McReynolds, *Seminoles*, 314–317.

75. Utley, *Indian Frontier*, 116.

76. Ibid.

77. Galonska, "Fort Smith Council of 1865," 4.

78. Bearss and Gibson, *Fort Smith*, 308.

79. Ibid., 309.

80. "Fort Smith National Historic Site," brochure, National Park Service, 2012.

81. Frost, *Never One Nation*, 26.

82. Ibid., 21.

83. Ibid., 22.

84. Fort Smith Museum of History vertical files, "Historical Markers, Civics Club Project—1930s." More information on specific people involved in the erection of this and other such monuments can be found in this file.

85. Thanks to Mike Crane for the insightful conversation regarding this point.

Chapter 4. The Hanging Judge's Injustices

Epigraph: Portis, *True Grit*, 63.

1. Curtiz, *Dodge City*; McLaglen, *Chisum*; C. L. Sonnichsen, "Roy Bean," *Handbook of Texas Online*, modified July 28, 2015, http://www.tshaonline.org/handbook/online/; DeMille, *The Plainsman*.

2. For a variety of perspectives on Parker's career see Brodhead, *Isaac C. Parker*; Croy, *He Hanged Them High*; Emery, *Court of the Damned*; Harman, *Hell on the Border*; Harrington, *Hanging Judge*; and Tuller, *Let No Guilty Man Escape*.

3. This approach to dismantling mythic narratives will follow that of Roland Barthes as outlined in the "Myth Today" essay in *Mythologies*.

4. Paskowsky, *Peacekeeper of Indian Territory*.

5. Bearss and Gibson, *Fort Smith*, 315.

6. Higgins, *Fort Smith*, 56.

7. Bearss and Gibson, *Fort Smith*, 315.

8. J. Burton, *Indian Territory and the United States*, 253.

9. For jurisdictional boundaries see Brodhead, *Isaac C. Parker*, 104–105; J. Burton, *Indian Territory and the United States*, 121, 152; and Tuller, *Let No Guilty Man Escape*, 44, 124, 139.

10. Bearss and Gibson, *Fort Smith*, 319; Higgins, *Fort Smith*, 56; Tuller, *Let No Guilty Man Escape*, 48–49; Benjamin DuVal, "Congressional Investigation," DuVal Family Papers.

11. Bearss and Gibson, *Fort Smith*, 319.

12. Ibid., 319.

13. Akins, *Hangin' Times*, 35.

14. Tuller, *Let No Guilty Man Escape*, 71.

15. See Akins, *Hangin' Times*, for a description of each trial and execution.

16. J. Burton, *Indian Territory and the United States*, 200.

17. Brodhead, *Isaac C. Parker*, 45; Tuller, *Let No Guilty Man Escape*, 42.

18. Harman, *Hell on the Border*, 88.

19. Bowden, "United States District Court."

20. See J. Burton, *Indian Territory and the United States, 1866–1906*, 3; and Maher, "Jurisdiction Matters," 7.

21. A. Burton, *Black, Red, and Deadly*, 1.

22. This is the same fundamental alibi unveiled regarding the *Peacekeeper of Indian Territory* video. Of the alibi contained in myths, Barthes says that "the ubiquity of the signifier in myth exactly reproduces the physique of the *alibi* (which is, as one realizes, a spatial term): in the alibi too, there is a place which is full and one which is empty, linked by a relation of negative identity ('I am not where you think I am; I am where you think I am not')"; "Myth Today," in *Mythologies*, 109.

23. In Ada Patterson, "Judge Isaac C. Parker," National Park Service, http://www.nps.gov/fosm/historyculture/1896-interview-with-judge-parker.htm.

24. Kopel, "Self-Defense Cases," 297.

25. Ibid., 298.

26. Ibid.

27. Brodhead, *Isaac C. Parker*, 151.

28. J. Burton, *Indian Territory and the United States*, 199.

29. Tuller, *Let No Guilty Man Escape*, 137.

30. Brodhead, *Isaac C. Parker*, 151.

31. Harman, *Hell on the Border*, 521–522.

32. Ibid., 523.

33. Ibid., 524.

34. Ibid., 521–552.

35. Kopel, "Self Defense Cases," 298.

36. Brodhead, *Isaac C. Parker*, 156.

37. Kopel, "Self Defense Cases," 324–325.

38. Ibid., 298.

39. Ibid., 300–301.

40. Ibid., 302.

41. Brodhead, *Isaac C. Parker*, 154–155.

42. Kopel, "Self Defense Cases," 304.

43. Ibid., 306.

44. Tuller, *Let No Guilty Man Escape*, 151.

45. Brodhead, *Isaac C. Parker*, 155.

46. Kopel, "Self Defense Cases," 322.

47. Tuller, *Let No Guilty Man Escape*, 162.

48. Ibid., 156.

49. Gross, "Rate of False Conviction."

50. American Civil Liberties Union (ACLU), "The Case against the Death Penalty," 2012, https://www.aclu.org/capital-punishment/case-against-death-penalty.

51. Tuller, *Let No Guilty Man Escape*, 161.

52. J. Burton, *Indian Territory and the United States*, 67.

53. Ibid., 67. For Parker's appointment of two commissioners and his staunch objections to the practice, see 190.

54. Ibid., 67.

55. Ibid., 230.

56. Daily, "Judge Isaac C. Parker," 682.

57. Tuller, *Let No Guilty Man Escape*, 10.

58. Brodhead, *Isaac C. Parker*, 19.

59. Tuller, *Let No Guilty Man Escape*, 10.

60. Ibid., 120.

61. For discussions on whiteness see Hartigan, *Odd Tribes*; Lipsitz, *Possessive Investment in Whiteness*; Omi and Winant, *Racial Formation in the United States*; and Pfeil, *White Guys*.

62. Brodhead, *Isaac C. Parker*, 19.

63. J. Burton, *Indian Territory and the United States*, 253.

64. Harman's *Hell on the Border* has been published in various guises over the years. While scholars and many tour guides acknowledge its flaws, it is still prominently used within the frontier complex.

65. Turk, "Hell, Grit, and Justice."

66. Harman, *Hell on the Border*, 88.

67. Ibid., 88.

68. Ibid., 94.

69. Ibid., 96.

70. Ibid., vi.

71. Ibid., xvii.

72. Ibid., xvii.

73. Turk, "Hell, Grit, and Justice."

74. Harman, *Hell on the Border*, 111.

75. J. Burton, *Indian Territory and the United States*, xiii.

76. Harman, *Hell on the Border*, 112–113.

77. Ibid., 115.

78. Higgins, *Fort Smith*, 58.

79. Kidder, "Who Took The Trees?" (2007), 9; see also his "Who Took the Trees" (2006).

80. Higgins, *Fort Smith*, 58.

81. J. Fred Patton, "Newspaper Trumpeted First Railroads," in *Insight 2000*, ed. Steel, 72. *Insight 2000* is a compilation of previously published articles that appeared in the *Southwest Times Record*.

82. "Speeches and Proceedings at the Bridge Banquet of the Chamber of Commerce, Fort Smith Arkansas, Wednesday, May 27th, 1891," pamphlet (St. Louis: Ev. E. Carreras, 1891), vertical files, Fort Smith Public Library.

83. Ibid., 23.

84. Ibid., 23–24.

85. "Population of Oklahoma and Indian Territory, 1907," Department of Commerce and Labor, U.S. Bureau of the Census, 8, http://www2.census.gov/prod2/decennial/documents/1907pop_OK-IndianTerritory.pdf.

86. Wickett, *Contested Territory*, 186.

Chapter 5. The Invincible Marshal's Oppression

Epigraph: "John Wayne Interview," *Playboy*, May 1971.

1. See Bhabha, *Nation and Narration*; Connerton, *How Modernity Forgets*; Franklin, *Vietnam and Other American Fantasies*; Friedman, "Myth, History, and Political Identity"; and Sturken, *Tourists of History* and *Tangled Memories*.

2. These figures come from the Patterson Report of 1877. Data from and discussion on the report can be found in Burton, *Indian Territory and the United States*, 119–120.

3. Akins, *Hangin' Times*.

4. In the past forty years the number of Southeast Asians and Latin Americans living in the city has significantly increased. This important change in the composition of the Fort Smith area is being written about by Perla Guerrero at the University of Maryland. She is currently working on a manuscript with the tentative title *Nuevo South: Latinas/os, Asians, and the Remaking of Place*.

5. In April 2014 Chief Baker of the Cherokee Nation commemorated an "Act of Union" between the tribe he represented and the Keetoowah band of Cherokee. Baker publicly acknowledged this union although the Keetoowahs have not

agreed to it in the past or today. The ceremony was an act of political theater that subsumes all Cherokees under one banner, whether they want to be or not; Anita Reding, "Cherokees Commemorate Union," *Muskogee Phoenix*, July 9, 2014, http://www.muskogeephoenix.com/local/x1760125239/Cherokees-commemorate -union, and United Keetoowah Band Chief George Wickliffe, "We Should Celebrate Our Distinctions, Not the Act of Union," *Native News Online*, July 12, 2014, http://nativenewsonline.net/opinion/celebrate-distinctions-act-union/.

6. Gorman, *Building a Nation*.

7. Murray Evans, "Chickasaw Cultural Center Seeks to Preserve Tribe's Heritage," (Oklahoma City) *Oklahoman*, http://newsok.com/chickasaw-cultural-center -seeks-to-preserve-tribes-heritage/article/3483613.

8. In Bearss and Gibson, *Fort Smith*, 131.

9. Harman, *Hell on the Border*, 701–702.

10. *The Trail of Tears Exhibit*, January 2013, Cherokee Cultural Heritage Center, Tahlequah, Oklahoma.

11. Wickett, *Contested Territory*, 46.

12. Ibid., 19.

13. Ibid.

14. Ibid., 28.

15. Ibid., 29.

16. Hartigan, *Odd Tribes*, 496, and "Establishing the Fact of Whiteness," 502.

17. Bhabha, "Of Mimicry and Man," 126, emphasis in the original.

18. Wickett, *Contested Territory*, 36.

19. Allen, "McAlester, James Jackson."

20. For more historical discussion on coal, oil, and gas deposits in Oklahoma see Morris, *Drill Bits, Picks, and Shovels*.

21. Debo, *The Rise and Fall of the Choctaw Republic*, 128, and Faiman-Silva, *Choctaws at the Crossroads*, 58.

22. Wright, "Wedding of Oklahoma and Miss Indian Territory," 255–256.

23. Ibid., 255.

24. Ibid., 259.

25. Mihesuah, *Choctaw Crime and Punishment*, 36.

26. Benjamin T. DuVal, "Address at the Opening of the Sixth Annual Fair of Western Arkansas," October 13, 1885, DuVal Family Papers, 2.

27. Tuller, *Let No Guilty Man Escape*, 121.

28. "Fort Smith Fair," *Arkansas Gazette*, October 4, 1883. These newspaper articles on the Fort Smith Fair were retrieved from archival materials in the Pebley Historical and Cultural Center, Boreham Library, University of Arkansas–Fort Smith.

29. "The Pawnee Braves," *Arkansas Gazette*, July 29, 1884.

30. "Over the State," *Arkansas Gazette*, October 19, 1884.

31. For a history of this period see Chang, *Color of the Land*; Foreman, *Five Civilized Tribes*; Strickland, *Fire and the Spirits*; Strum, *Blood Politics*; and Wickett, *Contested Territory*.

32. Holly Wall, "How We Mark the Anniversary of the Oklahoma Land Run," April 22, 2013, This Land Press, http://thislandpress.com/roundups/how-we-mark-the-anniversary-the-oklahoma-land-run/.

33. Wickett, *Contested Territory*, 31.

34. Littlefield and Underhill, "Black Dreams and 'Free' Homes," 349.

35. Wickett, *Contested Territory*, 31.

36. Woodward, *Origins of the New South*, 303.

37. Paul Ausick and Michael B. Sauter, "The 10 Most Oil-Rich States," *USA Today*, August 3, 2013, http://www.usatoday.com/story/money/business/2013/08/03/the-most-oil-rich-states/2613497/. For frequency of earthquakes see "Oklahoma Earthquakes" on the *Oklahoman* website, NewsOK, http://newsok.com/earthquakes.

38. Littlefield and Underhill, "Black Dreams and 'Free' Homes," 345.

39. Wickett, *Contested Territory*, 34.

40. Ben Boulden, "Lynching Left Blemish on Town's Good Name," in *Insight 2000*, ed. Steel, 90.

41. Littlefield and Underhill, "Negro Marshals in the Indian Territory"; Williams, "History of the American Southwest."

42. Charles Mooney, "Bass Reeves—Black Deputy U.S. Marshal," *Real West*, July 1976, 48.

43. Ibid., 49.

44. A. Burton, *Black, Red, and Deadly*, 165.

45. Ibid., 217.

46. Art Burton, "Bass Reeves: Deputy U.S. Marshal," *True West* 38, December (1991): 40–43.

47. Ibid., 41.

48. "Invincible Lawman," *Monumental Mysteries*, June 2014, Travel Channel, http://www.travelchannel.com/video/the-invincible-lawman.

49. Jordan Grummer, "Bass Reeves," *Times Record*, May 23, 2012.

50. For an example of such works see Johnson, *Apartheid in Indian Country*, 126.

51. A. Burton, "Bass Reeves," *True West*, 40; A. Burton, *Black, Red, and Deadly*, 156.

52. A. Burton, "Bass Reeves (1838–1910)," in *Encyclopedia of Arkansas History and Culture* and in *Oklahoma Encyclopedia of History and Culture*.

53. Littlefield and Underhill, "Negro Marshals in the Indian Territory," 80.

54. Ibid., 77.

55. A. Burton, "Bass Reeves," *True West*, 42.

56. "Negro Deputy Marshal at Muskogee a Good One," *Chickasaw Enterprise*, November 28, 1901. I obtained a copy of the article through the Center for Oklahoma History, Oklahoma City.

57. See again Littlefield and Underhill, "Negro Marshals in the Indian Territory," and Williams, "History of the American Southwest."

58. Burton, *Black Gun, Silver Star*, 297.

59. Ibid., 301.

60. Ibid., 295.

61. Ibid., 341.

62. Brady, *Black Badge*, 167.

63. Burton, *Black Gun, Silver Star*, 242.

64. Ibid., 242.

65. Ibid.

66. Ibid., 300.

67. Ibid., 243.

68. A. Burton, "Bass Reeves," *True West*, 42.

69. Littlefield and Underhill, "Negro Marshals in the Indian Territory," 83.

70. Williams, "United States vs. Bass Reeves," 156.

71. Ibid., 156–157. See also Williams, "Black Men Who Wore the Star" and "History of the American Southwest."

72. Williams, "United States vs. Bass Reeves," 157.

73. Ibid., 159.

74. Burton, *Black, Red, and Deadly*, 217.

75. Williams, "United States vs. Bass Reeves," 156.

76. Burton, *Black Gun, Silver Star*, 297.

77. Ibid., 301.

78. Ibid., 11.

79. Ibid., 13.

80. Ibid., 14.

81. Author's field notes, Art Burton lecture, May 26, 2012, Fort Smith Museum of History.

82. Scott Smith, "Unveiling of Bass Reeves Statue Voted No. 6 Story of 2012," *Times Record*, December 26, 2012.

83. Henry Louis Gates Jr., "Was the Lone Ranger Black?" *The Root*, http://www.theroot.com/articles/history/2013/12/was_the_lone_ranger_black.html?wpisrc=mostpopular; "Invincible Lawman," *Monumental Mysteries*, Travel Channel, http://www.travelchannel.com/video/the-invincible-lawman.

84. Parsons and DeArment, *Captain John R. Hughes*.

85. For critiques of colorblind racism and neoliberal racial ideologies see

Bonilla-Silva, *Racism without Racists*; Gilroy, *Black Atlantic*; S. Hall, *Representation*; and Jensen, *Heart of Whiteness*.

86. Du Bois, *Souls of Black Folk*.

87. In Freeman, "City Director's Remark Stirs Racial Feelings."

88. In ibid.

89. In "Racial Remarks Again Part of Fort Smith Board of Directors Meeting (Updated)," *City Wire*, August 8, 2009, http://www.thecitywire.com/node/5976#. UYJLBrWYZQU.

90. In ibid.

91. In ibid.

92. In Freeman, "City Director's Remark Stirs Racial Feelings."

93. The *City Wire* is an exclusively online media outlet in Fort Smith. In the interest of full disclosure, I was a paid freelance writer of music reviews for it from April 2012 to January 2013. I did not write about this incident or any of the ensuing controversy in the paper, nor was I employed by the paper at that time. Since January 2015 I have contributed commentaries, unpaid, as part of a University of Arkansas–Fort Smith collaboration with *City Wire*.

94. "Latest Incident Creates Ugly Looking Pattern," editorial, *Times Record*, September 10, 2009.

95. "Our Character Test," editorial, *City Wire*, September 13, 2009, http://www. thecitywire.com/node/6049#.UYJNorWYZQU.

96. Cash, *Mind of the South*, 205.

97. Ibid., 188.

98. Fort Smith Convention and Visitors Bureau, http://www.fortsmith.org.

Chapter 6. The Hello Bordello and Brave Men Matrix

Epigraph: Portis, *True Grit*, 175.

1. For a discussion of gender see Bederman, *Manliness and Civilization*; Butler, *Gender Trouble*; Herzfeld, *Poetics of Manhood*; Foucault, *History of Sexuality*; Gilmore, *Manhood in the Making*; Kimmel, *Manhood in America*.

2. Butler, *Gender Trouble*, 179.

3. Paskowsky, *It Took Brave Men*. The video is shown for visitors to the site in the context of a jail exhibit.

4. In J. Burton, *Indian Territory and the United States*, 63.

5. Ibid., 65.

6. Littlefield and Underhill, "Negro Marshals in the Indian Territory," 78.

7. In J. Burton, *Indian Territory and the United States*, 63.

8. Ibid., 65.

9. Wickett, *Contested Territory*, 36.

10. J. Burton, *Indian Territory and the United States*, 34.

11. Benjamin DuVal, "Congressional Investigation," DuVal Family Papers.

12. Bearss and Gibson, *Fort Smith*, 319; Higgins, *Fort Smith*, 56; Tuller, *Let No Guilty Man Escape*, 48–49; "History," First National Bank of Fort Smith, http://www.fnbfs.com/aboutus/history.asp.

13. Benjamin DuVal, "Congressional Investigation," 6, DuVal Family Papers.

14. "History—Line of Duty Deaths Prevalent in Old West," U.S. Marshals Service, http://www.usmarshals.gov/history/line-of-duty-old-west.htm.

15. Hylton in my field notes and transcription of audio recording, cornerstone dedication ceremony, Fort Smith, November 9, 2013.

16. "Equal Opportunity in the Old West," *U.S. Deputy Marshals: 200 Years of Grit*, video, Fort Smith Advertising and Promotion Commission, 2005.

17. Ibid.

18. Author's field notes, "How the West was Worn: Women's Clothing at Fort Smith from 1817-1896," presentation, Fort Smith National Historic Site, June 30, 2012.

19. *John and Mary Rogers*, exhibit, Fort Smith Museum of History, 1986.

20. Radcliff, "Miss Laura's Social Club."

21. Reynolds, "Miss Laura's Social Club," in *Crackerjack Positioning*, 139–146.

22. Ibid., 139.

23. Ibid., 142.

24. Ibid., 144.

25. Ibid., 146.

26. "Miss Laura's Social Club," brochure, Fort Smith Convention and Visitors Bureau.

27. Ben Boulden, "Living under the Red Light," Arkansas Historic Preservation program, 1994, archive, Fort Smith National Historic Site; Ben Boulden, e-mail to author, April 17, 2013.

28. Marilyn Collins, "Carolyn Joyce: Yesteryear's Madam Today's Lady," 2*NJOY*, August 2012, 25.

29. Ibid.

30. Ibid.

31. Ibid., 28.

32. Russell, "Fort Smith City Government."

33. These police dockets are in storage at the Fort Smith Museum of History. I thank Connie Manning, Leisa Gramlich, and Caroline Speir at the museum for providing access to them.

34. Ben Boulden, "Fort Smith Had Strict Prostitution Rules," in *Insight 2000*, ed. Steel, 86.

35. Ibid.

36. Ibid.

37. Kay Dishner, "Miss Laura's Still Providing Hospitality," in *Insight 2000*, ed. Steel, 86.

38. Ibid.

39. Kay Dishner, "End of War Brought Last Hurrah to Bordello Row," in *Insight 2000*, ed. Steel, 169.

40. C. Smith, "Diluting an Institution," 23.

41. Dishner, "End of War Brought Last Hurrah," 169.

42. "Police: Fort Smith Hotel Manager, Employee Promoted Prostitution," *Times Record*, January 17, 2013.

43. Aric Mitchell, "'Pleasures by Kasey' Seeks Acceptance, TV Show," *City Wire*, May 10, 2012, http://www.thecitywire.com/node/21939#.U_qD5PmwLdd.

44. Shirley, *Belle Starr and Her Times*, 5, 6, 10, 17, 20, 27.

45. Ibid., 6, 10, 11, 14.

46. Ibid., 17, 180.

47. Ibid., 18.

48. Ibid., 3.

49. Ibid., 4–5.

50. For further sensationalized accounts of Belle Starr see Booker, *Wildcats and Petticoats*; Rascoe, *Belle Starr*; Rau, *Belle of the West*; and Steel, *Starr Tracks*.

51. Author's transcription, introduction to a skit about Belle Starr's trial performed at the Clayton House, October 14, 2012, in honor of the birthday of prosecuting attorney William Henry Harrison Clayton.

52. Shirley, *Belle Starr and Her Times*, 38.

53. Ibid., 234–236.

54. Bouvier, *Women and the Conquest of California*.

55. Ibid., 5.

56. Ibid., 17.

57. Ibid.

58. Kaplan, *Anarchy of Empire*, 23.

59. Foucault, *History of Sexuality*.

60. For the poetics and performance of gender see Gilmore, *Manhood in the Making*, and Herzfeld, *Poetics of Manhood*.

61. Kimmel, *Manhood in America*, 134.

62. Ibid.

63. Ibid.

64. Ibid., 103.

65. See Deloria, *Playing Indian*, 95–127.

66. In Bederman, *Manliness and Civilization*, 131.

67. Kimmel, *Manhood in America*, 136, on men's clubs; Deloria, *Playing Indian*, on children's camps, 108, and on urbanism, 96.

68. Scaff, *Max Weber in America*, 73–97.

69. For Weber's thoughts on Protestant ethic while in Oklahoma, see ibid., 74; Weber quoted in Kimmel, *Manhood in America*, 104.

70. In Kimmel, *Manhood in America*, 150.

71. Ibid., 151.

72. Ibid.

73. Ibid., 148.

74. Wister, *The Virginian*, viii.

75. Trouillot, *Silencing the Past*, 74.

76. Littlefield and Underhill, "Divorce Seeker's Paradise."

77. Ibid., 21.

78. Ibid., 23.

79. Ibid., 24.

80. Ibid., 30.

Chapter 7. Performing "Frontier in the Attic"

Epigraph: McMurtry, *Last Kind Words Saloon*, 50.

1. Rothman, *Devil's Bargains*, 15.

2. Croy, *He Hanged Them High*, 229–230.

3. Ibid., 230.

4. The Paul Wolfe Collection contains numerous newspaper clippings from 1954 to 1964 as well as handwritten notes from meetings and presentations given to the community for raising money for the restoration. The collection is available at the Fort Smith Museum of History, accession number 1999.6, 200.6, Wolfe Collection. Current museum director Leisa Gramlich was kin to Paul Wolfe; Caroline Speir, who also works at the museum, was kin to Mayor H. R. Hestand. Thanks to them for their assistance with this collection. There is also a collection of Paul Wolfe documents at the Pebley Historical and Cultural Center, Boreham Library, University of Arkansas–Fort Smith.

5. Folders in the Paul Wolfe Collection, Fort Smith Museum of History, contain news clippings from the period but often lack specific source information. Articles, letters to the editor, and personal notes are interspersed in the collection.

6. The subhead "Relive the Heritage, Restore the Pride" is the tagline for Fort Smith's Western Heritage Month program.

7. A segment of this 1957 brochure that has been completely washed from local history is that without volunteer labor contributed by the AFL-CIO building-trade unions, the restoration would not have been completed as quickly. In a city where many are proud of the state's right-to-work status, the unions' contribution has been quietly left behind.

8. A Coke Hill folder, accession number 2012.1.80, derived from the Chamber

of Commerce files can be found in the Pebley Historical and Cultural Center, Boreham Library, University of Arkansas–Fort Smith.

9. Nancy Steel, "Coke Hill Leveled in 1958," in *Insight 2000*, ed. Steel, 189; Eddie Hicks, "Meanderings of a Meanie, Prying into People's Privacy," *Times Record*, March 19, 1939, Coke Hill folder, accession number 2012.1.80, Pebley Historical and Cultural Center, Boreham Library, University of Arkansas–Fort Smith.

10. Urry and Larsen, *Tourist Gaze 3.0.*

11. "R. K. Rodgers," Fort Smith Historical Society, http://www.fortsmithhistory.org/archive/bios/rkrodgers.html.

12. I have not been able to find this quote anywhere besides the National Historic Site webpage, http://www.nps.gov/fosm/historyculture/national-park-service-1961present.htm, and I suspect it to be part of the folklore of the site.

13. "The Judge Parker Saga," August 14, 1963. This quote is from the transcript of a prerecorded skit that was played during the "Ceremonies Transferring the Judge Parker Courtroom to the National Park Service by Public Historical Restorations, Inc." The transcript is archived at the Fort Smith National Historic Site research library, file box Janie Glover, Chamber of Commerce, accession no. 440.

14. This was the figure in an anonymous handwritten note in the Paul Wolfe Collection. The figure of 62,000 is also cited in a newspaper clipping in this collection but with no source cited.

15. Britz, "Long May Their Legend Survive."

16. Rothman, *Devil's Bargains*, 20–21.

17. "Miscellaneous" file, document F, Paul Wolfe Collection, Fort Smith Museum of History.

18. Rothman, *Devil's Bargains*, 11, 21.

19. "First Lady of Tourism in Fort Smith, Ark.," *Group Tour Magazine*, September 26, 2012.

20. Ibid.

21. Marilyn Collins, "Carolyn Joyce: Yesteryear's Madam Today's Lady," 2NJOY, August 2012, 27.

22. "First Lady of Tourism in Fort Smith, Ark."

23. "Fort Smith: Scoundrels Welcome," Group Travel Leader, April 7, 2010, http://grouptravelleader.com/articles/fort-smith-scoundrels-welcome.

24. "Fort Smith 'Hangin' Judge' Gallows Demonstration," video, uploaded to YouTube by chandarchandar, January 20, 2011, http://www.youtube.com/watch?v=g3oKtKDOmfQ.

25. This exhibit was created in 1998 by Leslie Przybylek, then curator of the museum, and Juliet Galonska, then historian at the Fort Smith National Historic Site. The exhibit was on display from 1998 to 2001. Przybylek and Galonska both moved out of state soon after the exhibit's installation. In 2009 the exhibit was

reinstalled. It was confirmed via e-mail with Leslie Przybylek that some original aspects of the exhibit were excluded in the second exhibit. All my citations from and descriptions of the exhibit come from the second installation unless otherwise stated.

26. McMurtry, *Last Kind Words Saloon*, 50. See Maddra, *Hostiles?*, 82–84, for a critique of how Buffalo Bill's Wild West shows strove to strike this same balance between the real and the unreal.

27. This picnic basket and noose were removed in 2013.

28. Franklin, *Vietnam and Other American Fantasies*, 26.

29. Each of these letters is on file at the Fort Smith National Historic Site archives.

30. "Roosters by the Dozen," calendar event announcement, December 2011, https:/www.facebook.com/Gritapalooza.

31. Mr. Sandy Sanders, Fort Smith mayor, is married to Ms. Sandi Sanders, former Marshals Museum director.

32. "Gritapalooza!," video, uploaded to YouTube by FortSmithNPS, June 9, 2011, https://www.youtube.com/watch?v=tbT34RsCAsg.

33. "True Grit," *The Real Story*, video, Smithsonian Channel, n.d., http://www.smithsonianchannel.com/sc/web/series/679/the-real-story/141166/true-grit.

34. Portis, *True Grit*, 63.

35. Ibid., 79.

36. Ibid., 87.

37. Bakhtin, *Dialogic Imagination*, 84.

38. Events included a May 17, 2012, reception for Harold T. Holden, a May 24 meet-the-artist reception, a May 25 lunchtime talk by Vaunda Nelson, author of *Bad News for Outlaws*, and that evening an "Oscar Awards" party at Movie Lounge event center. On Saturday, May 26, the monument was dedicated and unveiled in the morning, and presentations followed at the Fort Smith Museum of History. Art Burton spoke, actors at the National Historic Site reenacted the trial of Bass Reeves in the Judge Parker courtroom, and the Bass Reeves Troupe of Muskogee performed at the Clayton House. On Sunday, May 27, Baridi Nkokheli was interviewed at the Clayton House, and a wrap-up discussion took place at the Fort Smith Public Library.

39. Transcript of author's field recordings, Burton's talk, May 27, 2012, Fort Smith Public Library.

40. Lofaro, introduction to *David Crockett*, by Shackford, xii.

41. Nkokheli, "Affirmation in the Face of Adversity."

42. Sturken, *Tourists of History*, 12.

43. See Slotkin's works *Gunfighter Nation*, *Fatal Environment*, and *Regeneration through Violence*.

44. "Richard Slotkin on Guns and Violence," *Moyers and Company*, December 13, 2013, http://billmoyers.com/segment/richard-slotkin-on-guns-and-violence.

45. Vonnegut, introduction to *Mother Night*, v.

Chapter 8. Doubling Down on the Wager of Frontier Tourism

Epigraph: In Hathaway, *True Grit*.

1. See Carson, "End of History Museums."

2. Joseph Brennan and Mike Konz, "Kearney Arch Files for Bankruptcy Protection," *Omaha World-Herald*, March 6, 2012, http://www.omaha.com/news/kearney-arch-files-for-bankruptcy-protection/article_8d2cf7dd-0695-531c-b6fa-20db4bb24531.html.

3. In Richard Green, "Efforts to Fund Oklahoma City Indian Museum and Cultural Center Move to Appropriations Process," *Oklahoman*, April 28, 2014, http://newsok.com/efforts-to-fund-oklahoma-city-indian-museum-and-cultural-center-move-to-appropriations-process/article/4569026; Janelle Stecklein, "Indian Museum Just a Façade," *Muskogee Phoenix*, June 8, 2014, http://www.muskogeephoenix.com/archives/sunday-extra-indian-museum-just-a-facade/article_e1877e83-af89-5738-95e2-b87bb09c467e.html.

4. Woronkowicz et al., *Set in Stone*.

5. See Harvey, *Brief History of Neoliberalism*.

6. Carson, "End of History Museums," 11.

7. "Evidence Museums Matter," *Museum Audience Insight*, December 10, 2014, http://reachadvisors.typepad.com/museum_audience_insight/2014/12/evidence-museums-matter.html.

8. Ritchie and Goeldner, *Travel, Tourism*, 234–237.

9. For a discussion of global imaginaries see Salazar and Graburn, *Tourism Imaginaries*.

10. Interview with author, field notes, June 18, 2014.

11. See Berlant, *Cruel Optimism*, for an analysis on how beliefs about social change have not kept pace with real changes in the economy.

12. "About the Marshals Museum Project," U.S. Marshals Museum, 2015, http://usmarshalsmuseum.org/about.

13. "Fort Smith Named 'True Western Town' by True West Magazine," *City Wire*, December 12, 2012, http://www.thecitywire.com/node/25519#.VbJgCrNVhBc.

14. "Sun Hasn't Set on Fort Smith's Western History, Heritage," *Arkansas Business*, December 16, 2013, http://www.arkansasbusiness.com/article/96179/sun-hasnt-set-on-fort-smiths-western-history-heritage.

15. "Old West Status Brings Tourists, Jobs, Revenue, Pride," editorial, *Times Record*, December 14, 2012.

16. Mark Boardman, "Fort Smith, Arkansas, Is *True West* Magazine's Top True Western Town," *True West*, press release, December 12, 2012.

17. "NPS Stats," National Park Service, https://irma.nps.gov/Stats/.

18. Caroline Speir e-mailed me the Fort Smith Museum of History figures, Carolyn Joyce e-mailed me Miss Laura's figures, and Julie Moncrief messaged me on Facebook the data for the Clayton House.

19. Catherine Cullinane Thomas, Christopher Huber, and Lynne Koontz, "2013 National Park Visitor Spending Effects," National Park Service, http://www.nature.nps.gov/socialscience/docs/NPSVSE2013_final_nrss.pdf, 31, 38.

20. "A Comprehensive Plan for the City of Fort Smith, Arkansas," Wallace Roberts and Todd, December 2014, http://www.fortsmithar.gov/Planning/files/14_FinalCompPlan.pdf, 20.

21. 2012 Annual Report Executive Summary, Arkansas Department of Parks and Tourism, 2013, http://www.arkansas.com/!userfiles/editor/docs/apt-annual-report-financials-2012.pdf.

22. A comparison of the 2013 Annual Report Executive Summary reveals very similar data to the 2012 results; Arkansas Department of Parks and Tourism, 2014, http://www.arkansas.com/!userfiles/editor/docs/apt-2013-annual-report.pdf.

23. 2012 Annual Report Executive Summary, 86.

24. DuVal, *Native Ground*, 101; "Arkansas Tourism Officials Announce 2014 Henry Awards Nominees," *City Wire*, December 17, 2013, http://www.thecitywire.com/node/30977#.U8rUYvldUrc.

25. "Fort Smith Wins Community Tourism Development Award," *Times Record*, March 19, 2014.

26. John Lovett, "2014 GRIT Awards Recipients Announced," *Times Record*, April 26, 2014.

27. Author's field notes, April 25, 2013.

28. "GRIT Award Winners Named by Fort Smith Convention and Visitors Bureau," *City Wire*, April 25, 2013, http://www.thecitywire.com/node/27565#.U8rZ_PldUrc.

29. Lynn Wasson, "GRIT Awards Honor Tourism Contributions," *Entertainment Fort Smith*, 2012. http://www.efortsmith.com/features/index.cfm/GRIT-Awards-honor-tourism-contributions/-/aid/34/.

30. Author's field notes, Movie Lounge event center, Fort Smith, April 25, 2013.

31. In actuality, they gut the interiors and retain only the appearance of the old façade.

32. Rusty Garrett, "CBID OKs Retail/Residential Project for Downtown Fort Smith," *Times Record*, April 25, 2013, http://swtimes.com/sections/news/cbid-oks-retailresidential-project-downtown-fort-smith.html.

33. Self-disclosure: the author served on the board of Next Step Homeless

Services from 2008 to 2014. The other two agencies are the Salvation Army and the Community Rescue Mission. So-called point-in-time counts consistently show sixty to eighty individuals experiencing homelessness on a given night.

34. "Fort Smith Board Agrees to Pursue Homeless Task Force Ideas," *City Wire*, March 20, 2010, http://www.thecitywire.com/node/9251#.U8rqgPldUrc.

35. Ken Pyle, "Commentary: Riverview Hope Campus 'Better Way' to Address Homelessness," *Times Record*, September 30, 2014, http://swtimes.com/opinion/commentary-riverview-hope-campus-better-way-address-homelessness.

36. Flores, *Remembering the Alamo*, 160.

37. News briefs, *Oklahoman*, July 19, 2003, http://newsok.com/tests-confirm-body-is-missing-womans/article/1938031.

38. Kristen Inbody, "Museum Considers Fort Smith," *Times Record*, October 3, 2003.

39. Alison Vekshin, "Senators Wed City, Museum," *Times Record*, October 25, 2003.

40. "Fort Smith Natural Site for Museum," editorial, *Times Record*, December 14, 2003.

41. In Mary Crider, "Fort Smith Considered for U.S. Marshals Museum, *Times Record*, January 29, 2004.

42. "Fort Smith a 'Natural' Museum Location," editorial, *Times Record*, February 2, 2004; "City Deserves U.S. Marshals Museum," editorial, *Times Record*, April 5, 2004.

43. *U.S. Deputy Marshals: 200 Years of Grit*, DVD.

44. Mary Crider, "Marshals Service Plans to Visit Museum Site," *Times Record*, November 10, 2005; "It's Show Time!" editorial, *Times Record*, November 11, 2005; Rusty Garrett, "Marshals View Possible Site for Museum," *Times Record*, November 18, 2005; "City Perfect Location for Museum," editorial, *Times Record*, November 27, 2005.

45. "Project's Goal: Bring Museum Home to Area," editorial, *Times Record*, May 31, 2006.

46. In Steve Tetreault, "City Pitches Marshals Museum," *Times Record*, June 28, 2006.

47. "City Named Museum Finalist," editorial, *Times Record*, July 25, 2006.

48. In Aaron Sadler, "Fort Smith Rival Makes Museum Pitch," *Times Record*, December 4, 2006.

49. Pam Cloud, "Residents Cry, 'Bring It Home,'" *Times Record*, November 16, 2006.

50. Pam Cloud, "City Makes Case; Marshals Museum Site in Panel's Hands," *Times Record*, November 18, 2014.

51. "Marshals Select Fort Smith for Museum," *Arkansas News*, January 4, 2007.

52. In Pam Cloud, "City Hosts Victory Celebration," *Times Record*, January 8, 2007.

53. "Federal Funding May Be Possible for Museum," *Times Record*, January 17, 2007; "Surplus Trough Is Open in Little Rock," editorial, *Times Record*, February 22, 2007; "Beebe Signs Bills Funding Museum," *Times Record*, April 5, 2007.

54. Pam Cloud, "Marshals Director to Visit," *Times Record*, February 19, 2007.

55. Amy Sherrill, "Panel Eyes Museum's Location," *Times Record*, August 6, 2007; Amy Sherrill, "Panel Picks Riverfront for Museum," *Times Record*, September 18, 2007.

56. Mary Crider, "Heritage Tourism Grows," *Times Record*, May 2, 2005.

57. Amy Sherrill, "Beebe Cuts Museum Check," *Times Record*, February 29, 2008.

58. "Building Design Photos Provided by Marshals Museum Architect," *City Wire*, April 24, 2009, http://www.thecitywire.com/node/3806#.U9ZnM_ldUrc.

59. "Walton Foundation Gives $2 Million to Marshals Museum," *City Wire*, August 19, 2014, http://www.thecitywire.com/node/29103#.U9ZktvldUrc, with the Walton Family Foundation Report, 2013, http://2013annualreport.waltonfamilyfoundation.org/walton-family-foundation-2014-annual-report.pdf?v=1.

60. U.S. Marshals Museum Board of Directors meeting, June 10, 2014, board agenda and author's notes.

61. The *City Wire* consistently prints the cost of the museum to be $53 million, while the *Times Record* uses the figure $50 million. At the June 2014 Marshals Museum board meeting it was made clear that the board would not have a definite figure until contracts for construction came in. Three months from the September 24, 2014 official groundbreaking there was still a great deal of ambiguity regarding costs. For an updated financial picture see "Our Progress," U.S. Marshals Museum, http://usmarshalsmuseum.org/our-progress.

62. "Marshals Museum Director: 165,000 Visitors Possible," *City Wire*, May 25, 2011.

63. Author's transcription, Hylton's November 9, 2013, speech at the cornerstone dedication.

64. Stacy Ryburn, "Fallen Marshals Honored," *Times Record*, November 9, 2013; Ryan Saylor, "US Marshals Director: Fort Smith Is 'Sacred Ground,'" *City Wire*, November 11, 2013, http://www.thecitywire.com/node/30434#.VEop_fl4rdc.

65. Mary Crider, "Museum Unveils Sept. 11 Attack Artifact," *Times Record*, September 11, 2012.

66. Quotations from the video are my transcription; "Your Marshal: Yesterday's Legends—Tomorrow's Heroes," video, uploaded to YouTube by U.S. Marshals Museum, August 27, 2012, https://www.youtube.com/watch?v=EH5uKUdiVeo.

67. Ibid.

68. Peter Urban, "Experts Don't See Sellout for Marshals Coin," *Times Record*, June 29, 2014.

69. "'A Lot to Accomplish' in 2014 for Marshals Museum," *City Wire*, December 10, 2013, http://www.thecitywire.com/node/30860#.U7mrKvldUrc; "U.S. Marshal Historian Brings Weapon to Museum Meeting," *City Wire*, March 9, 2010, http://www.thecitywire.com/node/8823#.U7mr3_ldUrc; personal e-mail correspondence between the author and the James Preservation Trust, June 6, 2014; "The Hangman and His Winchester," Marshals Museum Guns of the Frontier Lecture Series, April 14, 2014, author's transcription and field notes.

70. Author's notes and transcription of audio recording, Marshals Museum board meeting, June 10, 2014.

71. Author's transcription, recorded Marshals Museum groundbreaking ceremony, Fort Smith, September 24, 2014.

72. "Army Corps of Engineers Says It Will Not Give up Land for U.S. Marshals Museum," *40/29 News*, March 26, 2015, http://www.4029tv.com/news/army-corps-of-engineers-says-it-will-not-give-up-land-for-us-marshals-museum/29730232.

73. "124-Year-Old Warner, Smith and Harris Firm to Close Doors," *City Wire*, June 21, 2011, http://www.thecitywire.com/node/16382#.VEotIvl4rdc.

74. Woronkowicz, "Feasibility of Cultural Building Projects."

75. Lisa C. Jones, "Six-Gun Gallery East St. Louis Site Is a Finalist for Marshals Museum," *Post-Dispatch*, July 29, 1990.

76. *America's Star*, news release, Wyoming Territorial Park, August 1991, archives, Wyoming Territorial Prison State Historic Site.

77. "National U.S. Marshals Museum," brochure, Wyoming Territorial Park, archives, Wyoming Territorial Prison State Historic Site.

78. Gretchen Glick to Senator Malcolm Wallop, July 29, 1991, Director of Development, archives, Wyoming Territorial Prison State Historic Site.

79. In Julia Prodis, "Wyo Wins Bid for Marshals Museum," *Casper Star-Tribune*, August 2, 1991.

80. See Schnack and Wilson's *We Always Lie to Strangers*.

81. Steven Rosen, "Laramie Will Pin on Badge as Home for Marshal's Artifacts," *Denver Post*, August 11, 1991.

82. "Vision Plan: The United States Marshals Museum," July, 1995, archives, Wyoming Territorial Prison State Historic Site.

83. "November 12, 1998, National U.S. Marshals Museum Trustees Minutes," archives, Wyoming Territorial Prison State Historic Site.

84. Stanley E. Morris to David Manuel, undated, archives, Wyoming Territorial Prison State Historic Site; program, 1989 United States Marshals National Memorial dedication.

85. "National U.S. Marshals Museum Trustees Minutes," July 19, 1998, archives, Wyoming Territorial Prison State Historic Site.

86. "Laramie Park Still in Midst of Financial Problems May Close," *Sheridan Press*, October 27, 2000.

87. Goodman to Reyna, August 21, 2002, archives, Wyoming Territorial Prison State Historic Site.

88. Wyoming Territorial Park to U.S. Department of Justice, September 4, 2002, archives, Wyoming Territorial Prison State Historic Site.

89. Angela Brooks, "Territorial Park to Get Rid of Marshals Exhibit," *Laramie Boomerang*, September 6, 2002.

90. Angela Brooks, "Wyoming Territorial Park Forecloses Storage Lien," *Laramie Boomerang*, October 9, 2002.

91. Ollie Hill to Jamie Newbrough, April 11, 2003, archives, Wyoming Territorial Prison State Historic Site.

92. "Marshals Service Sues Territorial Park over Artifacts," unidentified newspaper, October 29, 2002, archives, Wyoming Territorial Prison State Historic Site.

93. Angela Brooks, "Park Ironing out Problems with U.S. Marshals Service," *Laramie Boomerang*, November 14, 2002.

94. Amy Sherrill, "City Welcomes Marshals Artifacts," *Times Record*, November 9, 2007.

95. "About" page, Wyoming Territorial Prison State Historic Park website, http://www.wyomingterritorialprison.com/about/.

96. For how the transition of the Marshals Museum from Laramie to Fort Smith was glossed see Rusty Garrett, "City on Short List for Museum," *Times Record*, November 18, 2005; Aaron Sadler, "Marshals Museum Coming Home: Officials Cite City's Legacy, Support of Community," *Times Record*, January 5, 2007.

97. "United States Marshals Foundation Bicentennial Stamp and Print Edition by Frederic Remington," brochure, date unknown, produced by Ambassador Graphics and Wildlife Gallery, North Charleston, SC.

98. Bellmon quoted in Tim Ray, "Memorial to U.S. Marshals Planned near Cowboy Hall/6.5 Million Project," *Journal Record*, May 26, 1988; second quote is from Ed Godfrey, "Marshals Coming to City Memorial, Museum Planned," *Oklahoman*, May 26, 1988, http://newsok.com/marshals-coming-to-city-memorial -museum-planned-near-cowboy-hall/article/2227022.

99. Jon Denton, "Memorial Will Honor Marshals Plans Unfolding for Site Near City's Cowboy Hall of Fame," *Oklahoman*, September 11, 1988, http:// newsok.com/memorial-will-honor-marshals-plans-unfolding-for-site-near-citys -cowboy-hall-of-fame/article/2238840.

100. First quote in Jack Money, "Exhibit Honoring U.S. Marshals Arrives at Cowboy Hall of Fame," *Oklahoman*, March, 22, 1989, http://newsok.com/

exhibit-honoring-u.s.-marshals-arrives-at-cowboy-hall-of-fame/article/2259826; second quote in Ed Godfrey, "Marshals Coming to City Memorial, Museum Planned," *Oklahoman*, May 26, 1988, http://newsok.com/marshals-coming-to-city-memorial -museum-planned-near-cowboy-hall/article/2227022.

101. Dignitary list, "United States Marshals National Memorial Dedication Program," program, November 8, 1989, Oklahoma City; Bellmon quote in Jack Money, "Memorial Honors Slain Marshals, Bellmon Says Oklahomans Must Remember Sacrifices of 400," *Oklahoman*, November 9, 1989, http://newsok.com/memorial-honors-slain-marshals-bellmon-says-oklahomans-must-remember-sacrifices-of-400/article/2291194.

102. Blankenship quoted In Jack Money, "Memorial Honors Slain Marshals, Bellmon Says Oklahomans Must Remember Sacrifices of 400," *Oklahoman*, November 9, 1989, http://newsok.com/memorial-honors-slain-marshals-bellmon -says-oklahomans-must-remember-sacrifices-of-400/article/2291194.

103. "Long-Standing Debt May Force Loss of Site for U.S. Marshals Memorial," *Dallas Morning News*, October 20, 1992.

104. In Jack Money, "Marshals Memorial Blame Denied, $347,000 Debt Forces Construction Halt," *Oklahoman*, August 3, 1990, http://newsok.com/marshals -memorial-blame-denied-347000-debt-forces-construction-halt/article/2326145.

105. Penny Owen, "Weeds, Neglect, Debt Entangle Law Memorial," *Oklahoman*, October 19, 1992, http://newsok.com/weeds-neglect-debt-entangle-law-memorial/ article/2409806.

106. "History," United States Marshals Service, http://www.justice.gov/ marshals/history/frontier.

107. Jim Spears, "Marshals Museum Update," presentation, Sixth Annual Fort Smith History Conference, January 25, 2013, author's transcription of recording.

108. Ryan Saylor, "City 'Resiliency' Noted at 125th Fort Smith Chamber Anniversary," *City Wire*, November 5, 2013, http://www.thecitywire.com/node/30367#. U8wkS_IdUrc.

109. Woronkowicz, "Feasibility of Cultural Building Projects."

Bibliography

Abdul-Jabbar, Kareem. *Black Profiles in Courage*. New York: William Morrow, 1996.

Allen, LaRadius. "McAlester, James Jackson (1842-1920)." In *Encyclopedia of Oklahoma History and Culture*. 2009. http://www.okhistory.org/publications/encyclopediaonline.

Akins, Jerry. *Hangin' Times in Fort Smith: A History of Executions in Judge Parker's Court*. Little Rock: Butler Center Books, 2012.

Baggot, King, dir. *Tumbleweeds*. Film. William S. Hart Productions, 1925.

Bakhtin, Mikhail. *The Dialogic Imagination*. Austin: University of Texas Press, 1981.

Baker, Lee. *Anthropology and the Racial Politics of Culture*. Durham, NC: Duke University Press, 2010.

Barnes, Jeff. *Forts of the Northern Plains*. Mechanicsburg, PA: Stackpole Books, 2008.

Barthes, Roland. *Mythologies*. New York: Hill and Wang, 1972.

Bauman, Richard. *Verbal Art as Performance*. Prospect Heights, IL: Waveland Press, 1984.

Bearss, Edwin, and Arrell Gibson. *Fort Smith: Little Gibraltar on the Arkansas*. 2nd ed. Norman: University of Oklahoma Press, 1988.

Bederman, Gail. *Manliness and Civilization: A Cultural History of Gender and Race in the United States, 1880–1917*. Chicago: University of Chicago Press, 1995.

Berlant, Lauren. *Cruel Optimism*. Durham, NC: Duke University Press, 2011.

Bhabha, Homi. *Nation and Narration*. New York: Routledge Press, 1990.

———. "Of Mimicry and Man: The Ambivalence of Colonial Discourse," *October* 28, special issue (1984): 125–133.

Bodnar, John. *Remaking America: Public Memory, Commemoration, and Patriotism in the Twentieth Century*. Princeton, NJ: Princeton University Press, 1993.

Bold, Christine. *The Frontier Club: Popular Westerns and Cultural Power, 1880–1924*. New York: Oxford University Press, 2013.

Bolton, S. Charles. *Arkansas, 1800–1860: Remote and Restless*. Fayetteville: University of Arkansas Press, 1998.

Bonilla-Silva, Eduardo. *Racism without Racists: Color-Blind Racism and the Persistence of Racial Inequality in America*. Lanham, MD: Rowman and Littlefield, 2009.

Booker, Anton. *Wildcats and Petticoats*. Girard, KS: Haldeman-Julius, 2010.

Bouvier, Virginia. *Women and the Conquest of California, 1542–1840*. Tucson: University of Arizona Press, 2001.

Bowden, David. "United States District Court for the Western District of Arkansas." In *Encyclopedia of Arkansas History and Culture*. Modified July 23, 2009. http://www.encyclopediaofarkansas.net/.

Brady, Paul. *The Black Badge: Deputy United States Marshal Bass Reeves from Slave to Heroic Lawman*. Los Angeles: Milligan Books, 2005.

Brandon, Jamie, and Jerry Hilliard. "Zachary Taylor and the Sisters of Mercy." In *Historical Archaeology of Arkansas: A Hidden Diversity*. Edited by Carl Drexler. Knoxville: University of Tennessee Press, 2015.

Britz, Kevin. "Long May Their Legend Survive: Memory and Authenticity in Deadwood, South Dakota; Tombstone, Arizona; and Dodge City, Kansas." PhD diss., University of Arizona, 1999.

Brodhead, Michael. *Isaac C. Parker: Federal Justice on the Frontier*. Norman: University of Oklahoma Press, 2003.

Brownlee, Susan. *The 1904 Anthropology Days and Olympic Games*. Lincoln: University of Nebraska Press, 2008.

Bruner, Edward. *Culture on Tour: Ethnographies of Travel*. Chicago: University of Chicago Press, 2005.

Burton, Art. "Bass Reeves (1838–1910)." In *Encyclopedia of Arkansas History and Culture*. Modified May 29, 2012. http://www.encyclopediaofarkansas.net/.

———. "Bass Reeves (1838–1910)." In *Oklahoma Encyclopedia of History and Culture*. 2009. http://okhistory.org/publications/encyclopediaonline.

———. *Black Gun, Silver Star: The Life and Legend of Frontier Marshal Bass Reeves*. Lincoln: University of Nebraska Press, 2006.

———. *Black, Red, and Deadly: Black and Indian Gunfighters of the Indian Territory, 1870–1907*. Austin: Eakin Press, 1991.

Burton, Jeffrey. *Indian Territory and the United States, 1866–1906: Courts, Government, and the Movement for Oklahoma Statehood*. Norman: University of Oklahoma Press, 1995.

Butler, Judith. *Gender Trouble: Feminism and the Subversion of Identity*. New York: Routledge, 1999.

Carson, Cary. "The End of History Museums: What's Plan B?" *Public Historian* 30, no. 4 (2008): 9–27.

Cash, W. J. *The Mind of the South*. New York: Vintage Books, 1941.

Chambers, Erve. *Native Tours: The Anthropology of Travel and Tourism.* Prospect Heights, IL: Waveland Press, 2000.

Chang, David. *The Color of the Land: Race, Nation, and the Politics of Landowner-ship in Oklahoma, 1832–1929.* Chapel Hill: University of North Carolina Press, 2010.

Cogburn, Brett. *Rooster: The Life and Times of the Real Rooster Cogburn, the Man Who Inspired* True Grit. New York: Kensington Books, 2012.

Coleman, Sylvia. "The Quartermaster: Vital Link to Survival." *Journal of the Fort Smith Historical Society* 12, no. 2 (1988): 7–13.

Connerton, Paul. *How Modernity Forgets.* Cambridge, England: Cambridge University Press, 2009.

Croy, Homer. *He Hanged Them High: An Authentic Account of the Fanatical Judge Who Hanged Eighty-Eight Men.* New York: Little, Brown, 1952.

Cruze, James, dir. *The Covered Wagon.* Film. Famous Players–Lasky, 1923.

Curtiz, Michael, dir. *Dodge City.* Film. Warner Brothers, 1939.

Daily, Harry. "Judge Isaac C. Parker." *Chronicles of Oklahoma* 11, no. 1. (1933): 673–690.

Debo, Angie. *The Rise and Fall of the Choctaw Republic.* Norman: University of Oklahoma Press, 1934.

Deloria, Philip. *Playing Indian.* New Haven, CT: Yale University Press, 1999.

DeMille, Cecil B., dir. *The Plainsman.* Film. Paramount Pictures, 1936.

———, dir. *Union Pacific.* Film. Paramount Pictures, 1939.

Desmond, Jane C. *Staging Tourism: Bodies on Display from Waikiki to Sea World.* Chicago: University of Chicago Press, 1999.

Du Bois, W.E.B. *The Souls of Black Folk.* New York: Oxford University Press, 2007.

Durkheim, Emile. *Emile Durkheim: Selected Writings.* Edited by Anthony Giddens. Cambridge, England: Cambridge University Press, 1972.

Du Val, Kathleen. *The Native Ground: Indians and Colonists in the Heart of the Continent.* Philadelphia: University of Pennsylvania Press, 2006.

Dwan, Allan, dir. *Frontier Marshal.* Film. Twentieth Century Fox Film, 1939.

Emery, J. Gladston, *Court of the Damned.* New York: Comet Press Books, 1959.

Etulain, Richard. *Does the Frontier Experience Make America Exceptional?* Boston: Bedford/St. Martins, 1999.

Faiman-Silva, Sandra. *Choctaws at the Crossroads: The Political Economy of Class and Culture in the Oklahoma Timber Region.* Lincoln: University of Nebraska Press, 1997.

Flores, Richard. *Remembering the Alamo: Memory, Modernity, and the Master Symbol.* Austin: University of Texas Press, 2002.

Ford, John, dir. *Fort Apache.* Film. Argosy Pictures, 1948.

———, dir. *The Iron Horse.* Film. Fox Film, 1924.

————, dir. *The Man Who Shot Liberty Valance*. Film. Paramount Pictures, 1962.

————, dir. *The Searchers*. Film. Warner Bros., C.V. Whitney Pictures, 1956.

————, dir. *Stagecoach*. Film. Walter Wanger Productions, 1939.

Foreman, Grant. *The Five Civilized Tribes: Cherokee, Chickasaw, Choctaw, Creek, Seminole*. Norman: University of Oklahoma Press, 1934.

Foucault, Michel. *The History of Sexuality*. Vol. 1, *An Introduction*. New York: Random House, 1978.

Franklin, H. Bruce. *Vietnam and Other American Fantasies*. Amherst: University of Massachusetts Press, 2000.

Frazer, Robert. *Forts of the West: Military Forts and Presidios and Posts Commonly Called Forts West of the Mississippi River to 1898*. Norman: University of Oklahoma Press, 1965.

Friedman, Jonathan. "Myth, History, and Political Identity." *Cultural Anthropology* 7, no. 2 (1992): 194–210.

Frost, Linda. *Never One Nation: Freaks, Savages, and Whiteness in U.S. Popular Culture, 1850–1877*. Minneapolis: University of Minnesota Press, 2005.

Galonska, Juliet L. "Fort Smith Council of 1865." In *Proceedings: "War and Reconstruction in Indian Territory: A History Conference in Observance of the 130th Anniversary of the Fort Smith Council."* Edited by Juliet L. Galonska. National Park Service, Oklahoma Historical Society, and Arkansas Historical Association. September 14-17, 1995, Fort Smith, AR.

Geertz, Clifford. *Works and Lives: The Anthropologist as Author*. Stanford, CA: Stanford University Press, 1989.

Gibson, Arrell. *The Chickasaws*. Norman: University of Oklahoma Press, 1972.

Gilmore, David. *Manhood in the Making: Cultural Concepts of Masculinity*. New Haven, CT: Yale University Press, 1990.

Gilroy, Paul. *The Black Atlantic: Modernity and Double Consciousness*. Cambridge: Harvard Press, 1993.

Gmelch, Sharon Bohn, ed. *Tourists and Tourism: A Reader*. Long Grove, IL: Waveland Press, 2004.

Goffman, Erving. *Presentation of Self in Everyday Life*. New York: Anchor Books, 1959.

Gorman, Joshua. *Building a Nation: Chickasaw Museums and the Construction of History and Heritage*. Tuscaloosa: University of Alabama, 2011.

Grey, Zane. *The Lone Star Ranger*. New York: Grosset and Dunlap, 1915.

Gross, Samuel R., Barbara O'Brien, Chen Hu, and Edward H. Kennedy. "Rate of False Conviction of Criminal Defendants Who Are Sentenced to Death." *Proceedings of the National Academy of Sciences of the United States of America* 111, no. 20 (May 20, 2014): 7230–7235. http://www.pnas.org/content/early/2014/04/23/1306417111.full.pdf+html.

Gruen, Phillip. *Manifest Destinations: Cities and Tourists in the Nineteenth-Century American West*. Norman: University of Oklahoma Press, 2014.

Hall, Jonathan. *Reconstructed Forts of the Old Northwest Territory*. Westminster, MD: Heritage Books, 2008.

Hall, Stuart. *Representation: Cultural Representations and Signifying Practices*. London: Sage Press, 1997.

Handley, William, and Nathaniel Lewis, eds. *True West: Authenticity and the American West*. Lincoln, NE: Bison Books, 2007.

Harman, Samuel. *Hell on the Border*. Fort Washington, PA: Eastern National, 1898/2007.

Harrington, Fred Harvey. *Hanging Judge*. Norman: University of Oklahoma Press, 1996.

Hart, Herbert. *Tour Guide to Old Western Forts* (Johnstown: Old Army Press, 1980.

Hartigan, John. "Establishing the Fact of Whiteness," *American Anthropologist* 99, no. 3 (1997): 495–505.

———. *Odd Tribes: Toward a Cultural Analysis of White People*. Durham, NC: Duke University Press, 2005.

Harvey, David. *A Brief History of Neoliberalism*. New York: Oxford University Press, 2007.

Hathaway, Henry, dir. *True Grit*. Film. Paramount Pictures, 1969.

Herzfeld, Michael. *The Poetics of Manhood: Contest and Identity in a Cretan Mountain Village*. Princeton, NJ: Princeton University Press, 1985.

Higgins, Billy D. *Fort Smith: Vanguard of the Western Frontier History*. Lawrenceburg, IN: Creative Company, 2007.

———. *A Stranger and a Sojourner: Peter Caulder, Free Black Frontiersman in Antebellum Arkansas*. Fayetteville: University of Arkansas Press, 2004.

Hine, Robert, and John Mack Faragher. *The American West: A New Interpretive History*. New Haven, CT: Yale University Press, 2000.

Horwitz, *Confederates in the Attic: Dispatches from the Unfinished Civil War*. New York: Vintage Books, 1998.

Hymes, Dell. "Breakthrough to Performance." In *Folklore: Performance and Communication*, edited by Dan Ben-Amos and Kenneth Goldstein. Hague: Mouton, 1975.

Jakle, John. *The Tourist: Travel in Twentieth-Century North America*. Lincoln: University of Nebraska Press, 1985.

Jefferson, Thomas. *Notes on the State of Virginia*. East Rutherford, NJ: Viking Press, 1985.

Jensen, Robert. *The Heart of Whiteness: Confronting Race, Racism, and White Privilege*. San Francisco: City Lights, 2005.

Johnson, Hannibal. *Apartheid in Indian Country: Seeing Red over Black Disenfranchisement*. Waco, TX: Eakin Press, 2012.

Kansas Historical Society. "Home on the Range." In *Kansapedia*. Modified December 2014. http://www.kshs.org/portal_kansapedia.

Kapczynski, Amy. "Historicism, Progress, and the Redemptive Constitution." *Cardozo Law Review* 26, no. 3 (2005): 1041–1117.

Kaplan, Amy. *The Anarchy of Empire in the Making of U.S. Culture*. Cambridge: Harvard University Press, 2002.

Karp, Ivan, and Steven Lavine, eds. *Exhibiting Cultures*. Washington, D.C.: Smithsonian Institution Press, 1991.

Kidder, Bradley Sr. "Who Took the Trees." *Journal of the Fort Smith Historical Society* 30, no. 2 (2006): 7–21.

———. "Who Took the Trees? The End Game." *Journal of the Fort Smith Historical Society* 31, no. 1 (2007): 9–13.

Kimmel, Michael. *Manhood in America: A Cultural History*. New York: Free Press, 1996.

Kirshenblatt-Gimblett, Barbara. *Destination Culture, Tourism, Museums, and Heritage*. Berkeley: University of California Press, 1998.

Kopel, David. "The Self-Defense Cases: How the United States Supreme Court Confronted a Hanging Judge in the Nineteenth Century and Taught Some Lessons for Jurisprudence in the Twenty-First." *American Journal of Criminal Law* 27, no. 3 (2000): 294–328.

Lipsitz, George. *The Possessive Investment in Whiteness: How White People Profit from Identity Politics*. Philadelphia: Temple University Press, 1998.

Littlefield, Daniel, and Lonnie Underhill. "Black Dreams and 'Free' Homes." *Phylon* 34, no. 4 (1973): 342–357.

———. "Divorce Seeker's Paradise." *Arizona and the West* 17, no. 1 (1974): 21–34.

———. "Negro Marshals in the Indian Territory." *Journal of Negro History* 56, no. 2 (1971): 77–87.

Lofaro, Michael. Introduction to *David Crockett*, by James Shackford. Lincoln: University of Nebraska Press, 1992.

Lowenthal, David. *The Heritage Crusade and the Spoils of History*. New York: Cambridge University Press, 1998.

MacCannell, Dean. *The Tourist: A New Theory of the Leisure Class*. Berkeley: University of California Press, 1976.

Maddra, Sam. *Hostiles? The Lakota Ghost Dance and Buffalo Bill's Wild West*. Norman: University of Oklahoma Press, 2006.

Maher, Daniel R. "Jurisdiction Matters." *Journal of the Fort Smith Historical Society* 38, no. 1 (2014): 7.

———. "The Men behind the Badges." *Journal of the Fort Smith Historical Society* 35, no. 2 (2011): 17–20.

McLaglen, Andrew V., dir. *Chisum*. Film. Warner Brothers, 1970.

McMurtry, Larry. *The Last Kind Words Saloon*. New York: Liveright, 2014.

McReynolds, Edwin. *The Seminoles*. Norman: University of Oklahoma Press, 1957.

Mihesuah, Devon Abbott. *Choctaw Crime and Punishment 1884–1907*. Norman: University of Oklahoma Press, 2009.

Morris, John W. *Drill Bits, Picks, and Shovels: A History of Mineral Resources in Oklahoma*. Oklahoma City: Oklahoma Historical Society, 1982.

Nelson, Vaunda Micheaux. *Bad News for Outlaws: The Remarkable Life of Bass Reeves, Deputy U.S. Marshal*. Minneapolis: Carolrhoda Books, 2009.

Nkokheli, T. Baridi. "Affirmation in the Face of Adversity." February, 22 2011, University of Arkansas–Fort Smith. Audio recording, 60 minutes. Pebley Historical and Cultural Center, Boreham Library, University of Arkansas–Fort Smith.

Nora, Pierre. "Between Memory and History: Les Lieux de memoire." *Representations* 26 Spring (1989): 7–25.

Oliva, Leo. *Fort Scott: Courage and Conflict on the Border*. Topeka: Kansas State Historical Society, 1984.

Omi, Michael, and Howard Winant. *Racial Formation in the United States: From the 1960's to the 1990's*. 2nd edition. New York: Routledge, 1994.

Parker, Bradley J., and Lars Rodseth. *Untaming the Frontier in Anthropology, Archaeology, and History*. Tucson: University of Arizona Press, 2005.

Parsons, Chuck, and Robert DeArment. *Captain John R. Hughes, the Lone Star Ranger*. Denton: University of North Texas Press, 2011.

Paskowsky, Michael, dir. *It Took Brave Men*. Video. National Park Service. Author's transcription. Uploaded to YouTube by FortSmithNPS, May 25, 2011. https://www.youtube.com/watch?v=5VXvMp4uGdg.

———, dir. *Peacekeeper of Indian Territory*. Video. National Park Service, 2000. Author's transcription. Uploaded to YouTube by FortSmithNPS, May 25, 2011. https://www.youtube.com/watch?v=MJ5Cpq4gsA4.

Paulsen, Gary. *The Legend of Bass Reeves: Being the True and Fictional Account of the Most Valiant Marshal in the West*. New York: Laurel Leaf, 2008.

Penny, H. Glenn. *Kindred by Choice: Germans and American Indians since 1800*. Chapel Hill: University of North Carolina Press, 2013.

Pfeil, Fred. *White Guys: Studies in Postmodern Domination and Difference*. London: Verso, 1995.

Pomeroy, Earl. *In Search of the Golden West: The Tourist in Western America*. New York: Knopf, 1957.

Porter, Edwin, dir. *The Great Train Robbery*. Film. Edison Manufacturing, 1903.

Portis, Charles. *True Grit*. New York: Overland Press, 2004.

Post, Ted, dir. *Hang 'Em High*. Film. Leonard Freeman Production, Malpaso, 1968.

Rabinow, Paul. "Representations Are Social Facts." In *Writing Culture: The Poetics and Politics of Ethnography*, edited by James Clifford and George Marcus. Berkeley: University of California Press, 1986.

Radcliff, Maranda. "Miss Laura's Social Club." In *Encyclopedia of Arkansas History and Culture*. Modified June 11, 2015. http://www.encyclopediaofarkansas.net/.

Rascoe, Burton. *Belle Starr*. Lincoln: University of Nebraska Press, 2004.

Rau, Margaret. *Belle of the West*. Greensboro, NC: Morgan Reynolds, 2001.

Reynolds, Don Jr. *Crackerjack Positioning: Niche Marketing Strategy for the Entrepreneur*. Tulsa: Atwood, 1993.

Ritchie, J. R. Brent, and Charles R. Goeldner. *Travel, Tourism, and Hospitality Research*. Hoboken, NJ: Wiley, 1994.

Rosler, Michael, and Tobias Wendl. *Frontiers and Borderlands: Anthropological Perspectives*. New York: Peter Lang International Academic.

Rothman, Hal. *Devil's Bargains: Tourism in the Twentieth-Century American West*. Lawrence: University of Kansas Press, 1998.

Russell, Phillip. "Fort Smith City Government and the Progressive Era in Urban Reform." Master's thesis, University of Arkansas, 1981.

Salazar, Noel B. "Imaged or Imagined? Cultural Representations and the 'Touristmification' of Peoples and Places." *Cahiers d'études africaines* 49, no. 1–2, (2009): 49–71.

———. "Imagineering Otherness: Anthropological Legacies in Contemporary Tourism." *Anthropological Quarterly* 86, no. 3 (2013): 669–696.

———. "Tourism Imaginaries: A Conceptual Approach." *Annals of Tourism Research* 39, no. 2 (2011): 863–882.

Salazar, Noel B., and Nelson H. H. Graburn, eds. *Tourism Imaginaries: Anthropological Approaches*. New York: Berghahn Books, 2014.

Scaff, Lawrence. *Max Weber in America*. Princeton, NJ: Princeton University Press, 2011.

Schieffelin, Edward. "Performance and the Cultural Construction of Reality." *American Ethnologist* 12, no. 4 (1985): 707–724.

Schnack, A. J., and David Boone Wilson, dirs. *We Always Lie to Strangers*. Film. Spacestation Productions, 2013.

Selwyn, Tom, ed. *The Tourist Image: Myths and Myth Making in Tourism*. New York: John Wiley and Sons, 1996.

Shaffer, Marguerite. *See America First: Tourism and National Identity, 1880–1940*. Washington, D.C.: Smithsonian Books, 2001.

Sheller, Mimi, and John Urry, eds. *Tourism Mobilities: Places to Play, Places in Play*. New York: Routledge, 2004.

Shirley, Glenn. *Belle Starr and Her Times: The Literature, the Facts, and the Legends.* Norman: University of Oklahoma Press, 1982.

Slotkin, Richard. *The Fatal Environment: The Myth of the Frontier in the Age of Industrialization, 1800–1890.* Norman: University of Oklahoma Press, 1998.

———. *The Gunfighter Nation: Myth of the Frontier in Twentieth-Century America.* New York: Antheneum, 1992.

———. *Regeneration through Violence: The Mythology of the American Frontier, 1600–1860.* Norman: University of Oklahoma Press, 2000.

Smith, Calvin. "Diluting an Institution: The Social Impact of World War II on the Arkansas Family." *Arkansas Historical Quarterly* 39, no. 1 (1980): 21–34.

Smith, Valene, ed. *Hosts and Guests: The Anthropology of Tourism.* Philadelphia: University of Pennsylvania Press, 1977.

Sonnichsen, C. L. "Roy Bean." In *Handbook of Texas Online.* Modified July 28, 2015. https://www.tshaonline.org/handbook/online/.

Souther, J. Mark, and Dagen Bloom, eds. *American Tourism: Constructing a National Tradition.* Chicago: Columbia College Chicago Press, 2012.

Steel, Nancy. *Insight 2000,* Fort Smith: Southwest Times Record, 2000.

Steel, Phillip. *Starr Tracks: Belle and Pearl Starr.* Gretna, LA: Pelican, 1989.

Stevens, George, dir. *Shane.* Film. Paramount Pictures, 1953.

Strickland, Rennard. *Fire and the Spirits: Cherokee Law from Clan to Courts.* Norman: University of Oklahoma Press, 1975.

Strum, Circe. *Blood Politics: Race, Culture, and Identity in the Cherokee Nation of Oklahoma.* Berkeley: University of California Press, 2002.

Sturges, John, dir. *Gunfight at the O.K. Corral.* Film. Paramount Pictures, Wallis-Hazen, 1957.

———, dir. *The Magnificent Seven.* Film. Mirisch, Alpha Productions, 1960.

Sturken, Marita. *Tangled Memories: The Vietnam War, the AIDS Epidemic, and the Politics of Remembering.* Berkeley: University of California Press, 1997.

———. *Tourists of History: Memory, Kitsch, and Consumerism from Oklahoma City to Ground Zero.* Durham, NC: Duke University Press, 2007.

Thoburn, Joseph. "Centennial of the Tour on the Prairies." *Chronicles of Oklahoma* 10, no. 3 (1932): 426–433. http://digital.library.okstate.edu/CHronicles/v010/v010p426.html.

Tilghman, William, dir. *Passing of the Oklahoma Outlaws.* Film. Eagle Film, 1915.

Trouillot, Michel Rolph. "Anthropology and the Savage Slot: The Poetics and Politics of Otherness." In *Recapturing Anthropology: Working in the Present,* edited by Richard G. Fox. Santa Fe, NM: School of American Research Press, 1991.

———. *Silencing the Past: Power and the Production of History.* Boston: Beacon Press, 1995.

Tuller, Roger. *Let No Guilty Man Escape: A Judicial Biography of Isaac C. Parker.* Norman: University of Oklahoma Press, 2001.

Turk, David. "Hell, Grit, and Justice." Paper presented at the Fort Smith National Historic Site Conference, July 1–3, 2011, Fort Smith, AR.

Turner, Edith. "An Interview with Edith Turner." By Matthew Engelke. *Current Anthropology* 41, no. 5 (2000): 843–852.

Turner, Frederick Jackson. "The Significance of the Frontier in American History." Essay. 1893. Reprinted in *Does the Frontier Experience Make America Exceptional?*, edited by Richard Etulain. Boston: Bedford/St. Martins, 1999.

Turner, Victor. *The Anthropology of Performance.* New York: Performing Arts Journal, 1988.

Urry, John, and Jonas Larsen. *The Tourist Gaze 3.0.* London: Sage, 2011.

Utley, Robert. *Frontier Regulars: The United States Army and the Indian, 1866–1891.* Lincoln: University of Nebraska Press, 1973.

———. *The Indian Frontier of the American West 1846–1890.* Albuquerque: University of New Mexico Press, 1984.

Verbinski, Gore, dir. *The Lone Ranger.* Film. Walt Disney Pictures, 2013.

Visweswaran, Kamala. *Un/common Cultures: Racism and the Rearticulation of Cultural Difference.* Durham, NC: Duke University Press, 2010.

Vonnegut, Kurt. *Mother Night.* New York: Dell, 1999.

Wallis, Michael. *David Crockett: The Lion of the West.* New York: Norton, 2012.

Wayne, John, dir. *The Alamo.* Film. Batjac Productions, Alamo, 1960.

Whisnant, Anne Mitchell, Marla R. Miller, Gary B. Nash, and David Thelen. *Imperiled Promise: The State of History in the National Park Service.* Bloomington, IN: Organization of American Historians, 2011.

Wickett, Murray. *Contested Territory: Whites, Native Americans, and African Americans in Oklahoma, 1865–1907.* Baton Rouge: Louisiana State University Press, 2000.

Williams, Nudie. "Black Men Who Wore the Star." *Chronicles of Oklahoma* 59, no. 1 (1981): 83–92.

———. "A History of the American Southwest: Black United States Deputy Marshals in the Indian Territory, 1870–1907." Master's thesis, Oklahoma State University, 1976.

———. "United States vs. Bass Reeves: Black Lawman on Trial." *Chronicles of Oklahoma* 68, no. 2 (1990): 154–167.

Willoughby, Robert. *The Brothers Robidoux and the Opening of the American West.* Columbia: University of Missouri Press, 2012.

Wister, Owen. *The Virginian.* New York: Grosset and Dunlap, 1904.

Woodward, C. Vann. *Origins of the New South, 1877–1913.* Vol. 9 of *A History of the*

South. Edited by Wendell Holmes Stephenson and E. Merton Coulter. Baton Rouge: Louisiana State University Press, 1951.

Woronkowicz, Joanna. "The Feasibility of Cultural Building Projects." Working paper. December 2011. In *Set in Stone,* by Woronkowicz et al. http://culturalpolicy.uchicago.edu/sites/culturalpolicy.uchicago.edu/files/setinstone/pdf/feasibility.pdf.

Woronkowicz, Joanna, D. Carroll Joynes, Peter Frumkin, Anastasia Kolendo, Bruce Seaman, Robert Gertner, and Norman Bradburn. *Set in Stone: Building America's New Generation of Arts Facilities, 1994–2008.* Chicago: Cultural Policy Center, University of Chicago, 2012. http://culturalpolicy.uchicago.edu/sites/culturalpolicy.uchicago.edu/files/setinstone/index.shtml.

Wray, Matt. *Not Quite White: White Trash and the Boundaries of Whiteness.* Durham, NC: Duke University Press, 2006.

Wright, Muriel. "The Wedding of Oklahoma and Miss Indian Territory." *Chronicles of Oklahoma* 35, no. 3, (1957): 255–264.

Wrobel, David, and Patrick Long, eds. *Seeing and Being Seen: Tourism in the American West.* Lawrence: University Press of Kansas, 2001.

Zinnemann, Fred, dir. *High Noon.* Film. Stanley Kramer Productions, 1952.

Index

Daniel Maher is associate professor of anthropology and sociology at the University of Arkansas–Fort Smith. He is a past recipient of the Lucille Speakman Excellence in Teaching Award.

CULTURAL HERITAGE STUDIES

Edited by Paul A. Shackel, University of Maryland

The University Press of Florida is proud to support this series devoted to the study of cultural heritage. This enterprise brings together research devoted to understanding the material and behavioral characteristics of heritage. The series explores the uses of heritage and the meaning of its cultural forms as a way to interpret the present and the past.

Heritage of Value, Archaeology of Renown: Reshaping Archaeological Assessment and Significance, edited by Clay Mathers, Timothy Darvill, and Barbara J. Little (2005)

Archaeology, Cultural Heritage, and the Antiquities Trade, edited by Neil Brodie, Morag M. Kersel, Christina Luke, and Kathryn Walker Tubb (2006)

Archaeological Site Museums in Latin America, edited by Helaine Silverman (2006)

Crossroads and Cosmologies: Diasporas and Ethnogenesis in the New World, by Christopher C. Fennell (2007)

Ethnographies and Archaeologies: Iterations of the Past, by Lena Mortensen and Julie Hollowell (2009)

Cultural Heritage Management: A Global Perspective, by Phyllis Mauch Messenger and George S. Smith (2010; first paperback edition, 2014)

God's Fields: An Archaeology of Religion and Race in Moravian Wachovia, by Leland Ferguson (2011; first paperback edition, 2013)

Ancestors of Worthy Life: Plantation Slavery and Black Heritage at Mount Clare, by Teresa S. Moyer (2015)

Slavery Behind the Wall: An Archaeology of a Cuban Coffee Plantation, by Theresa A. Singleton (2015; first paperback edition, 2016)

Excavating Memory: Sites of Remembering and Forgetting, edited by Maria Theresia Starzmann and John R. Roby (2016)

Mythic Frontiers: Remembering, Forgetting, and Profiting with Cultural Heritage Tourism, by Daniel R. Maher (2016; first paperback edition, 2019)

Critical Theory and the Anthropology of Heritage, by Melissa F. Baird (2018)

Heritage at the Interface: Interpretation and Identity, edited by Glenn Hooper (2018)

Cuban Cultural Heritage: A Rebel past for a Revolutionary Nation, by Pablo Alonso González (2018)

The Rosewood Massacre: An Archaeology and History of Intersectional Violence, by Edward González-Tennant (2018)

Race, Place, and Memory: Deep Currents in Wilmington, North Carolina, by Margaret M. Mulrooney (2018)

An Archaeology of Structural Violence: Life in a Twentieth-Century Coal Town, by Michael Roller (2018)

Colonialism, Community, and Heritage in Native New England, by Siobhan M. Hart (2019)